Folklife
along the
Big South Fork
of the
Cumberland River

Folklife *along the* Big South Fork *of the* Cumberland River

Benita J. Howell

with contributions by
Susan Stonich

THE UNIVERSITY OF TENNESSEE PRESS
Knoxville

Originally published as *A Survey of Folklife along the Big South Fork of the Cumberland River*. Report of Investigations 30, Department of Anthropology, University of Tennessee, Knoxville, 1981.
Copyright © 2003 by The University of Tennessee Press / Knoxville.
All Rights Reserved. Manufactured in the United States of America.
Paper: 1st printing, 2003; 2nd printing, 2024.

Unless otherwise noted, the illustrations are in the collection of the author.

Fieldwork conducted and reported under auspices of the Anthropology Department, University of Kentucky, in accordance with National Park Service Contract CX500090902, 1979–81. Report preparation and revision completed under auspices of the Anthropology Department, University of Tennessee.

Library of Congress Cataloging-in-Publication Data

Howell, Benita J.
Folklife along the Big South Fork of the Cumberland River / Benita J. Howell; with contributions by Susan Stonich.— 1st ed.
    p. cm.
Rev. ed. of: A survey of folklife along the Big South Fork of the Cumberland River. Knoxville: Dept. of Anthropology, University of Tennessee. 1981
Includes bibliographical references and index.
ISBN 978-1-57233-231-7
1. Cumberland River, Big South Fork, Valley (Tenn. and Ky.)—Social life and customs. 2. Folklore—Cumberland River, Big South Fork, Valley (Tenn. and Ky.) 3. Cumberland River, Big South Fork, Valley (Tenn. and Ky.)—Social conditions. 4. Big South Fork National River and Recreation Area (Tenn. and Ky.) I. Stonich, Susan. II. Howell, Benita J. Survey of folklife along the Big South Fork of the Cumberland River. III. Title.
F442.2 .H74 2003
976.8'6053—dc21   2003004085

*To the people of the Big South Fork
past, present, and future,*

and in memory of

*my grandfather Sam Burton
and
my aunt Dorothea Burton.*

Contents

Preface	xiii
Introduction	1
Regional Background	1
The Folklife Study	3
Postscript: Cultural Heritage Conservation	10
Changes in the Revised Edition	13
For Further Reading	13
1. Historical Overview of the Big South Fork Area	15
The Physical Environment	15
Euro-American Settlement History	18
Economic Development	23
2. Environmental Knowledge and Resource Use	33
Traditional Use of Resources	33
Weather Lore	39
Working by the Signs	40
3. Subsistence Economy	46
Tools and Their Use	47
Shelter	48
Textiles and Clothing	53
Housekeeping	55
Foodways	56
4. The Cash Economy and Industrial Development	67
General Stores	67
The Timber Industry	70
Coal Mining	79
Early Oil Exploration	91
5. Short Line Railroads	94
Kentucky and Tennessee Railroad	94
The Stearns Logging Railroad	98
Oneida and Western Railroad	100

viii   Contents

6. COMMUNITY AND SOCIETY   111
    Communities   111
    Churches   122
    Schools   127
    Law and Lawlessness   132

7. CULTURAL EXPRESSION IN MUSIC, ORAL TRADITION, AND HANDCRAFTS   141
    Music   142
    Folk Dance   159
    Oral Tradition   162
    Handcrafters   166

8. FOUR FAMILIES IN A CHANGING ECONOMY   170
    A Farm Family: Chester and Bertha Ledford   171
    A Logging Family: Morgan and Nellie Skidmore   177
    A Coal Mining Family: Seldon and Jennie Lacey   179
    A Railroad Family: Jim and Dottie Farmer   182
    Conclusion   185

CONCLUSION AND RECOMMENDATIONS   187
    The Past   187
    The Future   189
    Interpretive Themes and Resources   190
    Additional Folklife Documentation   193
    Land Acquisition, Relocation, and Social Impact Assessment   196
    Construction Phase   198
    Operations and Management   200
    Summary   201

POSTSCRIPT 2002   203
    Cultural Heritage Interpretation   203
    Facilities   204
    Change and Cultural Persistence   205

APPENDIX 1.   HOUSEHOLD SURVEY   207
APPENDIX 2.   CEMETERY INVENTORY   216
APPENDIX 3.   TABLES   236
APPENDIX 4.   BIBLIOGRAPHIC RESOURCES   276

REFERENCES CITED   299
INDEX   308

Illustrations

Figures

Following Page 66

Front View of Parch Corn Hunting Camp Lodge
Rear View of Parch Corn Hunting Camp Lodge
Four-Crib Log Barn at Parch Corn Hunting Camp
Old Blacksmith Shop at Parch Corn Hunting Camp
Corn Crib on Oscar Blevins Farm
John Blevins House on Oscar Blevins Farm
Front Corner View of Lora Blevins House
Back Corner View of Lora Blevins House
Log Barn on Lora Blevins Farm
Log Outbuilding on Lora Blevins Farm
Rear View of William Peter Tapley House
Smokehouse behind William Peter Tapley House
Sunday School Building, Beech Grove Baptist Church
Sewell House on Maxine Loudin Property
Log Barn on Alfred King Property
Oscar Blevins Barn
Typical "Tenant" House
I-House with Ell Addition
Farmhouse in Allardt
Bruno Gernt House
Thomas Hughes Public Library
Loudin House
Barn behind the Lindens, Rugby
Ben Stockton House
Contemporary Folk Architecture
Travel Trailer with Frame Addition

x Illustrations

Root Cellar and Storage Building
Root Cellar with Simple Hex Sign on Door
Garrett Store
Interior of Wright's Store
Interior of Mrs. Avo Rains's General Store
Interior of the Kidd Store and Post Office
Kidd Store and Post Office

Following Page 140

White Pine United Baptist Church
Beech Grove Baptist Church
Mt. Helen Baptist Church
Bethel Baptist Church
Christ Church Episcopal
Coffin-shaped Grave Markers in Bethel Baptist Church Cemetery
Stockton Family Graves in Stockton Cemetery
Thompson Cemetery
Benches for Graveside Rites at Helen Blevins Cemetery
Shed Replacing Log House over Roysdon Family Graves
Grave of Elizabeth Williams, Troxel Cemetery
Natural Stone Marker, Powell Kidd Cemetery
Cast Concrete Marker with Dove Motif, Barrs Cemetery
Cast Concrete Marker, Nancy Graves Cemetery
Concrete Marker with Painted Lettering, Blevins Cemetery
Slaughtering at No Business, 1919
Marion Miller, Will Miller, and Harve Winchester at No Business
School March at No Business
Stearns Coal and Lumber Company
W. O. Frogge, Robert Deal, and "Coon" Latham
Stearns Logging Railroad
Derailment on the Stearns Logging Railroad
Miners at Worley camp of Stearns Coal and Lumber Company, 1905
Worley School and Class of 1905
Kentucky and Tennessee Railroad Bridge across the Big South Fork
The Blue Heron Tipple
Contemporary Coal Tipple
Tennessee Stave and Lumber Company's Wolf River Incline
A Pedal-Powered Handcar on the Tennessee Stave Logging Railroad

Boardinghouse and Store at Tennessee Stave and Lumber Company Logging Camp
John Tays Store
Oneida and Western Railroad
Webb–Hammock Company Supply House, Bathhouse, and Company Store
Johnboat Excursion on North White Oak Creek
John and John H. Tays at the Louvain Bandmill
Members of the O & W Section Crew Using a Track Jack
Oneida and Western Railroad Depot
Truckload of Pulpwood at Southern Railway
Everett Boyatt Filing the Headsaw at his Sawmill
Everett Boyatt Squaring a Log to Be Sawed
Everett Boyatt Sawing Boards
Everett Boyatt Feeding a Board into an Edger
Everett Boyatt at the Conveyor
Forge Built in 1918
Woodworking Shop, Kentucky Hills Industries

Maps

Vicinity Map	xviii
Big South Fork National River and Recreation Area	xix
Locations of Inventoried Cemeteries	218–19

Preface

The Big South Fork folklife survey was conducted in 1979–80 under National Park Service contract CX500090902 and was first published by the University of Tennessee Anthropology Department in 1981 as Report of Investigations 30. National Park Service staff at Big South Fork and residents of the area encouraged reissue of this work. Readers should bear in mind that except for minor corrections and revisions to turn a technical report into a book, this volume was written more than two decades ago. Many aspects of the research and reporting would be handled differently today in light of my subsequent experience and developments in applied ethnography and cultural heritage conservation. With the passage of twenty years, however, the descriptive content has gained additional value as a record of local history, lore, and lifeways. Many of the elderly contributors have passed away and many of the landmarks they described have vanished from the cultural landscape. The report holds additional historical value as a pioneering example of applied ethnography in the National Park system. This kind of research has become a recognized tool for park planning and cultural resource interpretation during the past two decades, but it was somewhat novel in the late 1970s.

The folklife survey was funded as an adjunct to the survey of archaeological resources required during environmental impact assessment and development of the original master plan for the Big South Fork National River and Recreation Area. Both the archaeological and folklife surveys were conducted for the U.S. Army Corps of Engineers, Nashville District, the agency responsible for planning and constructing the recreation area facilities. Personnel in both of these agencies deserve special commendation for their enthusiastic endorsement of a folklife project. Their willingness to fund it as an integral part of cultural resource management helped set a new precedent for federally sponsored attention to intangible cultural resources. Without advocacy from planners and cultural resource specialists in these agencies, the project never would have been authorized.

It was a pleasure to work with personnel from the various governmental agencies involved in the Big South Fork project. Special thanks go to these individuals: from the Corps of Engineers Planning Branch, planners Susan Neff and Jim Spear, staff archaeologists Danny Olinger and Cathy Ganzel, and project director Mickey Sullivan; from the Southeast Archeological Center, director Richard Faust and staff archaeologist Robert Wilson; from the Oneida office of the

National Park Service, superintendent Doyle Kline, head ranger Glen Voss, and Anna Ruth Clark. Thanks to state historic preservation officers Nick Fielder of Tennessee and Phil Cochran of Kentucky for their advice and onsite visits, and to Bobby Fulcher of the Tennessee Division of State Parks for facilitating work with musicians. Barbara Stagg and the Rugby Restoration Association (now Historic Rugby, Inc.) graciously offered their hospitality and moral support.

The University of Kentucky Research Foundation administered the contract during the fieldwork period (July 1979–February 1980) and early stages of report preparation. Within the Anthropology Department, Virginia Slattery was responsible for administrative paperwork, and her assistance was invaluable. Others associated with the University of Kentucky who contributed to the project were J. P. Noffsinger of the School of Architecture, who conducted preliminary evaluation of structures for National Register eligibility; Bill Marshall and Terry Birdwhistle of the M. I. King Library, who arranged for the oral history tapes for this project to be incorporated into the library's existing Appalachian Oral History Archives; and colleagues within the Anthropology Department, especially Billie DeWalt and John van Willigen, who shared their ideas and supported the project from the earliest planning stage.

In the years following this work, I gained immeasurably from the opportunities it brought me to collaborate with colleagues in anthropology and folklore, especially Muriel Crespi, the late John Peterson, Melinda Wagner, Mary Hufford, and Alan Jabbour.

The Kentucky colleagues who contributed most to this project were my coworkers in the field, Susan Stonich (then Duda) and Robert Tincher, both graduate students in the Department of Anthropology at that time. They were involved at every stage of planning and executing the project and were responsible for substantial areas of fieldwork. Robert Tincher concentrated on documenting the secular and sacred music and exploring its cultural context. He produced the music tape collection and catalog. I made extensive use of his paper "Old-Time Music and Musicians of the Big South Fork" (University of Kentucky, Anthropology Department, July 1980) when writing the discussion of music and musicians included in this report. Susan Stonich (then Susan Duda) based her master's thesis on intensive work with five area families, focusing on the economic aspects of family history. Her thesis, "The Big South Fork Basin: Economic Adaptation in an Appalachian Context" (University of Kentucky Anthropology Department, 1980), provided substantial contributions to this report. Historical and statistical data from the thesis appear in chapter 1, and a condensation of four of the five family economic histories presented in the thesis appears here as chapter 8. Susan's thorough and painstaking work in preparing statistical tables and figures is especially appreciated. With the exception of the contributions noted above, I authored the report and edited chapters 1 and 8. Thus I assume responsibility for the report's errors and shortcomings.

I joined the anthropology department at the University of Tennessee following fieldwork and completed the report's preparation in Knoxville. Christine Cox, Gary Womble, and Sherry Crisp facilitated that process. I appreciate the support of my colleagues in the University of Tennessee anthropology department, especially Terry Faulkner, who drew the maps and figures at a time when this work was done by hand, not by computer.

I am grateful to Jennifer Siler and Scot Danforth at the University of Tennessee Press for their support of this project and to the manuscript readers for their constructive suggestions. Revision was greatly facilitated by Tom Des Jeans, staff archaeologist at Big South Fork National River and Recreation Area, who arranged for the original typescript to be scanned. Tom Howell scanned the original photographs and line drawings to prepare new plates for this edition. Throughout this project, from fieldwork on, Tom has unfailingly given material and moral support to my work. He has my deepest gratitude.

Finally, credit for this work belongs most of all to the scores of Big South Fork area residents who contributed information, particularly those who made oral history tapes. Our greatest debt of gratitude is to these individuals, to their family members, and to many others who contributed to the survey in various ways. Your hospitality, generosity, and cooperation made the folklife survey possible.

Folklife Survey Oral History Participants

Acres, Audney
Acres, Milford
Acres, Thelma Rosser
Akers, J. D.
Akers, Bessie Tays
Blevins, Ermon Smith
Blevins, Oscar
Burchfield, Irene
Duvall, Clyde
Easley, Hilda Gernt
Elliott, Arthur
Frogge, Willie Osville
Garrett, Lucille Draughn
Hicks, Effie Sweet
Hicks, Joe
Kimbrell, Arnold
Ledbetter, Jim T.
Ledbetter, Stella Buck
Lominac, Lattie Buck, Sr.
Lourie, Helen
Lowery, Tom
Martin, Allen and Oscar

Miller, Ellen Burke
Miller, Will J.
Peercy, O. N.
Rains, Keith
Ross, Smith
Sheppard, Ben
Simpson, Joe
Slaven, General
Slaven, Mary Miller
Spradlin, Esther
Spradlin, Oren
Stewart, Cecil
Taylor, Nell Crouch
Terry, John
Terry, Verna
Thompson, Frona Smith
Troxell, Anna Davenport
Waters, Henley
Waters, Lillie Ledbetter
Watson, Rebecca Ross
Whitehead, Elsie Coffee
Whitehead, Luther

The following individuals were taped in 1976 by Karen Kasmauski and Mrs. Wilma Watters for the McCreary County Library oral history collection.

Gallimore, Foster
Gregory, Steve
Morrow, Charity
Perkins, N. B.
Spradlin, Esther
Spradlin, Rettie
Stephens, Chester
Watson, Cephus
Watson, Ivory
Watson, Rebecca
Watters, Clarence
Watters, Lula

Thanks are also owed to the following people who generously shared their skills and knowledge or facilitated the project in various important ways.

Acres, Arzo
Anderson, Virgil
Baese, Frank
Baese, Jennie
Baker, James Toomey
Beaty, Joe
Beech Grove Baptist Church
Blevins, Viola
Boggs, Elmer
Booher, Mrs. N. D.
Boyatt, Everett
Brooks Store, Rugby
Brooks, Ogle
Brooks, R. O.
Byrd, Alfred
Colditz, Arnold
Colditz, Rudolph
Conatser, Evelyn Sharp
Crabtree, Carl
Crabtree, Dean
Crabtree, John S.
DeBord, Abigia
Doss, Willie
Douglas, Nancy Hicks
Draughn, Janice
Eacret, Judy Tipton
Easley, Virgil
Ellis, Gladys
Gentry, Tom
Gernt, Oscar
Gernt, Willie
Goad, Clifford
Goad, Luster
Gregory, Alpha
Gregory, Guy
Gunter, Roy
Hammond, Eland
Hatfield, Wanda
Hicks, Dee
Hicks, Delta
Hicks, Lillie Mae
Historic Rugby, Inc.
Huffines, H. H.
Hull, Hershal
Human, Lillard
Hurst, Elmer
Hurt, Elmer
Jones, Doyle
Jones, June
Keene, James
Kentucky Hills Industries
Kidd, Jewel

Kidd, W. S.
King, Christopher "Crit," Sr.
King, Wilma
Lawhorn, Effie
Marcum, Ezra
Marcum, Mrs. Ezra
McCreary Co. Library
Miller, Lillard
Millsap, Ira
Morgan, Joyce
Neal, Fannie
Norris, Jerry
Odum, Oscar
Owens, William G.
Parker, Mary
Parker, Rowe
Parker, Tom
Pearson, Obed
Perry, Alvin
Qualls, Cathy
Rains, Avo
Range, Fayette
Range, Julie
Reagan, Margaret
Rosenbaum, Junior
Scates, Dorothy
Sewell, Elval
Slaven, Robert
Smith, Eldridge "Slim"
Smith, Mary Belle
Souders, Louella Sharp

Souders, Ray
Speck, Wilda
Speck, Wilda
Stagg, Barbara
Stanley, Harold
Stearns Company
Stephens, Robert E.
Stewart, Linda
Stonecipher, Ira
Storie, Cleopha
Strunk, Herman
Terry, Charlie
Thomas, Frank
Thomas, Tolbert
Thomas, Walter
Thompson, Luther
Tipton, Willie
Tompkins, Anna
Tompkins, Clarence
Tompkins, Clifford
Tompkins, Hollis "Ted"
Tompkins, Ovid
Troxell, Clyde
Troxell, Ralph
Walker, Beulah
Watters, C. L. "Trigger"
Weaver, Ralph
West, Bessie
Wheeler, Hazel
Wright Store, Jamestown

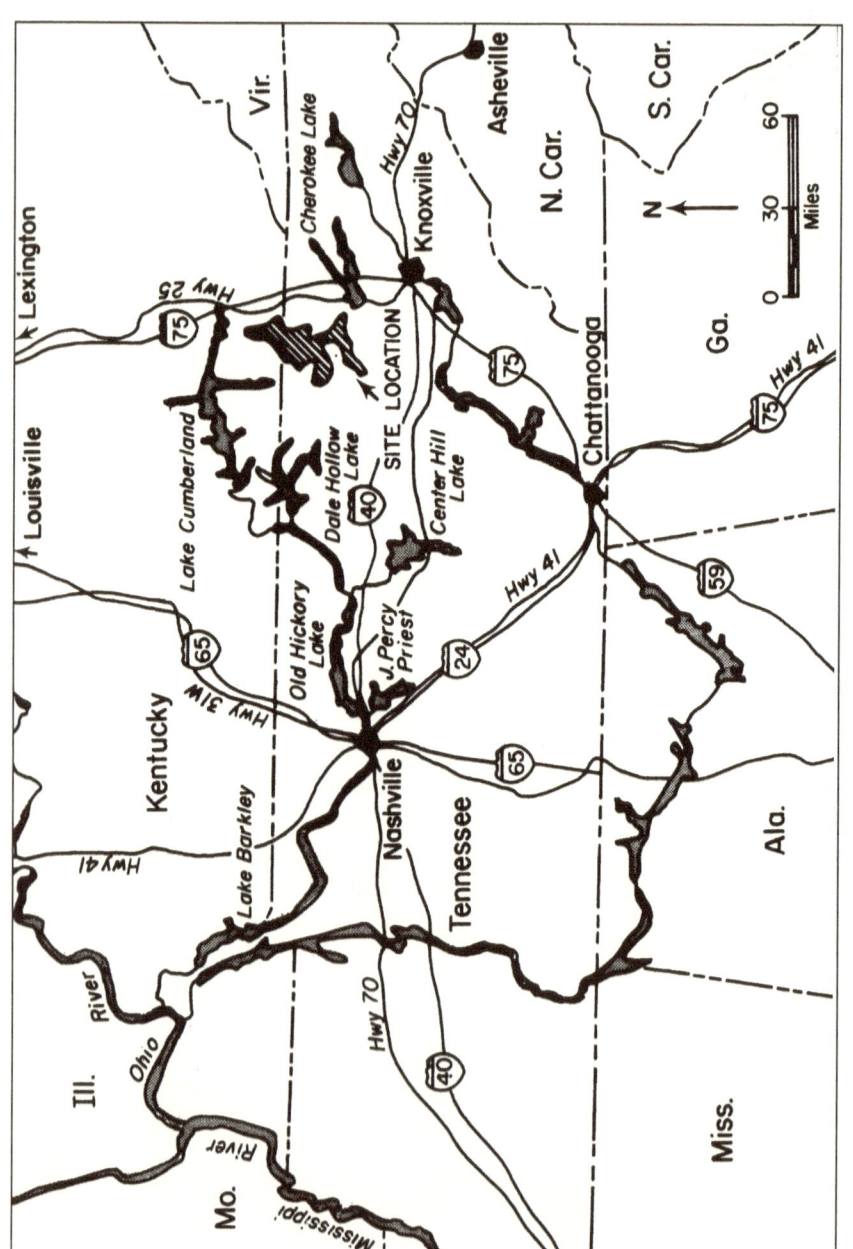

Vicinity map.

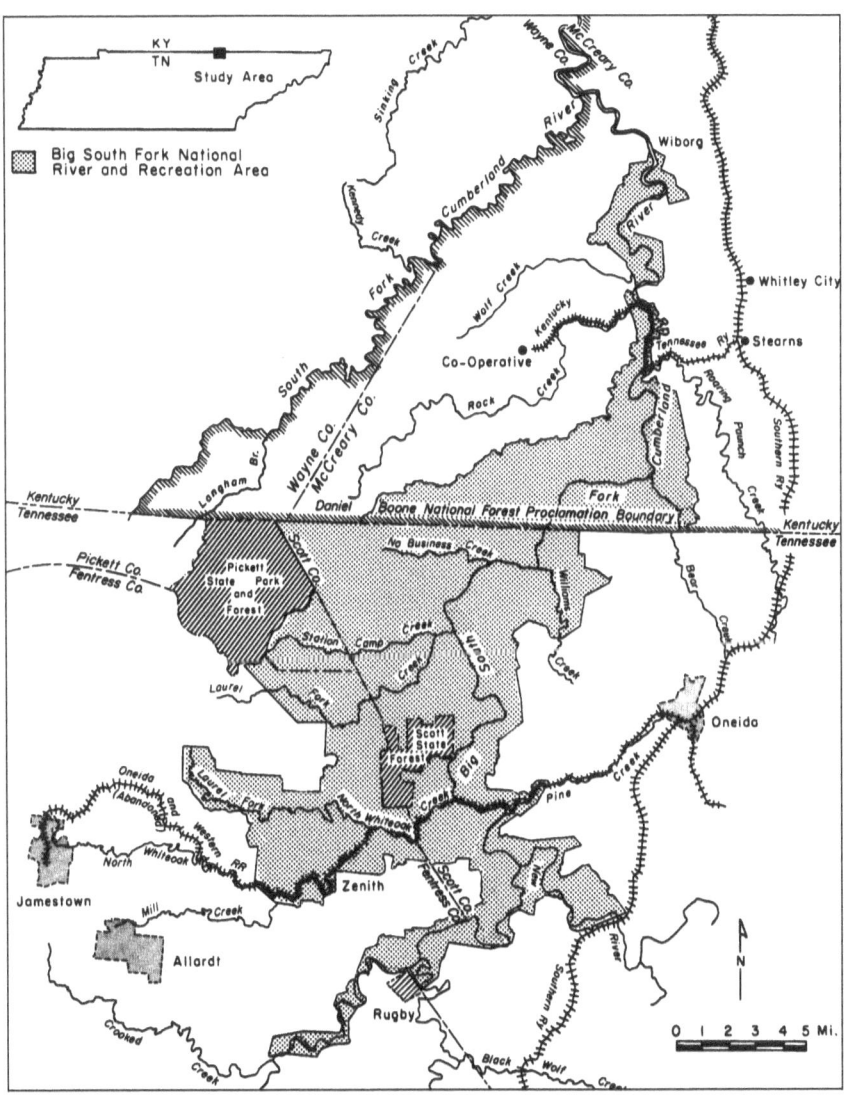

Big South Fork National River and Recreation Area boundaries.

Folklife *along the* Big South Fork *of the* Cumberland River

Introduction

The Big South Fork of the Cumberland River originates at the confluence of its major tributaries, New River and Clear Fork, in Scott County, Tennessee, and flows northward into McCreary County, Kentucky. On March 7, 1974, Congress authorized the Big South Fork National River and Recreation Area in Section 108 of PL93-251. The authorized boundaries encompassed approximately 123,000 acres of the Big South Fork drainage basin, portions of Morgan, Scott, Fentress, and Pickett Counties in Tennessee and McCreary County, Kentucky.

Beginning in the mid-1930s, local legislators spearheaded repeated attempts to gain congressional authorization for a dam on the Big South Fork at Devils Jump, Kentucky. The alternative of wild river preservation and compatible recreational development began to take form in the 1960s and was effectively promoted by conservationists. Thus the enabling legislation specified these purposes for the combined national river and recreation area:

> *conserving and interpreting an area containing unique cultural, historic, geologic, fish and wildlife, archaeologic, scenic, and recreational values, preserving as a natural free-flowing stream the Big South Fork of the Cumberland River, major portions of the Clear Fork and New River stems, and portions of their various tributaries for the benefit of future generations, the preservation of the natural integrity of the scenic gorges and valleys, and the development of the area's potential for healthful outdoor recreation.*

Regional Background

The Big South Fork region officially was opened to Euro-American settlement after the Third Tellico Treaty of 1805, and many land grants for parcels in what was then Wayne County, Kentucky, were issued during the first half of the nineteenth century. Settlers included Revolutionary War veterans compensated through land grants for their services and some of the Long Hunters who were already familiar with the area. Primary corridors for westward settlement, however, avoided the Big South Fork area, providing access to the Kentucky bluegrass via Cumberland Gap or following the Cumberland River westward to the rich, gently rolling country around French Lick, later to become Nashville. The Walton Road from East Tennessee across the Cumberland Plateau skirted south of the Big South Fork area. Subsistence farmers and hunters who established homes along the Big South Fork and its tributaries found a rugged terrain of ridges and knobs separated by a latticework of winding streams that had carved their valleys into steep gorges. Farming was confined to the narrow bottomlands; the broad, relatively flat tablelands extending beyond the gorge rim were not effectively brought under cultivation until farmers came on the scene with the capital to purchase the equipment and fertilizer needed to begin large-scale livestock and grain operations. In learning to adjust to the limitations of this environment, many of the earliest Euro-American settlers continued to emphasize hunting and foraging, developing adaptive strategies similar to those of prehistoric Native Americans and the Cherokee and Shawnee whom they displaced.

Early maps and travel accounts indicate that the Big South Fork area lay along a major north–south Indian trail that connected the Tennessee River Basin to Ohio and the Great Lakes region (Myer 1971). This upland corridor became the route of the Cincinnati Southern Railroad and, later, U.S. Highway 27. Small groups of Archaic peoples foraged on the plateau between 10,000 and 2,500 years ago. Human presence intensified during the Woodland period (2,500 to 1,000 years ago), but plateau sites dating to this period suggest that Woodland peoples occupied temporary hunting camps for only a few weeks from late summer to early winter. Their primary villages, major ceremonial sites, and horticultural fields were located along the Emory River and in the Tennessee Valley. As horticulture and elaborate ceremonialism increased during the Mississippian period (1,000 to 400 years ago), use of the plateau seems to have diminished. By the time of European contact, both the Cherokee and the Shawnee of the Ohio Valley claimed the plateau, primarily as a hunting ground and travel corridor (Ferguson et al. 1986; Ferguson 1988).

Two east–west Indian trails passed through the Big South Fork area. One extended from Monticello to Williamsburg, Kentucky, generally following the route of Kentucky Highway 92. The other, the Monticello–Jacksboro (Tennessee) pike, crossed the Big South Fork River near Rock Creek and continued through Scott County south of Huntsville (Myer 1971). Troops moved along this corridor and there were minor skirmishes during the Civil War, but local unrest had more serious consequences for Big South Fork residents than did official military activity. The populace had divided loyalties and suffered at the hands of both Confederate and Union guerrilla partisans. After the Civil War, outside capital funded ventures such as the Cincinnati Southern Railroad, the Rugby colony, and Allardt settlement, thereby shaping postwar economic development in the region.

The English author and educator Thomas Hughes established a colony at Rugby in Morgan County, Tennessee, in 1880, hoping especially to attract younger sons of British gentry. Though short-lived, Rugby opened a window on the outside world and generated some employment and markets for native Tennesseans living nearby. Many would-be Rugby colonists were ill prepared for rural life and soon moved elsewhere, but a few were absorbed into the local population.

The German community of Allardt in Fentress County had more lasting effects on the area's economy. During the 1880s, Allardt residents established flourishing farms that demonstrated the agricultural potential of tableland soils. The German settlers also began exploiting the timber and mineral resources of Fentress County. Middle Tennesseans who formed the Tennessee Stave and Lumber Company and various northern capitalists (foremost among them the founders of the Stearns Coal and Lumber Company) discovered the area's natural resources and developed extensive lumber and coal operations. By 1920, two short line railroads, the Kentucky and Tennessee and the Oneida and Western, had been built to ship coal and lumber out of the area. They also linked the people of the river gorge to cities along the Cincinnati Southern (by then the Southern Railroad).

The Big South Fork area prospered during the opening decades of the twentieth century. The population grew through natural increase and through immigration of workers with the specialized skills required by the lumber, coal, and railroad industries. But inevitably, the accessible timber was cut over. Coal mining suffered from national economic downturns, depletion of the most easily worked coal seams, and labor-management conflict. World War II brought a brief resurgence to the area's extractive industries but also began the stream of labor out-migration that persisted into the 1970s. Postwar curtailment of logging and mining activities ultimately forced abandonment of the Oneida and Western Railroad in Tennessee, removal of the Stearns logging railroad, and shortening of the Kentucky and Tennessee Railroad in McCreary County.

The Folklife Study

RATIONALE AND GOALS

To comply with federal requirements for environmental impact assessment in conjunction with planning the recreation area, a team of archaeologists from the Southeast Archeological Center of the National Park Service conducted initial surveys to locate and evaluate the area's prehistoric and historic sites and structures. The survey field director, Robert Wilson, encountered many of the region's old-timers in the course of his work and was fascinated by their stories and personal experiences. He realized that they had preserved a rich body of regional lore and custom into the late twentieth century. Alongside the mute physical remains of past lifeways retrieved through archaeology, these people seemed to be cultural resources in their own right. With the encouragement of center director Richard Faust, Wilson proposed that a portion of the funds available for cultural resources research be used for a folklife survey. In light of the recreation area's mandate to conserve and interpret cultural and historic resources and values, and because the Nashville District's involvement in the Tennessee-Tombigbee folklife project already had set a precedent for such research, his arguments were convincing. Fifty thousand dollars of the funding for cultural resource management was allocated to a folklife project.

In early 1979, the chief of the Southeast Archeological Center, National Park Service, solicited proposals for folklife research, citing as legislative mandates 36 CRF 800, 36 CRF 63 and guidelines, the Antiquities Act of 1906 (PL59-209), the Historic Sites Act of 1935 (PL74-292), and the Historic Preservation Act of 1966 (PL89-665). The folklife project was conceived as an adjunct to archaeological investigation and resource management. The rationale for such a project was stated as follows: "The proposed developments of various facilities and the increase in land use (for recreational purposes) could adversely affect unknown or unidentified cultural resources. Information on these resources must be recorded in order to determine: 1) their eligibility for inclusion in the National Register of Historic Places; 2) the potential effects of development and increased land use on these resources; and 3) the possible mitigation of any adverse effects to these resources" (Wilson 1978).

The scope of work called for a diverse array of material and intangible cultural resources to be investigated, including structures, cemeteries, foodways, medicine, speech, folklore, oral history, music and dance, and social customs. The resulting technical report was intended to provide "a guide for all future interpretation of the local history and thus provide data for any programs presenting this way of life to the American people" (Wilson 1978).

RESEARCH STRATEGY

The University of Kentucky proposal drew upon general concepts from ecological anthropology to organize the project and set priorities among the diverse topics listed in the scope of work. By focusing on humans' changing relationships to the land and natural resources, we hoped to develop a story line for interpretation of cultural heritage that would complement interpretation of the area's natural resources. We hoped that this approach would contribute to visitors' awareness of environmental issues and their appreciation for both cultural and natural resource conservation. In light of the project's emphasis on oral history and recent directions in environmental studies, "folk environmental history" now seems the most appropriate label for the research strategy we chose.

That approach yielded a great deal of valuable information and directed the project toward a focus on socioeconomic and cultural change in the region. Consequently, without explicitly addressing images of Appalachia, our work tended to counter persistent conventional wisdom that explained Appalachian culture in terms of either psychocultural or environmental determinism. Cultural determinists typically had identified a constellation of distinctive values and personality traits transmitted from Euro-American, chiefly Scots-Irish, pioneers to their descendants (Campbell 1921; Kephart 1913). Environmental determinists, on the other hand, viewed Appalachians as "contemporary ancestors" whose pioneer lifestyle had persisted into the twentieth century because of geographic, socioeconomic, and technological isolation from the American mainstream (Pearsall 1966).

Industrialization came to the Big South Fork with the Cincinnati Southern Railroad later than in some other parts of Appalachia, but it would be misleading to characterize even this area as isolated and culturally stagnant. Scots-Irish and English settlers came from North Carolina and Virginia in the late eighteenth century along with Germans from Pennsylvania, and new groups of settlers continued to arrive throughout the nineteenth century. These included German immigrants who were settling in Morgan County by 1840, an abortive Welsh colony in Scott County in the 1850s, the British (and Yankee) colony established at Rugby in 1880, and the German settlement at Allardt a few years later. Industrial development brought additional outsiders who filled managerial and skilled technical positions on the railroads, in the coal mining industry, and in logging and sawmill operations. Contact with outsiders increased native awareness of alternative cultural practices; at the same time, outsiders who adjusted successfully and remained in the Big South Fork region did so in part by borrowing from and adapting to local lifestyles.

In the post–Civil War period when outside capitalist interests discovered and developed means to extract the region's timber and mineral resources, the Big South Fork area suddenly found itself drawn into the nation's economic mainstream. The railroads that shipped out coal and lumber also brought in manufactured goods and processed foods, and they made possible convenient travel within and outside of the area. Towns sprang up, posing different social relations problems than had life on farmsteads loosely joined into settlements. Finally, extensive labor out-migration following World War II affected virtually every family in the area by bringing Big South Fork natives into direct contact with mainstream urban culture. The few individuals lacking prolonged personal experience with city life at least absorbed much information from city-dwelling relatives who returned home on visits or for more prolonged stays. This history of increasing ethnic diversity and socioeconomic change suggests that traditional culture elements still viable in the late twentieth century had persisted because they remained integral to overall cultural adaptation in the Big South Fork area, not because of isolation or ignorance that artificially preserved quaint, old-fashioned lifeways.

RESEARCH METHODS

The Big South Fork folklife survey required a variety of research methods to develop statistical and historical background information on the area, to obtain a general picture of contemporary lifeways, and to document specific folklife elements. Because the project entailed responding to a specific scope of work within tight time constraints and focused on territory within proposed recreation area boundaries, this report does not offer comprehensive treatment of the region. In particular, readers should consult other reports for details concerning prehistoric and protohistoric American Indian occupation of the area (Ferguson, Pace, Gardner, and Hoffman 1986, 1988), architectural and engineering resources (Hutchinson, Dugan, and Levy 1982), and specific development areas (Miller, Wihry, and Lee 1980; Building Conservation Technology 1984; McBride 1993).

Fieldwork began in July 1979 and continued intensively through November 1979, with some additional visits in January and February of 1980. The researchers lived in a small farm community in eastern Fentress County near the recreation area boundary. Impressions and information gathered informally through the activities of daily life thus provided a valuable supplement and check against the data gathered through formal research.

Statistical and Documentary Sources. Statistical sources consulted include federal census publications from 1850 to 1978 and reports of the regional development districts and state agencies. Census data were extremely useful in identifying changing economic alternatives, but their use posed several difficulties. Categories of data included in the decennial census and methods of measurement have changed through time and have varied from one location to another. Therefore, it was difficult to compile comparable data for the several counties of two states, especially for a period stretching back to the mid-nineteenth century. Furthermore, county political boundaries do not correspond to the cultural and ecological boundaries of the Big South Fork area. Conditions in this area often were substantially different from those in distant sections of these counties. Therefore, information obtained from county-level statistics had to be interpreted with great care. This problem is especially acute for the period before 1912 when McCreary County was formed, because statistical information on the Kentucky portion of the project area had to be drawn from the census data for Wayne, Whitley, and Pulaski Counties.

The bulk of historical writing on the Cumberland River basin slights the Big South Fork, but county and local histories have provided a great deal of valuable information. County and post office records, private company records, and family history materials and photograph collections also were consulted, as were contemporary and historic newspapers published in the Big South Fork area. Inspection of a variety of historic, railroad, transportation, topographical, and soil maps helped us ascertain settlement patterns and the development of regional transportation routes.

Household Survey. The primary purpose of the household survey conducted during the first month of fieldwork was to gather baseline data on natural resource utilization and land management practices, subsistence and cash economy activities, purchasing patterns, family and community organization, and social activities. The survey permitted a rough estimate of the extent to which traditional cultural practices were actively maintained, and it helped to identify the key subsistence patterns, occupations, and activities that needed to be explored through subsequent research. Survey respondents were asked to identify potential oral history interviewees, craftspeople, musicians, and storytellers who might contribute to the project. A number of the survey respondents were themselves identified as future key consultants.

The household survey schedule and a tabular summary of the quantitative results appear in appendix 1. The survey was pretested on households lying outside of the project boundaries, then administered to the head or other adult member of twenty-three households still living inside the recreation area boundaries when the folklife project began. Two additional household heads accepted the survey schedule and said that they would complete and return it at a later time (but did not do so); three households refused to participate in the survey; and seven households were not contacted in two attempts to visit them. Because five of these seven households belonged to the children or the parents of household heads who were interviewed, at least some of the information they could have given was picked up in interviews with their close relatives. The household survey was handled as a structured interview rather than as a questionnaire. One or two researchers asked the questions orally, and one of us recorded the responses on a printed survey schedule.

Work with Key Consultants. Key consultants were identified through the household survey, through references from U.S. Army Corps of Engineers and National Park Service personnel, and through referral from local residents. In the course of interviews, each interviewee was asked to suggest others whom we should consult. This snowball approach yielded an extensive list of potential contacts for various topics and activities.

Not every potential contact referred in these ways could be followed up, given the limitations of time and resources for the project. Elderly persons received priority, both because they could supply a broader time perspective and because serious illness or death might turn postponement into permanent loss of their valuable contributions. Preference also was given to persons intimately connected with communities and activities located within the proposed boundaries of the recreation area, even though much could have been learned about more distant sections of the region had time and resources permitted. Finally, prime prospects for interviews were selected to provide coverage of the specific kinds of information needed to reconstruct area lifeways as they changed from early settlement through the mid-twentieth century.

Topics explored with interviewees and other local consultants included the following: technology of subsistence farming and forest utilization; hunting and trapping; foodways, including use of game and wild plant foods; folk medicine; handcrafts and domestic skills; wage work activities; education; religion and church life; family and community activities; folk music and oral genres; and the history and occupational lore of specific settlements, commercial logging and mining companies, and railroads. Research activities with key consultants included informal conversation, formal interviews and oral history taping sessions, field trips to sites within the recreation area, demonstrations of domestic skills and crafts, and music making. Home visits offered some opportunity for observing and participating in daily life activities on an informal basis. The local practice of visiting frequently with relatives and friends and the enjoyment many interviewees got from remembering and talking about old times smoothed the way for work with key consultants. Some, but very few, of the people approached for interviews declined to participate in the project.

The Special Collections Division of Margaret I. King Library at the University of Kentucky, Lexington, is the repository for fifty-five oral history interviews (some spread over multiple sessions) and forty tapes of local musicians and preachers recorded during this project. The Big South Fork collection also includes copies of fifteen oral history interviews recorded during 1976 and 1978 for the McCreary County Library Oral History Project. The music collection also was incorporated into an extensive archive of folklore and folk music recordings held at the Tennessee State Library and Archives in Nashville.

Architectural Evaluations. Folklife study personnel identified standing structures that were potential candidates for National Register nomination and referred these to Professor J. P. Noffsinger, an architectural historian with the University of Kentucky School of Architecture. Based on his onsite evaluations, the Corps of Engineers contracted for an exhaustive evaluation of architecture in the recreation area (Hutchinson, Dugan, and Levy 1982).

Three approaches were used to identify structures that needed to be included in the architectural evaluations: (1) Persons already familiar with the Big South Fork area were asked for information regarding structures in the area. These included local residents, Corps of Engineers Land Acquisition personnel, and National Park Service archaeologists working in the project area. (2) Houses and outbuildings were screened and preliminary information noted during the initial survey of households located inside the recreation area boundaries. (3) All nonresident landowners were sent a questionnaire requesting information about any pre-1930 buildings still standing on land being acquired for the recreation area. This questionnaire produced a response rate of 25 percent and some potential interviewees on topics of general interest, but it failed to turn up any additional structures.

Cemetery Survey. Active cemeteries were avoided wherever possible in establishing the recreation area boundaries, but there are a number of cemeteries, some small and inactive, within the boundaries. Several inactive cemeteries, small family plots, or isolated graves not indicated on county highway and U.S. Geological Survey maps were discovered through conversations with local residents and during the initial survey of households located within the project area. Several of these sites were visited with local residents; however, in some cases these people knew the general location of individual graves or small family plots but could no longer find them.

Appendix 2 is a cemetery inventory containing observations recorded to gather evidence of recent use (interments and visitation for upkeep and decoration). The survey also provided an opportunity to document burial practices and augment other data on settlement history by establishing when and by which families the various cemeteries had been used. Because of these historical objectives, and because of potential impacts of recreational development on cemeteries near but not within the area boundaries, the cemetery survey included a number of cemeteries lying outside the project boundaries. County historical society cemetery inventories, much of the information available online, have largely superseded this aspect of the project.

DATA SOURCES

The overview of Big South Fork regional history presented in chapter 1 was drawn primarily from published historical and statistical source materials. Chapters 2–7 rely heavily on oral history sources to reconstruct a picture of daily life. The time frame of this account is approximately 1900–1950; however, ethnographic observation confirmed the persistence of many traditional lifeways into the late 1970s. Chapter 8 reiterates and integrates the information presented in earlier chapters through describing the details of economic activities and decision making carried out by particular families engaged in farming, logging, mining, and railroad work. These accounts, assembled from recollection and in some cases from documentary records, illustrate the range of variation in adaptive strategies used by area residents.

Anthropologists studying cultures undergoing rapid modernization typically have reconstructed earlier lifeways from verbal accounts. There is just cause for concern that the resulting "memory culture" may be inaccurate and certainly is selective, but there are means of evaluating information obtained through interviews. No single account need be taken at face value; several accounts of an event or several descriptions of a process are collected and cross-checked against one another.

In some cases external data sources provide a further check on the accuracy of oral history data. For example, Stearns Coal and Lumber Company records can be used to confirm employee statements concerning hours, wages, and dates when mines were opened and closed. Unfortunately, the facts and figures contained in documentary sources alone shed only a little light on the mundane details of everyday life as experienced by miners and their families. In that respect, oral narrative is an irreplaceable source of knowledge.

Unless a written source is cited, the reader should assume that statements are based on a compilation of information from all of the oral history interviewees who discussed the topic in question. Information and insights peculiar to one individual are noted as such, but the individual's identity is not revealed. This practice was adopted to protect individuals from local controversy and criticism. Although all oral history interviewees signed written releases making their tapes available to the public, they did not have the opportunity to review the contents of those tapes to correct misstatements or to delete sensitive material.

Travel and fictional accounts from the past, although they must be used with extreme caution, may have recorded just the kind of ethnographic information needed to flesh out the facts and figures recorded in census reports. In the case of the Big South Fork, Harriette Simpson Arnow, a Pulaski County native who was a historian as well as a novelist, set her *Hunter's Horn* on the Big South Fork only a few miles north of the recreation area boundary. Her 1949 account of this area during the Great Depression agrees substantially with the ethnographic detail recalled by interviewees, a fact that strengthens the case for accuracy in both accounts. Similarly, ethnographic data and the general outlines of oral histories previously collected elsewhere in Appalachia are consistent with data collected during the folklife project. That consistency is another general indicator of accuracy.

Although there was a compelling rationale for giving priority to collecting the oral accounts of elders, readers should bear in mind that this description of life along the Big South Fork is mostly a folk history. In the years since this research was done, anthropologists generally have rediscovered the importance of history, both situating ethnographic studies in historical context and undertaking historical studies that address cultural phenomena in the past rather than through conventional ethnographic fieldwork. Judged by the standards of recent work in Appalachian history and historical anthropology, it is obvious how much more use could have been made of documentary sources had the project time frame permitted extensive documentary research. Two audiences, however, persuaded me to republish the 1981 work despite its limitations: local residents whose history is represented here, and folklorists and cultural anthropologists aware that the report itself has acquired some historical significance because of its association with subsequent developments in cultural heritage conservation and applied ethnography.

Postscript: Cultural Heritage Conservation

The process of carrying out provisions of the folklife survey scope of work raised important questions about its goals and rationale. What aspects of culture were to be preserved? What would constitute acceptable mitigation for adverse impacts caused by the national recreation area? Only if one accepted a shreds-and-patches view of culture—that Big South Fork residents had merely preserved a few interesting but quaint cultural anachronisms into the late twentieth century—would documentation on tape or in print constitute an adequate response to anticipated cultural loss. Instead, traditional knowledge and practices seemed to be thoroughly integrated into daily life. Conservation of a lively and still viable cultural system through active support and encouragement of local culture was still possible and desirable in order to honor the broad spirit of the National Environmental Policy Act of 1969 (PL91-190), specifically the directive to "preserve important historic, cultural, and natural aspects of our national heritage, *and maintain, wherever possible, an environment which supports diversity and variety of individual choice*" (italics mine).

In response to section 102 of PL91-190, draft environmental impact statements for the proposed recreation area had been submitted in May 1973 and in September 1975. Discussion of current economic and social conditions in these statements was quite limited and was based on county-level statistical data and a few interviews with large-scale landowners. The reports did not address the immediate situation of the thirty-four households (some 125 individuals) believed to be living within the proposed boundaries in 1975, nor did it assess the possible social and cultural impacts of their impending relocation. The folklife survey team found it necessary to explore these issues in order to understand the current situation, assess the nature and viability of surviving traditional culture elements, and make useful recommendations directed toward minimizing adverse impacts and enhancing preservation *and perpetuation* of traditional culture.

In the original introduction to this report, I wrote the following:

> *Museum collection and documentation is one approach to heritage preservation. Whether the collection consists of material culture artifacts or ballad texts and tunes, the collector assumes that the traditional culture fabric is fast disintegrating and that these fragments of it must be preserved in a display case, on film, or on recording tape before they too vanish forever. The broader folklife approach to heritage preservation looks beyond cultural artifacts to examine the behavior associated with the changing traditional culture. It traces the thread of continuity between past and present and finds viable traditions that can be perpetuated* in vivo, *not merely preserved* in vitro. *Such a study is the first step in designing development policies that build on the past to support diversity and variety of individual choice and thereby help to maintain a living cultural heritage in rapidly changing areas like the Big South Fork.*

This stance aligned the Big South Fork folklife project with efforts to extend the scope of existing historic preservation legislation to protect intangible aspects of culture as well as material resources. Led by public sector folklorists at the American Folklife Center (AFC) in Washington, D.C., this movement adopted the label "cultural heritage *conservation*" and argued that still viable cultural knowledge and practices must be supported and encouraged in order to conserve cultural diversity. An AFC-commissioned policy report on cultural heritage conservation (Loomis 1983) cited the Big South Fork folklife survey as an example of the kind of research into "community life and values" that should become part of thorough impact assessment for federally funded development projects.

Soon after the Loomis report was published, I alerted applied anthropologists to the significance of its recommendations (Howell 1983b) and took every opportunity to reiterate the importance of ethnographic research to fill what I saw as a huge gap of unaddressed cultural issues between conventional historic preservation research and social impact assessment. I shared what I had learned through the Big South Fork project in conference presentations and publications directed to various audiences: social scientists working in the field of environmental planning (Howell 1984), international conferences on cultural parks convened in 1984 (Howell 1988) and 1988 (Howell 1998), National Park Service cultural resource management staff and contract researchers (Howell 1987), a 1989 conference assessing the National Environmental Policy Act twenty years after its passage (Howell 1993), and practitioners and students in public sector folklore (Howell 1994).

The folklife survey research team was in the field and interacting daily with local residents during real estate assessment prior to land acquisition for the recreation area. We attended public meetings in which Corps of Engineers planners presented their 1978 general master plan to the public. The reactions, questions, and complaints I heard from local people who attended those meetings (and especially from potential relocatees who were not heard in public meetings) sensitized me to the importance of genuine rather than token public participation in land use planning (see Howell 1989, 1990, 1993, 1998). Cultural conservation depends upon participation of directly affected citizens, not simply as sources of information, but also as respected collaborators in the decisions that affect their well-being.

The Big South Fork project was a formative experience for Susan Stonich and for me. In her doctoral research and throughout a distinguished career, Susan has continued to focus her research, teaching, and applied work on environmental anthropology issues. For me, the project established a career-long interest in cultural impacts of land-use policy and the cultural history of Appalachia, especially development of tourism in the region. While conducting the research and writing the 1981 report, I could not have foreseen how much notice the Big South folklife survey would attract beyond the immediate audiences of Big

South Fork planners and local residents. In the context of efforts to expand the scope and utility of the historic preservation and cultural resource management that were standard practice in the late 1970s, this project was held up as an instructive case example for two separate but related initiatives: a multidisciplinary cultural heritage conservation effort supported by federal, state, local, and private-sector programs, and an applied ethnography program for the national park system

Changes in the Revised Edition

Since the 1981 report has historical importance because of its contribution (albeit modest) to the cultural heritage conservation initiative and to institutionalizing applied ethnography for national parks, the original report is reissued here with minimal changes aside from this new introduction. I have resisted the impulse to revise extensively based on all that I have learned in more than twenty years of additional work in Appalachian Studies and anthropology. The original technical report was intended to become a part of the Big South Fork master planning documents. As such, it contained some detailed information omitted from this revision because it is out of date and would be more misleading than enlightening. The sections have been reorganized somewhat to make the book more readable for a general audience. Otherwise, most changes in content correct errors, improve style, or reword statements to provide readers a clear time frame. What the research team saw and experienced firsthand and described in present tense in the original report is now as much a part of history as the events and landmarks described in residents' anecdotes. In the "Recommendations" chapter I have added a few impressionistic comments to indicate whether recommendations have been implemented. Thorough, systematic assessment of the recreation area's impact on the culture, society, and economy of the region would be a major project in its own right, however.

The bibliography of the 1981 report is reproduced in its original topical arrangement followed by a single alphabetical listing of references cited in this book. For general readers interested in finding other material on the Big South Fork area, the following is a selected list of books published since 1980 that should be readily available from regional libraries or bookstores.

For Further Reading

Baker, Howard H., and J. Netherton
1993   *Big South Fork Country.* Nashville, Tenn.: Rutledge Hill Press. Building Conservation Technology, Inc.

1984 *Master Plan for the Development, Management, and Protection of the Rugby Colony Historic Area.* Nashville, Tenn.: U.S. Army Corps of Engineers.

Coleman, Brenda D., and Jo Anna Smith
1993 *Hiking the Big South Fork.* Knoxville: University of Tennessee Press.

Deaver, Brenda G., Jo Anna Smith, and Howard Ray Duncan
1999 *Hiking the Big South Fork.* Knoxville: University of Tennessee Press.

Dickinson, W. Calvin
1987 *Morgan County.* Memphis, Tenn.: Memphis State University Press.

Hogue, Albert R.
1994 *History of Fentress County, Tennessee.* Baltimore: Genealogical Publishing Co.

Manning, Russ, and Sondra Jamieson
1990 *The Best of the Big South Fork National River and Recreation Area: A Hiker's Guide to Trails and Attractions.* Norris, Tenn.: Laurel Place.

McBride, Kim A.
1993 *A Background Archival and Oral Historical Study of the Barthell Coal Camp, McCreary County Kentucky.* Lexington: Program for Cultural Resource Assessment, University of Kentucky.

McCreary County, Kentucky Historical and Genealogical Society
2000 *McCreary County, Kentucky, History and Families.* Paducah, Ky.: Turner Publishing Co.

McDade, Arthur
2000 *The Natural Arches of the Big South Fork: A Guide to Selected Landforms.* Knoxville: University of Tennessee Press.

Roy, Jean
1996 *Over the Hill: Collected Newspaper Columns from the Pages of the Independent Herald, Oneida, Tennessee, 1976–1992.* Oneida, Tenn.: *Independent Herald.*

Scott County Historical Society
1992 *A Pictorial History of Scott County, Tennessee.* Huntsville, Tenn.: Scott County Historical Society.

Stephens, Robert Ernest
1989–90 *McCreary County, Kentucky Cemeteries.* 3 vols. Utica, Ky.: McDowell Publications.

Historical Overview of the Big South Fork Area

From the perspective of cultural ecology, the fundamental elements shaping the course of events along the Big South Fork have been changing human responses to a changing environment. Change has been stimulated by introduction of new technologies making possible exploitation of additional environmental resources and modifying the nature of social interaction. Economic development built upon these technologies and brought new groups of people to the area. Together, the old and new residents continued the process of interacting with their environment and devising new cultural responses to the opportunities and problems they created for themselves.

The specifics of human adaptation in the Big South Fork area are described in the following chapters in which individual technological systems such as subsistence farming and coal mining are treated separately. In reality, these systems and their effects have been interdependent. This brief introduction to the region provides a framework for integrating the information that follows.

The Physical Environment

TOPOGRAPHY AND GEOLOGY

The Big South Fork basin covers 1,382 square miles of the Cumberland Plateau in north-central Tennessee and southeastern Kentucky and includes three major tributaries of the Big South Fork River: Clear Fork, New River, and the Little South Fork. The lowest basin elevation, 673 feet, is the confluence of the Big South Fork and the Cumberland River, now inundated by Lake Cumberland. As one travels southward toward the confluence of New River and Clear Fork, the course of the river becomes increasingly tortuous where it has carved out steep gorges. The highest basin elevation, 3,534 feet, occurs in the southeastern section (U.S. Army, Corps of Engineers 1976, 14).

The recreation area includes the gorge and rim areas of Clear Fork, New River, and Big South Fork. Terrain near streams is rugged, characterized by highly dissected mesas capped with resistant sandstone. As streams eroded the rock they formed steep-walled canyons; flood plains are poorly developed. Resistant rock in the stream channels and rock falls from adjacent cliffs form rapids and obstructions at various points. Differential erosion and weathering have produced caves and arches in the less resistant shale and siltstone of the valley walls (U.S. Army, Corps on Engineers 1976, 60).

The Big South Fork drainage basin formed in generally flat Carboniferous sediments of the Cumberland Plateau. During the Mississippian and Pennsylvanian, the area consisted of tidal deltas, flats and lagoons, and near shore swamps associated with an oscillating shoreline. Sedimentation created predominantly sandstone and shale, with lesser amounts of siltstone, conglomerate, and coal. Limestone is found only in the lowest exposures of Mississippian rocks (U.S. Army, Corps of Engineers 1976, 21–22).

MINERAL RESOURCES

Big South Fork basin mineral resources include coal, petroleum, and natural gas. Of these, coal has been the most important commercial resource. Most of the thickest exposed coal seams along the Big South Fork in Kentucky have been mined out, but a considerable amount of coal is still thought to be present in thinner exposed seams and in subsurface seams (Pomerence 1964).

Petroleum and natural gas resources are found primarily in Mississippian rocks underlying the region. Most oil and gas producing zones are located within 2,000 feet of the surface. When oil and gas prices are strong, numerous wells are dug. These may reach maximum production levels of several hundred barrels of oil, or 3,000 cubic feet of gas, per day, but production tapers off fairly rapidly.

Although the U.S. Geological Survey finds it unlikely that additional shallow oil reserves of substantial size will be discovered, the Tennessee Division of Geology believes that pools yielding one to three million barrels will be found. Deeper Ordovician and Cambrian rocks are the most promising field for exploration (U.S. Army, Corps of Engineers 1976, 27). These had been relatively untapped because of the high cost of initial drilling. In the late 1970s, however, several abandoned wells were revived by secondary recovery methods. Scarcity and strong prices periodically revive the region's petroleum industry.

Other mineral resources of the area include silica, limestone, and commercial grade clay deposits. These resources have not been exploited commercially.

SOILS

A detailed soil survey of the McCreary County portion of the recreation area (Byrne et al. 1970) lists three soil associations: Tate-Trappist, Tate-Clymer-DeKalb, and Tate-Shelocta. Tate and Shelocta soils generally are found at the lowest elevations on slopes of between 12 percent and 35 percent. These are the only soils of the area developed from calcareous shale and limestone. Historically these soils supported subsistence farming and pasture; the land is now mostly forested.

The steeper valley slopes at higher elevations are occupied either by Tate soils (on slopes of from 39 percent to 50 percent) or by Tate-Trappist soils (on slopes of from 25 percent to 45 percent). Trappist soils also occur on the ridge tops. Acid shale and sandstone underlie these soils. Their agricultural potential is limited by slope and, especially in the case of Trappist soils, by slow permeability. Nevertheless, the wider ridge tops, now mostly forested, once supported farms.

DeKalb soils are found on steep slopes beneath narrow ridge tops where Clymer or Trappist soils occur. Beds of sandstone and shale underlie the Clymer and DeKalb soils, and yellow pine and oak dominate their forest cover.

According to data compiled by the East Tennessee Development District (1980), soils in the Tennessee portions of the Big South Fork basin include Hartsells-Ramsey, Ramsey-Jefferson-Hartsells, Rockland-Hermitage, Ramsey-Jefferson, Waynesboro-Cumberland, and Bodine-Montview-Baxter. These sandstone and slate-based soils are deficient in phosphoric acid and lime. Throughout the recreation area, moderate soil fertility, steep slopes, and rapid runoff created adverse conditions for agriculture.

CLIMATE

Moist, hot summers and mild winters are typical for the Big South Fork drainage. Temperatures average lower and precipitation is greater on the Cumberland Plateau than in adjacent lowlands lying below the plateau escarpments. Highest average temperatures recorded at Rugby, Tennessee, between 1880 and 1949 occurred during July (high, 86.9° F; low, 61.6° F). Lowest average temperatures were recorded during January (high, 47.5° F; low 26.2° F).

Prevailing winds from the south and southwest bring moist air from the Gulf Coast into the area. Based on the Rugby data, average monthly precipitation varies from a low of 3.4 inches in October to a high of 6 inches in March. Snowfall averages 17 inches a year, but snow seldom stays on the ground longer than a few days. Flooding is most common during December through March, but summer thunderstorms may cause local flash flooding (U.S. Army, Corps of Engineers 1976, 15–16).

Within the recreation area, atmospheric inversions cause temperatures in the valleys and canyons to be higher in summer and lower in winter than those on adjacent highlands (U.S. Army, Corps of Engineers 1976, 58). Microclimatic variation extends to precipitation and humidity as well.

WATER RESOURCES

Stream flow data have been collected from twelve gauging stations in the Big South Fork basin since 1908. Seasonal variability in stream flow has been much greater than the seasonal variability in precipitation. Surface runoff is high in the recreation area because of the relative impermeability of exposed rocks, the steepness of slopes, and the thinness of soils. In spite of abundant rainfall, stream flow in small drainage areas is not adequately sustained by groundwater during periods of minimum precipitation (Kernodle et al. 1974). Within the region, evaporation rates are least during periods of greatest precipitation. Thus the highest stream flow values are recorded from January through March when precipitation is greatest, and the lowest values are recorded during September and October (U.S. Army, Corps of Engineers 1976, 64).

A survey of water resources in the Tennessee portion of the recreation area (Kernodle et al. 1974) located groundwater in interconnected joints, cracks, and bedding planes in Pennsylvanian sandstone and conglomerate. Although early settlers located and used natural springs, interstitial waters tend to be unavailable because of low permeability. Yields from modern wells and their depths vary considerably. The Kernodle survey determined that 80 percent of the wells yield at least two gallons per minute, sufficient water for an electric pump system supplying a household without all of the modern conveniences. However, fewer than 40 percent yield ten gallons per minute, the flow needed to ensure a dependable water supply for a modern house and some associated commercial agriculture, such as a broiler house. Water supply has been a limiting factor affecting settlement location, agricultural development, and household improvements.

Euro-American Settlement History

EXPLORATION

Although maps of early exploration leave the area south of the Cumberland River a blank (e.g., Caruso 1959), it is possible that Euro-Americans entered the Big South Fork basin as early as the spring of 1749–50, when Dr. Thomas Walker penetrated Cumberland Gap and discovered the Cumberland River (McCague 1973, 26). The Long Hunters, most famous among them Daniel Boone, lost no time exploiting this virgin territory. McCague (1973, 37) describes their activities in detail.

> The long hunt was not sport but business, and the hunters went about it in that spirit. They went out in parties of as many as forty or fifty, partly for protection against the Indians but mainly because large parties could cover more country more efficiently and kill more animals. Since each man customarily had at least two packhorses to carry out the skins he took, plenty of provisions for a long stay could be packed in, and were. Otherwise the men traveled with the bare necessities: ample powder and lead, of course; bullet molds; axes and a few additional tools; spare parts for rifles that might need repairing—and that was about it. The station camp set up in some selected location became a more or less

permanent base. A rude, open-faced hut of poles covered with peeled bark, buffalo hides, or whatever was at hand provided shelter. In many places along the Cumberland, a cave or the lee of a shelving rock, still called a rock house in regional parlance, served more admirably than any hut.

One Long Hunter story widely told involved two brothers, Abraham and Isaac Bledsoe, who returned to their station camp to find that Indians had stolen their entire cache of skins. Their loss was memorialized with a tree-trunk inscription: LOST 2300 DEERSKINS RUINATION BY GOD. McCague (1973, 36) states that the Bledsoes were hunting on the Big South Fork when this incident occurred; however, Caruso (1959, 66) places them at Bledsoe's Lick in Middle Tennessee.

Whatever the undocumented facts of early exploration by the Long Hunters, settlers interested in agricultural land bypassed the Big South Fork for the Kentucky bluegrass or the Cumberland Country of Middle Tennessee. Later, some of these early Middle Tennesseans pushed back eastward into the relative wilderness of the Cumberland Plateau, where their family names survive today. Among such settlers named by McCague are an Isaac Crabtree (1973, 44), John Rains (1973, 61–62), and Abednego Llewellen (1973, 84). Obediah Terril did not marry or produce descendants, but he gave his name to the Obey River (McCague 1973, 34).

EARLY SETTLEMENT, 1780–1820

Extensive Euro-American occupation of the Big South Fork area first developed in Kentucky between 1780 and 1820. Land grant records, historic maps, early census data, and the family histories told by local residents are in mutual agreement on this fact. Factors stimulating settlement were the opening of transportation routes (Speed 1886, 63), the Tellico Land Grants (Johnson 1939, 17), and legislative encouragement from the State of Kentucky (Johnson 1939, 65).

Three Indian trails also used by pioneer Euro-Americans ran through the Big South Fork area. Two trails ran east–west; one of these connected points near modern-day Williamsburg and Monticello, and the other ran southeastward from Monticello, crossing the Big South Fork near its confluence with Rock Creek. The third trail ran north-south between Lexington, Kentucky, and Crab Orchard, Tennessee, paralleling the later route of the Cincinnati Southern Railroad and U.S. Highway 27 (Myer 1971). An early publication with maps, *Description of Roads in the U.S., 1814* (Melish 1814), indicates that this trail had become a road as far south as Chitwood, a community on the Kentucky–Tennessee border. Verhoeff (1911, 101) attributes maintenance and continued extension of this road to economic influence from Ohio that began expanding into southeastern Kentucky and north-central Tennessee in the early 1800s.

Land grants encouraged settlers to follow these transportation routes into the area. The Big South Fork basin was included in the Cherokee Territory shown on the 1794 map. Although settlers everywhere along the frontier pushed into Indian territory before it was legal to do so, most of the Big South Fork basin was not officially open for settlement until the Third Tellico Treaty was signed in 1805. Between 1803 and 1853, 572 "Tellico Grants" were issued, many of them for land between the Big South Fork and the Little South Fork in Wayne County, Kentucky. Most were small grants of 100 to 200 acres, but they ranged in size from 9 to 1,029 acres (Jillson 1925, 9).

In what is now McCreary County, John Mounce took up a large grant that included the future site of Stearns, Kentucky. Elisha Slaven supposedly sold his grant around Oil Valley for a hog rifle and a pair of horseshoes. He then moved south to Tackett Creek, a tributary of No Business Creek in Scott County, Tennessee. According to Sanderson (1958, 20), early Scott County settlers who received land grants in consideration of their Revolutionary War service included a West and a Chambers on Cherry Fork and Richard Harve Slaven, who held land from the mouth of Bear Creek to the mouth of Parch Corn. Jonathan Blevins, a Long Hunter who moved from place to place, gradually worked his way south from Oil Valley to Station Camp Creek in Scott County, where his children settled down to farming, mostly self-provisioning.

These early settlers cleared the narrow bottomlands for crops and raised hogs, cattle, and sheep in the ridge top woods. Hunting continued to contribute greatly to their diet, and most other necessities came from the area's natural resources as well. Sales of wood products and furs generated the little cash income that was needed. Despite the "unsuitability" of the land for farming—its rugged topography and its thin, sandy, acid soil—the 1850 census recorded 126 people living along Station Camp Creek. By 1900, families were living on farms from one-half to one mile apart along Station Camp from its headwaters to its mouth.

Commercial inducements to settle the Big South Fork area date from 1813. In that year, Kentucky and Ohio business interests persuaded the Kentucky Legislature to issue land grants in Wayne and Pulaski Counties on very favorable terms in order to encourage salt exploration and manufacture. Their policy was in response to severe salt shortages that developed following the War of 1812. Grant holders were not required to pay for their land until after they had manufactured 1,000 bushels of salt; then they paid the State of Kentucky ten cents per acre (Johnson 1939, 65). Huling and Zimmerman, the salt prospectors who brought in Kentucky's first commercial oil well, had become landowners under this program.

LATER SETTLEMENT, 1820–80

Family history related by interviewees agrees with Freytag and Ott's (1970) Morgan County history in suggesting that a second wave of settlers pushed into the Big South Fork area from the southern end of the Cumberland Plateau. Knoxville was established by the 1790s and was linked to Nashville by a road crossing the Cumberland Plateau, passing through Crab Orchard. Population in Anderson and Roane Counties was large enough that in 1817 Morgan County was created from the northern sections of old Anderson and Roane. Morgan County contained parts of what would become Fentress and Scott Counties. As population shifted further northward, Fentress County was created in 1823 and Scott County in 1849.

Named settlements and trails linking them begin to show up on maps of the Big South Fork area in the 1820s (e.g., Tanner 1829; Young 1826). Maps published between 1855 and 1874 (Colton 1855, 1859, 1863, 1866, 1869, 1874; Mitchell 1860) already show all of the important highway corridors of the late twentieth century. In many cases, however, the development from trail, to wagon road, to gravel road, to paved highway was completed only recently. Old-timers whose families settled the bottomlands along the Big South Fork and its tributaries say that the tablelands that now support feed crops, pasture, livestock, and some truck farming were not productive before chemical fertilizers became available. Historical records, burials, and family stories nevertheless point to fairly extensive settlement in northern Morgan County and adjacent parts of Fentress and Scott Counties by the late 1840s.

It is likely that some formerly occupied lands fell into disuse during and immediately after the Civil War. Almost no official military activity occurred near the Big South Fork, but divided loyalties gave rise to both Confederate and Union guerrillas who preyed upon the civilian populace, wantonly destroying what they did not appropriate for their own use. Families at variance with their neighbors often were harassed so that they left their property during the conflict and were permanently dispossessed at its end. At any rate, during the 1870s and 1880s there were extensive tracts of plateau land awaiting development and a new railroad, the Cincinnati Southern, to bring settlers into the area. Tennessee and Kentucky governments joined private entrepreneurs in advertising for settlers (e.g., Killebrew 1876; Hughes 1881; Hawkins 1882; McWhirter 1885).

In 1880, the English author and educator Thomas Hughes established a colony for younger sons of English gentry at Rugby in Morgan County, Tennessee. Though short-lived as a British colony, Rugby provided a window on the outside world and some employment for native Tennesseans. From a maximum population of about 350, the community had dwindled to a handful of families by 1900 (Rugby Restoration Association 1972). Most of the colonists were ill prepared for rural life in this isolated location and moved on to Chattanooga, Knoxville, and other urban centers, but a few married into the indigenous population.

The community of Allardt in Fentress County, Tennessee, started about the same time as Rugby. Named for the German emigration officer who promoted its development, Allardt was a planned community that attracted some settlers from German communities in northern Michigan and others directly from Germany. A grid pattern of roads was laid out, and land was sold to the arriving immigrants in rectangular tracts of 100, 50, or 25 acres. They began extensive agricultural exploitation and later added large tracts of undeveloped Fentress County land to their holdings. Logging and coal mining operations were established on these landholdings. In addition to farmers and entrepreneurs, the community attracted individuals skilled in a variety of crafts and commercial sectors (*Allardt Neighbor* 1925). Allardt flourished and is still the home of many descendants of the original settlers. It is the only incorporated town in Fentress County other than the county seat, Jamestown.

POST-1900 POPULATION TRENDS

Population figures for the period 1850 to 1880 show healthy increases throughout the region (see appendix 3, tables 1 and 2). Even Fentress County increased 33.4 percent despite the ravages of the Civil War, but the greatest increase, 216 percent, occurred in Scott County. Cincinnati Southern Railroad construction, which began during the 1870s, may explain this population growth.

During the period 1880–1900, the largest percentage increases in population occurred in Scott County (84 percent) and in Whitley County (109 percent). These increases are well above the average population gains of Tennessee (31 percent) and Kentucky (30 percent) during the same twenty years. Development of the coal mining, logging, and railroad industries is reflected in these increases, but they are only a shadow of the population growth to come in the early decades of the twentieth century (see appendix 3, table 1). Large-scale industrial development between 1900 and 1920 brought the last sizable groups of immigrants—management personnel and skilled workers required by the railroads, mines, and lumber concerns.

These decades were boom times for the area, but dwindling supplies of easily accessible timber and coal coupled with the general economic slowdown and labor unrest of the depression years dealt these industries a heavy blow. World War II demand for coal and wood products provided a temporary boost to the local economy but also introduced local workers to the opportunities and drawbacks of out-migration. Recruited first as workers in defense plants, area residents joined the general Appalachian migration to northern cities, chiefly Muncie, Indiana, as local jobs disappeared.

Beginning in 1950, Fentress, Scott, and McCreary County census figures began to reflect high rates of out-migration. The highest was a 43 percent out-migration rate in McCreary County between 1950 and 1960 (see appendix 3, table 3). From 1950 to 1970, primarily because of out-migration, all three counties experienced population decline: Fentress County, 16 percent; Scott County, 8 percent; McCreary County, 25 percent.

Among those who stayed at home, residents of the river gorge area began to move to the surrounding tableland communities. Their exodus was hastened by the closing of logging and mining operations, rural schools, country stores, and post offices, and by the deterioration of unpaved county roads that never had been engineered for automobile travel. Abandonment of many miles of short line railroad removed the only convenient mode of transportation available to many of these communities. By 1960, it would have been difficult to realize that the Big South Fork gorge and adjacent area had once supported dozens of logging and mine camps and rural settlements, each with its own school enrolling fifty to eighty students per session. Fewer than thirty-five year-round households remained within the recreation area boundaries when land acquisition began.

In contrast to the project area, overall population of Fentress, Scott, and McCreary Counties increased more than 10 percent between 1970 and 1975. Census estimates for 1978 projected continued increases. Several factors were responsible: (1) the return of retirees who had left the area earlier; (2) decreased employment opportunities in northern and midwestern industrial cities, especially following the mid-1970s economic recession; (3) a very high regional birth rate; and (4) expanding local employment opportunities, which have slowed out-migration. In particular, increased demand and higher prices for domestic energy revitalized the local coal and oil industries in the late 1970s.

Economic Development

THE SUBSISTENCE FARMING BASE AND EARLY COMMERCE

Permanent settlers who followed the Long Hunters into the Big South Fork region continued to rely heavily on hunting to supplement subsistence farming. The transition to farming was gradual if family stories about Jonathan Blevins (1779–1863) are typical: "That old man carried his frying pan . . . I'm just trying to tell you that they moved from one place to another to get into better hunting grounds . . . he just mostly hunted . . . These younger ones did farm more; they didn't hunt as much." Samuel Hall, a Morgan County resident who lived a generation later than Jonathan Blevins, was a prodigious hunter whose exploits were recorded in his epitaph (Freytag and Ott 1970, 92): "Samuel Hall, Born Dec. 20, 1820, Died Oct. 7, 1887. He was a farmer and a hunter by trade. Road (sic) and hunted. He killed 1800 deer with 1 gun. He cared (sic) in about 4 at a time on his mule and he marked it on his gun stock. He had 4000 or more squirrels and turkeys, and coons not to be numbered. He willed his gun to his younger son A. L. Hall."

Descriptions of "one-horse farms" along the Cumberland River drawn from Harriette Simpson Arnow's *Flowering of the Cumberland* (1963, 210–60) apply equally to early farming practice along the Big South Fork. Horses rather than oxen were the common draft animals, but mules were introduced early in the nineteenth century and came to be preferred by many farmers for their strength, endurance, and modest food requirements. Middle Tennessee's original pattern of open-range grazing continued on the plateau until the 1950s, when counties there began to enact fence laws. Under the open-range pattern, the average farmer could maintain large herds of cattle and flocks of sheep as well as hogs and milk cows. Each farmer devised a distinctive combination of ear crops to mark possession of his animals and registered his mark with the county clerk. By burning the underbrush each spring, farmers aimed to turn the woods into grassy parklands for their cattle and sheep. Acorns and chestnuts provided mast for domestic hogs and the razorbacks that were still plentiful.

Crops rather than livestock were fenced. These included corn, some wheat, flax, and occasionally cotton. Among the vegetables, beans, potatoes, and cabbage were most common because they could easily be preserved for future use. Beans were dried or pickled, potatoes and cabbage were holed up in pits or kept in root cellars, and cabbage was made into kraut. Apple and peach trees provided fresh fruit in season and dried fruit through the winter. With the addition of chickens for eggs and meat, geese for feathers, several stands of bees originally captured from the wild, and the many natural resources that provided additional food, fuel, and building materials, the farmer had few purchases to make.

The farm family also tanned hides and made shoes and other leather goods; created their clothing and household linens from raw flax, cotton, and wool; turned timber and stone into houses, outbuildings, and chimneys; produced gunpowder and bullets, tar and turpentine, and lime; and made and repaired tools, wagons, furniture, and many other household implements. Little besides salt, coffee, and the metal stock used in blacksmithing had to be bought. One family story suggests that coffee was a mystery to some as late as 1840. It seems that the women who were preparing dinner for a "working" delayed and delayed serving the meal. When the men became impatient, one of the women explained that everything else was ready, but the coffee beans just would not get soft. She was trying to cook them up like any other dried beans.

By the time Thomas Hughes arrived on the scene in the 1880s, socioeconomic differences among the native Tennesseans whom he encountered were readily apparent. Hughes (1881, 62–63) described his neighbors thus:

> *When all is said and sung, there is nothing so interesting as the men and women who dwell on any corner of the earth.... Let me introduce you to our neighbors, so far as I have as yet the pleasure of their acquaintance.... They are poor almost to a man, and live in log-huts and cabins which at home [Great Britain] could scarcely be rivaled out of Ireland. Within ten miles of this place [Rugby]*

there are possibly half-a-dozen which are equal in accommodation and comfort to those of good farmers in England. The best of these belongs to our nearest neighbor, with whom a party of us dined. . . . He has been on his farm twenty years, and has cleared some fifty acres, which grow corn and vegetables and he has a fine apple orchard. We should call his farming very slovenly, but it produces abundance for his needs. . . . The vast majority of these mountaineers are in very different circumstances. Most, but not all of them, own a log cabin and minute patch of corn round it, probably also a few pigs and chickens, but seem to have no desire to make any effort at further clearing, and quite content to live from hand to mouth. They cannot do that without hiring themselves out when they get a chance.

Various means of earning cash income had developed by the 1880s. As early as 1826, commercial activity was under way in Morgan County. Manufacturing concerns were producing whiskey and turpentine, wool and fur hats, leather, and sugar maple sap (Freytag and Ott 1970, 29). The 1860 Census of Manufacturers (see appendix 3, table 5) listed two coal mines, two gristmills, one tanyard, and three sawmills for Morgan County. This census listed no manufacturing concern for either Fentress or Scott County, although information collected from interviewees suggests that commercial gristmills and sawmills were operating by that date. Pulaski, Whitley, and Wayne Counties in Kentucky (in that rank order) supported a greater number and variety of manufacturing establishments. However, these activities were centered in Somerset, Williamsburg, and Monticello, not in the outlying sections that would later be merged into McCreary County.

EXTRACTIVE INDUSTRY, 1880–1930

Completion of the Cincinnati Southern Railroad through the Big South Fork region in 1880 marked the beginning of intensive commercial exploitation of timber and mineral resources. The railroad and the companies attracted to the area once this transportation link was in place greatly expanded existing opportunities for wage employment. Many farmers who did not take jobs earned extra cash by cutting and hewing railroad cross ties. Local entrepreneurs like John Morgan of Pine Knot who were situated near the railroad could turn themselves into middlemen, buying such commodities as tanbark, animal pelts, and medicinal herbs from local farmer-producers and exporting them from the region. This trade expanded the subsistence farmer's opportunities for cash income and created stronger markets for the commercial foodstuffs and manufactured goods that became readily available once the railroad was in operation. The railroad also provided improved transportation within the region and linked its residents to more distant population centers. Last but not least, the railroad swelled county tax revenues.

Outsider capitalists who realized the economic potential in the region's forest and mineral resources had begun construction of the Cincinnati Southern Railroad through the area in the 1870s. With the opening of the section served by the Pine Knot, Kentucky, terminal in February of 1880, the route was complete between Cincinnati, Ohio, and Monroe, Louisiana (McWhirter 1885, 62).

In 1881 two coal mines were opened in Scott County along the route of the Cincinnati Southern, the Crooke Coal and Coke Company in Glenmary and the Helenwood Coal Company in Helenwood. For the year ending December 31, 1881, the Crooke Company employed an average of 175 men and shipped 45,000 tons of coal north to Lexington, Kentucky, and south to Macon, Georgia (Colton 1883, 55).

In 1884 a branch line was built from Flat Rock, Kentucky, to Barren Fork, two miles to the east, where the Barren Fork Mining and Coal Company (later the Eagle Coal Company) began operations that continued until the labor disputes of 1935 (Perry 1979, 98). A few miles farther south along the route, the Bryant mines were opened both in Kentucky and in Tennessee.

WAGE WORK AND EXTRACTIVE INDUSTRY

Based on data from the 1900 Census of Manufacturers (see appendix 3, table 4), one can estimate the relative importance of wage and agricultural labor. Eighty-seven percent of the households in Fentress County and 82 percent in Wayne County were classified as farm households, while only 68 percent of those in Scott County and 70 percent in Whitley County were so classified. In 1900 the "average number of wage earners" (undefined in the census) ranged from 0.2 percent of the population in Fentress and Wayne Counties to 2 percent of the population in Scott County.

At that time, timber products were still sold primarily by small landowners who cut their own timber and either turned it into rough lumber, barrel staves, and cross ties, or floated the logs, especially tulip poplar for veneer, down the Big South Fork to mills at Burnside, Kentucky.

Beginning in 1902, the Stearns Coal and Lumber Company became the predominant force shaping economic development in the northern two-thirds of the Big South Fork area. Although top and middle management were sent from northern Michigan, where the company owner, Justus S. Stearns, had lumber and salt mining interests, supervisors, miners, and loggers were recruited from the local population. By 1910 the company owned vast areas of McCreary, Scott, Fentress, and Pickett Counties.

Laws protecting squatters' rights were liberal, especially in Tennessee, where a squatter could acquire title to land that he cleared, fenced, planted, and lived on for a period of seven years. Stearns therefore made a practice of leasing timberlands, especially those in Tennessee, to tenants who cleared and fenced boundaries and built homes and farm buildings there. In return for protecting the land under their charge from vandalism and the encroachment of squatters, tenants lived there rent-free. They could use down wood, cut limited amounts of standing timber for construction purposes, fish, hunt, trap, collect wild plants, etc. Their presence as legal tenants helped Stearns perfect its own land titles.

Yet while Stearns was encouraging, even subsidizing, the continuation of a subsistence farming lifestyle, it was also creating a sizable nonfarm population. As the Kentucky and Tennessee Railroad, a subsidiary company established by Stearns in 1902, laid track westward along Rock Creek, permanent settlements of mining families grew up along the rail line. After a logging railroad southwest from Bell Farm was begun in 1925, a number of temporary logging camps were established along that line. The Stearns Coal and Lumber Company grew until 1929, when it produced 970,000 tons of coal and 18 million board feet of lumber. The company employed two thousand miners and an unknown number of loggers (Stearns archives).

Local problems and nationwide economic conditions contributed to Stearns Coal and Lumber Company's decline during the Great Depression. First, Stearns was far from any of the great potential coal markets, so that their product had to be either more expensive to consumers or less profitable to produce. Second, the coal deposits themselves were thin and irregular, and the technology available at the time did not allow processing within manageable cost limits. Labor disputes closed the mines from 1935 to 1936, and when they reopened they were operated for only one or two days a week. By 1935, coal production had fallen to less than 400,000 tons (Stearns archives). In 1937 Fidelity, along with other smaller mines, was closed; however, a new mine, Blue Heron (Mine 18), was opened that year (Stearns archives). Increased coal demands during World War II brought a temporary recovery, but by 1950 annual coal production was again less than 400,000 tons. The mine at Cooperative closed that year, and Mine 4 was to close two years later (Stearns archives).

Most of the company's easily accessible timber had been logged out by 1935, when the U.S. Forest Service bought surface rights to 47,000 acres of cutover timberland. The State of Tennessee bought the land for a nominal sum and created Pickett State Park and Forest. By 1950 the logging railroad had been scrapped.

In the 1910s and 1920s, mines and lumber companies also flourished in Tennessee south of the Stearns holdings. The Oneida and Western Railroad (O & W) in Scott and Fentress Counties performed many of the same functions as the Kentucky and Tennessee, but for smaller independent coal and lumber companies. Organizers of the O & W included officers of the Tennessee Stave and Lumber Company, whose major stockholders were based in Monterey,

Tennessee. Railroad construction began in 1913 from Oneida and was completed to East Jamestown by 1921. A spur and incline joined the main line to a logging railroad in the Wolf River area. Tennessee Stave had its peak production year in 1929 but declined rapidly thereafter. Although the O & W was extended nine miles to Jamestown in 1930, economic conditions and a developing highway system steadily diminished its importance as a freight carrier. The O & W was abandoned in 1953. For most of its existence the O & W had been the only convenient link between Oneida and Fentress County, but WPA road building projects changed that. Although they provided additional employment, the road-building projects hastened the O & W's decline as trucks and automobiles began to assume the railroad's functions. But because no improved road followed the railroad's route, the coal mines located along North White Oak Creek had to be abandoned also.

FARMING, 1900 TO 1930

From 1900 to 1930, while Stearns and other companies were actively acquiring land and extensively extracting the area's natural resources, the three-county population continued to increase at a rate equal to, or in the case of Scott County, three times the average increase for their states (see appendix 3, table 1). At the same time, the number of farms remained relatively stable (see appendix 3, table 6) while decreasing approximately 50 percent in average size (see appendix 3, table 7). By 1930 the farm population represented 52.5 percent of the total Fentress County population, 44.6 percent of the Scott County population, and 42.9 percent of the McCreary County population (see appendix 3, table 8).

Detailed statistical data on nonagricultural employment from 1900 to 1930 are not available, but the relative stability in the number of farms during that period suggests that despite increased potential for wage work, farmers continued to farm their smaller landholdings. Data from the 1930 Census (see appendix 3, table 9) offer some confirmation of this: 86 percent of all farms in the three-county area were classified either as "self-sufficing" or as "part-time," designations which in practice were not mutually exclusive. Approximately 62 percent of the farms were identified as "self-sufficing," that is, farms on which the family used 50 percent or more of the total of all farm products produced. "Self-sufficing" farms were most numerous in Fentress County (67.4 percent of all county farms). "Part-time" farms constituted 24 percent of the total farms in the three-county area. A "part-time" farmer spent 150 or more days working for pay at jobs not connected with his farm.

Thus farming continued despite increased opportunity for wage work; wage work became a supplementary source of income for many noncommercial farmers.

In 1930 (see appendix 3, table 10) farmers in Scott, Fentress, and McCreary Counties consumed about two-thirds of their products and sold or traded only one-third, primarily livestock and livestock products.

THE GREAT DEPRESSION AND WORLD WAR II

A farmer describing the 1930s said, "That Depression just blew by us." Regional economic conditions could hardly have "blown by" the 50 percent who were classified as "nonfarm" residents in the 1930 census (see appendix 3, table 8). By 1935 many of the mines had closed because of economic conditions and because of labor disputes; the remaining mines were operating only one or two days a week. The Oneida and Western Railroad also was running only two days per week.

In spite of the reduction in opportunities for wage work, population of the three counties continued to increase during the decade from 1930 to 1940 (see appendix 3, table 1). During that same decade the farm population increased from 46 percent to 58 percent of the total population (see appendix 3, table 8). The number of farms increased 55 percent (see appendix 3, table 6), and the percentage of farm products used by farm households increased from 66 percent to 74 percent despite a threefold increase in commercial crop production in Fentress County (see appendix 3, table 10). As opportunities for wage work diminished, residents chose to emphasize agricultural production rather than out-migration.

Census data on industrial employment (see appendix 3, tables 11, 12 and 13) show that in 1940 agricultural and forest industries constituted the greatest percentage of industrial employment in the three-county area: Fentress County 63.8 percent; Scott County 50.7 percent; McCreary County 35.9 percent. In McCreary County, however, mining was equally important (35.9 percent). Although not contributing as many jobs as in McCreary County, mining was also present in Fentress and Scott Counties, contributing, respectively, 11.2 percent and 11.3 percent of the total industrial employment in those counties.

World War II temporarily bolstered employment in the coal industry by increasing the demand for coal, but by 1950 wartime demands had slackened and conversion to diesel further weakened the bituminous coal market. By 1950 McCreary County had 27.6 percent fewer miners than in 1940 (see appendix 3, table 14). Forest employment declined drastically between 1940 and 1950 (see appendix 3, table 15) as Stearns discontinued hiring its own loggers and shifted entirely to a contract arrangement. Increased wartime demand for forest products hastened depletion of the available resources, and when there were no more harvestable trees there were no more jobs. Reforestation began in the 1950s, but contract logging revived only during the 1970s.

POST-1950 DEVELOPMENTS

By 1950, patterns of wage work, some of which had been established for fifty years, had begun to change through the introduction of new alternatives. All three counties experienced employment increases in manufacturing, trade, and service industries but also decreases in agriculture, forestry, and mining. Manufacturing contributed 15 percent (in McCreary County) to 25 percent (in Scott County) of regional job opportunities. At that time most manufacturing was in wood products; diversification within the manufacturing sector occurred during the following decade (see appendix 3, table 16).

Between 1940 and 1950 the agricultural trends of the previous decade reversed. There was a regional decrease in the number of farms, an increase in average size of farms, and a decrease in the farm population from 58 percent to 48 percent of total population (see appendix 3, table 8). By 1974 there were only 958 farms remaining in the area, an 80 percent decrease since the historic high of 4,922 farms in 1940. The percentage decreases ranged from 91 percent in McCreary County to 70 percent in Fentress County (see appendix 3, table 6). Simultaneously, average farm size increased to 134 acres—almost a 100 percent increase since the 1930 historic low (see appendix 3, table 7). A measure of the extent of commercial agricultural production in 1974 is the percentage of farms that have sales greater than or equal to $2,500. In Fentress County this was 49 percent of all farms; in Scott County, 37 percent; and in McCreary County, only 21 percent (see appendix 3, table 17). In 1974 McCreary County had the fewest farms, the smallest farms, and the lowest percentage of farms with agricultural sales greater than or equal to $2,500.

In 1974, although the same kinds of farm products were sold in all three counties, the relative percentage distributions of these products differed among the counties (see appendix 3, table 17). Poultry products were most important in Fentress County, accounting for 50 percent of all farm products sold. In Scott County livestock sales were most important, accounting for 46 percent of all sales. In McCreary County crops accounted for 50 percent of all farm products sold.

Between 1950 and 1974, the farm population in Fentress County decreased from 61 percent of the total population to 20 percent; in Scott County, from 45 percent to 7 percent; and in McCreary County, from 41 percent to 3 percent (see appendix 3, table 8). Of the remaining farmers in the region, almost 50 percent worked more than 100 days off their farms every year (see appendix 3, table 18). Conversely, from 1950 to 1974 the sources of nonfarm industrial employment diversified (see appendix 3, tables 11, 12, and 13); the manufacturing and service sectors each accounted for 25 percent to 36 percent of the industrial jobs in the three-county area. The manufacturing sector produced principally wood products and textiles; poultry processing was an important additional source of employment in Fentress County. By the late 1970s, mining was once again becoming an important source of employment in Scott County, contributing 25 percent of the jobs in that county. Mining and quarrying also paid the highest wages of any industrial sector (East Tennessee Development District 1979).

It is important to realize that even though there was diversification and redistribution in the types of available industrial employment after 1940, the absolute number of jobs at any one time did not change very much (see appendix 3, tables 11, 12, and 13). New jobs did not keep pace with population increase. The 1978 average unemployment rate in Scott County was 8.1 percent; in Fentress County and in McCreary County, 10.3 percent. All these rates were well above the Tennessee unemployment rate of 5.8 percent, the Kentucky rate of 6.2 percent, and the national unemployment rate of 5.8 percent for the same period. Although high, 1978 unemployment rates were below 1975 levels (see appendix 3, table 19).

In 1970, 54 percent of the families in McCreary County and 42 percent of the families in Fentress County and in Scott County had incomes below the family poverty level of $3,400 (see appendix 3, table 20). At the same time, 10.1 percent of families nationally and 18 percent of Tennessee families had incomes below this level.

Per capita personal income in 1970 ranged from 50 percent of the state per capita income in McCreary County and in Fentress County to 60 percent of the state per capita income in Scott County. Between 1974 and 1977 per capita income increased rapidly but, even so, remained $2,000 to $3,000 lower than the state averages (see appendix 3, table 21).

Based on data collected in February 1976 (see appendix 3, table 20), 37 percent of the population of McCreary County and of Scott County and 31 percent of the population of Fentress County received public assistance payments. These were either federally administered aid to the aged, blind, and disabled; old age, survivors, disability, and health insurance; or Aid to Families with Dependent Children. At the same time, 28 percent of the area's residents were receiving food stamps.

Since 1880 the commercial development of the Big South Fork area, which began with exploitation of mineral and forest resources, seems to have come full circle. In 1980, because of national energy demands, increased prices, and technological developments within the mining industry, these resources were once again commercially important. Oil exploration and drilling activity, which was a minor source of employment as early as the 1920s, intensified. Wells in this area are not heavy producers, but improved secondary recovery methods enhance their economic importance whenever petroleum commands higher prices.

By 1980, government land acquisition for the recreation area had preempted some of these efforts to rebuild the area's economy through a new era of primary resource extraction. Certainly a diversified economy more insulated from industrial cycles of demand for primary resources would provide more stable employment for local residents. Residents were waiting to see whether government and private development associated with the recreation area would bring them the benefits of a diversified economy.

2

Environmental Knowledge and Resource Use

Urbanization has insulated many Americans from their natural environment, but Appalachia's early settlers were forced to live in intimate association with theirs. They learned to take advantage of its resources and adjust to its demands and limitations. Rural people living in the Big South Fork area preserved much of this knowledge into the twentieth century.

The first part of this chapter discusses traditional uses of mineral resources, timber resources, wildlife resources, and wild plants used for food and medicine. The second section discusses two areas of folk knowledge or folk belief that reflect farm people adapting to the environment: weather lore and living by the signs. Although sign lore has received no convincing scientific validation, many items of traditional weather lore do have an empirical basis and scientific explanation. For example, whether smoke rises or falls from the chimney is a folk measure serving the same function as a barometer. Both the mercury and the smoke are affected by atmospheric pressure; however, the smoke also may be affected by relative humidity.

Traditional Use of Resources

MINERAL RESOURCES

Early settlers in the Big South Fork area tended to establish their homesteads in the bottomlands along the river and its main tributaries. The narrow alluvial deposits were more easily farmed with primitive tools and without chemical fertilizers than were the flat upland areas now used for agriculture. As Arnow (1960, 37) has noted, the homestead centered in the stream bottom also included a slice of gorge escarpment and upland so that the various resources found in each of these micro-environments would be available to the homesteader.

Mineral and geologic resources of the early hill-and-valley farms included limestone for fences and lime; sandstone for chimneys, gravestones, and grindstones; and saltpeter for the manufacture of gunpowder. The rock house formations provided storage and temporary shelter. Of these resources, only saltpeter had fallen into disuse by the turn of the century, although one interviewee reported that her grandfather manufactured gunpowder on Pine Creek in Scott County during the Civil War.

Farmers who could not afford to buy fertilizer during the Great Depression actually revived lime manufacture. Lime kilns were constructed by piling up alternate layers of logs and limestone. These pyres were burned to produce lime, and the intermixed wood ash added potash to this homemade fertilizer. In addition to sandstone, sand from weathered sandstone outcroppings was still used to scrub floors as recently as the 1920s. Local sand deposits were dug out for construction and various other uses until recently.

Although there are pottery-grade clay deposits near the Big South Fork, no pottery was made in this area until the craft was introduced by Kentucky Hills Industries in the mid-1960s. In the old days, crocks and other ceramic items were always purchased.

Salt was a mineral resource of great importance to the early homesteaders, for it was essential to meat preservation. Salt springs are found at various locations in the Big South Fork area. The Williams who gave his name to Williams Creek is supposed to have operated a saltworks in that vicinity; and the area's first oil well was an unexpected by-product of salt exploration. As was the case with saltpeter and powder manufacture, the local salt industry did not survive after it became relatively easy to obtain the commercial product from large-scale salt works.

From time to time, settlers stumbled on other mineral deposits that could be exploited. Lead was found on Tackett Creek, gouged out with knives, melted down, and molded into bullets. Whether inspired by lead ore or something else, the Lost Silver Mine legend is still very much alive along the Big South Fork.

Intensive exploitation of the area's major mineral resources, coal, oil, and natural gas, required industrial rather than small-scale technology and had to await development of adequate transportation systems. During the nineteenth century, crude oil was used medicinally rather than as a fuel; the substance was daubed on stock to repel vermin and on humans to cure arthritis.

The rock house has continued to be used for storage and shelter. In at least two instances described by interviewees, shelters were fashioned into permanent homes. Other documented uses during the period 1890 to the present include schoolhouse, shelter for graveside services during inclement weather, stock pen, household storage and laundry house, hideaway for moonshine stills and "scouting" outlaws, and camping quarters for hunting and fishing trips.

Water supply was another critical resource affecting early settlement patterns. Springs were sought where rock outcrops are exposed on the steep sides of gorges or hills. As long as homes were located in the stream bottoms, water could be carried downhill from springs, or piped down through hollow log sections pieced together, or later through pipe. A good spring was an important resource not only for the cool, pure drinking water it furnished but also because the spring house was the only available means of refrigerating perishable food like milk and butter. When settlement shifted to the plateau zone, some families found themselves carrying spring water uphill to their homes. Others built more convenient, but less dependable, wells. Use of cisterns was limited to some homes in the Rugby colony; the natives generally looked with disfavor on this kind of water supply because they realized its greater potential for contamination.

In contrast to the lower reaches of the Cumberland River, the Big South Fork and its tributaries must be regarded more as a barrier than as a means to transportation and commerce. Aside from shipping poplar logs downstream by floating and poling them through the rough areas, the river was not used for commerce. Rather, the problem of fording was a formidable one, as many anecdotes attest. Johnboats were occasionally used when wagons could not ford, or for fishing and recreation in quiet stretches of water, but there is no highly developed local tradition of boating. Knowing from experience the very real possibility of flash flooding and its consequences, local people in the 1970s were hardly enthusiastic about the recreation area bringing more rafters and paddlers to the Big South Fork.

TIMBER RESOURCES

Appendix C of the Final Environmental Impact Statement for the recreation area (U.S. Army Corps of Engineers 1976) lists more than fifty tree species indigenous to the area. Most have some commercial value. Logging proceeded in the Big South Fork area as elsewhere in stages; first the tallest and straightest trees were cut selectively, primarily tulip poplar and white pine. Then white oak and red oak increased in importance as sawmill requirements for stump diameter were reduced. Later logging operations extended to all of the area's important hardwoods. These included maples, birches, ironwood, hickory, beech, chestnut, the oaks, the hickories, sweet gum and black gum, walnut, ash, basswood (linden), elm, and cherry.

Before large-scale logging operations were established in the area, farmers obtained some cash income from their woodlands by cutting tulip poplar logs, turning white oak into stave bolts, white and red oak into cross ties, and chestnut oak or hemlock bark into tanbark.

Home manufactures used a great variety of hardwoods. For construction purposes, oak logs were split by hand and rived into boards and shingles. Later, they were processed at sawmills, the earliest of them water powered. Before sawed lumber became available, floors were constructed of thick puncheons, four- or five-foot lengths of split logs turned flat side up and then planed smooth with a foot adze. As was the case with cross ties, white oak was preferred to red in home construction because the wood has a finer grain and is more rot resistant. Chestnut was the preferred material for fence rails, and it was sometimes rived into slats for picket fences as well. Where strength and resilience were required as in tool handles, chair rungs, or wheel spokes and hubs, hickory was the wood of choice. Black walnut was used for gun stocks, and both walnut and cherry for furniture and woodenware. White oak splits were fashioned into baskets and chair seats, and a scrub broom could be made by splitting one end of a length of hickory into fibrous strands, then whittling and smoothing the remainder to form a comfortable handle.

Among the softwoods, tulip poplar was especially prized for log construction because of its long straight boles, light weight, and often gigantic diameter. White pine logs were also common. Red cedar was used for furniture and woodenware, the bark of hemlock was gathered for tanbark, and pitch pine was used for torches and in the manufacture of tar.

WILDLIFE RESOURCES

The fish resources of the many streams in the Big South Fork area seem not to have been an important food resource, probably because time could not be devoted to intensive fishing during spring and summer when most agricultural work had to be done. Fish traps built across streams and on occasion dynamiting produced a big return on a small time investment. However, methods such as salting or smoking to preserve surplus catch for future use were not practiced. Fish that could not be consumed immediately were released from the traps, but dynamiting was of course tremendously destructive to all stream life. For the most part, fishing seems to have been recreational in the past just as it is today. It provided a special food treat, often consumed on the spot. A brief article by a Scott County resident (Reed 1979) describes both the technology of a New River fish trap and the social aspects of its use.

Catfish, bass, walleye, and bluegill were the principal food fish sought by most old-timers; trout has been stocked in the streams more recently. Boys used to enjoy gigging for frogs as well as fishing, and old frog gigs are included in local tool collections.

Hunting and trapping were more universal pursuits than fishing. Deer hunting is popular now and attracts many hunters who grew up in this area but who now live and work in urban environments. The old-timers agree that their fathers hunted deer in the late nineteenth century, but that the native deer population was wiped out by disease. The current deer population is the result of stocking that began fifteen or twenty years ago. By that time, the traditional art of preparing venison was lost and methods had to be learned from cookbooks.

Rabbit, squirrel, raccoon, and woodchuck (groundhog) have continued to be favorite game meats. Most people consider opossum unfit to eat. Wild turkey, once plentiful, were not common enough in the 1970s to be an important game food. Other game fowl—ducks, grouse, and quail—have not been exploited as commonly as their abundance might suggest.

Trapping fur-bearing animals fits nicely into the farmer's slack time and continues to be practiced by some. Pelts of raccoon, skunk, mink, and red fox are sold for supplementary income. Bobcats are occasionally caught, and these tend to find their way to the taxidermist's shop to be transformed into trophies for the lucky trapper.

Along with other forms of wildlife, wild bees deserve mention as an important resource. Domestic honey production was quite widespread, and wild bees have been an important source of new colonies. A number of men in the area know how to track the bees, capture them, and bring them home. The object of the chase invariably is to capture the bees, not simply to take their honey.

WILD PLANT FOODS

In appendix 3, table 22 lists eighty-six edible plant species that occur in the Big South Fork area. These potential food sources have not been extensively exploited in the recent past, but one may assume that the earliest Euro-American settlers along with the Indians once made much fuller use of these resources.

Among the potherbs or "sallet" greens, poke is most frequently mentioned and is still collected by a good many interviewees. However, some families used to gather other greens also—yellow dock, sour dock, old field lettuce, pigweed, lamb's quarters, crow's foot, mustard, dandelion, and bullweed. Wild sage rather than cultivated sage sometimes was used to season game and as an ingredient in sausage and souse meat. Roots were used almost exclusively for medicine; however, meadow garlic may have been used in sausage making, and one woman reported that her family collected and roasted the Indian turnip, Jack-in-the-Pulpit, when she was a girl.

Beechnuts, black walnuts, hickory nuts, and chestnuts were gathered in the fall, and chestnut mast also fattened the semiwild, semidomestic hogs ranging free in the woods. Old-timers contend that the chestnut-fattened hogs yielded better-flavored pork than animals finished off on grain. The chestnuts are no more, but black walnuts are still a popular wild food.

Among the wild fruits and berries collected both in the past and currently are persimmon, papaw, blackberry, huckleberry, frost grape, and muscadine. The two wild grapes are quite sour but produce flavorful jellies. Muscadines used to thrive in the cleared areas along the O & W railroad tracks, but reforestation has destroyed that former habitat.

Various plants were used to prepare table beverages. Sassafras tea was brewed from sassafras root bark, and Oswego tea was made from spicewood bark and twigs and the leaves of bee balm. Many other teas were prepared for medicinal purposes. Persimmons were turned into mildly alcoholic persimmon beer. First the persimmons were baked in cornbread. Then the bread was crumbled into a crock, covered with water, and allowed to ferment for a few days.

Big South Fork residents have been able to use a variety of substitutes for refined sugar. Honey and sorghum molasses are still quite popular, but in the early decades of the twentieth century, maples were tapped and the sap was boiled down into maple syrup and sometimes maple sugar. In the process of logging the area's hardwoods, some fine old sugar groves were lost. An additional natural sweet for children was the balsam exuded from sweet gum trees. This balsam was chewed like chewing gum.

MEDICINAL PLANTS

In appendix 3, table 23 lists medicinal plants present in the Big South Fork environment and compares the officially recognized use of each plant with its local use. The table indicates which of the available medicinal plant resources actually were used and whether their folk use appears to coincide with chemical properties of the plants that have gained them acceptance in the U.S. Pharmacopoeia (USP), the National Formulary (NF), or the Homeopathic Formulary (HF).

Of the ninety-six plants included in table 23, only twenty of the locally used plants are not included in Youngken's *Pharmacognosy* (1950), a source published about midway through the 1900 to 1980 period that interviewees were able to discuss based on firsthand knowledge. Most folk uses of medicinal plants conform closely to the scientifically recognized uses reported by Youngken. A disproportionate number of remedies that lack a recognized scientific basis were used to treat childhood ailments such as hives, thrush, measles, and asthma. Childhood illness was also the area in which herbal treatments most often gave way to magical treatments—for example, imbedding a lock of the asthmatic child's hair in an oak sapling.

There are thirty plants of potential medicinal value that occur in the Big South Fork area but for which there is no evidence of use in local folk medicine. Failure to use some of these is understandable: Conium and Apocynum would be deadly unless the dosage was very carefully controlled, and Corydalis and Solanum have quite specialized uses. Because there are many diuretic, laxative, and expectorant substances to choose from, it is not surprising that some of the plants producing these effects were passed over in favor of more effective or more plentiful ones. Among the medicinal plants not used locally are several that were gathered and sold to pharmaceutical companies. Root and herb collectors might not always know the commercial use of the plants they gathered for sale.

Among the medicinal plants for which there is no report of local use are several that act as menstrual regulators or uterine stimulants. One cannot discount the possibility that women knew the effects of these substances but chose not to share their knowledge with male collectors of medicinal lore like Rogers (1941).

Weather Lore

Early settlers learned the resources of the Big South Fork area and how they could be put to use to provide almost all the necessities of daily life. Still, a killing frost or flood might spell disaster. Anxiety toward the end of a long, severe winter must have been great as food stores dwindled. Enough but not too much rain was critical for a successful growing season. Because the weather was of such vital interest, prognostication lore developed from close observation of the environment, primarily existing weather patterns and animal behavior that might be related to future weather events.

Weather lore is one aspect of Big South Fork folklore that retained widespread currency into the 1970s. Many old-timers observed that the weather had changed noticeably since the 1910s or 1920s, when they were young. They observed that spring generally comes later now, and some old dependable guidelines for predicting rain or shine no longer seem to work. Some held that Ground Hog Day, the traditional time for forecasting the arrival of spring, should be observed February 14, not February 2.

The items below are a sample of local weather lore, guidelines vouched for by a single individual with an unusually curious turn of mind who tried to check out the sayings he heard over eighty years, qualifying them if necessary and rejecting ones that did not work. Thus these items are one man's actively used store of weather lore.

CHANGING SEASONS
> It will be three months from the first time you hear a katydid until frost.
> If the groundhog sees his shadow on Ground Hog Day (February 14),
>   there will be forty more days of bad weather; if not, winter is broke.
> Every day it thunders in February, it will frost the same day in May.
>   (If the weather is cloudy, it may not frost, but the temperature
>   will be cold enough for frost.)

SEVERITY OF WINTER

> The number of fogs in August determines how many snows there will be the following winter.
>
> Thick corn shucks mean a severe winter. Count the layers of shucks to find out how many snows there will be.
>
> More dark than light woolie worms presages a severe winter. (If most of the woolie worms seem to be headed southward, it will be a bad winter.)
>
> A popping wood fire is a sign that snow is coming soon.
>
> If a rabbit stirs early on a snowy day, it will snow again the next day.

RAIN OR SHINE

> A ring around the moon with no stars inside is a sign of a week's pretty weather, but there will be as many rains as there are stars inside the ring.
>
> Warm wind in summer means rain is in store.
>
> Rain before seven will end by eleven. (This rule was no longer reliable.)
>
> Smoke rises when fair weather is coming and falls when bad weather is coming.
>
> If smoke from the chimney goes toward the ground, there will be falling weather.
>
> When maple and poplar leaves turn upside down, rain is on the way.
>
> Red sky in morning, sailor's warning; red sky at night, ship's delight.
>
> If the sun shines when it is raining, it will rain again the next day.
>
> When dew is on the grass, rain will come to pass.

Working by the Signs

The farmer has a great deal of freedom to plan his planting, cultivating, and harvesting of crops; caring for livestock; maintaining his tools and equipment; building or repairing fences or buildings; harvesting timber; and countless other tasks. But mistakes in management of these many activities or simply bad luck with the weather could ruin him. It was only natural, then, that farmers looked beyond themselves for guidance in planning their work and for reassurance in the face of the uncertainty and risks involved.

Working according to the signs of the zodiac and the phases of the moon has provided the needed guidance and reassurance. One believer in signs explained: "There's a whole lot in them signs. It's Nature I suppose, the way the Lord intended. He thought they's just smart enough to catch onto them things." The biblical justification for following the signs is found in Gen. 1:14: "Let there be lights in the firmament of the heaven to divide the day from the night; and let them be for signs, and for seasons, and for days, and years." And again, Ecclesiastes refers to the ordering of life according to the signs. "To everything there is a season, and a time to every purpose under the heaven: a time to be born, and a time to die; a time to plant, and a time to pluck up that which is planted" (Eccles. 3:1–2).

A farmer's almanac or an almanac calendar is used to determine when the moon enters and leaves each of the twelve zodiac signs. The local farmers' co-ops distribute such a calendar. Zodiac charts and interpretations from T. E. Black's booklet, *God's Way*, are presented in the *Foxfire* article "Planting by the Signs" (Wigginton 1972, 212–27). Other almanacs may vary from Black in the details of planting rules presented.

Rules for planting by the signs collected in the Big South Fork area are sometimes contradictory, and there seem to be two different principles underlying the logic of appropriate signs. One is the association of the zodiac signs with the elements fire, earth, air, and water according to the scheme shown in the *Foxfire* article (Wigginton 1972, 216). The other principle involves a correspondence between some characteristic of the sign and the kind of growth pattern that is desired or to be avoided. According to the first principle, planting in the head, Aries, should be avoided because this is a barren, masculine sign associated with fire. According to the second principle, however, cabbage should be planted in the head so that it will form well-shaped, compact heads.

The most consistent rules for planting by the signs collected in the Big South Fork area concern moon phases rather than zodiac signs. And while *God's Way* and similar sources give rules for conducting various activities such as digging and laying foundations, slaughtering, or cutting hair according to zodiac signs, almost all such rules collected in this area relate to moon phase. The sole exception is the belief that any operation involving bloodletting, such as pulling teeth, docking, or castrating, should be done when the sign is away from the affected body part in order to avoid excessive, possibly fatal, bleeding.

An almanac is necessary for following the zodiac signs, and the system is complicated to remember. The principles associated with the waxing and waning moon are less complex, and simple observation will suffice to keep track of the moon's phase. Excerpts from a conversation with a couple who plant by the signs confirm these points:

Hus: *We also kind of go by the moon.*
Wife: *We don't plant in every one of these [zodiac] signs, you see. We try to plant—*
Hus: *—beans when the sign's in the feet.*
Wife: *Yeah, and another good sign is when, is in the bowels.*

Hus: *The different things works different.*
Wife: *Now, a lot of your calendars will tell you when to plant stuff above the ground or underneath the ground . . . planting days by the moon . . . If you sow cabbage seed, you want to do that when the sign's in the head—yeah, for sure—and then not plant corn when the sign's in the arms . . .*
Hus: *. . . in the knees.*
Wife: *Well, for it to come up not plant in the knees cause it'll just curl up and not come up through the ground. But the way it grows, it grows too tall [when planted in the arms].*
Hus: *No, that's on the new of the moon.*
W: *Oh, yeah, when the moon is new the corn grows tall and the ears high and stand right straight up at the end of the stalk.*
Hus: *And it don't yield as good.*
Wife: *[Plant] Irish potatoes when the sign, when the moon is . . .*
Hus: *. . . full.*
Wife: *Yeah. If you plant on the new of the moon, they'll come right to the top of the ground and get sunburned . . . . We always heard it said not to plant nothing when the sign was in the heart, but we planted corn one time and forgot to look, and we had a good crop.*
Hus: *And a lot of it just depends on the season anyway. My grandmother, she couldn't read or write, but she could tell you the day the moon changed, and the way she'd do it—on her fingers. I couldn't tell you how it was, but she could tell you when it'd change again.*
Wife: *Well, it was done from watching and learning it just as it was. There were no calendars or almanacs then.*

The following list of rules for working by the signs was compiled from local sources: folklife study interviewees, rules collected by folklore students of Mrs. Linda Stewart at Oneida High School (n.d.), and items included in Esther Sanderson's *County Scott and Its Mountain Folk* (1958). For purposes of comparison, rules published in the *Foxfire* article (Wigginton 1972) are noted if they conflict with the local material.

PLANTING BY THE SIGNS

General

    Transplant trees when the moon is new in early fall or very early spring.

    Plant seed for crops that yield above ground on the new moon and for plants that yield root crops on the old moon.

Peas

    Plant peas on the new moon in March.

Cabbage
>Plant cabbage in the head.
>Do not plant in the head because it is a barren sign. (Foxfire)

Beets
>Plant beets in the feet.
>Plant beets in the heart to keep the string out of them.
>Do not plant in the heart because it is a death sign. (Foxfire)

Potatoes
>Plant Irish potatoes on the full moon. If planted on the new moon they will make potatoes on top of the ground and the potatoes will be sunburned and turn green.
>Plant potatoes on the first quarter of the moon in April.
>Plant potatoes in the heart and not in the new moon.
>Don't plant potatoes on the new moon because they will go to vine instead of making potatoes.
>Don't plant potatoes in the feet or they will form lots of toes.

Cucumbers
>Plant cucumbers on the new moon in May, and they will make earlier than if you plant them in April.
>Plant cucumbers in the arms, and they will grow as long as your arm.
>Plant cucumbers in the feet or arms.
>Don't plant cucumbers in the feet, or they'll curl up like toes.
>Don't plant cucumbers in the bowels.

Beans
>Plant beans in the arms or in the thighs.
>Plant beans in the feet or secrets.
>Plant beans in the feet or bowels.
>Don't plant beans in the bowels or they will have black spots. (Foxfire)
>Plant beans in the heart.
>Do not plant in the heart because it is a death sign. (Foxfire)

Corn
>Plant corn in the arms.
>Don't plant corn in the head or it will all go to stalk.
>Don't plant corn in the bowels or it will rot without coming up.

Don't plant corn in the knees or it will buckle and not come out of the ground.

Plant corn on the full of the moon so it won't grow so tall.

Don't plant corn on the new moon or it will all go to stalk.

HARVESTING BY THE SIGNS

When the New Year falls on the dark of the moon, there will be a good fruit harvest.

Don't dig potatoes on the new moon or they will rot.

Dig sweet potatoes on the first quarter so they won't rot.

Harvest in the old moon for keeping. (Foxfire)

Dig sweet potatoes on the third or last quarter of the moon so they won't rot.

BUILDING FENCES AND MAKING BOARDS AND SHINGLES

Split fence rails on the old moon; otherwise they will curve.

If you lay the rock foundation for a rail fence on the new moon, it will sink and let your rails down onto the ground where they will rot.

Dig post holes on the old moon and you will be able to tamp them tight. If you dig post holes on the new moon, there will be a big mound of dirt left over and the post will be loose.

Rive boards on the old moon, and they will lay down flat.

Make shingles and nail them on in the old moon. If you put shingles on a roof in the new moon, the shingles will cup up and the roof will leak.

SOAP MAKING

Make soap on the old of the moon, or it will be too strong. If you try to make soap on the new moon, it will boil over.

Soap made on the new moon jells best. (Foxfire)

Make soap on the increase of the moon, or it won't lather.

KRAUT MAKING

Make sauerkraut on the new moon to have it firm and white.

SLAUGHTERING

Kill hogs on the increase of the moon, or the meat will not shrink.

Slaughtering on the full moon makes meat swell; on the new moon, it shrinks.

Slaughtering on the new moon makes the meat puffy and hard to render. (Foxfire)
Kill hogs on the dark of the moon to make a large quantity of lard.
Slaughter in the knees or feet. (Foxfire)

ANIMAL HUSBANDRY AND PERSONAL CARE

Wean colts, calves, and children on the new moon.
Wean a child or animal in a sign that does not rule the vital parts of the body. (Foxfire)
Make ear crops to mark stock when the signs are in the legs or feet.
Dock lambs' tails when the sign is in the heart.
Castrate pigs in the feet, when the sign has gone past the affected part. (Foxfire)
Cut your hair in the new of the moon and put it under a rock. It will grow twice as long.
If you cut your hair in Libra, Sagittarius, Aquarius, or Pisces, it will grow stronger, thicker, and more beautiful. (Foxfire)

3

Subsistence Economy

Among the folk culture regions of the Eastern United States, the Upland South region in which the Big South Fork area is located retained the greatest number of traditional culture elements (Glassie 1968). Glassie contended that traditionalism on the "small nearly self-sufficient farm" of the Upland South did not result from conscious conservatism but from preservation of material arrangements that "make sense in a setting where, though money is scarce, people are not desperately poor" (Glassie 1968, 200).

Glassie quoted a traveler's comments on the primitive conditions of life in backwoods Kentucky in 1835; stories collected near the Big South Fork suggest that the situation there was little changed in 1935.

> The farmer . . . makes almost everything that he uses. Besides clearing the land, building houses, and making fences, he stocks his own plough, mends his wagon, makes his ox-yokes and harness, and learns to supply nearly all his wants from the forest. The tables, bedsteads, and seats in his house are of his own rude workmanship . . . . There are thousands scattered over the west, who continue, to this day, to make all the shoes that are worn in their families. They universally raise cotton, and often cultivate also hemp, and flax; the spinning-wheel and the loom are common articles of furniture; and the whole farming and hunting population are clad in fabrics of household manufacture (James Hall, Sketches of History, Life, and Manners in the West, 2:68–69; quoted in Glassie 1968, 196).

In the 1970s few people under eighty had firsthand familiarity with the traditional survival tools and the skills needed for log construction, wagon building and repair, spinning and weaving, or shoemaking. It was no longer necessary to process primary raw materials from scratch. But many households did still build their own houses and outbuildings, make part of their clothing and household goods, and produce much of their food.

This chapter describes some of the primary elements of the traditional subsistence economy that survived to a greater or lesser extent among residents of the Big South Fork area in the late 1970s: tools and their use; shelter; textiles and clothing; housekeeping; and foodways.

Tools and Their Use

Traditional hand tools have become collector's items. The Museum of Appalachia in Norris, Tennessee, offers a comprehensive collection for viewing. Mechanized farm equipment replaced the old horse- or mule-drawn equipment. Logging also was mechanized, although small-scale operations sometimes continued to use draft animals into the 1970s. Builders and woodworkers use modern materials and power tools, and the auto mechanic and welder have taken over many of the functions of the old blacksmith shop. Although the materials, tools, and processes have changed, the tradition of acquiring and using a variety of technical skills is still flourishing. Many men are versed in the building trades, automotive or small engine repair, welding, or some comparable skill that satisfies household needs and earns income on a full- or part-time basis.

In the early 1970s, the Foxfire series published several valuable articles on traditional tools and their use. *The Foxfire Book* (Wigginton 1972) contains articles on basic woodworking tools and building skills (38–52), log cabin building (53–107), and chimney building (108–14). Articles in *Foxfire* 2 (Wigginton 1973) explain the construction of tub wheels for turbine gristmills (142–63) and wagon wheels (118–41). Butter churn construction is described in *Foxfire* 3 (Wigginton 1975, 369–97. *Foxfire* 4 (Wigginton 1977) contains articles on knife making (51–67) and on wooden sled construction (134–49). There are lengthy articles on blacksmithing (106–207) and on gun and ammunition manufacture (208–390) in *Foxfire* 5 (Wigginton 1979). The latter article includes a profile of deceased Scott County gunsmith Charlie Blevins.

Of the skills described in *Foxfire* articles, the construction skills like riving boards and notching-up logs were still known by a few older men in the Big South Fork area in the 1970s. Their skills were sometimes demonstrated at county fairs and similar celebrations although no longer practiced on a regular basis. At least one farmer made a variety of household tools, including knives similar to the ones made by Troy Danner, whose work was featured in *Foxfire* (Wigginton 1977, 60–65). Several men still made hickory tool handles by hand both for sale and for home use.

A generation earlier, there were still several practicing blacksmiths, but the only forge operating in the late 1970s belonged to Ted Tompkins of Armathwaite in Fentress County, Tennessee. Four generations of the Tompkins family have operated this business. In the old days, the blacksmith made his shop tools, farming implements, logging equipment, household tools, and hardware for wagons and buildings (Wigginton 1979, 129–30). Repairing wagons and wagon tires was an important part of the work. The Armathwaite shop was located beside the old wagon road, facing northward toward the old road rather than south toward the present Highway 52. The blacksmith not only made necessary wagon repairs but also kept wagon grease on hand to service the axles, so that his establishment was the garage and service station of its day. When the paved road was under construction, the Tompkins blacksmith shop provided maintenance for the highway construction equipment, and later Ted Tompkins's father built the first truck flatbed used in this area.

Once wagons and animal-drawn farm equipment became mostly nostalgia pieces, logging equipment was the mainstay of the blacksmith shop's business, supplemented by miscellaneous repairs and custom work. The shop was known throughout the area, even in McCreary County.

Many young blacksmiths throughout the United States have developed a specialized business based on decorative wrought-iron craftsmanship and have kept the craft alive in this way. The Tompkins shop was unique because it retained the community-based technical and economic functions of the traditional blacksmith shop into the 1970s.

Shelter

This section situates vernacular buildings of the Big South Fork area in the context of regional architectural development and describes building practices of the late twentieth century that represented a continuation of "folk" tradition despite sweeping changes in construction materials and technology.

HISTORIC SIGNIFICANCE OF ARCHITECTURAL RESOURCES

The blend of Tidewater English, Pennsylvania German, and Scots-Irish traits underlying Appalachian culture is especially pronounced in the region's traditional architecture. Glassie traced Appalachian log construction to central Europe via Pennsylvania, but the Tidewater hall-and-parlor house type seems to have inspired the form of the dogtrot cabin (see Glassie 1968, 89–98). The double-pen cabin form that evolved into both the saddlebag cabin and the "tenant house" (Montell and Morse 1976) or "Cumberland house" (Riedl et al. 1976) had Scots-Irish origins (Glassie 1968, 78).

In the 1970s, there were few extant examples of log construction in the recreation area, partly because the oldest settlements were depopulated shortly after World War II and subject to vandalism during the intervening years. A series of tornadoes that struck the area on April 3, 1974, destroyed many of the remaining structures. The houses and outbuildings still standing were not unusual in style, materials, quality of construction, or historic associations. Nevertheless, taken as a whole they provided an important sample of the typical folk architectural forms of the area, especially as these forms were used in the Big South Fork area for many years after they had been replaced by popular architectural forms in other sections of Tennessee and Kentucky. Forms generally associated with the nineteenth century (Montell and Morse 1976) were still being constructed in the Big South Fork area as late as 1930.

BARNS AND OTHER OUTBUILDINGS

The recreation area contains late examples of building types that have long since disappeared from the scene elsewhere in Tennessee and Kentucky. Barn types are a case in point. Glassie (1968, 88–89) describes the evolution of the transverse crib barn at the beginning of the nineteenth century.

> *The Tennessee Valley farmer found himself in need of a large barn. The Pennsylvania barn would have served him, but he seems not to have known it; he did, however, know the double-crib barn, a type found in Central Europe and with regularity from south central Pennsylvania down the Alleghenies of Virginia, West Virginia, and Kentucky, and through the Blue Ridge of North Carolina and Tennessee. He built a pair of double-crib barns facing each other, roofed the whole, and had a four-crib barn. As it was built, the four-crib barn developed its own symmetry, one of its two passageways was blocked off to provide additional stabling, and this painfully neat evolutionary sequence resulted in the transverse crib barn.*

Although it was built as late as 1930, the old Blevins barn at Charit Creek is a traditional four-crib log barn. Montell and Morse (1976, 68) reported that barns of this type were quite rare in Kentucky and that all extant examples known to them were in very bad condition at the time of their survey. The old Blevins barn was still in a very good state of repair in 1980.

The double-crib barn type is represented by one of the outbuildings near the Lora Blevins house. This log structure dates from about 1929. Nearby is a log crib with shed addition; a similar structure can also be found on the Oscar Blevins farm. The crib types described by Montell and Morse (1976, 54–58) generally date from the nineteenth century in Kentucky, but the Big South Fork examples noted here date from the 1920s.

An unusual transverse crib barn composed of three log cribs and frame additions was found on Blue Heron Road in McCreary County; however, extraneous notches indicate that the logs had been moved from another site or rearranged.

The U.S. Department of Agriculture through its extension agents first began offering plans for hay, stock, and tobacco barns to Kentucky farmers in the 1920s (Montell and Morse 1976, 53). While the older log barns remained in use in the Big South Fork gorge area, on the adjacent tablelands modern types replaced such structures.

Among other traditional outbuilding types, springhouses and smokehouses were no longer built since refrigeration and chemical meat curing processes had taken over their functions. Within the recreation area boundaries there were two examples of smokehouses, one on the Tapley property in McCreary County, another at Charit Creek. The latter had been converted into the Parch Corn Hunting Camp bathhouse. Root cellars were still being built in the 1970s, and numerous modern concrete block examples could be seen throughout the area, even inside the city limits of incorporated towns. Impending land acquisition for the recreation area caused one resident to halt construction of a traditional stone root cellar.

HOUSES

The simple cabin constructed by pre-Revolutionary Kentucky settlers was a one-room unit with a fireplace in the gable end, often with a small window near the chimney, a puncheon floor, a loft, and a shed attached to the rear (Montell and Morse 1976, 10–11). This description fits the John Blevins cabin on the Oscar Blevins farm. The original cabin was built around 1879 and augmented by the rear lean-to and a second room of frame construction around 1900. It continued to be used as a dwelling for many years thereafter and later served as a tobacco barn.

The Tapley house in McCreary County, probably built between 1900 and 1910, was also a single-room cabin in its original form, but it had doors leading to open porches on both the north and south sides. Frame additions were added to the west side rather than to the back of the house. This arrangement maintained the breezeway effect of the opposite doorways while shielding the main part of the house from direct rays of the summer sun. Unfortunately, the Tapley house burned soon after it was documented.

According to Glassie (1968, 89) the dogtrot house type developed as a subtype of the Tidewater hall-and-parlor house. When frame construction was replaced by log construction on the frontier, it became necessary to build the house in two separate sections because logs long enough to extend the full width of the house were difficult to find. In Virginia the hall was framed in, but farther south it was left as a breezeway, creating the dogtrot house. This house type developed in the Tennessee Valley and spread northward through Tennessee and Kentucky (Glassie 1968, 99).

No extant example of a dogtrot house was found within the recreation area, but the survey did find a house nearby in Fentress County that began as a dogtrot.

The owner reported that her grandfather first built a one-room cabin around 1870 and added the second cabin and breezeway about seven years later. During subsequent renovations, the original cabin and breezeway were torn down. This information was interesting in light of the general belief that the dogtrot type was a single unit concept (i.e., a variant on the hall-and-parlor house) rather than the result of adding a second cabin to an original single-pen structure.

Current building practices in the area suggest that this debate (Glassie 1968, 98; Montell and Morse 1976, 21) concerning origins of the dogtrot, and for that matter the saddlebag and other double-pen types, may be moot. The most adaptable house types have continued to be modular ones; the builder has a complex end product in mind but is able to build the whole in sections as a growing family requires and as available time and resources permit.

Concerning the saddlebag house, Montell and Morse (1976, 22) write: "A number of saddlebag houses in Kentucky have a single door in the front center—this seems to be the oldest form. In such cases exposed chimney stones loom directly ahead as one enters the structure. Interior doors lead from this short, narrow hallway into the room located to the left and to the right."

A saddlebag house, lacking this central door, is found in the original house at Charit Creek, now the core of the lodge building. Although a modern kitchen lean-to was added to the front of the building, the original entrance arrangement was preserved inside. Based on Blevins genealogy, this structure might date back to 1816. Montell and Morse (1976, 25) confirm the plausibility of this early date. They note that the saddlebag type spread from New England down the seaboard to the Watauga settlements and into Tennessee and Kentucky. They recorded an early example in Monroe County, Kentucky, dating to 1820.

The Lora Blevins house is a double-pen log structure without the central chimney. Its chimney, originally sandstone but replaced by concrete block, is in the east gable end; the west room, built after the family had already occupied the east room, has no chimney.

The double-pen house type designated "tenant house" by Montell and Morse (1976, 25) is a story-and-a-half house with two front rooms and a central chimney or stove flue, the downstairs rooms serving as parlor and guest room and the upstairs as sleeping rooms. A lean-to rear addition housed the kitchen and dining area, although by the late nineteenth century additions might be placed to form a T or ell-shaped house. The early form of tenant house according to Montell had only one front door, but separate entrances to each of the main rooms became the typical form. Riedl et al. (1976) use the presence of two doors to distinguish their "Cumberland House" from their "double-pen house" (the single-door type). Both of these forms occurred in the Big South Fork vicinity.

Affluent farmers who were able to afford the farm machinery and fertilizers needed to make their land productive settled the tableland beyond the gorge and escarpment zones. There they built more substantial two-story houses. At the time of the folklife survey, there was one example of the two-story single-pen log house on the Maxine Loudin property in Fentress County. Only the log original, said to be more than 100 years old, was still standing (in very poor condition); frame additions attached to the back of the house had been torn down.

Several examples of the I-house (two-rooms high, two rooms wide, and one room deep), often modified by additions, could be seen in Wayne County, Kentucky; in Fentress County, Tennessee, near Allardt and Armathwaite; and in Scott County, Tennessee, near Helenwood and on the outskirts of Oneida.

The most striking contrast between indigenous folk architectural forms and mainstream architecture is seen in the buildings at Rugby designed and built under the supervision of Cornelius Onderdonk. By the turn of the century, however, the more substantial homes in Allardt and other large communities were no longer products of folk architecture.

CONTINUITY OF FOLK TRADITION

Among less affluent residents, folk architecture has persisted. Modern materials and the associated tools and building techniques have been adopted, but some basic principles underlying folk architecture have continued to operate, resulting in new folk forms. These principles are (1) working from a traditional design carried in the head rather than from written plans and specifications, (2) building by family members and friends rather than by specialists, and (3) completing a building, especially a house, in stages rather than all at once. These practices have persisted because they are economical. Mobile home modification, commonplace in the area, illustrates this point.

Mobile homes are popular because they are the least expensive way to equip a home with modern plumbing and appliances, but they lack the space and other features of traditional homes, such as porches. Mobile homes are sometimes set on concrete block foundations over an excavated cellar that is used for storing canned goods and root crops. The first modification to the mobile home exterior is the addition of a front porch across its entire length, often of traditional post-and-beam construction with a metal roof. Occasionally a fiberglass-panel shed with generous overhangs is erected over the entire mobile home. When the porch is built, the mobile home's narrow stoop is replaced by broad wooden steps leading up to the porch. The next addition is usually two rooms across the back to provide more bedroom space. According to interviewees, further frame additions have completely surrounded some mobile homes in the Big South Fork area so that the passerby cannot detect the original core within.

In the 1970s, local building supply stores carried a large variety of standard house plans. It was not unusual for property owners to call in a contractor only to excavate and build the foundations, while family members and more distant relatives or friends who possessed the needed building skills completed the rest of the structure. Even if a contractor framed up the house and completed the exterior, the family often did its own interior finishing work. In some cases, the house basement had been finished and roofed so that this underground house could be occupied for an extended period of time before construction of the superstructure even began. Late 1970s developments in underground housing as an energy conservation measure attracted the interest of some Big South Fork residents, suggesting that economy and efficiency rather than sheer conservatism shaped housing design and building practices in the past and continue to do so.

Textiles and Clothing

Women in the Big South Fork area still make much of the clothing and textile home furnishings their families use. Home sewing of women's and children's clothes, knitting, crocheting, and quilting are very widely practiced domestic skills, and small shirt factories provide many women employment based on sewing skills. All of the sewing and needlework now employs store-bought thread, yarn, and fabric, however. Even the handful of weavers affiliated with Kentucky Hills Industries use commercial threads and yarns in their work.

In the past, textile manufacture began with raising sheep and growing fiber crops, flax and cotton. The fiber was processed, spun into thread or yarn, and woven into cloth or used in knitting. Weaving as a domestic enterprise disappeared before spinning. No one presently living learned to weave as a child, although some of the older women remembered their mothers weaving. The few craftswomen now weaving for Kentucky Hills Industries learned to weave as adults in formal workshop training sessions.

Only a few people over eighty years old vaguely recalled how flax fibers were processed before spinning them (see Arnow 1963, 250–62). Some of these interviewees reported that small patches of cotton were grown in this area when they were children. The cotton was not spun into thread, but was simply picked over and formed into quilt batting. One man recalled that the seeds were picked out of the cotton bolls by hand and that each child sat down after supper with a shoe full of cotton to be picked over before bedtime.

Interviewees also recalled how wool was carded and spun into yarn. Domestic wool was knitted into socks and other clothing items long after home weaving had been abandoned in favor of store-bought cloth.

While home-woven fabrics were still the rule, women's clothes were made from linsey-wolsey, a fairly soft, warm fabric of linen and wool. Sturdier twilled jean cloth was fashioned into men's clothes. Weavers made both solid-color and striped cloth for dress goods. The stripe was formed in the process of warping the loom; filling in the weft was then a mechanical process that could be done without reference to a pattern. The soft colors achieved with natural dyes such as walnut hulls, madder, or indigo (the latter purchased rather than grown locally) produced lovely fabric, but the more elaborate weaving designs used by Appalachian coverlet makers apparently were not known to local weavers.

Laodicia "Aunt Dicie" Fletcher of Rugby did weave traditional coverlets and was able to interpret the notation of old English parchment pattern drafts, but she was not a local woman. Reports of her origins vary, but she grew up and learned to weave in either West Virginia or North Carolina, both centers of coverlet making. She brought her loom to Rugby with her and marketed her work at the Tabard Inn. Rugby residents tried to help her also market in Cincinnati, where several pieces were displayed at the Art Museum. Historic Rugby, Inc., owns several examples of her work, but her loom and patterns have not survived.

Home sewing, either with home-produced or store-bought fabric, typically was guided by homemade patterns based on existing clothing. The more expert seamstresses could cut with no pattern at all. Commercial patterns like the ones in use today were unknown. Hand sewing of the entire garment was replaced first by the treadle sewing machine and later by electric models. A reliable sewing machine remains a prized piece of equipment in most households. Various textile household furnishings as well as clothing were made at home. Many women still make decorative needlework items and quilts.

Because there are so many available published sources for quilt patterns, it is difficult to determine which of these may have been passed down traditionally and which have been picked up from published sources. It is certain, however, that the utility quilt pieced of large, irregular-sized squares and rectangles is a traditional form. Winter versions of this utility quilt used dark-colored woolen squares, an extra-heavy filler (sometimes layers of blanket), and typically a flannel lining. Because these quilts were very thick, they were tacked rather than quilted. The custom of making quilts from sewing scraps or the good areas of worn-out clothing persisted through changes in fabric preferences; in the 1970s polyester knit had replaced the traditional cotton and wool in much of the local quilting. The custom of using scraps influenced pattern choice, so that patterns using small quantities of several different fabrics, for example Trip around the World and Double Wedding Ring, were quite popular.

While the women were providing for the family's textile needs, the men tanned hides for leather to make not only tack for their draft animals but shoes for the family as well. One older woman recalled that her father-in-law owned a set of hardwood shoe lasts and made shoes for several families in his community, receiving his pay in produce or some other service. The uppers of these shoes were fashioned in moccasin style, and the thick leather soles were attached with wooden pegs. Another person volunteered the information that tanned groundhog hides made the strongest shoelaces.

Housekeeping

Laundry and house cleaning were done with homemade lye soap. As water dripped through an oak hopper full of fireplace ashes, lye was formed. It was caught in a stoneware vessel set under a trough at the bottom of the hopper. Grease left over from cooking mixed with lye and boiled in a big kettle made a soft soap that varied in color from brown to almost pure white depending upon how carefully the grease had been strained. One soap maker added birch water to her soap kettle to give the soap a pleasant aroma. The homemade lye was caustic enough to produce a very effective cleaner, but it was not strong enough to form hard cake soap; that requires the commercial lye favored by contemporary soap makers. With commercial lye, it is even possible to eliminate the laborious boiling process from soap making. Procedures for making soap with homemade lye and with commercial lye are described in *The Foxfire Book* (Wigginton 1972, 151–58). These same procedures were familiar to many Big South Fork residents, both male and female.

Clothes washing also called for a big iron kettle suspended over an outdoor fire. The clothes were boiled and battling sticks were used to beat the stubborn dirt out of them (see Wigginton 1973, 256–65). If possible, the washing operation was set up near a stream that was used for rinsing. It is a tribute to the strength and quality of the home-woven fabrics that they could withstand the rigors of these laundering methods and the strong lye soap. The first improvement in this pioneer laundry system was introduction of the washboard as a substitute for battling sticks. Later, old-fashioned wringer washing machines became fixtures on many porches. The earliest models had wooden agitators and wringers.

Lye soap was also used in scrubbing floors. Although many cabins originally had dirt floors, thick oak puncheons were installed when time permitted. These floors were scrubbed clean with lye soap and sand. There were two kinds of brooms, the ordinary sweeping broom made of broom corn and a scrub broom made by cutting apart the fibers in a hickory plank to form the head of the broom and shaping the remainder into a comfortable handle. These scrub brooms were quite durable even when strong lye soap and sand were the scouring agents. An article in *Foxfire 3* (Wigginton 1975, 437–50) demonstrates the manufacturing process for both kinds of brooms. Big South Fork residents definitely preferred hickory to white oak as the raw material for scrub brooms, however. At least one Big South Fork broom maker finished his sweeping brooms by clamping and sewing them into the flat shape of commercial brooms rather than leaving them round as shown in the *Foxfire* article.

Foodways

Diet in the past was shaped by a combination of available food resources and preservation methods. Traditional food preservation methods have changed because the technology has changed; sources of knowledge have expanded to include canning instruction booklets, published cookbooks, and home demonstration presentations as well as the traditional mode of learning through helping older relatives. Nevertheless, many of the preserved foods that once were necessary parts of the diet were retained in the face of new technology because of taste preferences and traditional associations.

Old-timers compared the diet they grew up with and the diet of the younger generation with all of its highly processed junk foods and commented that they ate better in the old days when an abundance of vegetables and fruits was always on the table. The diet was high in animal fat, but it supported a great deal of strenuous physical activity and prolonged exposure to the cold in winter.

The big meals were breakfast and dinner at midday. Breakfast might consist of bacon or chops, eggs, potatoes, fried apples, and biscuits served with gravy and molasses or honey. Dinner might include meat and potatoes or sweet potatoes accompanied by other cooked vegetables, cornbread, and canned fruit or a more elaborate dessert such as fried pies or stack cake for special occasions. Supper was a light meal of leftovers from dinner or bread and milk. "Crumble in" (cornbread crumbled into sweet milk and eaten like cereal) is still a favorite light supper for several interviewees.

FOOD RESOURCES

From the time the Big South Fork area was first settled well into the twentieth century, most of its farms produced more for home consumption than for sale. In the last quarter of the twentieth century, a few farmers still kept workhorses or mules, but most used tractors. Elderly interviewees from communities near the river remembered when extensive numbers of hogs and cattle ranged free before the enactment of fence laws made it necessary to clear and maintain large areas of pasture. Sheep were fairly common prior to World War I, and occasionally farmers kept wool-bearing goats. By the 1970s, sheep and goats (the dairy variety) were rarely kept and beef cattle were raised only on a commercial basis. Commercial dairying developed after World War II, especially in Fentress County, but this activity was abandoned when enactment of more stringent sanitation regulations increased the cost of equipping milking sheds and dairies. Broilers became an important commercial farm product.

On the small self-provisioning farms of the 1970s hogs were the most common livestock, and some families still kept milk cows, but many who used to keep livestock restricted themselves to a vegetable garden and perhaps a small flock of chickens. Growing a vegetable garden was an almost universal food production activity in the Big South Fork area; many families who had given up every other form of food production maintained this subsistence skill.

The most popular garden crops were beans, tomatoes, cabbage, potatoes, corn, onions, and cucumbers. Other crops included sweet potatoes, beets, okra, carrots, peas, lettuce, turnips, peppers, melons, mustard, and strawberries. Apples and peaches were very common orchard crops, and grapes often were grown, especially in Fentress County. Some farmers also had small tobacco allotments.

Fence laws forced a shift from open foraging in the woods for much of the year to reliance on pasture and feed crops such as corn, soybeans, and hay. Before farmers began growing a wide range of feed crops, the leaves of corn plants were stripped while still green and tied into bundles for feed. This "fodder pulling" occurred in late summer shortly after the school session began. A school vacation was called so that everyone could work in the fields.

Wild foods were a supplement to food produced on the farm. Of the wild plant foods, poke shoots, blackberries, and walnuts were most commonly used in the 1970s. According to older interviewees, a much wider variety of greens, nuts, and fruits had been used in the past.

Fish had become a more important food in the late twentieth century than earlier. Some old-timers' answers to questions about fishing imply that industrious farmers did not have much time for it, but railroad workers and other nonfarmers did enjoy fishing in their time off work. Catfish, bass, walleye, and bluegill were the principal food fish.

Game was an important part of the diet even after the populace shifted from commercial hunting to relying primarily on farming. *The Foxfire Book* (Wigginton 1972, 264–73) contains an interesting article on dressing and cooking game. Rabbit, squirrel, raccoon, and woodchuck (ground hog) were prepared similarly by parboiling and then frying with pepper and sage seasoning. Most interviewees considered opossum unfit for human consumption because the animals have filthy habits and the meat is tough and fatty, but there is a strong psychological basis for this food taboo. This point was beautifully illustrated by one man's story about tricking his family into eating opossum. He chopped off the telltale tail, dressed the animal, and brought it home for his wife to prepare. The family ate what they thought was raccoon meat with the usual relish, but as soon as the hunter announced the trick he had played on them, everyone immediately got sick.

FOOD PREPARATION AND PRESERVATION

In the Foxfire series and a full-length popular book, *Mountain Cooking* by John Parris (1978), traditional recipes based on locally available wild and domestic food products have been printed for the tourist trade. *Mountain Cooking* was a useful source because it combined essays on foodways with a recipe section. Although

Parris wrote from personal experience in southwestern North Carolina, his information corresponded closely with what Big South Fork residents had to say about foods and food preparation. *The Foxfire Book* (Wigginton 1972) contains articles on these topics: cooking on the open hearth and woodstove (159–64); mountain recipes and preservation of fruits and vegetables (159–84); butter making (185–88); slaughtering hogs and preserving meat (189–207); and game (264–73). *Foxfire 2* (Wigginton 1973) contains articles on honey and beekeeping (28–46) and on wild plant foods (47–94). *Foxfire 3* (Wigginton 1975) contains articles on wild plant food (274–353); apple butter (416–23); and sorghum molasses (424–36).

Recipes collected locally are included in the *Mountain Magic* folklife booklets compiled by Oneida High School students (Oneida High School n.d.) and in cookbooks published from time to time by local organizations. Especially noteworthy among the latter is a cookbook compiled by women of the Allardt Presbyterian Church, because it featured many recipes for German dishes that were still favorites in Allardt. Descendants of the original German settlers lost their language, their Lutheranism, and many other culture traits, but distinctive foodways persisted to mark their ethnic origins.

More fundamental than recipes are the basic processes by which raw products are turned into food staples and preserved for future use. Traditional recipes necessarily had to make use of these available foodstuffs. Included here is information on processing meat, grains, fruits and vegetables, and making sweeteners and beverages. Food preservation was a problem that demanded ingenious solutions before refrigerators and pressure canners were available. Old-time food preservation techniques continued in use along with modern methods because people still enjoyed foods like kraut, pickled eggs, fodder beans, and dried apple pies.

Meats. Elderly interviewees remembered when farmers commonly slaughtered cattle and sheep as well as hogs for the family's meat supply. They recalled that beef was smoked like pork. Mutton was consumed immediately. Local farmers sometimes sold fresh mutton to the English families at Rugby. One woman commented on differences between the English and native practices regarding meat. The English seemed to prefer slightly "high" meat and poultry. She had been shocked by the practice of letting a killed chicken hang for a couple of days, supposedly so that it would be easier to pluck. She had turned down the offer of a housekeeping job in Rugby largely because of such food-handling practices.

Hogs have long been the principal source of meat for home consumption because they are efficient converters of feed into meat and do not require extensive pasturage. Native families were careful to slaughter during the coldest part of the year, generally from Thanksgiving through February, and to concentrate all their energies on processing the meat immediately.

The first task at slaughtering time was locating and shooting the hogs that were running loose in the woods. One man explained:

> *We had to be careful and see that we had the right hog, because everybody had hogs at that time. Everybody knowed pretty well how many he had . . . you'd look at the mark in their ears. And sometimes they'd go wild in the woods. That way we usually took a dog and he would bay the hog to where we could get up and see if it was our hog, because there would be so many hogs . . . the same color . . . We shot the hog and took it to the house. They'd weigh anywhere from 200 to 400 [pounds]. They didn't get as big, I don't believe, as the later hogs we have nowadays.*

After shooting the hog, the next step was to plunge the carcass into a big kettle of boiling water. After scalding, the hair was scraped off the carcass. Then a gambrel stick was run between the tendons and bone of the hind ankles, and the carcass was hoisted into the air, head down, to drain after being stuck in the jugular vein with a sharp knife. If desired, the blood could be collected in a vessel and combined with meal, salt, and sage to make blood pudding; this food seems to have been rare but not unknown in the Big South Fork area. There was an art to sticking the hog properly so that the carcass would drain thoroughly in about twenty minutes. After draining, the carcass was opened and the entrails removed. The carcass was then taken down and butchered into shoulders, hams, chops, ribs, and side meat.

The standard method for preserving meat was smoking. A curing compound was sometimes applied to finish the drying process after smoking. One elderly woman recalled that her father used borax, or sometimes wood ashes, for this purpose and then packed the meat in boxes full of shelled-out corn to provide insulation. Black pepper was often rubbed on the meat to discourage skippers (maggots). In the 1970s grocery stores carried commercial curing compounds.

Some meat was canned rather than smoked or chemically cured. Pressure canners and the conventional cold pack method had replaced an earlier form of storage in crocks, described thus: "We just smoked what we would fry—the bacon and sides . . . Now this side meat, it would get old and strong on us if we didn't fry it up, and we would fry it up and put it in a stone jar, a crock. We'd pour grease over that meat and cover it up. We'd just scratch it out, put it in a skillet and fry and heat it, and it was just like you went out and got a piece out of the smokehouse. It would last for a year like that, maybe some longer."

There were various ways to use other parts of the hog. Scrap meat was ground for sausage and seasoned with sage and red pepper. Before refrigeration, sausage was pre-fried and stored in crocks or canned to extend its keeping time. Souse meat was made also. It was prepared by boiling the hog's head until the meat fell off the bones, then grinding or chopping the cooked meat, seasoning it like sausage, and pressing it into a mold. The high gelatin content of this mixture bound it together so that it could be unmolded and sliced after cooling. It was used like sandwich meat. Intestines cleaned, chopped, and fried crisp were called chitterlings (chittlins). Liver mush was a liver sausage made with meal and sausage seasonings. Finally, all excess fat was removed from the meat, placed in a big kettle, and rendered into lard. Commercial lard remained the general-purpose cooking fat of many Big South Fork families.

Pressure canning revolutionized meat preservation in the depression, when local home economics teachers as part of the WPA programs taught workshops in canning methods. Subsequently, freezers made it even easier to preserve home-slaughtered meat and meat products.

Grain Products. Farmers used to grow both corn and wheat, in a few cases rye as well. The many streams of the Big South Fork drainage were dotted with water-powered gristmills that could accommodate both corn and the small grains. Some used a water wheel like the Davis Mill at Parmleysville, Kentucky, which still operates each summer as a tourist attraction. Others, like the Adkins-Hurt Mill near Mt. Pisgah, Kentucky, were turbine or tub mills.

Carrying a turn of corn to the mill on foot or on horse or mule back was a pleasant chore for women and children because they had fewer opportunities to get away from home than did the men. Customers at the mill had time to chat and catch up on local news while waiting their turns. The miller took a measure of the finished flour or meal as payment; he could resell this or use it in his own household.

A few water-powered mills were located where they were not affected by low water following a drought, but most of the mills had to shut down periodically. Thus steam-powered mills tended to supplant the old water mills. Farmers, however, stopped growing wheat and rye, and eventually the millers did not have enough trade to maintain their businesses. The few farmers who would have liked to produce their own cornmeal had to begin buying the commercial product.

Cornbread has been a staple of the area since the earliest days, but as cooking methods have changed so has the bread. The woman who cooked over an open hearth baked corn pones or hoecakes, which got their name from being baked on a greased hoe blade placed directly on the hearth. The wood-burning stove lent itself to cornbread baked in a skillet. Either way, white cornmeal was used for bread. Yellow corn was grown only for animal feed. The addition of cracklings, the crispy residue left from rendering lard or frying meat, made cracklin' bread or shortenin' bread. Gritted bread could be made late in the summer when the meal from last year's harvest might be running low. That recipe replaced meal with grated corn that was past the roasting ear stage but still milky.

Hominy provided still another corn dish. A special large-kernel dent corn was grown for hominy. After the kernels were taken off the ears they were soaked in a lye solution to loosen the hulls. The stripped kernels were washed to rinse away the lye, and the hominy was ready to eat immediately or to can. It was served like ordinary whole kernel corn. Further processing of hominy by drying and then grinding it into grits was common farther south but not in the Big South Fork area.

Sweeteners. In the old days, farm families bought very little cane sugar. It was used mainly for fancy baked goods and preserves. Sugar was not an ingredient in the best pure sour-mash corn whiskey, although it later came to be used in inferior whiskey. Families in the Big South Fork area had three home sources of sweetening: molasses, honey, and maple sugar. Of these, molasses is the most recent, dating from the Civil War period. Maple syrup and sugar making seems to have been fairly widespread as late as the turn of the twentieth century, but interviewees report that a number of good sugar maple groves were cut over for timber. Beekeeping has been practiced continuously from the earliest settlement period to the present.

Beekeepers used to capture colonies of wild bees to stock their hives. In the 1970s many still knew the art of tracking wild bees to their trees, smoking them out, and coaxing them into a prepared hive to carry home. In the past, beekeepers relied on knowledge of the bees' habits rather than protective clothing to avoid being stung. By the 1970s, books and pamphlets on beekeeping and commercial supplies were readily available. Supers had almost entirely replaced the old bee gums, sections of hollow tree trunk so named because they often were black gum wood. Honey sales were an important income supplement for several large-scale beekeepers. Relatives in Muncie, Indiana, and other urban areas developed good markets for the honey there. Many families who did not produce honey commercially kept bees to provide for their own needs.

Cane sugar from the southern states and the West Indies became scarce during the Civil War, and sorghum cane, which will grow under a much wider range of climate conditions, began to be used as a substitute (Arnow 1960, 17). After the war ended, residents of Appalachia continued to grow sorghum and make sorghum molasses.

The early molasses-making techniques involved stripping all of the fodder from the harvested cane stalks, then grinding them and pressing out the juice. A mule-powered turn-screw mill was used for this purpose. The collected juice was then boiled down with constant skimming to remove foam and a greenish scum of impurities until a clear golden color and proper consistency were achieved. This process was time consuming; to prepare enough syrup to last the family a year, the mill would be in operation at daybreak and the last of the stirring-off would go on into the night.

In later modifications of this technology, the mule-powered mill was replaced by a steam or gasoline mill; more important, the boiling-down process was hastened by introduction of the evaporator pan. The earlier models were wooden and later ones were stainless steel, but in both cases several compartments were linked so that the juice in each compartment could be transferred into the next as the syrup reached a certain stage of cooking. Raw juice was continually added to the first container, while finished molasses came out of the last. Old-timers claimed that the evaporator pan method was inferior to the older method of boiling down smaller batches in a single container, because some of the juice that passing through the pan would not be cooked thoroughly and skimmed long enough. Grinding the stalk without first stripping the fodder is another practice of mass producers that the old-timers decried. This shortcut and hurried processing in the evaporator would produce molasses hardly fit to eat because of a cloudy greenish cast and a strong, raw flavor to match. The old-timers claimed that proper sorghum molasses should approach a good dark honey in its appearance and flavor smoothness.

Vegetables and Fruits. Vegetable gardens and home orchards contained a fairly wide range of crops in the 1970s, and the modern pressure canner and home freezers made it possible to preserve most of these crops for winter use. Beans, potatoes, and cabbage were primary garden crops in the past, choices that were dictated in part by availability of appropriate methods of storage. Not only potatoes but also other root crops and apples with good keeping qualities could be stored in a root cellar, which was cool in summer but protected from frost in winter. If the family did not have a root cellar, pits dug in the ground and lined with hay would serve the same purpose.

Beans were dried in two ways, shelled and in the shell, the latter threaded onto long strings and hung from the ceiling like strings of red peppers. Beans dried in the shell, locally called fodder beans (also known as shucky beans or leather-breeches), were prepared by cutting the whole beans into bite-size lengths then boiling them for a long time with a little fat meat for seasoning. Some families still use this method to process part of their bean crop.

Apples and peaches were dried in the open air or inside near the heating stove. The fruit was peeled, cored, and sliced, then laid on boards and covered with cheesecloth or screening. Fruit cut into rings could be strung onto poles for drying, but this method was not observed in the Big South Fork area, nor was the method of sulfur bleaching (see Wigginton 1972, 181). Wild berries, once dried in the open air, were preserved by canning or freezing. One woman described crock grapes, a preserve made by pouring hot molasses over wild fox grapes (cf. Wigginton 1972, 183). Various more commonplace preserves were made with sugar or honey.

Brining produced cucumber and beet pickles, sauerkraut, pickled beans, pickled boiled eggs, and condiments like corn relish. Kraut and pickled beans were made in huge barrels and kept there through the winter. Mold might form on the surface, but the submerged food stayed wholesome. In the 1970s women were making their pickles and kraut in crocks and sealing them in canning jars after the fermentation process was complete. A still newer process called for fermenting dill pickles and kraut in the canning jars.

Table Beverages. Coffee was one of the few food purchases Big South Fork residents made in the nineteenth century. They bought whole unroasted coffee beans and parched and ground them at home. Native teas, especially spicewood and sassafras, were also common table beverages.

Milk cows of the past were not heavy producers but yielded enough to supply the family's needs for butter and milk. Buttermilk was drunk and used in recipes for biscuits, cornbread, and even custard pie. Before refrigeration was available, the springhouse was the only means of storing fresh milk; buttermilk kept longer.

Cheese making was not a part of local home food preparation except around Allardt, where the German settlers made cottage cheese. However, commercial dairymen did supply milk to cheese factories in the region, especially after the 1950s when regulations requiring new equipment caused many dairy farmers to lose their Grade A certification. Arnow (1960, 410) has commented that butter was made in preference to cheese because the byproduct, buttermilk, was usable whereas whey was not.

Persimmon beer was a table beverage sometimes made in the early fall when the milk cows were beginning to go dry. Persimmons were baked into cornbread, crumbled into a crock, covered with water, and allowed to work off. The beer was then strained and bottled for use at mealtime.

Apple cider was another popular drink. In the 1970s it was still being made with the old-fashioned wooden presses, both for home use and for sale. The best flavor comes from the blended juices of several different apple varieties. Unpasteurized, unrefrigerated cider becomes hard and at the end of that stage of fermentation turns sour, forming cider vinegar.

Alcoholic Beverages. Apple drinks more potent than hard cider were still made when older residents were children or young people. One man described the process of making applejack. "You know you can put that apple juice in a barrel, put it down in a basement where it won't get hot, put you a pipe, maybe a little rubber hose down in there and let that run off in a jar that's got water in it. Let that work off that way. As you drink it, put a little sweetened water back in there. First thing you know, you've got something real to drink . . . applejack." Another man described apple brandy.

> *I made some apple brandy one time. You just take a big whiskey barrel, fifty gallon barrel, and pick you apples up. You had a big trough that you throwed them in. You'd take a maul, a wooden maul and beat them up, then you'd dump it into the barrel till you got it full. Let 'em stay there so long till it worked off and settled back, then you'd just put it in your still and boiled it off and there come your brandy. It was good. It'd kick you—as strong as pure whiskey. Hit'd make you drunk and buddy, hit didn't just go off either. You got drunk on hit, you'd feel the effects for three or four days or a week.*

Moonshine is of course the most notorious of all Appalachian beverages. Pure corn whiskey was made at home following procedures quite like those used by ancestors of the Big South Fork settlers hundreds of years earlier in the British Isles. The sweet mash whiskey was kept on hand for medicinal purposes, as a general tonic, and for hospitality. Shortcuts that produced an inferior and often dangerous product were introduced once a cash economy created a booming market for whiskey. This conversation explains the differences between the two kinds of whiskey.

> A: *Why, they used to make whiskey around our part of the country there, everybody nearly made it. They made some good moonshine whiskey then. We'd sprout the malt and go to the barn and dig us a hole in the stables where the manure was—it couldn't never freeze—and bury that box down in there. It'd hold water. We'd put that corn in there—it'd have a lid to it, you see. We'd go every day or two and put warm water in that, and that's the way we sprouted the malt corn. See, we had to sorta watch about the revenue fellers too, you know, so whenever we let that lid back down, we'd throw some stalks and old hay over that, and maybe a mule in there [in the stall]. That's the way we sprouted that malt corn. Then you got one of these sausage grinders and run it through that, then it was ready to go in that still cap. They'd run a quill down through that cap and drink that [the still beer]. It's good, law yeah. See, it'd form a cap on top of it. You could tell when it got ready to work. The cap would get thinner and thinner. Directly it'd just break up, and she's ready to go in the pot and go to boiling it.*
>
> *They wouldn't put no sugar in that first. That was called the sweet mash, that first. That was the corn likker, nothing in it but just the corn. Whenever it got boiled off, it got weaker and weaker. Whenever it got down to what we called backin's, then they'd just empty that pot into barrels, and that's when they'd put the sugar in it. And it'd make more the next time than it did the first time, but it wouldn't be as good.*
>
> B: *That sugar whiskey's what gave people hard liver and everything, but that corn likker, old people used to drink that. They'd keep it in the home and*

drink it for medicine, maybe. Keep it on the table and all the family had to take a swallow every morning to keep 'em healthy. But after they got to putting that sugar in, it made 'em sick, poisoned 'em.

A: Gave 'em Jake leg.

B: Made their liver get hard.

A: The revenuers got so hard on 'em they wouldn't half make it. Made it on an old thump keg, they called it. They didn't run it through much of a copper pipe and take that grease [verdigris mixed with corn oil, called hardy grease] out of it.

B: My grandmother said that the way her daddy made it, he'd take a yarn sock and put that pipe, let that whiskey run through that yarn sock, and she said there'd be a great big ball of that old green stuff come off that copper. That was poison, and they'd [makers of bad whiskey] just let it go down in, pay no attention to it.

Here is another account of whiskey making after widespread bootlegging, fueled by demand from Stearns miners with cash on hand, became the order of the day in river gorge communities just across the state line in Tennessee.

Did you know that cane seed would make whiskey just the same as corn? This man had a still up yonder and wanted me to put up some with him. He had two big homemade barrels, riv out of chestnut flats big at the bottom and sloped up at the top, wooden hoops on 'em, helt 90 gallon apiece. Well, we put a bushel of meal in them, made two run out of that; the still held 45 gallons.

Well, one day he said, "Let's make some out of cane seed." We both had a big cane patch, had a barn and crib piled full of seeds.

I said, "That stuff won't make no whiskey."

"Yes, it will too."

I had a big gristmill in the creek there. We flew in and shelled us off a lot of these cane seeds and we'd go there and grind the seed of a night, then run some corn back through to keep people from knowing. We worked them up, and boys, it turned up the strongest whiskey, shoot fire. And he then wanted to put some sugar in it. I never had put no sugar in whiskey; you'd just cook the slop back and put you sugar in it.

I said, "They won't nobody buy that ol' sugar whiskey."

"Yes," said, "they will. I know a fellow'll take it every bit for $3.50 a gallon."

Well, we got a pair of mules and rode out here to Oneida and went across the railroad there to old man Bailey Cross's and bought 100 pounds of sugar, cost six dollars. We divided that and put it in a meal sack, each one of us just like we had a turn of meal. Throwed it across the mules and carried it back. We cooked them two big barrels back—the slop—divided that sugar, put fifty pounds in

> each barrel. Boy, that stuff worked off there and gosh, that'd gone two and three gallons of whiskey to the run, a hundred proof.
>
> You could buy your malt up here. Used to be a big store up here, Shannon Brothers, they got to ordering this barley malt. It was $7.00 a hundred back then, but a gallon of that would work a fifty-gallon barrel just rolling. Used to have to sprout the malt out of corn. It'd take you several days to sprout this malt, then you had to grind hit on a sausage mill.

Obviously, these men did not mind acknowledging their involvement in moonshine making back in the days of the Great Depression. Whiskey making continued on a much reduced scale in the 1970s, and stills were occasionally raided and publicized in local newspapers, but written accounts are the best source of detailed information on the technology of whiskey making. There is a fine article with detailed diagrams in *The Foxfire Book* (Wigginton 1972, 301–45).

Front view of Parch Corn Hunting Camp Lodge (Charit Creek Lodge), Scott County.

Rear view of Parch Corn Hunting Camp Lodge (Charit Creek Lodge) showing original saddlebag cabin.

Four-crib log barn at Parch Corn Hunting Camp (Charit Creek).

Old blacksmith shop at Parch Corn Hunting Camp (Charit Creek).

Corn crib on Oscar Blevins Farm, Scott County.

John Blevins House on Oscar Blevins Farm.

Front corner view of Lora Blevins house, Scott County.

Back corner view of Lora Blevins house.

Log barn on Lora Blevins farm.

Log outbuilding on Lora Blevins farm.

Rear view of William Peter Tapley house, McCreary County.

Smokehouse behind William Peter Tapley house.

Former Sunday school building of Beech Grove Baptist Church, McCreary County. Log construction under tarpaper.

Sewell house on Maxine Loudin property, Fentress County. Log construction under tarpaper.

Log barn built after 1930 on Alfred King property, McCreary County.

Barn built by Oscar Blevins in 1963 on his property in Scott County.

Typical "tenant" house, Fentress County.

I-house with ell addition, Wayne County.

Farmhouse in Allardt, Fentress County.

Bruno Gernt house, Allardt, Fentress County.

Thomas Hughes Public Library, Rugby, Morgan County.

Loudin house, Fentress County.

Barn behind the Lindens, Rugby, Morgan County.

Ben Stockton house, Fentress County.

Contemporary folk architecture, Fentress County.

Travel trailer with frame addition, Scott County.

Root cellar and storage building, Fentress County.

Concrete block root cellar with simple hex sign on door, Fentress County.

Garrett Store, formerly Hickory Ridge School, at Goad, Fentress County.

Interior of Wright's Store, Jamestown, Tennessee.

Interior of Mrs. Avo Rains's general store at Forbus, Pickett County.

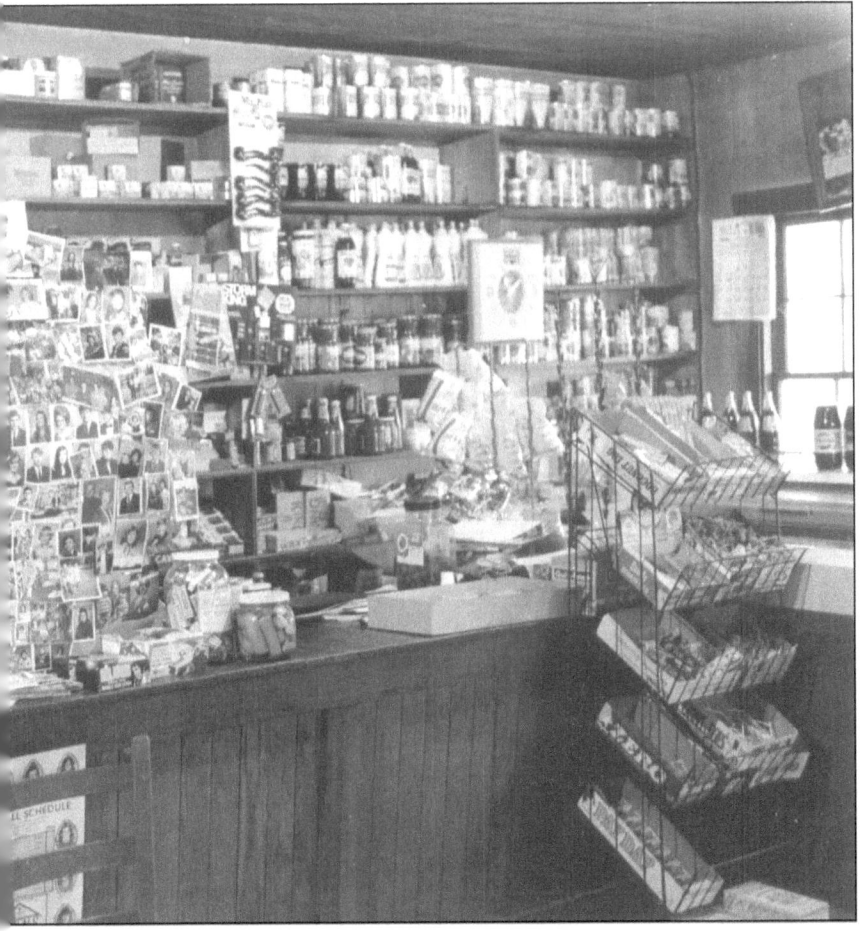

Interior of the Kidd Store and Post Office at Cooperative, McCreary County.

Kidd Store and Post Office, Cooperative, McCreary County.

4

The Cash Economy and Industrial Development

Before industrial development of timber and mineral resources intensified participation in the cash economy, most Big South Fork residents were subsistence farmers who needed little cash except to pay their taxes. Purchases at local stores could be accomplished through barter if necessary. Local specialists like blacksmiths and millers accepted payment in kind, and extra labor for clearing land, building, and other tasks was available on exchange instead of for hire. The farmer had various means of acquiring the cash he needed. He could sell forest products from his woods, medicinal roots and herbs, and furs. Livestock and surplus produce were also sold. Poor transportation and limited knowledge of urban ways created an opportunity for local entrepreneurs who kept general stores to become middlemen in most of the farmers' commercial transactions.

Industrialization turned many mostly self-provisioning farmers into full-time or part-time wage earners. As the cash economy expanded, the material conditions of life and social relationships changed profoundly. This chapter begins by examining the place of the general store in the traditional economy, then describes the occupational opportunities created by corporate development of the area's timber, coal, and oil resources.

General Stores

Enterprising local farmers established themselves as middlemen in their neighbors' commercial transactions by opening general stores. They saved others a great deal of laborious travel to town while benefiting themselves, both from profits made and from wholesale prices paid to suppliers for their own family needs. Their advantage came at the cost of much hard work: keeping the store open at all hours and often carrying on the usual array of farm and household tasks; suffering all the vicissitudes of wagon road travel on frequent trips to and from the railroad to pick up and deliver goods; and often assuming the duties of postmaster as well.

Around the turn of the century, France Miller and associates established a store on No Business Creek in Scott County. They carried the usual line of general merchandise and bought or accepted in barter chestnuts, eggs, and wool. These commodities had to be transported by wagon to Oneida, where the eggs were sold locally and the chestnuts and wool were loaded on the Southern Railroad for shipment to distant buyers. Wholesalers sent traveling agents called drummers to take the storekeepers' orders and shipped their merchandise to the nearest freight depot. Wagons returning to the No Business store were loaded with goods that had arrived at the Oneida freight depot.

Hauling goods for the store was exhausting work. The wagoner set out from No Business around 4:00 A.M. with a carbide lamp, hid the lamp beside the road at daybreak, and retrieved it in the evening to light the last part of the return journey. In winter, ice froze in the wagon wheels, and in summer the road turned to mud. The Big South Fork ford was often unsafe to cross with a wagon; for emergencies there was a dugout made from a big chestnut log stowed away near the river. First the cargo was ferried across, then the wagon was dismantled and taken across the river in three trips: wagon bed, front wheel assembly, and rear wheel assembly. After the wagon was reassembled and the team hitched up again after their swim across the river, the wagoner could proceed on his way.

About 1910 John "Woolyhead" Buck and his wife, Nancy, opened a store in a more developed area than No Business, the Fairview section northwest of Jamestown in Fentress County. At that time theirs was the only store for miles around, and they took in almost as much merchandise as they sold. They bought roots and herbs from local collectors for resale to the George P. Taylor Company of Burnside, Kentucky. Mrs. Buck was an expert fur grader; she sold the fox and raccoon pelts she bought from local trappers to agents of Louisville furriers who visited the store each year.

The Bucks also bought surplus farm produce such as corn, beans, peas, dried apples, and eggs. Farmwives made a point of selling surplus eggs each spring in order to buy hats and piece goods for new "May Meeting" dresses. Live chickens as well as eggs were accepted in trade. During the year the Bucks accumulated a large flock and sold it to a peddler who visited the store each spring. The store kept some of the produce it received in trade but found a better market for most of it in Jamestown.

The Buck store became a community social center. Although the post office was at Little Crab, mailboxes for Fairview families were lined up in front of the store. Tobacco-chewing storytellers congregated on the porch in summer or beside the stove in winter to wait for their mail and exchange local news. Because the Bucks had to provide room and board for the drummers who visited to take their merchandise orders, their home became a boardinghouse for any travelers needing a place to stay. Their hospitality was extended free of charge to the half dozen or so preachers who arrived in Fairview each September for the weeklong Baptist Association meeting. The Bucks periodically hosted a different kind of social event by providing space in the field beside the store for a traveling circus to pitch its tent.

While the Buck store was thriving, a wagoner was on the road all the time transporting merchandise shipments from the railroad depot to Fairview. Before the Oneida and Western Railroad was built, the nearest depot was at Glenmary in southern Scott County. Later, goods could be transferred from the Southern to the O & W and delivered to Louvain or East Jamestown.

The expanding railroad system made it easier for individual families as well as storekeepers to procure goods from outside the area. The national mail-order houses that began to flourish in the last decades of the nineteenth century had a delayed impact in remote sections of Appalachia, but eventually they helped undermine general stores there as they had done in other parts of the nation. Volume sales made it possible for the mail-order houses to undercut local merchants (Carson 1954). Later, improved roads and the automobile made it easier for merchants in towns to compete directly with country stores. Even before family cars became widespread in the Big South Fork area, Jamestown merchants began to capture more rural business by sending out rolling stores similar to bookmobiles. It is significant that the area's most authentic general store in 1979 was the Wright Store located in the heart of Jamestown.

Rural storekeepers survived as well as they did in the face of competition because lowest price was not the only drawing card for their customers. The availability of credit or barter and the storekeeper's role as middleman in the sale of medicinal plants and furs were equally important to many customers. One of the principal Nashville wholesalers, Block Brothers, gave Pickett County residents an additional means of earning cash income through the agency of the local storekeeper.

Each fall, Block Brothers delivered truckloads of unshelled walnuts to Byrdstown, Moodyville, and Forbus. Families interested in earning cash by shelling the nuts over the winter met the trucks at the store, and the storekeeper recorded the number of pounds let out for shelling to each family. The storekeepers sold participants a patented nutcracker ordered from a manufacturer in New Hampshire. The steel nutcracker stood upright; a cup held the nut in place while a lever like a pump handle was lowered, bringing the upper part of the cup down to crack the nut.

Families with many members earned substantial cash cracking walnuts and picking out the meats while they sat around the fire on long winter evenings. They returned the nutmeats to the store for cash, and the storekeeper handled delivery of the processed kernels to Block Brothers for reimbursement plus commission. The walnut business was an important source of income during the depression years, but steel shortages during World War II forced the nutcracker manufacturer out of business, and this cottage industry ceased soon thereafter.

Trade in medicinal plants and furs provided supplementary income for some Big South Fork families in the 1970s, but the local buyers were no longer storekeepers. Rural stores no longer carried a full line of general merchandise. Most sold food staples and a modest line of notions and hardware. Area residents typically made major purchases in town, including weekly grocery shopping, but picked up odd items and snacks at the local store.

Trading with the local store has retained its former social significance. Most rural storekeepers cannot rely on their business as a sole source of income, but they do gain from continuing to operate their stores. Their income from the store includes the advantage of obtaining personal merchandise at wholesale prices, and they also reap social rewards from continuing to provide a community center.

The Timber Industry

TIMBER SALES BEFORE INDUSTRIAL DEVELOPMENT

Before corporate lumbermen discovered the Big South Fork area, local farmers had marketed some forest products on a modest scale. Unlike the Cumberland River proper, the Big South Fork would not accommodate logs lashed together into rafts, but individual logs could be floated downstream on the flood tides to Port Isabel (later named Burnside) in Pulaski County, Kentucky. Men equipped with pikes walked the riverbanks and dislodged logs that jammed in the rocks. By 1880 Burnside was the site of several lumber companies, including Archer, Mancourt; Kentucky Lumber; and the A. C. French Company. The Chicago Veneer Company opened its Burnside mill in 1901 (Arnow 1977, 21–25). This company bought poplar logs that were comparatively easy to float downstream. Each man who cut logs and floated them to Burnside branded them with a distinctive mark so that the company could credit him properly for all logs that reached their boom. Several interviewees told of accompanying their fathers on log driving trips to Burnside when they were boys. After seeing the sights of the town, they caught the train back home.

Corporate development of the local timber industry was based on the railroads, but when the Cincinnati Southern Railroad was built through the area in the late 1870s, it first affected local forest product sales by creating a demand for cross ties. Construction and maintenance of the Kentucky and Tennessee and Oneida and Western Railroads helped to produce a steady market for cross ties in later years. Many farmers cut oak timber from their woods and hewed out cross ties by hand. Portable sawmills later took up the task of producing cross ties.

Tanbark was another important forest product until various chemical processes were developed for industrial tanneries. Morgan County census records indicate that there were tanyards there as early as the 1820s and that the local tanning industry continued to be important after the Civil War (Freytag and Ott 1970, 29, 110, 250). By the turn of the century, Pine Knot, Kentucky, storekeeper John Morgan was taking advantage of his strategic location near a Southern Railroad depot to export large quantities of tanbark to distant markets. Morgan bought tanbark from farmers who cut chestnut oak or hemlock trees in spring, stripped the bark, and stacked it to dry. They sold the dried, bundled bark to Morgan and other entrepreneurs by the wagonload.

Lumber was produced only in limited quantities for local use before lumber companies established sawmills in the Big South Fork area. Some of the local sawmills were the water-powered, sash-cut variety used from the early colonial period until the 1820s on the eastern seaboard. Steam was first harnessed to run circular saws in the Maine log woods in 1821; this technological advance radically improved sawmill efficiency (Holbrook 1961, 19–39). The water-powered saw ran at a very leisurely pace, simply mechanizing the operation of the ancient two-man pit saw. Low water forced these mills to stop operating. They typically were attached to a gristmill, and the miller devoted most of his attention to grinding grain. A man who recalled such a mill claimed that the miller only had to check the sawmill at his dinner break. The cut he had set up at the beginning of the workday would be complete by then, and he could set up another cut for the afternoon.

Local sawmills gradually adopted circular saws powered by steam and later by gasoline or electricity. The circular saw is portable, easy to maintain, and inexpensive initially; but it cannot handle the volume or accommodate the oversized logs that can be processed with a band saw. However, band mills were beyond the means of all but the biggest lumber companies in this area. The initial costs of equipment are very great, and expert maintenance is essential. Furthermore, a band mill is economical only when a large volume of timber is available to take full advantage of its speed. For the operation that can afford it, the band mill increases output while achieving greater accuracy and less wastage because of its thinner cutting edge.

DEVELOPMENT OF THE U.S. TIMBER INDUSTRY

Industrial exploitation of America's timber resources began in the Bangor and Penobscot River sections of Maine during the 1820s. The log boom, branding ax, snubbers, and Peavy hook were invented in the Maine log woods (Holbrook 1961, 22–25). The switch from ax to crosscut saw occurred in Maine about 1880 (Holbrook 1961, 48). By this time, the state's white pines had been cut over and a second harvest of spruce was under way.

By 1880, the center of the timber industry already had shifted from Maine to the Great Lakes. Many of the Maine loggers had gone west to Michigan, Wisconsin, and Minnesota, where the most significant technological contributions were the band saw and Horace Butters's Patent Skidding and Loading Machine. The latter was developed in Luddington, Michigan (home of the Stearns family), in 1886 (Holbrook 1961, 100–103).

Great Lakes timber resources were substantially depleted much more rapidly than Maine's had been, so that by the turn of the century the lumbermen were on the move again, this time to the forests of the Pacific Northwest and the Southeast. By 1905 these new centers rivaled the production of Wisconsin and Minnesota (Holbrook 1961, 152).

Lumber production nationwide peaked at something over 44 billion board feet per year in 1909; by 1945 annual production had dropped to less than 30 billion board feet (Brown 1947, 15). Since World War II, the national timber industry has experienced cyclic and seasonal fluctuations in demand. During boom times, especially in the South, numerous portable sawmills spring up. Truck transport for logs and lumber reinforced the trend toward small, portable mills.

Like many other parts of southern Appalachia, the Big South Fork was caught up in large-scale commercial logging between 1900 and 1920. Two big companies, the Stearns Coal and Lumber Company and Tennessee Stave and Lumber Company, established operations in the area during that period.

STEARNS COAL AND LUMBER COMPANY

Michigan-based Justus S. Stearns reflected widespread trends in the American timber industry when he acquired forested land in Kentucky, Tennessee, and Florida and a lumber mill at Hoquiam, Washington. The company applied technological expertise acquired in Michigan to their Big South Fork operations. Some middle-level supervisory personnel were brought in from Michigan, but inquiries failed to turn up any ordinary loggers who came south with the company. Presumably small-scale logging operations that antedated Stearns had taught local workers the basics, and they were readily able to adapt to the company's technological innovations. When Stearns logging operations ceased, a number of former employees who were natives of Kentucky and Tennessee went west to Washington or Oregon to continue working in the timber industry.

The Stearns Coal and Lumber Company was founded in 1902, and construction of the chief company town, Stearns, Kentucky, was begun the same year. By 1903 an electric band mill "unlike any other in the South" (Perry 1979, 108) was open for business. Initially the company leased both timber and coal rights from landowners, but by 1910 they owned vast amounts of Fentress, Scott, and Pickett Counties in Tennessee and what would become McCreary County, Kentucky.

Logging began along the Big South Fork River. The logs were floated downstream to a boom, then loaded on railroad cars for the last leg of the journey to Stearns. River transport worked for light poplar logs but was less satisfactory for oak. These heavy logs sometimes sank and caused horrendous logjams.

At first Stearns hired its own loggers, but the company shifted to a contract system in 1909 when they temporarily closed the electric band mill at Stearns because the volume of logs being processed had declined substantially. From 1909 until 1925, when extension of the Stearns logging railroad beyond the Kentucky and Tennessee terminus opened vast new areas for logging, individuals contracted with the company to log particular tracts, hired their own loggers, and set up small circular sawmills to produce rough lumber for delivery to Stearns.

While the logging railroad was under construction, the Stearns band mill was being refurbished; it reopened to handle logs shipped in by the new railroad, and company loggers were hired once again. The contract system continued in areas not accessible to the logging railroad and the various spurs constructed from its main line. Timber near the logging railroad was depleted by the end of World War II. Contract logging resumed, and the logging railroad was pulled out between 1949 and 1954.

Stearns timber cutters worked in teams of two, first notching the tree with an ax then finishing the job with long crosscut saws. The chain saw was not adopted until World War II. The earliest ones had extremely long bars and were designed to be handled by two men. Loggers did not think too highly of the early models, but wartime labor shortages and demand for timber put a premium on efficiency.

At first Stearns used Percheron horses and mules to snake logs out of the woods. In some places, chutes were built to carry logs down steep mountainsides to the river, but J-logging was more common. This method involved construction of J-holes at intervals along the steep sections. When the heavy log began to gain momentum on a hill, the horse ducked into a J-hole to escape injury. As the horse stepped aside, gravity uncoupled the J-shaped hook that secured the log to the drag chain and the log sped on down the hill. Overhead skidders later replaced the technology of chutes and J-logging.

Sleds or high-wheeled log carts were used to haul loads of logs along corduroy logging roads before mechanical equipment was invented. The Stearns Coal and Lumber Company acquired its first caterpillars in the 1930s but it had used steam-powered bulldozers with chain drive for some years before that. The first log trucks used in this area were old World War I army trucks with solid rubber tires.

The Stearns logging railroad was essential to accessing timber distant from the Big South Fork River in Pickett, Fentress, and Scott Counties. The logging railroad began at the terminus of the common carrier K & T line at Bell Farm, Kentucky. It gradually was extended twenty-five miles southwestward into Fentress

County. A number of temporary spurs were laid to open the various boundaries for logging. The Stearns Coal and Lumber Company controlled all logging along the K & T and its logging extensions. Albert Copeland, a Stearns contractor, operated a tram road near Bell Farm that delivered logs to the railroad. The M. I. Thompson Lumber Company logged some of the Stearns landholdings in what is now the Pickett State Forest. This company built narrow-gauge track and used motors rather than locomotives to pull log cars to a junction with the Stearns logging railroad, where the logs were loaded onto standard flatcars for shipment to Stearns.

While the logging railroad was operating, camps were provided for the company loggers, although many chose to rent houses with land and walk to and from work. This allowed their families to continue producing much of their own food. Other farmers worked only part time for Stearns after their harvest was in. They spent the week in boardinghouses and went home on weekends. Because the logging camps had to be moved periodically as new railroad spurs were laid, some of the camp housing was portable. Shacks were constructed so that they would fit on a flatcar; the roof was equipped with an iron hook so that a log loader could move the shacks onto and off of the flatcars. The same system was often used in the Pacific Northwest and was also used by the Tennessee Stave and Lumber Company to house employees who worked its timberlands near Head-of-Wolf in western Fentress County. In *Dorie, Woman of the Mountains*, Florence Cope Bush (1992) recounts her mother's vivid recollections of moving from camp to camp in identical portable shacks used by the Little River Lumber Company in the Great Smoky Mountains.

TENNESSEE STAVE AND LUMBER COMPANY

In the 1870s steamboats on the Cumberland River began hauling loads of rough lumber to finishing mills in Nashville. As the timber along navigable sections of the Cumberland was cut over, loggers turned to the tributaries, including the Obed River. Log rafts were put together and floated downstream after the late fall rains. Cordell Hull, who was to serve as Franklin Delano Roosevelt's secretary of state, helped his father "Uncle Billy" Hull cut and raft logs in Pickett County (DeLozier 1978).

Tennessee Stave and Lumber Company operations in western Fentress County represented a continuation of this incursion from Middle Tennessee into the timberlands of the Cumberland Plateau. The Ray, Speck, and Christian families who founded Tennessee Stave and were major stockholders in the Oneida and Western railroad came from Monterey, Tennessee. The Doss Spur from Stockton to Tennessee Stave's logging area at Head-of-Wolf was built in 1918. The Head-of-Wolf camp, containing a boardinghouse, commissary, and individual housing units, became the center of Tennessee Stave activities until the mid-1920s, when the timber was depleted.

An incline at the western terminus of Doss Spur connected that railroad with the network of logging railroad in Wolf River Valley below. This incline was so steep that special short cars had to be used on it. It was powered by a stationary steam engine or "donkey" and winch line.

Logs from Wolf River originally supplied the Hagemeyer Flooring Mill at Glenmary in Scott County. When that mill burned, the band mill at Verdun near Oneida replaced it. A second Tennessee Stave band mill was built at Louvain in Fentress County. Local residents recall that the building was completed and fully equipped with machinery but abandoned before even one log was sawed. None of them could explain the circumstances or date this event precisely. In the final phase of Tennessee Stave's operation, however, the mill at Verdun was converted to a planing mill. Rough lumber for finishing at Verdun was purchased from various small operators along the O & W railroad. These included the Whitson Lumber Company, Michigan Lumber Company, J. P. Pearson's Cumberland Valley Lumber Company, the M. I. Thompson Lumber Company, and sawmills near Oneida owned by Grover Pemberton and Jim L. Thompson. Former employees of the Whitson and Cumberland Valley Companies were interviewed and shared some vivid memories of their work experiences.

WHITSON POLE ROAD

The Whitson Company used a pole road to transport lumber from Slick Ford in Wayne County, Kentucky, to the O & W depot at Stockton, Tennessee. Pole roads were tracks of parallel peeled saplings, eight to ten inches in diameter, joined at the ends like sections of log pipe. Heavy flatbed wagons were pulled over these tracks by mules or horses. These cars had cast-iron wheels with a concave rolling surface that fit over the poles. Because the poles varied in size and shape and were not held in place by cross ties, the track did not have a constant gauge. Therefore, the axles were designed so that each wheel could move freely over a distance of about twelve inches to adjust for differences in gauge. Even so, "depolements" were common; an expert driver could expect to have to cope with at least one a day. Sometimes accidents occurred when the brittle cast-iron wheels broke under the weight of a heavy load. Men and animals were seldom hurt, but it was an inconvenience to have to lay down poles under the wheels of a disabled car and pull it back onto course.

The tram road was similar to the pole road. It used two-by-fours rather than poles for track, and tram cars had flat-surfaced, double-flanged wheels to fit. An experienced teamster asserted that tram cars were more dangerous than pole cars because their brakes were less effective. On steep-grades the mules had to be unhitched and the cars "wildcatted" to the bottom of the hill; that is, the teamster had to ride the car down, doing what he could with the brake to avert disaster. At least one man was killed on the Copeland tram road in Kentucky when his car overturned during such a maneuver.

The Whitson pole road was built in 1914 or 1915 and was used until 1925 or 1926. Before the O & W railroad was built, Whitson had shipped lumber from his Wayne County, Kentucky, sawmill to Burnside via the town of Cooper in Wayne County. When the new railroad made shipment via Stockton, Tennessee, more attractive than the old route, the pole road was built to the Stockton depot. Because the Whitson sawmill was located in a stream bottom, an incline was needed to lift loaded cars of lumber from the mill to the head of the pole road on the ridge above. At the top of the incline the cars were hitched to teams, four mules strung out single file. The driver rode the car and operated a brake attached to its wheels, but he used no reins, only voice commands, to control the mules.

The first leg of the pole road ran from Slick Ford to a halfway house located just west of Tennessee Highway 154 near the former site of Eve's Package Store. The halfway house was a boardinghouse with about six separate shacks nearby for employees. The company's mule barns were located there. Each day one crew made a round trip from the halfway house to Slick Ford, and a second crew made a round trip from the halfway house to Stockton. There were about twenty pole car drivers employed, a barn master, and a road maintenance crew. This crew was kept busy filling in mud holes with rock and replacing pole sections. Because there were no cross ties and the poles lay directly on the ground, they had to be replaced about once a year.

The boardinghouses used by some Stearns loggers were quiet, respectable places where drunkenness and rowdy behavior were not tolerated. The Stearns Coal and Lumber Company was concerned with maintaining law and order and laid off or fired disorderly employees. On the other hand, life at the Whitson halfway house seems to have fit the pattern of bunkhouse behavior historians and folklorists have described for loggers in other parts of the country (e.g., Holbrook 1961; Thornton 1973; Ives 1976).

A driver once stayed at the halfway house for seven months straight without a haircut or a shave. The food was rough—cornbread, beans, potatoes, "biscuits that would bounce," and "anything they could ketch." The workday lasted from dawn to dusk, but even so, the evenings were taken up with drinking, gambling, and, inevitably, fights. Those who did not play cards bet on the relative merits of their favorite mules. This was a man's world. The only women, the boardinghouse keeper's wife and daughter, kept their distance from the workers. Wages were $1.50 a day in the 1920s when the drivers struck for "$2.00 a day and a warm dinner on Sundays," their only day off. They stood together and easily thwarted Mr. Whitson's effort to break the strike with convicts from Knoxville who found that the mules were on strike along with the men who knew how to work them.

CUMBERLAND VALLEY LUMBER COMPANY

There were several loading points for logs and lumber along the O & W railroad, but Cumberland Valley Lumber Company was probably the largest of these operations. This company logged in the vicinity of Sharp Place in Fentress County and used gasoline tractors to pull wagonloads of logs to their sawmill on the ridge north of Gernt, an O & W depot and section crew camp. As many as fifty families lived near the Cumberland Valley mill. An incline carried lumber from the mill down to Gernt for shipment on the railroad. Residents of the Cumberland Valley camp sometimes rode the incline, which operated much like a ski lift, on their way to and from the store at Zenith, the next railroad stop west of Gernt.

> A: *There was lots of people rode it whenever I was running it. One car, the car loaded with lumber going down would pull the empty one back up. And they'd ride up and down on that. And I run that for pert near a year. Had a drum with a big cable...*
>
> B: *... and a car on each side.*
>
> A: *Had a big lever up there and a brake on that drum 'til you could hold it just going at whatever speed you wanted it to go, and right down at the foot of the hill, there was a curve went around that way and a person had to loosen up on the brake and give it a little speed so it'd go around that curve and on out to the lumberyard.*
>
> B: *There's where it broke loose and tore the store out.*
>
> A: *They told me that it had broke once and tore everything up down there, but as it happened there wan't nobody on it the time that the rope broke.*

This incline operator later worked in the Cumberland Valley sawmill and in a stave mill that was also part of the Cumberland Valley complex. He learned how to cut barrel staves and trim their edges, a task that required skill and dexterity.

> *After I'd done that sawing about two year, why I took a notion I wanted to work one of them jointer wheels. And so the man that owned the mill, I told him about it, and he said, "Well, they's one of my jointer men talking of quitting." He said, "If he does," said, "you can try it." Said, "You've learnt everything else."*
>
> *That feller quit, and he turned me onto that jointer wheel, and I put my own bits in—my shaving knives. They called 'em bits, but they's just a piece of steel about that [a foot] long, thick steel, real sharp on one edge. I'd set 'em, put 'em myself in there every time they had to be changed, so ... all I'd have to do would just be drop that stave, just drop it on that bench and let the edge of it just touch the knife and it would smooth it; and I'd just flip it over when the other man would take it and change hands with it. I'd just flip it over and just set the other edge to it and just drop it off there.*

And that man owned the mill, he stood there one day and watched me doing that, and he said, "Let me try that a little. That looks to me right easy." Said, "That other man said that was the hardest job that ever was."

I said, "Why, Price, it's a easy job." It was Price Pearson was who the man was. And so he took it. I said, "Now you've got to be careful, Price," I said. "That knife will take it right straight away from you and shave it every bit up into shavings."

An' he said, "I will." Well he couldn't jerk it back, get it back. It just went drawing it right on in.

I said, "Turn it loose, Price! It'll have your hands in there."

And he turned it loose and it just shaved it every bit up into shavings.

He said, "Now I've got you behind. You'll never catch up," said, "Now, now here it is."

And I said, "Why, I'll be caught up before they saw a dozen bolts." And so I was. I just caught up and cleaned up. Got so when I'd joint the last stave, I'd hold it up like it was a banjo and beat on it like and sing.

Like so many of the work stories told around the Big South Fork, this one has humor at the expense of the boss, but it also reveals a man who met the challenge of learning new occupational skills. Subsistence living already demanded many skills, and it was natural for men to learn still more when opportunities for industrial employment presented themselves.

POST-1950 EXPLOITATION OF TIMBER RESOURCES

Depletion of their vast timber resources ended Stearns logging after World War II. The Tennessee Stave and Lumber Company had not managed to survive the Great Depression. Between 1949 and 1954, the Stearns logging railroad was scrapped and the O & W was abandoned.

Stearns sold the land that became Pickett State Forest and Park and Scott State Forest to the State of Tennessee for a nominal sum in the early 1930s. Civilian Conservation Corps workers built the natural stone facilities at Pickett State Park. In 1937, Stearns sold 47,000 acres to the U.S. Forest Service, and this land was incorporated into the Daniel Boone National Forest. Thus, inclusion of the company's remaining timberland into the national recreation area completed a long period of transferring logged-over land from private to public ownership.

The Koppers Company purchased and reforested the former O & W right-of-way when that railroad was abandoned. In the late 1970s they cut the new growth. Further south in Scott and Morgan Counties, logging operations were conducted by the Rugby Land Company and the Hiwassee Land Company, which replaced the mixed hardwoods with pine to supply pulpwood for paper manufacture. In the 1970s, however, most loggers working around the Big South

Fork area no longer were company employees but rather contractors logging rather modest timber tracts for individual landowners. They hired small crews, often composed of relatives, and had little capital invested in equipment. Some still used mules to snake logs out of the woods.

Many small circular sawmills in the area bought logs from contractors. Wood industries located near the recreation area produced construction materials, flooring, railroad cross ties, tool handles, and charcoal. The small sawmills supplied these companies with rough lumber and stock, as well as sold retail to the public. One such mill near Oneida, for example, sold cross ties to Southern Wood Piedmont Company at Pine Knot, Kentucky; rough lumber to Tibbals Flooring of Oneida and to Oneida Wood Industries; and slabs to a charcoal factory at Somerset, Kentucky. By the late 1970s, waste slabs and sawdust that sawmills might have burned prior to enactment of air quality regulations were being transported to a charcoal factory at Somerset, Kentucky, or used as bedding material by broiler house operators.

Coal Mining

In the preindustrial period subsistence farmers exploited their timber resources for home consumption and limited cash income. There was considerable continuity between work in the timber industry and traditional skills. The same was not true in the case of coal mining. Big South Fork residents were unaware of the coal under their feet. It would have been possible to sink shallow pits in coal outcrops exposed by stream erosion; but if anyone ever discovered his coal and mined it for home use, the people interviewed had no knowledge of it.

Even before the Civil War, professional minerals prospectors realized the coal-producing potential of the Cumberland Plateau, and that factor weighed heavily in plans to link the area to the rest of the country by railroad. The war delayed railroad development, but during the 1870s construction began on what later became the Southern Railroad, ultimately part of the CXS system. The Whitley (now McCreary), Scott, and Morgan County sections of track were in place by 1880. Small mines at Glenmary and Helenwood in Scott County were the first to benefit from this vital link to industrial markets, but short line railroads later made it economically attractive to mine coal along the Big South Fork and its tributaries.

MINING TECHNOLOGY

Older interviewees who worked at Helenwood or at the early Stearns mines witnessed radical changes in mining technology over the years. An excellent introduction to the mining technology first used in the Big South Fork area is Joseph Husband's *A Year in a Coal Mine* (1910). Husband spent a year researching coal mining by actually working underground in a Midwestern mine. Despite the difference in geographical setting, his descriptions of tools and techniques provided background for talking with Kentucky and Tennessee miners who started work back in the pick-and-shovel days.

The primary technical difference between mines operated in this area and the situation Husband described is entrance layout. Mines along the Big South Fork and its tributaries tended to be drift mouth mines rather than slope or shaft mines. Instead of entering by means of a motor or man lift through a vertical shaft, the miner could walk into a drift mouth mine through a roughly horizontal entrance tunnel. Stream erosion along the Big South Fork and its major tributaries made it relatively easy and inexpensive to open mines; however, disadvantages resulted from the streambed location of mines in this area. There was a tendency for both water and noxious gases to accumulate in the mines.

Areas where water collected had to be drained by hand until pumps and pipelines were introduced. Miners dipped up the water in discarded powder kegs and poured it into a wooden wagon. Mules hauled these wagons out of the mine.

Before electric fans were available to circulate fresh air to the working faces, air circulation could be achieved only by using a furnace with a chimney extending through the mine roof so that the fire pulled fresh air into the mine entrance and exhausted bad air out the chimney. Interviewees report that this system was used at Worley in the early days and also at the Helenwood mines.

Channels called breakthroughs connected the working rooms and air tunnels inside the mine. As the working face was pushed forward, new breakthroughs had to be cut and the old ones had to be stopped up to force air to the ends of the tunnels. A canvas curtain could be installed to close an old air passage temporarily, but brattices of wood were built to block breakthroughs permanently. Any spaces between the passage wall and the wood framing were stuffed with burlap sacks to make the brattice as airtight as possible. Brattice construction crews were kept busy full time.

The mine foreman carried a safety lamp to detect dangerous methane and carbon monoxide accumulations, and another instrument to gauge the flow of air. The ill effects of breathing coal and rock dust were not fully understood when coal mining began in the Big South Fork area. Consequently, many retired miners suffered from black lung or silicosis. In later years masks with air filters were issued, but because they reduced the supply of air needed to do the strenuous work of shoveling coal, most of the men could not work comfortably while wearing them. If the retired miners interviewed express any regrets about their work, it was that they ruined their health without really knowing what was happening to them. They took the backbreaking work of loading coal in stride.

Before mining machinery was developed, the underground miner was not an hourly employee working on a shift but was regarded more as a free agent by the company. He had to furnish his own tools and supplies and he was paid by the ton of coal loaded. He was responsible for shooting his own charges to loosen the coal. Aside from assigning the miners their rooms to work and regulating the distribution of empty cars to be filled, supervision did not amount to much. Under the piecework system of payment, safety precautions were likely forgotten except when some recent accident made everyone newly aware of the extreme risks of the job. Piecework also meant that miners had to dispose of the slate in their rooms on their own time.

Before early cutting machines were introduced in the 1920s, coal was "shot on the solid." The miner used a breast auger if the coal was fairly soft or a crank-operated thread bar on a stand for harder coal. After he had drilled a row of deep holes, the miner placed charges of black powder, cap, and fuse in the bottom of each hole and filled the remaining space with "dummies" made of paper-wrapped clay. To save time, a man might scoop up coal dust and fill his dummies with it, but he created an explosion hazard in doing so. Once the fuses were lit, the area was cleared until the charges fired and the dust settled.

Coal was hand-loaded with pick and shovel. The older Stearns miners also recalled another tool, the punching machine, a pneumatically powered, two-pronged instrument used to create a fracture line across the working face, so that loosened coal could be popped out with a pick. The punching machine later was replaced by the same kind of jackhammer used by street repair crews.

When coal mines first opened in the Big South Fork area, mules were still used inside of the mines to pull wooden cars holding a ton or a ton and a half of coal to the mine opening. A stable master and a farrier as well as several teamsters were hired to tend the two dozen or so mules quartered at each mine. Motors were first used to haul coal cars only outside the mine opening. They collected coal cars brought to the opening by the mules and pulled them to the tipple where the coal was cleaned and graded by size. A miner who worked as a motor operator at the Davidson-Wilder mines in western Fentress County described early gasoline-powered motors. Stearns went directly to electric trolley motors, but mules were used inside the Stearns mines through the 1920s.

Both gasoline and electric motors posed safety hazards inside coal mines. Gasoline exhaust contributed to the problem of noxious fumes; but the exposed wires that served the electric motors were a shock hazard, and miners sometimes were electrocuted. Motors made possible a shift from wooden coal cars to steel cars that held twice the load. With the motors came a new set of workers paid an hourly wage: motormen, car couplers, and track men. The men who shoveled coal were still paid by the ton.

Cutting machines were introduced to the Stearns mines before motors had completely replaced the mine mules. The first cutting machines ran on track, but later versions had rubber tires so that delays for taking up and laying track could be avoided. Cutter bars on these machines were up to nine feet long. The Marlow mine operating near Zenith in the 1940s used a conveyor belt rather than cars to bring coal from the working face to the tipple. The Joy loader was phased into service during the 1950s, according to one retired miner. Stearns miners remember Sullivan and Blue Goose loading machines, designs that may have preceded the Joy loader. All of these devices were precursors of modern continuous mining machinery.

Retired miners who worked for Stearns rejected the notion that mechanization put miners out of work. Many of them were not inclined to learn how to operate the new machines, but other jobs inside the mines still were available, such as track crew and brattice construction work. Whereas each miner had been responsible for setting his own safety timbers and posts under the old shooting and loading system, mechanization meant that special timber crews had to prepare each area before the mining machines were moved in. The mine blacksmith who had sharpened individual miners' auger bits and picks turned his skills to maintaining and repairing the new machines. More important, hand loaders continued to work alongside the mining-machine support crews.

Mining machinery simply was not designed for seams of coal thinner than about four feet, and many seams in the Big South Fork area do not maintain that thickness throughout. Thus, some sections of the mines had to be shot and loaded by hand. However, the old system of allowing each man to fire his own shots was replaced by a safer procedure. Shot firemen who placed and detonated the charges worked an evening shift; the air cleared overnight, and the rooms were ready for loading by morning. The shot firemen kept track of the charges they prepared and counted them as they fired. If a shot failed to detonate, work might stop for as long as twenty-four hours, because a seemingly dead fuse might ignite the charge hours after it had been set.

The Stearns Coal and Lumber Company's Blue Heron Tipple was state-of-the-art technology when it was built in 1937. It operated until the mid-1960s. This tipple was a central sorting location for coal from several mine openings along both sides of the Big South Fork. A trolley bridge allowed electric motors pulling trains of fifty or more cars to cross the river, and another trolley track entered the tipple from the west. Each carload was weighed and inspected for excessive slate before it was dumped into the tipple. If the check weighman found too much slate in a loader's cars, that loader lost part of his pay.

A tipple is a giant sorting machine that separates coal into various commercial grades. Conveyors move the coal through a series of graduated sheet-iron grids. As each grid shakes back and forth, the coal small enough to pass through it falls into a collection pan. The coal dust falls through first, then the finest grade of coal. Coal too coarse to fall through the grid is passed to the next larger grid, and so on, until finally only the largest block coal remains.

A retired miner referred to the Blue Heron tipple as "the biggest thing that anybody knowed of in this country." It sorted four grades of coal, and a conveyor ran from each of the four collection pans to the railroad yard below the tipple, where gondola cars were loaded. Pickers sat beside each conveyor removing slate and waste rock. The Blue Heron complex included machinery to grind stoker coal.

MINE ACCIDENTS

Coal mines in the Big South Fork area have had relatively good safety records. Interviewees recalled only one fatality at the Zenith mines in Fentress County. A coal car came uncoupled, rolled back down the tunnel, and crushed a man to death. Noxious gas accumulations are common in damp mines located near streams, but this problem was not severe at Zenith or in the Stearns mines. Miners used carbide lamps for many years with few mishaps; these lamps are now prohibited as an explosion hazard.

Retired Stearns miners remember only a handful of explosions in over half a century of operation. There were dust explosions at Barthell around 1911 and at Fidelity in 1917. L. E. Perry (1979, 116–17) interviewed E. Rye West, sole survivor of the Barthell disaster, who described covering his face after the blast and stumbling over the bodies of six dead coworkers on his way to safety. At Fidelity two shot firemen were killed while detonating charges on their evening shift. Had the explosion occurred in the daytime, many men would have been killed by the blast that blew powder kegs out of the mine and over a hill to the tipple.

An explosion at Worley in 1932 killed three miners, and that explosion led to the most vividly recalled mining disaster in Stearns history. The Worley mine was closed after the 1932 explosion because carbon monoxide (the dreaded "black damp") follows explosions and fires inside of mines. Years later three supervisors were exploring inside the closed tunnels, hoping that they could be reopened for robbing (retrieving coal from the room pillars). When they removed a brattice, the invisible, odorless gas poured out. It overcame one man immediately, and when his two companions tried to get him out of the mine, they were also overcome. One lived long enough to be hospitalized but could not be saved. According to one miner who told this story, the tunnels of Blue Heron mines overlay those of Worley, and the possibility that black damp might seep through fissures into the mines around Blue Heron was a factor in closing them. This second Worley disaster occurred in 1964 (Perry 1979, 117).

The most frequent mine accident is the rock fall. Stories of near misses, injuries, and occasional fatalities are fresh in the minds of the victims, their work buddies, and their families, but the general public tends to forget the details of these accidents. Because of its unusual circumstances, one miner remembered and talked about a rock fall that caused no injuries. The foreman had a premonition that something was wrong and flagged the miners outside. Minutes later, the rock crashed down, about eleven carloads of it.

Much of the folklore of mining (e.g., Korson 1927, 1964, 1965; Green 1972) incorporates the theme of premonitions of disaster. One retired Stearns miner adds to his version of the 1964 Worley disaster his dream of a few days before laying out the events much as they happened, but with different victims. Although he believed that dream victims usually are not the real-life victims when a dream comes true, he nevertheless warned these men to be careful and described his dream to them. Ironically, one of the real victims was standing in the same room when this discussion took place, but out of earshot.

Safety was foremost in everyone's mind immediately after an accident, but in time the miners became lax again whenever foremen and safety inspectors were not around. Constant preoccupation with danger would have immobilized them. Trusting in timely warnings through dreams or other omens was one way to allay fear. Another was to treat a grim subject with humor, as in this story.

> At [Mine] Sixteen, why [the foreman] come in, and I was up next to the face turning out loose coal the loader didn't get. And the timber man was sitting there. And we'd knocked every timber down. Well, the main superintendent come in and got us down on our knees right there. Said, "I'm a notion to fire ever' one of you uns and then go home myself." 'Cause there warn't nary a timber in there. He didn't though. He bowed down on his knees and all of us come down on our knees like we was gonna have prayer. Maybe we needed to have a prayer or two.

STEARNS COAL AND LUMBER COMPANY MINES

Timber was foremost in his mind when Justus S. Stearns invested in land along the Big South Fork. The Bryant family had bought mineral rights near the river, including several tracts owned by the heirs of Huling and Zimmerman, who had attempted to market the oil discovered in what is now McCreary County. Louis Bryant studied mine engineering in Freiburg, Germany and returned to this country versed in the latest mining technology; but lack of transportation was an obstacle to developing the Bryant mineral rights along the Big South Fork. Once the Kentucky and Tennessee Railroad was chartered as a subsidiary of Stearns Coal and Lumber Company, the Bryants were in a position to lease their mineral rights to Stearns and receive royalties on the coal mined. This arrangement lasted from 1902 until 1923, when Stearns bought the Bryant holdings and began securing the surface rights as well. The Stearns policy of acquiring full ownership of surface and mineral rights contrasted with the practice of most Appalachian coal developers. Robert L. Stearns, Justus's son, also departed from the usual practice of northern absentee ownership when he built a fine residence and managed the company from the town of Stearns.

The Stearns mines opened in rapid succession as the K & T pushed north along the Big South Fork, then westward along Rock Creek (see appendix 3, table 24). The company bought out the Comargo Coal Company, the Premier Coal Company that had a camp at Buelli on Wolf Creek, and the Paint Cliff Coal Company that owned the Paint Cliff, St. Mihiel, and Oz mines. Coal camps sprang up along the railroad, and schools subsidized by the company promptly opened in each camp: Barthell in 1903, Comargo and Worley in 1905, Yamacraw in 1906, Paint Cliff in 1907, White Oak Junction in 1910, Fidelity in 1916, and Cooperative in 1922. Perry (1979, 113) described the early coal camp facilities in stark terms.

> *Box houses of cheap construction dotted the landscape at every mining camp, using all available space not needed for mining activity. These houses of two rooms and a kitchen were provided by the company for the convenience of the miners and their families at a monthly rental fee, withheld from their earnings. They were built of vertical boards and the thin walls had no insulation except the blue building paper tacked over the interior to cover the splintered surface of the rough lumber. There were two brick half-flues standing on the ceiling joists for a coal heating stove and a cooking stove. One electric light bulb in each room overhead was the only other luxury the company provided. There were no electric outlets, no plumbing, no running water.*

In addition to the men who worked at jobs inside and outside of the mine, each camp also had a mine superintendent, timekeeper, bookkeeper, a store manager and several clerks, a postmaster, and usually a doctor. According to Perry (1979, 113), the social elite of the camp comprised the superintendent, timekeeper, storekeeper, and doctor, and their position was physically reflected in the location of their houses on a hill overlooking the rest of the camp. However, retired miners' stories indicate that social distance between these groups was not rigidly maintained, particularly in the case of miners who came from the more prominent local families. A number of locals attained management and clerical positions within the company.

A miner who began working at Worley in the 1910s estimated that thirty or forty families lived at Worley in houses up and down the railroad and along the river. There was a post office, a company store, and later a school building that doubled as a church. Occasionally a family planted a small garden in the camp, but most relied on local farmers who peddled produce to the miners, or they arranged for garden space with relatives who lived outside the camps. The company stores did not stock perishable foods until much later.

Not all of the mine employees settled in the camps. Some who lived on farms chose to remain there and walk back and forth to work each day, sometimes distances of five to seven miles each way. Others lived in Stearns and commuted to work by train, leaving at 5:30 A.M. and returning at 5:30 P.M.

Some of the camps had boardinghouses as well as single-family dwellings. The Fidelity boardinghouse was located next to the bathhouse and across the tracks from the company store, where miners' supplies such as carbide and black powder were sold as well as consumer goods. On the ground floor of the boardinghouse were common rooms, including a barbershop. The boardinghouses were the scene of some spirited music making and dancing on weekends. Kentucky miners provided a solid clientele for moonshiners just across the state line in Tennessee settlements like No Business. Nevertheless, the company would not tolerate public drunkenness or Monday absenteeism brought on by the excesses of the preceding weekend. These policies probably reduced incidents of violence that often were associated with drunkenness.

Blue Heron was the last camp to be developed by Stearns. Several mine openings in the general vicinity were operated from the late 1930s until the late 1960s. The imposing tipple structure and the bridge across the Big South Fork dominated Blue Heron. The company store was near the foot of the tipple steps, and residents from outside the camp walked the bridge and used the tipple steps in traveling to and from the store. The church and school buildings stood on the hill above the tipple. Houses occupied the river bottom from the Roaring Paunch Creek bridge to well beyond the tipple and spread up the adjacent hillside. Space in the camp was set aside for organized recreation—baseball and horseshoes. The miners also liked to fish and hunt when they had the chance.

There was a large and active Baptist congregation at Blue Heron. The church organized a Sunday School and periodically held revivals. The only aspect of church life that seems to have been lacking in the camp was funeral and Decoration Day observances. There was no cemetery near the camp; residents were buried in family plots or cemeteries near their home churches, and the funerals were preached there.

Camp residents paid for rent and utilities—coal, electricity, water, and ice for iceboxes—through paycheck deductions. Whether or not they lived in the camp, all miners paid for the company doctor, the school, the bathhouse, and the mine shop where their tools were sharpened.

It is a common misunderstanding of outsiders that coal miners used to be paid exclusively in scrip honored only at company stores, and that because of this system, the company really did not have to part with the wages it paid. Stearns paid its miners on a biweekly basis in cash. However, if a man was short of funds he could get advance payment between paydays in the form of scrip. Numerous pay deductions left little take-home pay, so that scrip advances were inviting. Taking the scrip advance, however, produced even less take-home pay in the future, and so the vicious circle went.

Residents familiar with the situation in Fentress County agree with Stearns miners that company stores carried quality merchandise, but at inflated prices compared to those of independent merchants. A Fentress County miner explained how his coworkers might deal with a middleman who bought their scrip at a discount as high as 25 percent to 50 percent, thus supplying them with the cash needed to trade with independent merchants. Companies were obliged to honor their scrip when these middlemen traded it at the company stores even though they tried to restrain such middlemen from operating.

The situation was different in McCreary County. The Stearns Coal and Lumber Company through its various business enterprises—everything from the electric power plant to a large automobile dealership—held such a strong position in the countywide economy that, according to Perry (1979, 124), all consumer prices tended to be higher than elsewhere in Kentucky as a consequence. If so, the fact that most private merchants in McCreary County accepted Stearns scrip would not have been much of a boon to the financially hard-pressed miner and his family.

The most significant factor affecting the economic welfare of Stearns miners was retention of family farms. Coal mining never totally dominated the economy in the Big South Fork area as it did in the coal fields of Eastern Kentucky and West Virginia (see Caudill 1963). There was other work to be had and some land still to be farmed. Judging by the personal experiences of interviewees, Stearns did not pressure all its employees to live in company housing. Even in the Great Depression years when the mines operated only two or three days a week, part-time farmers who walked to work from their own homes were kept on the payroll along with the camp dwellers whose reduced earnings left them in debt to the company for rent and utilities.

Before coal-fired power plants created a year-round steady market for coal, even good years showed an imbalance between the heavy demand of the winter heating season and slack demand in summer. The man who made mining his only livelihood always fared better in winter than in summer, but the part-time farmer used his days without mine work to advantage, providing almost all of his family's food and saving the camp rent and utilities fees as well. A large family had no trouble taking care of farm chores when the miner of the family was working full time. Some could raise enough to meet their own needs and have surplus to sell in the camps. It was also to the company's advantage to have a local labor pool available for the high-production winter months but able to support themselves by other means in summer.

Despite lingering bitterness over the sale of the Justus Mine to Blue Diamond Coal Company and the subsequent strike, few McCreary County residents had anything negative to say about the old Stearns Coal and Lumber Company and its employee relations. The founders embarked on their enterprise in Kentucky and Tennessee in a spirit of benevolence quite unusual for the turn of the century (see Kinne 1929) and to a large extent put their ideals into practice in a program that might now be called community development for McCreary County. Interviewees realized that the company had exercised vast economic and political power but regarded its actions as generally benevolent rather than abusive. Although the company opposed union organization attempts, its former employees felt that the company provided better benefits than the Union could have done before it gained strength during World War II.

Fluctuations in annual coal production for Stearns closely paralleled figures for the United States as a whole (Stearns archives; Coleman 1969, 311). Production increased fairly steadily from 1900 through 1920. There was a recession in 1921 and 1922, but strong markets returned for the rest of the 1920s. Peak annual coal production for Stearns came in 1929 when a million tons were mined. Although production began to taper off the following year, the depression was not severe until 1932–33. The rest of the 1930s saw a gradual recovery until World War II created a boom. Men who had been working two or three days each two-week pay period during the worst of the Great Depression were able to work seven days a week during the war. Another slump followed the war as natural gas and fuel oil began to compete with coal as home heating fuel. This softening of markets coincided with dwindling supplies of recoverable coal in many of the Stearns mines. Some robbing was done, but finally by the 1960s only the Blue Heron mines and Paint Cliff were still open.

When these mines closed, the company invested heavily in developing a new deep shaft facility, the Justus Mine, described in detail in the *McCreary County Record* of October 16, 1975. Justus Mine opened in 1968 with the promise of revitalizing the county's coal industry and bringing renewed prosperity to its inhabitants, but in 1975 the mine was sold to the Blue Diamond Coal Company. This move ended the Stearns Coal and Lumber Company's long involvement in the coal industry and precipitated the kind of protracted and acrimonious strike that McCreary County had been spared in the days of "Bloody Harlan."

Early unionization attempts at Stearns had come in fits and starts. Each time, union sentiments and organizers spread into McCreary County from the coal fields further east. The first union activity occurred in 1908 and was met with stubborn resistance from the company. National Guard troops were called in. The company argued that it was paying a wage better than union scale and that union job safeguards would make it impossible to fire criminal types and thereby improve law and order. Most miners who were native to the area sided with the company. To avoid involvement in a violent labor struggle, many returned to full-time farming (Perry 1979, 109).

The most memorable incident of the 1908 struggle was the deliberate burning of the old Stearns Hotel during a Christmas Day attempt to flush out three union organizers who had barricaded themselves inside to avoid arrest. Rich Ross was killed as he left the burning building; Berry Simpson was captured and sent to prison but later pardoned, reportedly at the behest of Robert Stearns himself. Rube West escaped from the fire unscathed and was never apprehended, even though he made no pretense of hiding. In fact, he set up a notorious moonshine still on Troublesome Creek and trained several of the whiskey makers who took up the craft on No Business during the Great Depression.

The next abortive attempt at union organization came in 1922–23. It ended without violence, but every miner who had participated was fired and blacklisted for any further employment by Stearns (Perry 1979, 117). The union was a dead issue during the boom years of the 1920s, but the production slowdown during the depression was coupled with tonnage rates being cut from thirty-one cents per ton to twenty-two and twenty-four cents per ton. These conditions renewed interest in unions at a time when the UMWA was making strong efforts in neighboring Kentucky and Tennessee counties.

A union contract finally was signed in 1934–35 after passage of the Wagner Act and formation of the National Labor Relations Board had made blacklisting and other retaliation against unionization illegal. After the Stearns mines were organized, employees began picketing the Barren Fork mines in eastern McCreary County. The president of the Barren Fork Coal Company, J. B. Durrell, carried out his threat to close the mines rather than yield to the union (Perry 1979, 125–26). Several hundred jobs were lost, a blow that the county could ill afford in the mid-1930s. The following year, Stearns miners struck but returned to work without a contract when differences between the company and the union could not be resolved. Finally, a contract was signed in 1941, and the miners continued to be represented by the UMWA until 1953, when the company canceled the contract and closed the mines, claiming that it could no longer afford to operate under the contract conditions. The following year, the McCreary County Miner's Union was organized and mines reopened. This independent union continued to be acceptable until Stearns sold the Justus mine to the Blue Diamond Coal Company in 1975. This was a typical absentee coal corporation whose unenviable safety record elsewhere in Appalachia rekindled UMWA sentiment among Stearns miners. A long and bitter strike lasted until the spring of 1979 when a settlement, but not a reconciliation of all hard feelings, emerged.

MINES ALONG THE ONEIDA AND WESTERN RAILROAD

Coal mines along the O & W Railroad were concentrated in a seven-mile stretch from Potter (fourteen miles west of Oneida) to Hagemeyer (twenty-one miles west of Oneida). Ownership of these mines, as well as ownership of the various sawmills along the O & W, was held by various individuals who were stockholders in the O & W and in the Tennessee Stave and Lumber Company, later known as the Tennessee Coal and Lumber Company. Lack of access to historical records comparable to the Stearns Archives made it impossible to determine the exact nature of interlocking ownership and management between the railroad and the industries that benefited from it. Suffice it to say that from the perspective of employees in the mines and sawmills along the O & W, their employers were small, independent companies, not parts of a monolithic organization like the Stearns Coal and Lumber Company.

The Potter mine was a small outfit with no camp. All its employees walked to and from work. The Potter tipple was across North White Oak Creek from the main railroad line. Cable cars ran across the stream to bring coal to the railroad for loading.

The East Laurel mine, located two and a half miles west of Potter, was the first mine opened. It was worked out before the mines at Zenith were developed. When East Laurel closed, its operator, a Mr. Ligon, may have been associated with the Webb Hammock Company that ran the Zenith mines. East Laurel was the site of a thriving camp during the 1920s. The boardinghouse was a favorite stopover for traveling salesmen and railroad officials, but by the mid-1930s the camp was deserted except for the postmaster and his family. They stayed because the East Laurel post office also served neighboring Gernt, an O & W section camp and home of several mining families.

The original Zenith mine entrance was immediately south of the main railroad track, and the tipple was built over the main track. When new mine openings were developed across North White Oak Creek, a spur line was built to serve a new tipple. The creek was shallow with a rocky bed at that point, so the track was laid across the water on a rock bed rather than a bridge.

Also located at Zenith was a mine first operated by a Mr. Marlow and a Mr. Baldwin, a modern installation equipped with a conveyor loader. This mine opened in 1939 but ran only a short time because the operators refused to deal with union demands. After taking over the O & W in 1948, the Jewel Ridge Coal Company invested some money in reopening the Marlow mine, but they reconsidered and sold it to Robert Wilder of Williamsburg, Kentucky. Because the Marlow mine was so close to North White Oak Creek, water had been a constant problem. When the new owner ran a tunnel under the creek bed, water flooded the mine and the top fell. Just as the pumping and repairs were completed and the mine began to pay back the investment, plans to abandon the O & W were announced. The railroad was the only means of getting coal out of the river gorge, so Wilder was forced to stop mining and move out his heavy equipment as the railroad track was being pulled from Jamestown to Zenith.

The Hagemeyer mine run by a Mr. Laxton never showed the promise of the Marlow and Webb Hammock mines. Instead of the highly prized cannel coal found at Zenith, Hagemeyer produced small quantities of an inferior coal. Today a huge heap of "red dog" (burned slate waste) marks the location of the Hagemeyer mine.

As the land along the O & W railroad was being transferred to federal control, local people contended that there was still a great deal of high quality cannel coal at Zenith, but the mining era in the Tennessee section of the recreation area is remembered most for its failures. First technical problems—water and thin coal seams sandwiched between thick layers of slate—then the Great Depression followed by violent attempts at unionization, and finally the languishing railroad prevented establishment of a thriving mining industry. In the mid-1930s union organizers and sympathizers from Southeast Kentucky tried to close the Webb Hammock mines and resorted to violence when management ignored their demands. Miners who wanted to avoid the trouble went back to farming or logging. Even forty years later, they preferred not to discuss details of events at Zenith during the 1930s. Those who stuck it out as coal miners were forced to leave Fentress County and move to other coal fields. Consequently, the most vivid stories of those days come from railroad men who saw firsthand what was happening without being directly involved, and from men and women who were children growing up in the Zenith camp during the union troubles. Even though the children were in considerable danger (the schoolyard was a sniper's target on occasion), the Wild West–movie events going on around them seemed exciting and became indelible memories.

Snipers took to the bluffs overlooking Zenith. One shot Sheriff Taylor when he came into the camp to make arrests. Mine boss Ed Slaven took the sheriff's gun and went after the organizer. Instead of handing over his gun, the man shot Slaven at point-blank range. Before he died, Slaven grabbed his murderer's hair and shot him to death in the neck.

The trouble continued in 1937, and during one disturbance a stray bullet hit newly elected Sheriff Wolford Smith in the leg. Shortly after Smith was wounded, the supply manager for the Webb Hammock mines, Cap Woods, was ambushed and killed on the road from Armathwaite community to Zenith. The sheriff, still in a cast, directed the hunt for the assassins from the front porch of the county jail in Jamestown. Bloodhounds were brought in but proved ineffective, some say because the fugitives had filled their shoes with pepper. Many suspects were jailed, especially union organizers out of eastern Kentucky, but no firm case could be made against any of them.

Early Oil Exploration

The first commercial oil well in the United States is located on Oil Well Branch in McCreary County, Kentucky. Its story is told in the *Kentucky Petroleum Councilor* (March 1970, 5). Marcus Huling and Andrew Zimmerman were drilling for brine on the Martin Beatty farm with the intention of establishing a saltworks. Having drilled to a depth of about 200 feet using a wooden spring-pole rig, they struck oil in November of 1818. The "devil's tar" overflowed the well and spilled into the stream, arousing a public outcry against the venture, especially among farmers whose geese were coated with the sticky oil.

After trying unsuccessfully to float barrels of oil down the Big South Fork, Huling used mule trains to pack some of the oil out for sale to patent medicine manufacturers in the United States and Europe. However, by 1820, legal complications, continuing outrage over the pollution, and transportation problems caused Huling to abandon the well and resume salt exploration elsewhere. The well was plugged with a long section of log.

During the first decade of the twentieth century, a number of oil wells were brought in within the present boundaries of Wayne County, Kentucky. During the 1920s Stearns made some attempts to develop oil reserves within the company holdings. Hen Spradlin of Bell Farm, a farmer-blacksmith who did some blacksmithing for Stearns, became involved in the oil-drilling project. A man who helped move the steam-powered rig recalled it and the well in these words:

> *It was a big steam rig. You fired it with wood—steam boiler—moved it with mules—four head, I guess. We moved it about half a mile from where they drilled the first one up the creek in the bottom to where they drilled the next one.*
>
> *They struck oil about 850 feet down in the Lever sand they called it then; they call it the oil shale now. The last well they drilled there, hit stood up in the hole a way up. Well, I took one of these balls of wrapping twine and put me a cup on it and got me oil out to put on hogs. But then, there wasn't no way to get it out of there, no road in there only just old wagon roads. And they'd of had to laid a pipeline from there to Parmleysville, Kentucky. It was about thirty miles. And they said just a little stuff, wasn't enough to pay to fool with it. Stearns Company had it drilled.*

An octogenarian who worked in the oil fields near the common boundary of Fentress, Scott, and Morgan Counties during the late teens and early twenties recollected that the first oil well near Glenmary in Scott County was brought into production in 1918. It tapped relatively shallow deposits at 1,200 to 1,300 feet. In 1924, the Bone Camp Creek oil field east of Burrville in Morgan County was opened, tapping the Fort Payne deposit at 1,400 to 1,500 feet. Progress was slow with the equipment used at that time, and a great deal of heavy lifting was required of the workers. It might take a month to drill a distance that could be completed in a week using modern machinery.

In the aftermath of the 1974 oil embargo with its gas shortages and high prices, there was once again interest in developing oil and natural gas resources in Morgan and Fentress Counties. Anyone investing perhaps $30,000 in sinking an oil well wanted to do so with some confidence that it would produce oil. Knowing that geologists' opinions sought before drilling are not infallible, some turned to the old folk practice of dowsing to locate oil as well as water. The same implements could be used to dowse for oil and for water—a forked stick, preferably dogwood, or two wires bent at right angles. A stick should point toward water or oil as the dowser walks over the exploration area holding these implements loosely. The dowser should feel a strong tug downward when standing above the water or oil. The wires, held parallel to one another, one in each hand, should cross as one approaches the water or oil. Oil should affect the dowsing rod over a larger area than water, but there was no way to determine the depth of the deposit.

One elderly oil man used a hollow tube suspended from a wooden handle to dowse with. The tube was filled with crude oil and closed with a stopper. The points of the shuttle-shaped wooden handle were gripped between the tips of the forefingers so that the instrument could rotate freely. The tube would then rotate downward as the dowser walked over an oil deposit. Presumably the crude oil in the ground attracted the like substance in the tube.

5

Short Line Railroads

The preceding chapter makes it clear that industrial exploitation of timber and coal resources near the Big South Fork would not have been possible without the transportation provided by the Southern Railroad (formerly the Cincinnati Southern and later merged with the Norfolk and Western into the CSX system). The Kentucky and Tennessee and the Oneida and Western short line railroads were equally essential. Their functions, the technology mastered by railroad workers, and railroad work experiences form the focus of this chapter. Maps and additional information are now readily available in Elmer Sulzer's books on ghost railroads of Kentucky (1968) and Tennessee (1975), both of which were reissued by Indiana University Press in 1998. The railroads generated additional opportunities for wage work among natives of the Big South Fork area but also attracted skilled railroad men from outside. Thus the railroads had an important part in their own right in shaping the economic and social history of the Big South Fork area.

Kentucky and Tennessee Railroad

The Kentucky and Tennessee Railroad was chartered in 1902, the same year in which the Stearns Coal Company and the Stearns Lumber Company were first formed as separate entities. In 1904 when these companies were merged, the railroad was also reincorporated with an expanded prospectus. Although fully owned by the Stearns interests, the Kentucky and Tennessee Railroad was chartered as a common carrier. The original intention was to build the railroad toward Jamestown and from there to Chattanooga, Tennessee. However, when the line reached the mouth of Roaring Paunch Creek, the company became interested in developing the country along Rock Creek, and the track turned north along the Big South Fork instead of south (Dr. Frank Thomas, personal communication).

Construction of the railroad was accomplished by bringing in contract labor. By June 1, 1903, the line had been completed from Stearns to Barthell, and the first car of coal was delivered from Barthell on that date. As the railroad was extended, additional mines came into production (see appendix 3, table 24).

Seventeen miles of the K & T were already completed by 1915, according to an article in the Stearns *Co-operator* of November 15, 1915. At that time the officers of the railroad included J. E. Butler, general manager; A. J. Russell, general traffic manager; Leslie C. Bruce, assistant general freight agent; and Mark A. Gibbs, general superintendent. Mr. Butler had been associated with the Stearns operations in Michigan, and another Michigan native, Christian L. Larmee, was master mechanic in the railroad machine shop. Many of the K & T's employees were hired from the Southern Railroad.

Although Stearns began its logging operation without benefit of the railroad, rail transportation was a pressing need for that enterprise as well as for the mines. In *The Gum Tree Story* (1929, 12), W. A. Kinne described the company's early log transport system: "While the railroad construction was being continued to the mouth of Rock Creek, booms were constructed along the Big South Fork River below the mouth of Paunch Creek for the purpose of catching and holding logs to be loaded on railroad cars and taken to the mill at Stearns. Arrangements had been made for the buying of logs along the upper Big South Fork and its tributaries, and for a number of years many millions of feet were secured in this manner." A man who lived near the river contradicted this report of a smooth and efficient operation. He remembered the company's unsuccessful attempt to float white oak logs downstream.

> When Stearns Company first come in this country, they went across the river at the mouth of Station up the mountain there, and on top out up there. Didn't have no cars nor trucks nor nothing. Had these big Percheron horses. Put up a big camp there and logged there a year or two, and built a big chute from the top of the mountain to the river. Put that stuff in the river and floated it to Yamacraw. Well, they went to cutting this white oak, and the people told 'em, said, "Now this white oak timber won't float here, it'll sink, the butt logs of it."
>
> "No," [the company man] said. "Hell, it floated in Michigan."
>
> An old fellow said, "Yeah, and it's a helluva long ways from here to Michigan too."
>
> And they just put her in there and they just come very near going busted. Why, that river was just piled full of big white oak logs. And they moved out of there then and my brother-in-law and his old man moved in there and logged right smart bit of it out.

Soon after the Yamacraw Bridge was completed in 1907, a big flood destroyed the booms and sent a river full of logs crashing against the bridge. It fortunately withstood the onslaught, proving that this 600-foot-long solid concrete bridge, one of the longest of its kind, was sound in design and construction. However, workers had to be rushed to the boom at Tatesville above Burnside to reclaim the Stearns Company logs. They worked almost nonstop at this extremely dangerous task for two days and then the logs had to be shipped back to Stearns on the Southern Railroad at considerable additional expense (Kinne 1929, 12–13). This episode suggested that a better means of transporting logs was needed; acquisition of additional land far to the west of the river made rail transportation indispensable to the logging operation.

By 1922 and 1923, the K & T extended west as far as Cooperative and Mine 15. Stearns Coal and Lumber Company's original agreement to lease Bryant family mineral rights expired in 1923. Stearns then bought out the Bryant interests and began consolidating its landholdings on the east and west sides of the Big South Fork River. Acquisition of additional forested land sparked a massive resumption of logging operations that had been suspended in large measure in 1909.

A 1925 issue of the local newspaper (reprinted in the *McCreary County Record*, Oct. 16, 1975) announced this new development and plans for the logging extension to the K & T:

> *After having devoted all time and attention to the development of its coal production for the past ten years, the Stearns Coal and Lumber Company is again turning its attention to the timber end of the business, and the work of rehabilitating the mill at Stearns and beginning lumber operations on a large plane is well under way. It is estimated the cut will cover a period of twenty years, which should insure a permanence of work here for this generation, and lay a foundation for those reaching manhood.*
>
> *Of course the first work to be done is arrange for a means of bringing the logs to the Stearns Mill, and to this end the Kentucky and Tennessee Railway is constructing five miles of railway this fall and winter, extending same from Bell Farm, the present terminus of the road. The work is under the supervision of E. J. Telleschow, with Cal Schirmer to assist from a surveyor's viewpoint. The track will be of the standard-gauge variety and will accommodate regular engines and cars now in the service of the railway. It is the intention to push the railway further into the timber, but this first five miles will no doubt take care of present requirements.*

Remodeling of the Stearns Mill facilities included construction of two derricks used to unload log cars and a trestle built out over the holding pond to facilitate dumping logs there. At Bell Farm, nineteen miles from Stearns, the K & T proper ended. The first five-mile extension and all subsequent ones belonged to the Stearns Coal and Lumber Company rather than to the K & T Railroad. This arrangement left the K & T common carrier line short enough to be exempt from ICC regulation.

The company's estimate of a twenty-year cut in its western landholdings was fairly accurate. The logging railroad begun in 1925 was pulled out in 1949–50. As the Stearns mines closed, the K & T itself was pulled back to Cooperative, ten miles from Stearns. The last section to carry trains would become the Big South Fork Scenic Railway line to Blue Heron.

In its heyday, this railroad was the chain that held the vast Stearns operation together. Logs and coal were shipped to Stearns, supplies were shipped westward to the company stores, workers were transported to and from their work, mail traveled back and forth, and the company doctors used hand cars or small motors to make their calls. Employees and their families paid a low excursion fare to travel to Stearns for baseball games and holiday celebrations, and there were also excursions westward to Store 14 for employee picnics.

A Stearns Coal and Lumber Company (1938) public relations booklet described landmarks along the K & T route in glowing terms:

> The Kentucky and Tennessee Railroad, owned and built by the company through these timbered mountains and deep canyons, over turbulent streams and placid rivers, welds the vast area into one, from the logging camps at the far boundaries in the deep forests forty miles away, along beautiful Rock Creek to Exodus, which nestles in a wider valley. Truck gardens and mountain flowers intersperse the miners' homes as we roll through Fidelity and branch around to the mining village of Co-operative.
>
> At White Oak Junction oil derricks rise against the background of green. Then on to the village of Oz and to where Rock Creek joins the Big South Fork of the Cumberland. The ribbons of steel cross the river there on a bridge built in 1907. It was then the largest reinforced concrete railroad bridge ever built in the South. Surface-scarred by time and flood, its towering arches stand firm-rooted on the bed rock of the Cumberland and its hundred-foot spans link bank to bank in impressive artistry. A little farther on, homes dot the valley on both sides of the river at Worley. A giant tipple spans the rails there and busy electric mine locomotives shuttle cars back and forth across a big bridge over the river from the nearby mines. Three miles away on a spur track is the new great coal field at Blue Heron. On up the steep grade of the gorge another tipple bridges the tracks at Barthell, and then the four hundred and fifty foot climb to the terminus at Stearns to connect with the main line of the Southern Railroad from Cincinnati to New Orleans.
>
> The first locomotive for the Kentucky and Tennessee was heavier and more powerful than any of the big iron horses then used on the entire central division of the Southern system, and when they moved it in, they had to take off some of

its heavy parts and load them on flat-cars to distribute the weight for the mainline bridges in order to make delivery to the railroad at Stearns. Upwards of a thousand passengers a day move back and forth on the Kentucky and Tennessee Railroad between these busy and picturesque centers of work and life.

The Stearns Logging Railroad

Operation of the K & T Railroad was quite similar to that of the O & W, which is described in detail in the following section of this chapter; however, the logging railroad had more in common with logging railroads in other parts of the country. Construction on this extension of the K & T began in 1925, and at its longest, the line reached a distance of twenty-one miles from Bell Farm to Redmon Mountain above the Wolf River in Pickett County, Tennessee. Spurs were laid and taken up as needed to facilitate the logging of boundaries lying some distance from the main line of the logging railroad.

Unlike the K & T employees, the logging railroad engineer did not come from the Southern but from earlier experience on tortuous, steep logging railroads near Old Fort in Western North Carolina. His fireman, who later became a second engineer, also came from Western North Carolina. The second engine was not used for trips between Stearns and the logging area, but rather to set loaded cars out on sidings for pickup. Therefore, the principal engineer worked unbelievably long days and sometimes "worked out three crews of trainmen a week."

The K & T had an engine house near Bridge No. 2 (across Rock Creek). Orders were issued from that engine house, and the K & T usually picked up loaded cars from the logging railroad at that point. Once a month the logging engine continued on into Stearns so that it could undergo regular inspection and maintenance in the K & T shop. Because the engineer was responsible for engine maintenance between these monthly visits to the shop, he spent a period working in the shop during his early days with the company while the track was still under construction. This story indicates how carefully the master mechanic supervised work in his shop and trained apprentices.

> They had a pit there and this old man Larmee—he was the shop foreman—give me a fellow by the name of Rabbit to help me. An' I had to lower a driver—they had a place that you'd lower anything down, you know, and then there was a track down there, you'd run it out there where they could get to it with a crane, and you'd do the work on it.
>
> Well, I'd fixed my side and when I got around on the other side, Rabbit said, "Mr. Larmee's done fixed this, but I'll look at it." I said, "Mr. Larmee ain't the fellow's goin' to be in under thar." I said, "I don't care if he did fix it; I'm fixin' it different." So I throwed all o' that out and I fixed it the way I wanted it, you

know, an' this fella . . . he told me then at dinner time, he said, "I'm awful proud you done what you done this morning."

Course I didn't know what he was talkin' about, you know. I said, "What was that?" He said, "Throwin' all that stuff out." He said, "That ol' man was jus' tryin' you out. Now he never will be afraid of you from now on." And he [Larmee] was always awful sweet to me.

Among the repairs that the logging railroad engineer had to be able to make out on the road were the boilermaker's "hot" repairs. Spare parts to replace ones that broke frequently were always carried along on the train. The shop made special heavy-duty valve stems for the logging engine.

The old rod engine first used on the logging railroad proved unequal to the task, so the company bought a new Heisler engine. Unlike the Shay engines used in the Tennessee Stave logging operation, the Heisler had a gear mechanism that extended at right angles to the wheels with a tighter turning radius for negotiating extremely tight curves. The Heisler engine was also the super heater type in which the steam was dried to increase its energy output. Even with the extra power of the Heisler engine, it was necessary to "open up wide and rock the cars good" going over the state line. New trainmen and supervisors along for the ride had an unforgettable experience.

Some of the Stearns loggers described the logging railroad track as "pretty rough," but the steel was sixty-five to eighty pounds per yard, comparable to that used on the O & W, and the mine slate used for ballast made an excellent roadbed. Slate was gradually dumped under the pole trestles so that after a time they were filled in solid. In addition to his other duties, the engineer had to boss the logging railroad section crew. Section crew work is described below in connection with the Oneida and Western.

Aside from the loggers who rode to and from their workplaces and occasional picnickers on excursions to Store 14, there were no official passengers on the logging railroad; however, people did ride at their own risk. One such passenger was Jerome Boyatt, who used the train to transport bootleg whiskey. He attempted to avoid arrest by barricading himself inside a boxcar at Redmon Mountain. When the sheriff rushed the boxcar, Boyatt shot him dead. Subsequent events transformed Jerome Boyatt into one of the Big South Fork's best-known outlaw heroes (Howell 1983a).

Minor derailments occurred fairly frequently; the most serious involved nine log cars. The only accident that endangered the lives of the crew happened when a switch had been thrown by accident and the speeding train was shunted onto a siding that ended at a massive boulder. People did use the track as a path for walking or riding mules, but only one pedestrian was killed. He was drunk, and the train met him head-on inside a tunnel. Of course, free-ranging livestock were another matter. When asked about them, the engineer replied, "Honey, I wouldn't have no idea how many hogs I've killed in my time." The railroads certainly were an important factor in creating public sentiment for ending the traditional practice of allowing stock to range free.

Oneida and Western Railroad

The Oneida and Western Railroad was planned as an adjunct to the Tennessee Stave and Lumber Company's logging activities in the Big South Fork sections of Scott and Fentress Counties. The charter, issued August 5, 1913, authorized construction from Oneida, Tennessee, to Albany, Kentucky; however, actual construction by 1921 extended from Oneida to East Jamestown, Tennessee, a distance of thirty miles. A seven-mile section from East Jamestown to Jamestown was completed in 1930.

The O & W was owned and operated by the Andersons and Hagemeyers of Cincinnati, Oneida, and Harriman, Tennessee. O. H. Anderson was president and general manager; J. T. Anderson and Hall Hagemeyer were vice presidents; Bartlett Hagemeyer was secretary; and W. C. Anderson was treasurer. There were other shareholders related to the Hagemeyers or involved in the lumber business. These included William Bradley Ray, D. M. Speck, and Wales Christian from Monterey, Tennessee.

The headquarters of the O & W were in Oneida. The two-story red brick building across U.S. Highway 27 from the First National Bank was built for this purpose. Offices were on the main floor and Oneida living quarters for the Hagemeyers and the Andersons were upstairs. The depot stood on the First National Bank site. The general agent who ran the depot combined the work of freight agent, ticket agent, and dispatcher—jobs that would be assigned to three different people in a larger railroad company. The agent was also called to the scene of accidents, and sometimes he would be out all night on emergencies. Although the Oneida depot had been torn down, the Jamestown depot, located on the south side of Tennessee Route 52 west, was still standing in 1979.

The O & W was a thriving enterprise in its early years. Coal exploration along the railroad right-of-way was stimulated by the availability of transportation. During the 1920s the Tennessee Stave and Lumber Company became the Tennessee Lumber and Coal Company, reflecting the owners' diversifying interests. However, by 1930 when the company petitioned the Interstate Commerce Commission for permission to build the Jamestown extension, the best timber resources of the area already accessible to the railroad had been cut over. Depressed economic conditions and labor unrest at the Zenith coal mines during the 1930s further reduced the railroad's freight business and eventually forced the company into receivership under M. H. Davidson, a Cincinnati banker.

In the early 1940s the railroad's fortunes seemed to be improving when construction of a TVA dam on Wolf Creek was announced. Crown-Healy, a Chicago construction firm, bought the railroad with a view toward transporting construction materials to the dam construction site. However, the Wolf Creek project was suspended during World War II, and Crown-Healy lost out when new bids were taken in 1946. Abandonment of the O & W was first proposed at that time, but the Jewell Ridge Coal Company bought it intending to further develop the coal resources along the road. Dwindling business and mounting operation losses forced another application for abandonment in 1953 before the Jewell Ridge Company's plans could be implemented. Ironically, the last big freight hauling the O & W undertook was transport of cement to the Wolf Creek dam construction site in 1949. From a 1922 schedule of three daily round-trip runs that handled both passengers and freight, the 1953 schedule had dwindled to two or three trains per week.

Local citizens from all walks of life opposed abandonment of the O & W, and employees tried to fight the loss of their jobs in the courts. Construction of paved highways and bridges beginning in the 1930s let trucks compete for the railroad's freight business just when poor business conditions had reduced the volume of freight overall, but railroad workers tend to blame poor management under receivership rather than external business conditions for the railroad's demise.

The O & W had become an important part of life in Fentress and Scott Counties. It created jobs not only for railroad workers, but also in the logging outfits, sawmills, and mines along the right-of-way. The general freight, mail, and passenger services were appreciated by all of the citizens, because travel on the existing roads was still a time-consuming ordeal. The railroad link between the towns of Oneida and Jamestown was more direct than any automobile or truck route even after the roads were improved. And, finally, excursions on the railroad for picnics or fishing provided a particularly enjoyable form of recreation.

TRACK CONSTRUCTION AND MAINTENANCE

The O & W track was laid in several sections. The line was completed almost to the Big South Fork by June 1915, to Gernt in the summer of 1916, and to Christian by the end of 1916. This brought the railroad into the heart of "The Big Wilderness" timber. Further progress in railroad construction was slower. The track reached Stockton in 1918 and was extended an additional five miles to East Jamestown in 1921. The Doss Spur and incline built from Stockton opened up the extensive timber of the Wolf River Valley, and logging boomed there between 1918 and 1924. By the time the final leg of the O & W, the East Jamestown to Jamestown section, was built in 1930, the incline and spur had been pulled out and the economic picture looked decidedly less promising for the future.

Sulzer (1975, 189–99) reported that Tennessee Stave and Lumber Company used one of its affiliates, Eagle Construction Company, for the first two years of railroad construction. Local residents remembered that African American construction crews were brought in to lay the track. At that time, the memory of racial incidents that had occurred in Glenmary shortly after the turn of the century was still fresh. The workers were housed in camps along the track, and rolling stores supplied their needs. They were issued scrip rather than money to further ensure that they stayed in the camps. Local tradition includes accounts of several of these African Americans meeting with violent deaths at the hands of crew bosses or one another and being buried in unmarked graves along the railroad tracks.

Some local residents who helped lay track beyond Christian described some of the equipment and construction methods used in the late 1910s and early 1920s. A steam shovel operated by an engineer and a fireman was used to grade the right-of-way. Horse and mule teams hauled in ballast. Handcars hauled rail sections and tools over the completed rails to the construction site. A rail dog, similar to the logging dogs still in use, lifted the rails from the cars and dropped them over the cross ties. At first local farmers furnished hand-hewn cross ties; later sawmills supplied them.

The construction crews bolted together rail sections, whereas track joints now are welded. After setting the rail elevation (i.e., banking curves properly and setting the gauge) they spiked the rail to the cross ties. Boys not yet old and strong enough for this work carried water to the crews, and thus they followed their fathers and older brothers into railroad work. Many then stayed with the railroad in preference to any other kind of wage work.

Bridges were a special challenge in constructing a railroad across the Big South Fork and along Pine Creek and North White Oak Creek. A man who helped build some of the White Oak bridges reported that boxes were constructed from lumber and pumps used to drain these boxes while bridge foundations were being built. Apparently, a false bridge of timbers was built across the Big South Fork to serve as a scaffold for the workmen who were fitting and riveting the sections of the steel bridge.

Many of the men who helped build the railroad continued to do similar work on the track maintenance crews called section crews. Additional crews were deployed as the track mileage increased until there were four crews to cover the full thirty-seven-mile distance between Oneida and Jamestown. When the railroad began to pile up big operating losses, the fourth section was dissolved and boundaries between the other sections changed to absorb the additional miles.

Section 1 ran from Oneida to the Big South Fork Bridge, and after the number of sections was reduced extended all the way to Gernt. Section 2 originally ran from the Big South Fork Bridge to the Hagemeyer Mine and later handled the track from Gernt to Stockton. Section 3 first extended from Hagemeyer to East Jamestown; after the East Jamestown to Jamestown section (Section 4) was disbanded, Section 3's responsibility extended from Stockton to Jamestown.

A few families were attracted to the O & W from Harriman in Roane County, Tennessee, where they were already involved in railroad work, but many of the railroad workers were natives of Scott or Fentress Counties. In normal times, a section crew numbered five to seven men, but additional part-time workers were hired to handle emergencies such as washouts or derailments. An emergency crew might number twenty-five or more. Local farmers, loggers, and sawmill hands worked on the railroad off and on, filling these part-time jobs.

There were section camps at Gernt and East Jamestown, but many of the men preferred to live "out on top" and walk back and forth to the tracks. The section foreman might use his motor to pick up the workers. A number of section crew members who lived along the Leatherwood Road in Scott County met their crew foreman early each morning at the Big South Fork Bridge. In an emergency, the crew foreman had to walk from house to house rounding up workers, because no one had a home telephone at that time. Foremen had to live in the camps close by the track-side telephone shacks that provided communication with the agent in Oneida. Before leaving the camp in the evenings or on Sundays they had to call in their plans to the agent so that they could be reached quickly in case of an emergency.

During the 1910s and 1920s, the normal workday was ten hours. This left railroad men little time to spend with their families. The workday was reduced to nine hours sometime before World War II and to eight hours after the war. Back in 1921, water boys made fifteen cents an hour and section hands made twenty-five cents an hour.

The section crews had to keep a solid footing of ballast firmly tamped under the track, replace bad cross ties, maintain the proper gauge between the two rails, and maintain the proper banking on curves. Their task was made more difficult by the quality of materials used. The rail was generally 65 or 75 pounds per yard; 85-pound steel was used only in places subject to particular stress. In contrast, the usual track weight today is 140 to 150 pounds. The maximum life of cross ties was about seven years, because they were not treated with creosote to prevent rotting. Cinders and local rock served as ballast. The section men dynamited rock near the track and crushed it with knapping hammers. This sandstone rock soon crumbled into sand, allowing the track to shift.

A small gasoline engine powered the motor that was used to transport the crew, its tools, and supplies. It replaced the hand-pumped lever car that section crews originally had used. The tools included rail jacks, tamping picks, track gauge, level board (which operated like a spirit level), spike maul, a crowbar for lifting spikes, a cleaver to chisel out short rail sections, and a two-man hacksaw. The section crew also cut weeds and brush along the track with brush hooks.

When the railroad was abandoned, the steel was pulled up and sold for scrap. It was the section crew workers who broke out the bolts and lifted the spikes. The rail sections were loaded onto flatcars with a derrick and hauled to Oneida.

TRAINMEN AND ROLLING STOCK

O & W trainmen passed through the typical series of promotions, starting as brakemen, becoming either conductors or firemen, and moving from fireman to engineer. Promotion came much sooner than it might have on a major railroad like the Southern. For example, one O & W engineer started working as a water boy at the age of fourteen, then spent some time in the machine shop before going out on the road. He was working as an extra engineer by the time he was eighteen. Trainmen learned their jobs by accompanying a regular worker and observing, then assisting. They began working alone in the new job as "extras" for special runs and were then in line for promotion when a full-time vacancy occurred.

The schedule was set up so that the train crew could make a round trip during the day; therefore, the trainmen and their families lived in or near Oneida. Like section crew workers, the trainmen had a regular ten-hour day, but they might be called upon at any time to make special runs. This meant that their family time was often disrupted by work. At least, as one trainman's wife recalled, the families who lived near the tracks at Smith Switch could wave as the train went by.

At various times the company owned twelve different steam locomotives, as many as four at one time. They bore the numbers 18 through 29. Number 20 was a Baldwin locomotive designed especially for the sharp curves on the O & W, but all of the other engines came secondhand from other railroads. The locomotives steadily increased in size; numbers 18 through 22 were 600-class, and numbers 28 and 29 were 104 ton engines. The most powerful locomotives could haul six coal cars up the steep grade between the Big South Fork and Buck Ford known as "The Big Cut." Sometimes it was necessary to double up and use two smaller locomotives on this grade. The large engines were modified to negotiate tight turns by having the flange removed from the number two wheels.

Before his death, Willie Douglas, who had been a brakeman and conductor for the O & W, tracked down two of the old locomotives. Number 20 was being used somewhere in Vermont, and Number 29 was sitting on the campus of Walter College in Jasper, Alabama. Mr. Douglas himself owned one of the three cabooses (described in a feature article, Oneida *Independent Herald*, April 12, 1978).

Railroad officials used automobiles outfitted with railroad wheels to make inspection tours of the line. An A-model Ford so equipped figures in the most frequently recounted O & W anecdote. High water washed out a trestle and left the track sagging. The officials were afraid to ride across and tried to let the car over the trestle in low gear without a driver. The car shot into high gear, zipped across the trestle past the man who was supposed to catch it, and continued driverless into Oneida, where it crashed into a boxcar. Old-timers relished telling this story on the "big shots." Fortunately, no one was walking the track at that time, or the story might not seem so funny today.

Another unusual piece of rolling stock was the "mail bus." When passenger service was discontinued in the 1920s, the passenger coach was sold. A Chevrolet truck equipped with railroad wheels replaced it. This vehicle carried the mail and the small number of passengers who still used the railroad. Later the Chevrolet truck was replaced by the M-4, a gasoline-powered car similar to a streetcar in appearance. A motorman and a conductor operated both of these vehicles.

The old Chevy might have sufficed for the duration of the O & W's operation, but it was disabled in an accident. It collided with a locomotive near the mouth of Mill Creek, reportedly because the engineer's watch was wrong and he inadvertently overran his orders. The motorman was thrown onto the locomotive cowcatcher but lived to tell the story.

ACCIDENTS AND BREAKDOWNS

Retired railroad men reported few serious accidents other than the ones involving the A-model and the mail bus. There seems to have been only one fatality. One of the outside union organizers implicated in the killing of Cap Woods near Zenith returned to the mine camp after he was released from jail. He was walking along the railroad tracks drunk and stepped in front of an oncoming locomotive. The engineer was powerless to avert disaster in this kind of situation.

If there were almost no human fatalities, the same cannot be said of livestock. Negotiating the curves and grades took on added excitement for engineers while livestock were still free to range at will. They often got onto the tracks and sometimes even wandered onto the Big South Fork Bridge, where they became entrapped when they stepped down between cross ties. The O & W had to compensate many an irate housewife for the loss of a cherished milk cow.

The worst derailment on the O & W occurred on the Big South Fork Bridge when several cars came uncoupled from the locomotive and their emergency brakes failed to take hold. The cars and caboose went into the river, but the brakeman and conductor were able to jump to safety. The engineer on that run remembers dreaming about this accident and waking up jumping out of bed.

When there were breakdowns, the O & W was well equipped to get its trains running again. The machine shop in Oneida was shared with the Tennessee Railroad. When it was established, a Tennessee Railroad shop supervisor, E. W. Morris, was transferred from Rockwood to head the operation. Many of the employees came from Rockwood with Mr. Morris. The jobs in Oneida opened up just as an ironworks in Rockwood closed. These men had gained their railroad shop experience working in that mill's train yard.

The most skilled machine shop worker was the boilermaker. His job involved regular maintenance of the steam locomotives in the shop as well as emergency service. So that a disabled locomotive could be returned to service as quickly as possible, the boilermaker often made "hot" repairs. He went inside leaky boilers to replace rivets and bolts before the boiler was completely cool. In addition to his shop work, the O & W boilermaker was called on to inspect the secondhand locomotives the company was considering purchasing. This duty allowed him to make some memorable trips, including one to Canada.

STOPS AND FACILITIES

By piecing together information from Sulzer (1975), retired railroad men, and individuals who worked in the mines or sawmills along the railroad, it is possible to present fairly full descriptions of the stops along the O & W and the facilities at each of these locations.

Verdun. Verdun was two miles west of the Oneida depot. This was the site of the Tennessee Stave and Lumber Company's band mill. Logs collected at various points along the railroad were shipped to Verdun to be turned into lumber. Sometime around the end of the 1920s or in the early 1930s the Verdun mill was converted into a planing mill and rough lumber was brought to Verdun from numerous small sawmills for finishing..

Reed Station or Smith Switch. Three miles west of Oneida there was a spur line that passed the site of New Haven Church and ended at Cooper Pond, where Grover Pemberton operated a sawmill. This switch was named Smith Switch. It was also the terminus of an oil pipeline from the Grave Hill section. Oil from this line was loaded in tankers for rail shipment.

The alternative name of Reed Station came from the fact that a New York financier named Reed planned a rail line from this point along the Big South Fork to open up coal resources along the river. The spur would have followed the general route of Leatherwood Road to the river and then followed the eastern stream bank. Mr. Reed's plan was never implemented because he failed to secure financial backing.

Toomey. This stop, located six miles west of Oneida, was named for the prominent Scott County family. A telephone shack was located at this stop, where lumber from the Jim L. Thompson sawmill was loaded onto the train. The Thompson family had a large farm with a comfortable home as well as a few houses to accommodate hired hands.

Speck. Named for lumberman and O & W stockholder D. M. Speck, this stop was thirteen miles west of Oneida. There was an incline at Speck that may have loaded lumber from the M. I. Thompson Lumber Company. One older informant remembers that Stearns Coal and Lumber Company used the Speck incline to load lumber onto the O & W for shipment to Oneida, and presumably from Oneida to Stearns via the Southern Railroad. An employee of the Stearns logging railroad expressed doubt that the company would have dealt with its competitor Tennessee Stave or with that company's railroad, but this arrangement may well have been in force during the 1909–25 period of contract logging before Stearns developed its logging railroad.

Potter. Interviewees presume that Potter was named for another of the O & W shareholders, although they cannot identify him. Potter was located fourteen miles west of Oneida and was the site of a coal mine and two side tracks, one for loading coal and the other for lumber. An incline brought lumber to the railroad from a sawmill "on top." No one lived in Potter; the miners who worked there lived "out on top" and walked back and forth to work.

Gernt. Gernt, located sixteen miles west of Oneida, was one of the busiest stops on the line. The Gernt section camp included four houses and storage buildings for the railroad section crew. Some miners who worked at Zenith also lived in private houses at Gernt. A trestle built across Groom Branch near its confluence with North White Oak Creek led to the wye where engines were turned around. A swinging bridge allowed school children to cross White Oak on their way to and from the Mt. Helen School. There was no store in this camp; residents first used the store and post office at East Laurel and later patronized the Tays store at Zenith.

Gernt was a very active lumber loading stop. It was a depot for the Gernt Lumber Company, based in Allardt, and it was the site of two inclines that transported lumber from mills located above the north bank of the creek to the railroad below. One incline belonged to Ide and Herb Thompson. The other belonged to J. P. Pearson's Cumberland Valley Lumber Company.

East Laurel. Located sixteen and a half miles from Oneida, East Laurel was a busy camp in the 1920s while the Ligon Mine was still open. It was the site of a commissary, post office, boardinghouse, and several private homes. Some of the section hands based at Gernt lived at East Laurel. The boardinghouse accommodated a number of the miners, drummers doing business with the various stores along the railroad, and sometimes O & W officials out on inspection tours. After the mines closed, the post office remained open because it served Gernt and Zenith, but everyone except the postmaster and his family moved away.

Zenith. Zenith, located seventeen miles west of Oneida, was a mining camp for the Webb Hammock mines that operated during the 1920s and 1930s and the Marlow mine that opened and closed during the 1940s. Top-quality cannel coal was loaded onto the O & W at Zenith, first from a tipple spanning the main railroad track and later from a larger tipple built over a siding across North White Oak Creek.

Railroad facilities at Zenith included a telephone shack and a water tank. In 1979 the concrete foundations of this gravity-flow water tank were still standing just west of Zenith.

Christian. This stop was named for Wales Christian, one of the O & W shareholders. It was a lumber loading point located nineteen miles west of Oneida.

Briar Point. According to a 1922 schedule reproduced by Sulzer (1975, 189), Briar Point was twenty miles west of Oneida, but old-timers associate that name with the horseshoe bend in North White Oak Creek between Zenith and Christian. Some lumber may have been loaded at Briar Point. Not all of the lumber shipped on the O & W came from large companies; some was transported by wagon from small sawmills to the railroad.

Hagemeyer. This stop was named for the Hagemeyers who were O & W officers and held a substantial interest in the company. The mine located at Hagemeyer, referred to as the Hagemeyer Mine, seems to have been owned or at least operated by a Mr. Laxton. He batched there, but most of the miners commuted to work from the Armathwaite–Mt. Helen area, and none of them lived at Hagemeyer. A railroad section tool house was located at this stop, which was twenty-one miles west of Oneida.

Mill Creek (Old East Jamestown). The 1922 timetable placed East Jamestown at the twenty-three-mile mark, east of Stockton. Long-time railroad employees remembered that the depot and lumberyard at the mouth of Mill Creek were once called East Jamestown. Freight shipped from Oneida to this depot was distributed by wagon to various points in Fentress and Pickett Counties, and some went all the way to Albany, Kentucky. Westbound freight transferred to the O & W from the Southern included feed, general supplies, groceries, and shipments of various goods that traveling agents sold to general stores and commissaries in the area.

Stockton. After the railroad was extended, Stockton replaced Old East Jamestown as the principal terminus for local freight. It also was the end of the passenger line, twenty-six miles west of Oneida. This terminal took its name from the Stockton family who held extensive forested land in the area. A great deal of lumber delivered by wagon was loaded onto the railroad at Stockton, and this was also the loading point for lumber delivered via the Whitson pole road. The Doss Spur carrying Tennessee Stave logs from the Wolf River Valley joined the main O & W line near Stockton.

Westbound trains out of Oneida brought mail to the Stockton post office and, in later years, automobiles bound for Fentress County. In addition to the general freight that had earlier been shipped to Old East Jamestown, the Stockton freight depot handled supplies for the Michigan Lumber Company and the H. C. Whitson Company.

Doss Spur and the Wolf River Incline. The Tennessee Stave and Lumber Company logging camp, located in the Wolf River Valley near Pall Mall, was called Head-of-Wolf. It was served by a logging railroad with cog engines, but an incline was necessary to lift the logs from the valley to the plateau above, an abrupt climb of 2,800 feet. The Doss Spur, probably named for the Doss family who lived in the area, extended about six miles from the top of the incline, an area known as the Basin, to a point about four miles west of Stockton where it met the main O & W line.

While roads were being built in western Fentress County, the Wolf River incline was used to deliver asphalt from Oneida to the construction area. The asphalt had to be heated with steam from the incline engine so that it would flow from the standard tankers into the smaller cars used on the incline. After logging operations in the Wolf River area ceased, the logging track, incline, and spur track were scrapped. The spur had been pulled before the final section of the O & W proper was completed in 1930.

East Jamestown or Louvain
East Jamestown, thirty miles from Oneida, was the end of the line until 1930, when track was laid into Jamestown. A section camp with a boardinghouse and store was located there. John Tays ran these establishments after the camp at Head-of-Wolf closed and before he moved on to open a store at Zenith. There was also a freight depot at East Jamestown and a section of double track where trains could meet and pass one another.

Former railroad employees who refer to East Jamestown as Louvain are not sure where the name came from. Some believe it is a woman's name, possibly the name of a railroad official's wife. More likely, Louvain was chosen as a companion name for Verdun, the existing band mill that had already been given a French place-name. A second Tennessee Stave band mill was built at this site but never operated.

Hugarth

This unusual place-name must have been coined to honor Hugo and Arthur Gernt. Coal and lumber were loaded at this stop, thirty-five miles west of Oneida. Barite, barium sulfide, a mineral used in the manufacture of luminous paints, was mined on the Wolf River and trucked to Hugarth, where it was loaded onto the O & W for shipment to Oneida.

Jamestown

The final terminus of the O & W was a freight and mail depot in Jamestown, thirty-seven miles west of Oneida. In 1979 it was still standing, although in poor condition. In addition to receiving freight from Oneida, the Jamestown depot handled cross ties that were shipped east for the O & W's use and for delivery to other railroads.

6

Community and Society

In the oldest subsistence farming settlements of the Big South Fork area, kinship was the basis of community. Transition from the subsistence farming economy to one based on the extraction of timber and coal resources brought profound social changes as well as the technological and economic changes already described. This chapter discusses the traditional system of social relations within the community and comments on the persistence or disappearance of the elements that formed it.

Communities

Before commercial logging and coal mining transformed life along the Big South Fork, the area's mostly self-provisioning farmers occupied individual homesteads that were loosely clustered into settlements by the churches, general stores, and one-room schools that served each settlement. Homesteads along a single stream bottom could communicate with one another more easily than those separated by rugged ridges; in consequence, community boundaries were defined largely by the drainage system. The more easily traversed but less fertile tablelands were not favored sites for settlement early in the nineteenth century.

Pre-1900 settlements in McCreary County were near the east bank of the Big South Fork along Bear Creek and its tributaries and across the river in the Beech Grove–Bald Knob section along Laurel Crossing Branch, Newt Branch, and Trace Branch. The nearest town to these settlements was Pine Knot. Travelers from the west side of the river forded near the mouth of Bear Creek.

Still farther west in McCreary County, Rock Creek was the locus for farmsteads that communicated with the outside world via the Monticello–Huntsville Pike. The Laurel Ridge (sometimes called Laurel Hill) community was located near this old wagon road. Although virtually inaccessible now except by foot, Laurel Hill once attracted regular visitors from Bell Farm and from the No Business and Station Camp communities in Tennessee. They came to visit relatives and to attend church singings and revivals.

The Scott County, Tennessee, settlements centered along the Big South Fork near the mouths of Williams Creek, Station Camp Creek, and No Business Creek. The Monticello–Huntsville Pike passed this way and crossed the river at the Big Island ford. As late as the 1930s, the Station Camp community was thriving and had its own post office, named Elva, Tennessee. Black Oak, White Pine, and Alticrest, located along the Leatherwood Road near the Scott–Fentress boundary, represent a somewhat later chapter in settlement history. Many of the families who occupied these settlements in the 1970s had lived in the more remote river settlements a generation or two before. The automobile and the lifestyle changes it brought caused them to move closer to this relatively more accessible area.

In Fentress County, settlements established within the recreation area boundaries before development of the Oneida and Western Railroad were located along Joe's Branch of the Clear Fork, along Mill Creek near its confluence with North White Oak Creek, and along Big Creek and Crooked Creek to the south. All of these early settlements were based primarily on subsistence farming, although the men sometimes supplemented their incomes through "public works" (their term for any kind of wage employment) once that option became available. Workers commonly walked distances of ten or more miles each day on the round trip to and from jobs. The big timber and mining companies ultimately affected settlement patterning as well as economic opportunities and conditions in the area, however. Many families left the farm to move closer to jobs in logging, sawmills, mines, or on the railroads. These families, along with newcomers attracted to the Big South Fork area by plentiful work, settled in the company towns that grew up along the Kentucky and Tennessee and the Oneida and Western railroads.

The company towns had their churches, schools, and stores, but the bonds of common work and neighboring did not tie people to these new communities as closely as land ownership and kinship continued to tie them to the communities of their birth. Workers typically moved from camp to camp, these moves interspersed with returns to the home place, and they continued to participate in social activities at home. It is significant that large and active camp churches like those at Blue Heron and at Cooperative did not have attached cemeteries. One's proper final resting place was among kin in the family or home church graveyard.

The Big South Fork area differs substantially from the coal fields of Eastern Kentucky because one industry did not come to monopolize all of the land, supplant all farming, and absorb all of the population into its labor force. A range of occupational and lifestyle alternatives continued to be available to the people of the Big South Fork, and this was an important key to their relative success in preserving their traditional culture and surviving hard times with aplomb. Nevertheless, a close reading of Harry Caudill's observations on East Kentucky coal mining (1963) will help to point up significant differences between the traditional community and the camp and explain why the camp did not become a community in the traditional sense.

KINSHIP AND THE COMMUNITY

Initially a handful of families formed the core of each settlement and they usually produced many children. Given that some of today's octogenarians report making their first trips to town when they were past twenty, it is not difficult to understand why young people living in the stream bottom communities tended to find marriage partners among their close neighbors. It was not uncommon for sets of brothers to marry sets of sisters, creating "double-first-cousin" bonds among the offspring. Siblings and cousins remained in their home territory because they inherited a portion of the family founder's initial landholding. As relatives settled close to one another on land inherited from common ancestors, the community became an extended kinship unit. Kinship bonds were continually strengthened by the fact that almost all potential marriage partners in the vicinity were linked by some degree of blood relationship.

After a lengthy study of Tennessee ridge communities composed of a few intermarrying families, Elmora Matthews (1965) identified several benefits of marrying kin: it is a means of consolidating land ownership and conserving wealth within families; it strengthens cohesion within the community by continually reinforcing its kinship bonds; and it provides mates who share common experiences and aspirations, who are "expected" and therefore approved by the community at large.

Where kindred and neighborhood were largely coterminous, a formal organization to provide for governance and community services seemed unnecessary. Neighboring that carried the moral force of kinship obligation ensured mutual aid through informal cooperation. Such kin-based patterns of social interaction have persisted to a great extent in communities near the Big South Fork, although their residents agree that communitywide labor exchange began to decline many years ago in favor of waged labor.

The household survey of recreation area residents (see appendix 1) revealed that social interaction was more frequent with close kin than with neighbors related only distantly or not at all. With the exception of churches, organization memberships were almost nonexistent, and some church members did not attend regularly. Family activities tended to be nonspecific and unplanned with the exception of large family reunions that involved out-of-town relatives. Casual interaction with kin and exclusion of nonkin relationships were reinforced by the continuing practice of living near kin. Typically, adult siblings with families lived near one another and near surviving parents. Large collections of framed family photographs and snapshot albums proudly displayed in the living room of every home showed the continuing importance of kinship, even in the face of separations caused by labor out-migration.

COMMUNITY-CENTERED SOCIAL ACTIVITIES AND RECREATION

For as long as family farms remained the predominant means of livelihood along the Big South Fork, recreation was tied to work activities, especially labor exchange between kin and neighbors. "Workings" were organized for every task from clearing land, barn raising, and house building, to corn husking, bean shelling, and molasses making. Strenuous or technically complex work required more labor, more tools and implements, or more specialized expertise than a single household could muster. The lighter but monotonous food preparation tasks probably could have been accomplished without assistance of the community, but these workings were as much social as economic in function. They provided a socially approved setting in which young people could initiate a courtship. For all of the participants, the burden of monotonous work was relieved by conversation and rewarded by a big dinner spread by the hostess and other women whose families were present. In the more liberal households, the working often ended with square dancing.

Even the oldest interviewees had not personally participated in log rollings and barn raisings but had heard stories from parents or grandparents who described these events. Apparently the means of accomplishing heavy work had begun to change by the mid-nineteenth century. Informal mutual aid with unspecified obligations for future repayment was replaced by some more formal arrangement for hiring labor. Workers were paid in return services, goods, or cash. Corn huskings and bean shellings persisted as communitywide events until well after the turn of the twentieth century. "Candy-makings" also provided pretext for young people to meet.

School benefits provided additional opportunities for socializing and recreation. The following account describes the box or pie supper in detail and also points up the potential for troublemakers to spoil such amusements.

> Sometimes they'd have these pie suppers to raise money for something that they [the school] needed to buy. The girls, they'd bake pies and they'd take them in. They'd have 'em in boxes, and have their names wrote on the box. Well, there was one man that would get up and cry them pies off to the highest bidder. Sometimes maybe the girls—somebody'd get their box they didn't care about eating with, but still they had to go on and eat.

> One time, I know, they had a big box supper and there were some tough boys. They'd go in at anything; they wanted to be bullies, and they'd try to tear up things if they could.
> They selected [my husband] to cry the boxes off that night. Of course, we all went. They had music there that night, then they cried the boxes off, then after they cried the boxes off, they always put up two girls for the prettiest girl in the country, and two boys for the laziest man. The laziest man, he'd get a necktie or a pair of socks and the girls would get a box of jewelry or something like that. After the box supper was over, they put up our youngest girl and one of [a neighbor's] girls for prettiest girls in the country. Lord, [our girl] just ran way ahead. She got the box of jewelry that night. It made them tough boys mad because [the other girl] was their niece. They tried to take the box away from [my husband]. Said, "That ain't right." He said, "Yes, I guess it is; that's what the public says."
> Q: Was there any trouble?
> A: There would have been, but the law was there that night and showed 'em the door. But they shot around.
> Q: Was it pretty scary when they started shooting? Did everyone dive under the benches?
> A: No, everybody stood up. Oh, they wasn't shooting in the house. They was shooting in the ground or straight up one. They was bad people to try to run a bluff.

The transition from farming to wage work in the log woods or in the mines created changes in recreational needs and activities. Single men who lived in the camp boardinghouses were too tired for much recreation after work, but they might while away their weekends with drinking and gambling. They had to exercise some restraint, however, because the Stearns employee who did not show up ready for work Monday morning was laid off for the week. Repeated infractions were grounds for firing. The company did offer some recreational opportunities to its employees. Public dances were held each Saturday night at Bell Farm; and sports, especially baseball or softball and horseshoes, were popular in the Stearns camps. School consolidation and access to automobiles substantially enlarged young people's social networks and introduced a host of alternative social and recreational activities.

THE INDIVIDUAL IN THE COMMUNITY

In the past, an individual could count on community support during all life events—childbirth, marriage, illness, and death, as well as economic misfortune. Among the best accounts of this aspect of community life are Harriette Simpson Arnow's fiction works, *Hunter's Horn* (1949) and *The Dollmaker* (1954). All of

Hunter's Horn and the opening section of *The Dollmaker* are set during the 1930s and early 1940s in the Cowhorn section of the Big South Fork, not many miles north of the recreation area boundary. The ethnographic detail presented in these books rings true when compared with recollections of interviewees who experienced that period firsthand.

Birth. A woman in labor was attended not only by the local midwife but also by a group of female relatives. The husbands of these women often accompanied their wives and kept the father-to-be company while he waited. Arnow suggests that the men were not always kept out of the labor room, and at least one interviewee reported that his grandfather was a male midwife.

After the Stearns camps were established with company doctors in residence or on call, some women chose to have the services of a professional physician, even though their children continued to be born at home. Others preferred midwives, who by the 1970s were able to train and receive official state certification. One woman who had birthed sixteen healthy babies at home tried to interest her granddaughters in home birthing, but without success. Voicing a common attitude about hospitals, she said: "I had all my children at home. I reckon that's the reason I'm living, 'cause they'll kill you if they get you at the hospital. It shortens your days."

It would be simplistic to conclude that such attitudes toward the hospital merely reflected old-timers' conservatism or fear of modern medicine. Negative experiences with mainstream medicine were told and retold in stories that reinforced suspicion, but equally important was the belief that personal crisis, whatever its nature, should be faced at home with the support of the immediate family and the wider community of kin and neighbors.

Before adequate medical care was readily available, birth and the first few years of childhood were periods of great uncertainty. A rich body of folk belief helped to allay the anxiety surrounding birth and early childhood. Although prenatal care as we know it was nonexistent, mothers-to-be tried to avoid unusual experiences that they believed might mark their infants. After the child was born, it was carefully examined and its early behavior was observed and regulated in an attempt to determine or shape its future character. There were many magical cures for children's maladies and many good luck and bad luck omens relating to young children. Morton (1978) provides a well-rounded sample of such beliefs from East Tennessee. Older female interviewees were familiar with these beliefs but did not admit to following them personally during pregnancy and child rearing.

Marriage. Conn (1978) presents a detailed description of East Tennessee courtship and marriage customs. Wedding ceremonies were not elaborate social events. Most couples were married by justices of the peace, and elopements were common. Kentucky girls who were underage ran away with their prospective bridegrooms to Tennessee. Many female interviewees were married and mothers by the time they were fifteen or sixteen.

While family and friends often were not present at the simple wedding ceremonies conducted by justices of the peace, they did participate in the wedding through the infare dinner held afterward. Conn describes the East Tennessee infare celebration as a three-part event beginning at the bride's home, moving to the groom's home, and finally moving to the couple's new home (1978, 41), but Big South Fork residents spoke of a single dinner immediately after the wedding. The most lavish infare dinner ever held in the area almost certainly was the one honoring Sgt. Alvin C. York and his bride, Gracie. The meal was served outdoors near the rock outcropping where the Yorks were married. People attended from far and wide, and everyone contributed food and drink. A more typical infare dinner described by an interviewee took place at the groom's home. The couple returned there after going alone to a justice of the peace. The bride, who came from another community, was presented to the groom's family and friends at this dinner.

A less formal mode of community participation in the wedding was the shivaree. This was a late-night visit paid the newlyweds by the groom's bachelor friends and other practical jokers. They waited until the couple was in bed, then congregated outside the house using every noisemaker imaginable and making ribald jokes until they were invited in for refreshments. If they met with resistance and were especially sadistic, they might drag the groom out of the house and ride him on a rail. It was a game to avoid the shivaree just as today's newlyweds try to avoid having their car decorated.

A woman recalled her own wedding celebration, which took place around 1920, in these words:

> He borrowed a buggy—had a pair of mules—and he brought that buggy down there to my home and got me, and we come around through Moodyville to an old J.P. We wanted him to come out to the road and marry us in the road, and he wouldn't do it. Said he wanted us to come in. His wife was sick and she wanted us to come in and see us get married. Well, we got out and went in the house, and they had a hired girl there, and her and the hired girl was gonna hear it [be witnesses]. He turned in and married us; and about the time he got us married, we happened to notice he's up in one corner by the telephone and he had the telephone hook off, and everybody in the vicinity had heard. You could ring a little ring, and everybody in the country'd take the receiver down and eavesdrop. We's so outdone to think he'd played off on us that way.
>
> We got the buggy and went on to Wolf. They's waiting and had a big dinner cooked up, and some of the neighbors was in . . . They threatened to have a shivaree but never did. It was a common thing then, but we slipped off from up there and came back down to my Grandpa's and stayed the first night or two,

and nobody didn't know where we was at. It kindly died down and they never shivareed us. They hunted for us down the settlement that night, went to two or three places but they never did locate us.

Illness. Illness brought forth various expressions of community support. Whenever economically productive members of a family were disabled, neighbors took over their farm or household chores, brought in prepared food, helped with childcare, or did whatever else was needed to keep the family functioning. If the patient required intensive nursing, neighbors spelled the women of the immediate family at this task. Whether or not their help was needed to provide round-the-clock nursing, neighbors considered it a duty to visit the sick.

Local healers were the primary medical consultants. This was universally true before improved transportation and the Stearns company doctors made professional medical care reasonably accessible. Even after trained doctors were available, however, many families continued to prefer home remedies and the advice of local healers. The doctor was called only for the most serious problems or after less drastic forms of treatment had been exhausted without success.

Local medical practitioners included herbalists who treated a variety of ills, midwives, and home dentists who pulled teeth with pliers made by the local blacksmith or occasionally supplied by some overworked physician who hoped to avoid practicing dentistry. Although every family knew the most common herbal remedies and grew or collected materials needed for the common household remedies, each community had its specialist whose knowledge was more extensive. This person could be called upon to give advice or prepare special medicines when necessary. A number of the experts traced their special knowledge of herbal medicine back to Indian ancestors.

One Indian doctor, a man who called himself Dr. Medico, seems to have set up a commercial practice near the Wayne–McCreary County line around the turn of the century. He may even have traveled into Fentress County to practice on occasion, but he was exceptional. Most lay healers worked close to home and took no pay for their services. Rather, they could expect favors in return through the community system of mutual aid. In later years when commercial transactions began to supplant labor exchange, lay medical practitioners still did not accept payment because they knew they might be liable to criminal prosecution for practicing medicine without a license.

Recollections of early medical practices collected in interviews included a sketch of the country doctor's life as well as anecdotes from the patient's viewpoint. One may infer from these reminiscences that most doctors were conscientious but nevertheless limited in their training and in the equipment and pharmaceuticals available to them. In this context, reliance on local practitioners for primary care made practical sense. It also made sense socially as an expression of community values. Wherever possible, the community served its own needs through mutual aid. This principle strengthened community bonds while it minimized undesired interference from outsiders. Even in the 1970s when medical care had become relatively accessible, many old-timers continued to view hospitalization negatively because it separated the patient from home and family during personal crisis, when their support would be most important and most reassuring.

Death. Death, like illness, was handled by members of the community rather than by professionals. Close relatives or neighbors of the same sex as the deceased prepared the body. The eyes were closed and weighted down with coins; the body was washed and dressed as soon as possible so that rigor mortis would not make the task more difficult. The burial clothing might be the Sunday best of the deceased or a dress or suit made in advance and set aside to be used for the burial. If nothing appropriate was on hand, neighbors might donate clothing or sew it.

While the body was being prepared, a local coffin maker would begin the simple flat-topped wooden coffin. The box was made the proper length for the corpse; the sides were shaped so that the coffin was wider at the shoulders and tapered toward the feet. The lid was made separate rather than hinged. After the final viewing of the body, the lid was attached with nails or screws. In the graveyard, other men of the community gathered and took turns digging the grave. Because their work was an expression of regard for the deceased and the family, many more men participated than were actually needed to do the work.

There was no way to preserve the body, so burial usually took place the second or third day after a death. It was traditional for neighbors and relatives who had arrived for the burial to join the immediate family in sitting up with the corpse throughout the first night after the death. The visitors brought food and spent the time reminiscing and singing hymns. Many of the visitors left during the evening, but at least two or three stayed until dawn. Appalachian death lore includes many beliefs pointing to the need for the wake (e.g., see Long 1961; Montell 1966).

At the funeral, held in the church, the preacher eulogized the deceased; then everyone in attendance, closest relatives last, filed by the open coffin to view the remains. Very young children viewed the remains along with everyone else. Several of the people interviewed remember grandparents or great-grandparents only from this experience. Because of the difficulty and delay involved in informing relatives of a death and waiting for them to arrive at the home of the deceased, it was sometimes necessary to delay Appalachian funerals until long after the burial had occurred. Within the memory of interviewees, this was a common practice around the Big South Fork.

Whether or not the formal funeral service was held before burial, there was a simple graveside rite at the burial. Many cemeteries in the area had ranks of benches to accommodate the mourners during these graveside rites. Near the Powell–Kidd Cemetery in McCreary County, a rock house provided shelter for a set of log benches used for graveside rites during inclement weather, but no trace of the benches could be found in 1979.

Although by the late twentieth century professional funeral directors and funeral homes assumed the functions of preparing the body and coordinating the funeral, community support for the bereaved family remained very much in evidence. It was obligatory to attend the funeral, to visit the funeral home, and to bring gifts of food to the family of the deceased. In many cases, the tradition of the wake continued, transferred to the funeral home instead of taking place in the home of the deceased. Large parties of gravediggers might still be seen at work in some cemeteries. These memories of a woman who grew up in Kentucky during the 1930s show that traditional funeral practices remained unchanged well into the twentieth century.

> *If someone passed away, everybody in the community went and they pitched in and helped. They took food . . . They pitched in and made the burial clothes and helped put 'em away. They made their coffins and hauled them to the graveyard. If anybody got sick, people'd go in and set up all night with them 'til they got better or they passed away . . . And they'd go every day to see about 'em . . . I've helped put 'em away many times, made the burial clothes and things like that.*
>
> *My father always made the caskets in the community. Anything happened, they'd always come to him to make the coffin, and I helped him. I'd go out and take the hand saw and help cut the coffin. . . . I learned how they cut the wood to bend it and all. They used any kind of wood they could get; it'd have to be so many inches high and so many long, and they'd have to measure and fix it according. Then they'd saw the planks cattycornered about two-thirds through at the bottom, and they'd measure the person to make the middle.*
>
> *They had to pack the corpse to the graveyard. They'd pack it from Fidelity down here to the Kidd Graveyard, maybe. They'd have about six or eight men and they'd change every so often . . . Then they got to where they'd bring 'em in a wagon. Now, if they come from Fidelity, they'd [still] pack 'em up the mountain.*

Each year on Decoration Day, a Sunday in early summer, a memorial observance was held at each graveyard. This might be a church-sponsored event for the cemeteries attached to churches, but the same observance occurred in each family cemetery. The participants cleaned and decorated the graves, and a preacher memorialized everyone who had been buried during the past year. Here is one informant's account of Decoration Day in a family cemetery located in a very isolated section of McCreary County.

We used to buy this crepe paper and make our flowers. But now here of late years they buy these other flowers. Generally, they'd go to the graveyards, and most times they'd have preaching and singing and then decorate the graves.
Q: *Would you have dinner?*
A: *Well, they have had dinners, but that's one thing I don't like to do, is to eat around a graveyard. I just don't feel good about it. I'm afraid somebody laying there died hungry. Now used to, when we'd decorate over there at the graveyard, why we'd have singing out there and preaching, and then we'd come back to the house to set the tables to have dinner. And I have knowed as high as almost a hundred people being there. They'd come almost all the relatives that could get there and other people besides. And we'd set some awful [i.e., awe-inspiring] dinners there. Made a big long table out in the yard—about thirty feet long and three feet wide. And I saw that settin' full from one end to the other—all kinds of food.*

Before commercial grave markers could be obtained locally and even longer for those who could not afford commercial markers, family members created grave markers for loved ones. The simplest ones were unmarked fieldstones placed at the head and at the foot of the grave. Inscribed markers were made of sandstone or, more recently, of concrete. The sandstone slabs were squared or rounded into a symmetrical shape and carved with initials or name and the dates of birth and death. Occasionally these markers were decorated with a motif copied from commercial markers of the period, such as the hand or the dove, or they bore geometrical decoration. The poured concrete markers could easily be inscribed when the material was almost hardened. They sometimes bore a brief epitaph as well as a name and dates. No extant examples of wooden markers were found in the cemeteries within the recreation area, perhaps because sandstone was so abundant and so easy to shape and inscribe (cf. Ball 1977b). One example of a grave house (cf. Ball 1977a) was found in the Terry Cemetery southwest of No Business Creek. According to people who knew its history, the shed structure on the site in the 1970s replaced a more elaborate "house" that fell in years ago.

Two other burial practices may be related to the grave house. During the late nineteenth century, some families who seem to have been fairly affluent covered the entire grave with a monolith, sometimes dressing it to resemble the traditional coffin shape. Later examples combined the usual head and foot markers with a concrete pitched "roof" covering the grave from head to foot. Examples were found in Wayne County, Kentucky, and in Fentress and Morgan Counties in Tennessee.

In addition to these structures that protect the grave from water, the practice of grave cleaning entailed clearing every blade of grass from the top of the grave, mounding the earth, and packing it so hard that it sheds rather than absorbs water. In the Nancy Graves Cemetery, a very large cemetery in McCreary County near the recreation area boundary, grave cleaning was so thorough that no vegetation had been allowed to gain a foothold anywhere in the cemetery, either on top of graves or between them.

Use of commercial caskets, monuments, floral arrangements, and funeral homes later in the twentieth century changed the surface detail of death observances without really altering their underlying importance as community expressions of regard for the deceased and sympathy for the bereaved family. Likewise, the continuing prominence of death as a theme in Big South Fork folklore suggests that the population continued to approach death with much the same anxieties as their forebears did. Haint tales were perhaps the most universally popular traditional folklore genre in the area; violent or unjust death was the stuff of local legends, and most people interviewed during the folklife survey knew various death omens. Some of the most widely known death omens were the following:

> *If you dream of a wedding, there will be a death in the family.*
> *If you dream of someone naked, there will be a death in the family.*
> *If you dream of falling, there will be a death in the family.*
> *If you dream of muddy water, there will be a death in the family.*
> *If a bird flies into the house, there will be a death.*
> *A bird pecking on the window is a sign of death.*
> *A howling dog is a sign of death.*
> *If the rooster crows twice before breakfast, or if a hen crows, there will be a death.*
> *Cold shivers mean that someone is walking over your gravesite.*
> *To leave an open grave overnight invites misfortune.*

Churches

Many Big South Fork communities disappeared from the map when most of their residents moved away, their stores and post offices closed, and their one-room schools closed. The institution that remained most vigorous in the face of community dissolution was the church. As long as some residents remained to form a congregation nucleus, the small rural churches continued to function. An overview of church history and belief will help to explain why these churches survived in spite of small membership, limited activities, and the attractions of larger, more active churches in the towns.

In 1979 the denominations represented by churches in the Big South Fork area included Baptist, Methodist, Presbyterian, Congregational, Seventh Day Adventist, Jehovah's Witness, Church of God, Church of Christ, Church of the Nazarene, Mormon, and unaffiliated Pentecostal and Holiness groups. A majority of the churches and church members were Baptist. Because the Baptists dominated the Big South Fork area historically, the Baptists are the focus of this discussion. Baptist doctrine and church organization inherently preclude a single invariant theology and church doctrine, so conflicting schools of thought flourished and left their traces in the frequently encountered subdenominational labels: Regular Baptist, Separate Baptist, United Baptist, Missionary Baptist, Free Will Baptist, and Primitive Baptist. Still other labels are encountered elsewhere in the South but are not common in the Big South Fork area.

HISTORY OF THE BAPTIST DENOMINATION

A few English Baptists settled in colonial Virginia and North Carolina. They styled themselves General or Armenian Baptists and adhered to the doctrine of free will (Sweet 1931). The Great Awakening revival movement began in New England in the 1730s, although it did not gain a foothold in Appalachia until the last decade of the eighteenth century (Boles 1972; Johnson 1955). The New England revival greatly swelled the ranks of the Baptists; but in keeping with Great Awakening theology, the new converts were Calvinistic predestinarians rather than advocates of free will. These were Congregationalists who were reformed by revival spirit first to become "New Lights" and later to form Separate Baptist congregations when they gave up infant baptism in favor of adult baptism. Soon after 1750, Baptist converts began migrating southward from New England, where the Separate Baptists were strong, and from Pennsylvania, where the Regular Baptists had an active association. The Regulars shared a Calvinistic outlook with the Separates but were less involved in the evangelical revival movement.

Sweet (1931, 9–10) describes the antagonism the Separates aroused when they came in contact with the General Baptists in Virginia and North Carolina:

> *The older Baptists in Virginia and North Carolina, as well as other denominations in contact with them, generally disapproved of the Separates. This disapproval was largely based upon the pulpit mannerisms and type of preaching generally followed by the evangelists, and by the effects they produced upon the Congregation . . . One of the peculiar mannerisms developed by the preachers was the "holy whine," a sing song method of speaking which seems to have arisen with outdoor preaching, and which continued to be practiced by the less educated Baptist ministers of the frontier for many years . . . The Separate Baptists had the reputation for being an ignorant and illiterate set. As is generally the case, the people attracted to the kind of meetings conducted by the Separate Baptist evangelists represented the lower classes economically and educationally.*

Membership gains by the Separate Baptists during the 1760s and 1770s were in part the result of a popular reaction against civil persecution of Separate Baptist preachers and of general support for separation of church and state after the Revolutionary War.

Both Regular and Separate Baptists emigrated from Virginia and North Carolina to Kentucky and Tennessee when western settlement began. The Regular Baptists established more churches in Kentucky, and the Separate Baptists established more churches in Tennessee. Soon after the turn of the century, however, a new movement to achieve a compromise between the Calvinistic and Armenian positions touched both states. Adherents to the compromise formed the United Baptist Church in 1807–8 (Sweet 1931, 22–27).

Meanwhile, Andrew Fuller had organized the first Baptist missionary society in England in 1792. Sweet (1931, 61) reports that the missionary message was at first warmly received in Kentucky and Tennessee. The Great Awakening spread to Appalachia through the efforts of circuit-riding preachers imbued with missionary fervor. However, by the 1820s controversy over missionary activity began to develop, and churches split in consequence. Antimission sentiment, which Sweet (1931, 58) interprets as a frontier phenomenon, was especially strong in Tennessee. The antimission Baptists rejected the notion that clergy needed special education or that they should be paid salaries. The protest was also directed against what seemed to be a trend toward more rigid and centralized church organization. On theological grounds, the antimission congregations took an extreme Calvinist position that viewed any proselytizing as presumptuous tampering with God's foreordained will for each individual. These views were shared by the Primitive, or "hard-shell," Baptists; the Reformer Baptists, who were followers of Alexander Campbell; and the Two-Seed-in-the-Spirit Baptists, who subscribed to Daniel Parker's view that each individual was born with either the seed of good or of evil, and hence was either elect or damned from birth (Sweet 1931, 67–72).

Sanderson's (1958) history of Scott County shed some light on the history of the Baptist Church in the immediate Big South Fork area. The United Baptist Church was organized in the area in 1842 and flourished until the 1880s. At that time, controversy over the mission issue caused Scott County Baptists to split into Separate and Missionary Baptists. In 1979 several Missionary Baptist churches were located in the towns and along Highway 27, but farther west in the heart of the Big South Fork area, congregations were either Separate or United Baptist. Some communities had both United and Separate Baptist churches, suggesting factional splits in the past, but by the 1970s church members did not identify any major theological differences and freely attended one another's services. A Separate Baptist preacher who was asked to explain the origin of the label "Separate" referred to the scriptural injunction "Be ye separate." He interpreted this verse as a guide for contemporary behavior, not in terms of church history. A United Baptist lay member volunteered his understanding of the difference between Separate and United Baptists: the Separate Baptists believe that a person can be saved today and lost again tomorrow, so they permit repeated baptisms; the United Baptists believe in one baptism.

RELIGIOUS BELIEF

Despite their past or present doctrinal differences, all Baptists subscribe to these basic principles: (1) conversion as a condition of church membership, (2) adult baptism by immersion, (3) individual responsibility to God, and (4) a congregational rather than a centralized form of church governance. Encouragement of personal interpretation of the Bible and congregational autonomy insulated the Appalachian churches from outside influences and fostered schism of local congregations. Parker (1970) found in these circumstances a fertile field for the formation of folk religion, evident in widespread regional observances like Decoration Day, in less common practices like faith healing, and in the rare but heavily publicized serpent handling practiced by some Appalachian Pentecostal Holiness sects (see La Barre 1962; Kane 1974). Kane's work and some sketchy information obtained from interviewees suggested that serpent handling was practiced on the Cumberland Plateau, but not in the immediate Big South Fork area.

THE ROLE OF THE PREACHER AND THE LAY MEMBER

James Kerr in his analysis of Appalachian religion (1979, 71) argued that congregations wanted preaching, not pastoral care. The preacher who was a neighbor, kinsman, and who worked at the same tasks as the rest of the community during the week was a more credible figure than the outsider specialist. These values made a virtue of the necessity of using part-time, unpaid ministers.

The call to preach in a rural Baptist church might come to anyone, literate or not, but the novice preacher had to gain congregational approval in order to be confirmed in his work and ordained to preach by his fellow preachers. The call was a stimulus for many preachers to learn to read or to improve their reading in order to study the Bible in depth. Nevertheless, preachers expressed the belief that they are divinely inspired during their sermons; they do not prepare before they get up to speak. They generally begin quietly with a particular Bible text, but when they "get going good," they fall into the "holy whine" noted by Sweet and begin to arouse affirmative responses from the congregation. Despite the extemporaneous content of sermons, the oratorical style employed is highly stylized. Preachers acknowledged that as novices they modeled their preaching after successful preachers whom they admired.

The same egalitarian tendencies that favored the local part-time preacher also promoted full and equal participation by lay members in church services and church affairs. Their participation took the form of group singing, mass verbal participation in prayers, and lengthy personal testimony in addition to the affirmations interjected into the preacher's sermon. Each congregation as a democratic body conducted its own business affairs. In the early days, this function extended beyond church business into the regulation of members' conduct, an aspect of church life that will be discussed more fully as an informal means of social control.

CHURCH LIFE

Some of the smaller rural churches did not have a preacher available for services every week but participated in a circuit with other churches. Circuit churches might hold services only once a month, a situation that encouraged visiting at nearby churches on other Sundays. Regular services were held Sunday mornings or evenings, and prayer meetings might also be held on Wednesday evenings. Congregational business meetings and association meetings were often held on Saturday evenings. The smaller rural churches seldom provided special Sunday school programs for the children. One preacher rationalized this lack with the observation that Sunday school could not save anybody; only responding to the preached Word could do that. Emotional conversion rather than a prolonged program of religious instruction was the prerequisite for baptism.

Regular weekly and monthly church services and meetings might be attended by only a small core of faithful members, but the revivals that lasted a full week or longer drew larger crowds to the churches and might produce conversions to swell the membership rolls. In the 1970s most revivals were sponsored by a particular church and held in its building, but tent meetings and brush arbor meetings were not unknown. Kerr (1979) identified revivalism and emotional fundamentalism as important characteristics of Appalachian religion and noted that church participation that might dwindle at other times of the year was stimulated by revivals. Perhaps the Pentecostal and Holiness congregations gained members in the twentieth century because they managed to satisfy these emotional needs on a more continuous, sustained basis than the older churches.

The following description from Sanderson matches these memories of the old-time revival in most particulars, but shouting was another characteristic discussed in interviews. One woman vividly recalled that as a small child she had to climb up on the bench in order to get out of the shouters' way. She observed that shouting was expected behavior and not always spontaneous; at least this was true of one old lady in the church who always tied her bonnet tightly on her head before beginning to shout.

> Many of these early revivals followed along the camp-meeting type of procedure. Whether or not the ministers could "carry a tune in a sack" they usually led off with a solo . . . The whole procedure was democratic in keeping with the ideas of the frontier people. Every minister participated in the services which held three or four hours. The entire congregation participated in the singing, and Christians and sinners joined in mass prayer. Some minister or devout man or woman usually led off with the prayer at the mourner's bench, but all joined in as the spirit led them. Sometimes fifty would be praying aloud at one time . . .
>
> The revivals usually lasted two to six weeks, depending upon the interest taken. At the close of the revivals the new converts were taken into the church. All

> the converts came forward, testified, and expressed their desire to join the church and be baptized. The baptizings were held in May the next spring. These were called the "May Meetings" (Sanderson 1958, 117).

One woman likened the May Meetings of her childhood to Easter because everyone attended and the women and girls decked themselves out in new Sunday clothes. The association meetings were usually held in September. Congregations loosely affiliated together into an association conducted their mutual business at that time, but the weeklong meeting also provided an occasion for the host community to entertain and hear all of the visiting preachers.

Another special church observance provided a time for former members of a congregation to reunite, whether they had moved away from the area or simply transferred membership from the family's church to one of the larger town churches. These reunions, called homecomings, were held at each church sometime during the summer, with a special church service and dinner on the grounds. Tables, sometimes covered by a shed, were built near many church buildings in the Big South Fork area to accommodate dinners on the grounds.

Religiosity and church membership might not necessarily indicate regular church attendance. Extremely religious individuals sometimes rationalized their lack of participation in organized church activities by stating that none of the churches nowadays strictly follows the Bible. Because their religion emphasized personal commitment rather than group ritual, Bible reading and listening to religious broadcasts were very important parts of their lives. Some of the gospel programs heard locally had a national or regional distribution, but the most popular were the broadcasts of local preachers and singing groups. Although many church buildings in and near the recreation area attracted only small congregations in the 1970s, the invisible radio congregations were large and strong.

Schools

School consolidation intensified after World War II, but the earliest attempts to transport children from small rural settlements to school by "bus" (an uncovered wagon with several rows of plank seats) occurred in Scott County as early as 1915 (Sanderson 1958, 149). Most of the information on the old one-room community schools was collected from older residents who attended school before 1920.

There was a time when each community had its own one-room school, housing grades one through eight. Although the Big South Fork area has its share of illiterates, older residents assert that these persons did have schools to attend but chose not to do so. Considering how brief school sessions used to be, how inadequate the facilities and teaching resources, and how poorly trained the teachers, the learning absorbed by Big South Fork old-timers is a real tribute to their motivation.

Many of them still remembered recitations learned for school sixty, seventy, or even eighty years earlier and derived much satisfaction from reading the Bible, religious tracts, newspapers, and a variety of other materials.

The school term used to be much shorter than it is today. As late as 1911, Tennessee required attendance at school for only four months of the year for children eight to fourteen (Sanderson 1958, 152). These short sessions began in late summer, recessed for two weeks at fodder pulling and "'tater" digging time, and resumed until bad weather. Even when the term was lengthened, attendance was often very low during winter because the pupils had to walk long distances to and from school. Children also had their full share of household and farm chores to handle, which made their school days very long and sometimes kept them away from school. Under these conditions, it was difficult for the average or slow learner to make much headway. Many students dropped out before finishing the eighth grade, the boys to work and the girls to marry.

THE ONE-ROOM SCHOOL

The first schoolhouses were log buildings with open hearths; white frame buildings equipped with potbellied stoves replaced them, but some interviewees attended more unusual schools. School for the No Business settlement was held in a rock house near the Terry Cemetery around 1900; some years later that school met out of doors on log benches set up under a big chestnut tree.

The old one-room schoolhouses were sparsely furnished with a row of desks for each grade, a blackboard, and a heating stove. Sanderson (1958, 135) described turn-of-the-century Scott County teachers being equipped with "zinc water pails, brooms, and a box of chalk." A McCreary County teacher recalled having to buy her own chalk as late as the 1920s. State-approved textbooks were used, but book selections did not change from year to year. Consequently, the family bought books and passed them down through the ranks. While younger generations used paper and pencils for their schoolwork, a few of the oldest interviewees remembered using slates.

After coal-burning stoves were installed in schoolhouses, school boards bought a supply of coal and had it delivered to the school; teachers and scholars had only to tend their fire. But when open hearths or woodstoves provided heat, the teacher and children also had to cut and split their own firewood. Water came from a spring or a well; several interviewees described the water bucket that sat on a shelf by the schoolhouse door. A single dipper was used until health regulations required that each student have a cup or glass. There were no indoor toilets, and in the early days, not even privies. The girls went one direction from the schoolhouse, and the boys the other. When leaving to be excused, a student put a book in the doorway, and its exact placement signaled which "facilities" were already occupied.

Old-timers remembered studying reading, writing, arithmetic, spelling, physiology (health), history, and geography. Their schoolwork included memorization and recitation of poems and prose selections. Recitations and spelling involved the whole community in school activities through special programs presented to visiting parents and through spelling bees. Former students had vivid memories of these special school events. A recitation for parents generally was held at the end of each school term. Another traditional end-of-term celebration was the school march. The students wore good clothes to school and walked two-by-two to some agreed upon location, turned and walked back. A flag bearer and sometimes a musician, perhaps a banjo picker, might lead the march, but music to walk by was not essential. With few opportunities for courtship, walking two-by-two with the object of one's affections was intrinsically interesting.

Spelling bees often pitted one school against another. The students enjoyed the walk to a nearby school and found the match exciting. Some interviewees also mentioned communitywide spelling bees including parents as well as the school children. It is not clear whether these were organized as school benefits, but other social events held at the school often were. Box suppers, pie suppers, or cakewalks provided entertainment and raised money for school supplies the board could not afford. The residents seem to have been quite interested in improving their local school through these benefits. They also supported the school by providing boarding accommodations for the teachers.

TEACHERS AND TEACHER TRAINING

The teacher in a one-room school had the difficult task of organizing the day into study and recitation periods so that time could be spent with each class. Advanced students sometimes helped by listening to the lessons of students in the lower grades. It was difficult to find trained teachers for isolated one-room schools like the ones along the Big South Fork, but local resources for teacher training improved steadily through the years.

Special teacher training institutes called normals were held in Huntsville beginning in 1890. Teacher certification examinations were given at the end of the normal session and the newly certified teachers were assigned their schools at that time (Sanderson 1958, 134–35). Hogue's (1950) *History of Fentress County* includes a photograph of an 1899 normal class. During the 1920s, professors from Berea College conducted normals in McCreary County. Teachers used this continuing education to maintain their certification and, because the course carried college credit, to raise their base pay.

Although some of the elementary school teachers had barely finished high school themselves, others were college students who paid for their education by teaching during the summer vacation and fall quarter; others were established community members with training who were able to supplement their modest teaching income through other occupations.

Some of the more accomplished teachers held subscription schools after the free term subsidized by the school board ended. The students paid tuition directly to the teacher. For a long time, such subscription schools were the only means poor rural students had of furthering their education beyond the minimum tax-supported elementary school offering. The first secondary schools in the region were private academies like the Presbyterian Academy founded at Huntsville in 1885. Huntsville did not have a public high school until 1908 (Sanderson 1958, 136–37).

In McCreary County, the larger towns like Pine Knot and Whitley City formed independent school districts and provided high schools for their children, but any rural child who was able to attend had to pay tuition. There was no free countywide high school until one was built under the WPA construction program. At about the same time, Sgt. Alvin C. York, who had returned from World War I a national hero, spearheaded a successful drive to have his York Institute financed and operated by the State of Tennessee. This move, together with school buses, opened up a unique opportunity for quality free secondary education in Fentress County. York Institute was also open to residents of other counties who could arrange transportation or boarding in Jamestown. Before the 1930s, rural youth who wanted a high school education had to choose the expensive route of boarding school; some traveled as far as Berea or Knoxville to attend school.

SCHOOL CONSOLIDATION

Consolidation and transportation systems made public secondary education for rural students possible. The Scott County superintendent urged school consolidation as early as 1912 so that the county could finance a longer school term and pay teachers a better salary (Sanderson 1958, 144). Transportation for school children in Scott County began in 1915, when "Lee Marcum was given a private contract to transport twenty children in a wagon from upper Straight Fork Community (in east Scott County) to Straight Fork Elementary School at a salary of two dollars per month per pupil" (Sanderson 1958, 149). By 1925, the first school bus had made its appearance in Scott County.

Perry (1979, 63–93) recounted the early history of McCreary County schools in detail. Modernization of the McCreary County school system received its biggest boost from Superintendent William O. Gilreath, who used the WPA public works construction program to good advantage. Gilreath worked overtime preparing the necessary project proposals, consulting with a Lexington architect, and administering the construction projects himself. In order to decrease materials cost and increase labor, which was fully funded by the federal government, the project included sawmills to manufacture lumber and local quarries to provide the native stone used for walls of all these WPA schools. While the WPA program was in place between 1934 and 1940, McCreary County built schools at Nevelsville, Parker's Lake, Eagle, Whitley City (both elementary and high schools), Beech Grove, Revelo, Pine Knot, Silerville, and Hill Ridge. Some of these buildings were still schools in 1979, but the one-room buildings, including the old Beech Grove School, had been converted to dwellings.

School consolidation affecting the Big South Fork section of McCreary County began in the late 1930s. Some of these closings, for example the 1939 closing of Fidelity School, followed mine closings that dispersed the population these schools had served. During the World War II economic recovery period, there were few closings and two schools opened. The frequency of school closings increased dramatically during the 1950s and 1960s, reflecting both the departure of mining families as the Stearns mines closed and the county's commitment to consolidation. Between 1968 and 1979, the twenty-eight local elementary schools that once served the Big South Fork section of the county were reduced to a single school at Smithtown.

It is probably misleading to compare pre-depression school age population figures with actual school enrollments recorded in the post-depression years, however a 39 percent drop in overall enrollment figures between the 1941–42 academic year and the 1955–56 academic year shows without question the effects of postwar labor out-migration. The schools that survived consolidation were located along the better roads. The disintegration of isolated communities set in motion by loss of population was intensified by loss of the local schools. As much as consolidation improved the quality and efficiency of education, its adverse impact on community life in small rural settlements must be acknowledged.

Fentress County appears to have moved toward school consolidation rather slowly. Hogue's (1950) county history lists forty-six elementary schools with their teachers for the 1949–50 term. If the list is complete (as its currency at the time of publication would suggest), then as late as 1950, Fentress County still had twenty-five one-room schools and fourteen two-room schools. At that time, the Big South Fork section of the county was served by these elementary schools: Sharp, Alticrest, Stockton, Armathwaite, Shirley, and Goad. These schools already were the product of some consolidation, however. For example, the Goad School had absorbed two earlier schools, Hickory Ridge and Mt. Helen. Of the schools open in 1949–50, only the Armathwaite and Sharp schools survived in 1979. One Armathwaite woman commenting regretfully on the loss of the community post office observed, "If we ever lose that school [which occurred only a few years later], it will be the end of Armathwaite."

Law and Lawlessness

Like most of Appalachia, the Big South Fork area was first settled under frontier conditions. It was some time before formal political and legal institutions followed the settlers. Reinforcing Fiske's popular mythology, Harry Caudill (1963) argued that as descendants of outlaws and social misfits who evaded the legal and social order of the seaboard colonies by seeking refuge in the mountains, Appalachian people were inherently lawless. Scholarly historians convincingly discredited this myth, however (see Caruso 1959; Leyburn 1962).

Informal social controls could be effective in Appalachia as in other "folk" societies so long as the settlement was a homogeneous unit based on kinship obligations and a shared moral code (Redfield 1947). But economic inequality had undermined this kind of traditional normative system of social control. Industrialization meant that the population grew and became more heterogeneous. New quasi-urban camps and towns sprang up, bringing together people who did not feel that they were members of a community in the traditional sense. Those who abandoned farming for wage work suddenly had extra cash and leisure time, and whiskey was the most convenient means of spending the two simultaneously. Disputation and lawlessness increased as the local economy was being transformed. Formal political and legal institutions were strengthened to deal with these problems, but they did not always coexist comfortably with the traditional pattern of kin loyalty.

COUNTY FORMATION AND COUNTY POLITICS

Organized government came slowly to the upper reaches of the Cumberland Plateau because the population dispersed into wilderness areas faster than roads could be built to connect new settlements with their county seats. The rough wagon roads that were built were impassible in bad weather. Eventually public pressure forced the formation of new counties with county seats more accessible to the pioneer settlements. Morgan County was created from western portions of Anderson and Roane Counties in 1817, and northward expansion over the plateau soon produced Fentress County (1823), then Scott County (1849). Both of these counties included territory that had been in old Morgan County. The northern boundary of Fentress and Scott was not established conclusively until almost 1860 (see Sanderson 1958, 3–4). Kentucky and Tennessee disputed jurisdiction over the territory from the present state line south as far as Oneida, even though this area contained some of the oldest settlements along the Big South Fork. State and county government must have seemed remote indeed to families living in the Williams Creek, Station Camp, and No Business settlements before the jurisdictional dispute was settled.

In Kentucky, it was not until 1912 that McCreary County was carved out of sections of Wayne, Whitley, and Pulaski Counties. Although Perry (1979, 47) held that the Stearns Company advocated the status quo and preferred to deal with the three counties rather than with a single local government, interviewees explained why Stearns officials favored the new county. They were concerned because the three sets of law officers, each based in a distant county seat, were not maintaining order effectively in the backcountry where Stearns camps were located. Population growth and concentration in the Stearns domain demanded effective formal means of social control.

Another force toward county formation was the desire of local politicians to strengthen their own position. Pine Knot citizens spearheaded the county-formation campaign, assuming that Pine Knot would become the county seat. However, Whitley City (then Coolidge) became a contender and won the referendum. Several interviewees were old enough to remember the special 1912 Fourth of July celebrations honoring the new county, the contention between Pine Knot and Whitley City, and the county's earliest referenda and elections. This account describes events in a community near the Wayne County line.

> Well, they had a big barbecue at Whitley; they killed beefs and barbecued the whole beef, maybe a hog or two, and plenty of whiskey. And then they had a barbecue at my Dad's [in western McCreary County]. A year later, me and my brother'd find pints of whiskey hid behind logs, where they'd hid it and got too drunk to go back and find it . . . Them used to be days back then. A feller'd be running when they had big barbecues, they'd maybe be three or four running for judge, three or four for clerk, three or four for jailer, and two or three for sheriff, and they really worked too—made big speeches you know. And they always had somebody out a giving out the whiskey, see, to vote for 'em.
>
> The toughest time they ever had in this county, the county seat when it first come, it was at Pine Knot. And they got a 'lection up to vote for it to come to Whitley. I remember there was two men voted for it to stay at Pine Knot. They [other residents of the community] found it out late that evening, and they cut them a pole and some hickory whips and followed them two men plumb home. Well, if they'd caught 'em afore they got home they'd a put 'em on that pole and killed 'em. They's two people voted for it to go to Pine Knot; that made 50 or 75 people mad; and if they'd caught 'em, they'd a killed 'em, there wasn't no question about it.
>
> Q: Politics was pretty wild and wooly back then, wasn't it?
> A: Oh, hit was tough back them days. Yeah, boy. You had to be very careful who you told you'd vote for. Now if you told them wrong man that the majority was for, you's in trouble. You either turned over and voted right, or left out, one. You didn't stay around.
> Q: Did people get in trouble selling their votes to both sides? What happened to them when they got found out?

A: *They'd usually have to leave the county. They'd take off to Wayne County or some other county. They couldn't stay around. That's the way with these two fellers who voted for the county seat to go to Pine Knot. They soon sold out and went to Wayne County.*

The local historians Sanderson (1958, 85–99) and Perry (1979, 180–204) frankly admitted that old-style politics was full of mud-slinging campaigns, vote buying, ballot box stuffing, and other strong-arm methods. The heat of the campaign might explode into violence at the slightest provocation, especially when whiskey was on hand to add fuel to the fire. Even law officers or potential law officers were not immune to these outbursts. In fact, back when western McCreary County still belonged to Wayne County, two candidates for sheriff met at a voting house on election day, exchanged a volley of insults, and finally shot each other dead.

LAW ENFORCEMENT

Law enforcement, like politics, has crept into stereotypes about Appalachian society, helped along by lurid press coverage of murder, feuds, and moonshine. At a time when little was known about this area and its people were considered to be near savages by many of their fellow Americans, Horace Kephart, a professional librarian from Boston and St. Louis, settled in western North Carolina near the Tennessee line and began to observe his neighbors with an open and inquiring mind. His impressions, gathered between 1904 and 1922 and presented in *Our Southern Highlanders* (1976 [1922]), were considered fair and insightful comments by the subjects themselves. The picture Kephart painted is consistent with reminiscences of older residents in the Big South Fork area, with the exception that until the mid-1930s, revenuers seldom pursued moonshiners vigorously as they did near the North Carolina–Tennessee border. Enforcement was left to local authorities who could be and were bribed to look the other way.

Kephart found a fundamental distrust toward government and law among his neighbors, and he identified several reasons for their attitudes. Historically, established governments had been eager to use frontier areas as buffers against the Indians but reluctant to furnish the settlers services or protection. Instead, government imposed a punitive tax on distilling, which was the most efficient means mountaineers had to make a living from their corn patches. Opposition to the tax produced the eighteenth-century Whiskey Rebellion and continued to underlie moonshining into the twentieth century. In the Big South Fork, the populace generally condoned 1930s moonshining because so many families could not have survived without that source of income. At that time, merchants openly stocked malt and sheet copper.

Kephart and others have repeatedly pointed to self-reliance and individualism as cardinal Appalachian values. Cooperation in large, organized social groups was unusual, but family loyalty and cooperation countered extreme individualism. Kinship connections and family loyalty loomed large in determining political affiliation. Unquestionably, the resulting nepotism in government led to unfair treatment of those without the right connections, so that resentment and suspicions about "bad law" often were confirmed in experience.

These attitudes came together in admiration for outlaws who have become legends because they were mistreated by the law. In the Big South Fork area, this tradition includes Cal Logsdon, a nineteenth-century convicted murderer whose hanging was followed by the flood he prophesied as a sign of his innocence (Allen and Montell 1981); Jerome Boyatt, a 1930s bootlegger who shot a sheriff while under siege and was lynched while awaiting trial in the Scott County jail (Howell 1983a); and, most recently, Billy Dean Anderson, a Fentress County fugitive shot by FBI agents in 1979. Anderson evaded capture for many months, hiding out in rock shelters near his home as many fugitives had done before. News of the shooting produced a wave of local resentment. Within hours of the event, allegations were circulating that Anderson never should have been on the most-wanted list; that he had been ambushed and shot in the back by a large number of agents; that he was treated inhumanely by the agents between his shooting and his death hours later; and that his mother had been harassed and abused by FBI agents. Within a month, a local songwriter had created a ballad to tell the story, and Billy Dean was being shaped into another legendary outlaw who became a victim of "bad law."

THE COURTS

Despite their mistrust of government and the law, Big South Fork residents were ready enough to carry disputes, especially those regarding property rights, to the courts. The Sunbright and Rugby newspapers of the 1880s and 1890s carried many notices of land dispute cases to be heard. Here is a typical report from the *Rugby Gazette* of Saturday, March 20, 1886:

> *The case of Leo McManus vs. the Board of Aid and several persons in Morgan and Scott Co. came up for hearing before the Hon. Judge Baxter at Knoxville on Tuesday last.*
>
> *This suit has caused considerable excitement in this neighborhood and along the C.S.R.R. from Helenwood to Lancing. It was commenced by the above named party, who hails from Texas, and who claimed the land by virtue of a grant, which his father, Thomas McManus, held, covering several thousand acres of land in this county.*

> As it was an action of ejectment, the defendants had the right to introduce other titles than their own covering the same land. So they introduced the titles of the Board of Aid, embracing the whole of the McManus claim. Judge Baxter promptly decided that the "Eastland and Lane" titles [which the Board of Aid hold under] were superior to the title of Leo McManus, and instructed the Jury to return a verdict for the defendants.
>
> This decision is a most important one for the Board of Aid; for it not only settles their title as against McManus, but against Fielder as well. This is the same land and the same title that Fielder also sets claim to, and upon which he has been harassing the Board of Aid for nearly five years, but his claim is now practically disposed of forever.

Lest the reader assume that only the well-educated Rugbeians could have grasped the intricacies of this case and appreciated its import, it should be noted that persons who grew up along the river had the same abilities. One such gentleman described in detail the history of John Toomey's and Thomas Lyons's land acquisition on behalf of the Stearns interests, the chain of ownership for many boundaries in "The Big Wilderness," and the circumstances surrounding various title transfers. He had made it his business to peruse public records in the courthouse at Huntsville in order to learn many of these details, as had his father before him.

The general public followed the particulars of cases closely and derived considerable entertainment from court proceedings. Recesses provided time for horse trading, swapping stories, and renewing old acquaintances. Court Day used to be an important countywide social event. Discounting the tone of disdain with which this Rugby reporter describes the natives, one can capture the spirit of excitement that attended legal events from this *Rugby Gazette* report of Saturday, July 4, 1885:

> Robbins—This little town was quite astir during the week, owing to the presence of two of Knoxville's distinguished lawyers, Col. Henderson and Mr. Templeton, who were busy taking depositions in some important land suits, such as the Board of Aid vs. Hughett et al., Board of Aid vs. Fielder et al., Fielder et al. vs. Leak et al. A number of witnesses were examined in the various cases, and the lawyers hope to see those cases disposed of at the July term of the U.S. Court.
>
> To a disinterested spectator—such your correspondent has been—it was really amusing to watch the conduct of some of the witnesses while their depositions were being taken—the readiness with which they answered some questions and the fresh recollections they had of events, and the hesitancy they manifested in answering others, as well as the total lack of memory they displayed. In cross-examination one witness, an old lady, when being pressed hard to reply to some

troublesome and embarrassing question put to her by Mr. Templeton, shook her umbrella at that gentleman and remarked that as he was "so powerful pert in axing questions he had better answer 'em hisself."

There seems to be a wonderful family connection in this county of Scott. The officers of the law are related to all the clients, and many of the clients "kinfolks" of the officers ad infinitum; and to show the effect of this injustice I will state that a number of summonses were issued for witnesses and placed in the hands of the Deputy Sheriff for service, but the witnesses not appearing at the proper time, the lawyer on that particular side of the case on making enquiry as to what had become of his witnesses was informed that the Deputy Sheriff had not summoned them at all—had in fact torn up the summonses. The D.S. was the son of the party on the other side; inferences are therefore in order.

INFORMAL MODES OF SOCIAL CONTROL

Before official law enforcement made itself felt in the isolated communities along the Big South Fork, and to a considerable extent afterward, the most effective mode of social control was community opinion rather than law. Churches exercised the most extreme peer pressure. Here is one interviewee's description of how churches attempted to enforce proper conduct.

The elders of the church would have to get together and they'd have a meeting or a conference and then they'd decide whether this person should be turned out of the church or whether he could be reconciled and stay in the church.
Q: What was cause for turning somebody out?
A: Different things. If they'd done something that they wasn't supposed to do and wouldn't quit, why, they'd first go to 'em and talk to 'em. If they wouldn't hear 'em, then they'd—at last they'd go three of the members and talk to 'em, and if they wouldn't come into the church and make their acknowledgement and ask for forgiveness and to stay in the church, then they had to bring 'em to the church and the church had to decide on it.

Most persons probably would have found it difficult to withstand this degree of peer pressure and would have made their confession and been reconciled to the other church members, an act that required forgiveness on the part of the church members as well as repentance on the part of the wrongdoer. However, the same woman went on to describe one case when the process of "churching" (turning an individual out of the church) was carried to completion because the accused man refused to make amends.

I remember one time they was a man—it's been so long, it was just after I joined the church—I believe they accused him of stealing a hog. He never would come

> in, you know, never would make no acknowledgement. But that day they called him to come in to say yes or no, whichever he wanted to do, and he never would. So they called on the members then to gather around and make their decision. You was supposed to hold up your right hand if you wanted it done [the churching], and if you didn't want it done, you'd stay silent.
>
> So then we decided, said, "Well he won't make no acknowledgement, nor he won't do nothing. All we can do is to put him out of the church." So the members held up their hands. Well, I did too, but I'll declare to goodness, that dawned on my conscience so bad I declare I said I'll never be guilty of that again, and I never did no more.
>
> Q: What happened to the person that had been put out? How did people treat him after that?
>
> A: Well, as far as that was concerned, they was friendly, but he never did come back to church any more. But if you met him or seen him anywhere, why people was friendly with him, you know, spoke to him like usual.

While the churches were not always effective in regulating the behavior of their members and others resisted the call to church membership altogether, few escaped the demands placed on them by kinship. Kin expected to deal with one another fairly, to give and receive services and material aid when necessary, and to enjoy one another's hospitality on visits, whether for a few hours or a few weeks. This was the positive side of kinship obligations. There was also a negative side to kinship bonds—the expectation that family loyalty would guarantee allies against the other party to a dispute, that the family would protect any member, even one known to be guilty, from arrest and conviction. Stories told by Big South Fork residents and newspaper accounts described isolated incidents of vengeance killing or maiming carried out by a relative of a murder or assault victim, but prolonged family feuds of the kind that made eastern Kentucky and West Virginia notorious were unknown in this area.

THE PROBLEM OF VIOLENCE

Elmora Matthews (1965, 107–15) in her study of kin-based communities in the Duck River Ridge area of Tennessee suggested some of the strains that might cause normally cooperative kin ties to turn sour at times. Disputes that might lead to violence occurred most often between in-laws and between kin belonging to different generations, such as fathers and sons or uncles and nephews. Marriage choices, property distribution, land transfers, and other economic matters were typical causes of conflict. Matthews noted that violence of this kind was most prevalent in the Duck River communities where there was greatest disparity between espoused egalitarian values and actual differences in economic status among the households comprising the community.

Within the Big South Fork area, localities most affected by economic boom conditions seem also to have been the most beset by violence. The relationship between alcohol and arguments ending in violence was equally striking. Recognition of this pattern aroused law-abiding citizens against saloons. For example, this item appeared in the *Plateau Gazette* of January 24, 1884:

> *The effort made by Glen Mary to rid the village of saloons, and their attendant disorders, assassinations and murders, was recently rewarded by the powers of the four-mile law. A school was started, and the saloons closed, and it was hoped the unenviable character of the village might, in time, be obliterated. Last Saturday, however, by order of the County Court an election was held to incorporate a municipal government in opposition to the incorporated school. The boundaries were so run as to take in but one resident of Glen Mary proper, and then out and in among the miners favorable to the scheme. To get the necessary twenty-one freeholder residents within the boundary, an 8 x 10 lot was deeded to that number of miners. That is how it was done. It is to be hoped the school can be maintained even though the saloons are reopened, and law and order once again seriously threatened. There seems, too, to be some defect in the four-mile law which is so highly valued in this State, when, as we have seen, it can be so cunningly evaded.*

The *Sunbright Dispatch* of January 2, 1897, carried this report of a series of shootings started because of drinking and carried on because family members became involved in the fray. This may have been one of the most sensational incidents of its kind in the area's history, but newspapers in the 1970s contained all too many similar stories.

> *Helenwood, Tenn., Dec. 30—(Special.)—Last Sunday afternoon at half past one o'clock two men were killed and one wounded at this place as a result of one man being half full of whiskey. That man was Louis Pemberton, who took a Winchester rifle out of his saloon and started down main street shooting it off, till it aroused Marshall Frank Hughett, who came upon the scene heavily armed. He asked Pemberton to lay down his gun, and Pemberton, holding on to the breech, dropped the muzzle to the ground, but as he did not drop his gun from his hands, Hughett fired upon him with a needle gun hitting him in the side, the ball going through his body.*
>
> *While all this was going on Jim Pemberton (Louis' father) was walking rapidly down the street and by the time Hughett had fired the elder Pemberton was*

upon him and fired two shots, one striking him in the shoulder, sidewise. Then they clinched and fell struggling. When the smoke cleared away, Hughett was up and Pemberton was on the ground with two bullet holes in his side, one supposed to have been made by Hughett's wife and the other by Hughett, from which he died thirty minutes afterwards.

After Louis Pemberton fell he rose upon his knees and fired back at Hughett and his deputy, John David, with his Winchester, but without effect. He then fell back in a dying condition when Deputy David shot three shots at him while he was down hitting him each time in the side.

He lived about fifteen minutes after being shot by David.

White Pine United Baptist Church, Scott County.

Beech Grove Baptist Church, McCreary County.

Mt. Helen Baptist Church, Fentress County.

Bethel Baptist Church,
Wayne County.

Christ Church Episcopal, Rugby, Morgan County.

Coffin-shaped ledger grave markers in Bethel Baptist Church Cemetery, Wayne County.

Stockton family graves in Stockton Cemetery, Fentress County.

Thompson Cemetery, Pickett County.

Benches for graveside rites at Helen Blevins Cemetery, Scott County.

Shed replacing a log grave house over Roysdon family graves, Terry Cemetery, Scott County.

Grave of Elizabeth Williams, 1829-1891, in Troxel Cemetery, McCreary County.

Natural stone marker, Powell Kidd Cemetery, McCreary County.

Cast concrete marker with dove motif, Barrs Cemetery, McCreary County.

Cast concrete marker, Nancy Graves Cemetery, McCreary County.

Concrete marker with painted lettering, Blevins Cemetery, Scott County.

Slaughtering at No Business, 1919. Will J. Miller, Harve Slaven, and Ellen Miller. Courtesy Will J. and Ellen Miller.

Marion Miller, Will Miller, and Harve Winchester at No Business. Courtesy Will J. and Ellen Miller.

School march at No Business. Ellen Miller, Tusco Winchester, Will Miller, Mandy Spradlin. Courtesy Will J. and Ellen Miller.

Stearns Coal and Lumber Company sawmill and log holding pond in Stearns, Kentucky. Courtesy McCreary County Museum.

W. O. Frogge, Robert Deal, and "Coon" Latham at a Stearns logging camp shack near Redmon Mountain. Courtesy of Lattie Buck Lominac Sr.

Working on the Stearns logging railroad. *Top*, Fred Williamson; left *to right*, engineer Buck Lominac, fireman Robert Deal, Supt. Bob Tellischow, and Mack Koger. Courtesy of Lattie Buck Lominac Sr.

Clearing a minor derailment on the Stearns logging railroad.
Courtesy of Lattie Buck Lominac Sr.

Miners at Worley camp of Stearns Coal and Lumber Company,
1905. Courtesy Crit King Sr.

Worley School and class of 1905. Courtesy Crit King Sr.

Kentucky and Tennessee Railroad bridge across the Big South Fork at Yamacraw, Kentucky.

The Blue Heron tipple photographed before it opened for business in 1937. Courtesy McCreary County Museum.

Contemporary coal tipple south of Pine Knot, McCreary County.

Tennessee Stave and Lumber Company's Wolf River incline, Fentress County. Courtesy of Bessie Akers and Mary Parker.

Julia and John Tays, storekeepers at Wolf River, riding a pedal-powered handcar on the Tennessee Stave logging railroad. Courtesy of Bessie Akers and Mary Parker.

Boardinghouse and store at Head-of-Wolf, the Tennessee Stave and Lumber Company logging camp. Courtesy of Bessie Akers and Mary Parker.

The John Tays store at Zenith, Fentress County. Courtesy of Bessie Akers and Mary Parker.

The Oneida and Western Railroad at Zenith. Courtesy of Bessie Akers and Mary Parker.

Webb-Hammock Company supply house, bathhouse, and company store at Zenith. Courtesy of Bessie Akers and Mary Parker.

Children on a johnboat excursion on North White Oak Creek, Zenith, 1930s. Courtesy Bessie Akers and Mary Parker.

John Tays and nephew John H. Tays at the Louvain bandmill, which Tennessee Stave and Lumber Company built but never operated. Courtesy of Bessie Akers and Mary Parker.

Charlie Terry watches while Bill Norris and Tom Parker, members of his Oneida and Western section crew, use a track jack. Courtesy of Bessie Akers and Mary Parker.

Oneida and Western Railroad depot, Jamestown, Tennessee.

Unloading a truckload of pulpwood beside a Southern Railway siding at Helenwood, Scott County.

Everett Boyatt setting and filing the headsaw at his mill near Oneida, Tennessee. Courtesy of Everett Boyatt.

Everett Boyatt squaring up a log to be sawed. Courtesy of Everett Boyatt.

Everett Boyatt sawing boards. Courtesy of Everett Boyatt.

Everett Boyatt feeding a board into the edger.
Courtesy of Everett Boyatt.

Everett Boyatt at the conveyor. Courtesy of
Everett Boyatt.

Forge built in 1918 by James and Robert Tompkins, Ted Tompkins blacksmith shop in Armathwaite, Fentress County.

Woodworking shop, Kentucky Hills Industries, Pine Knot, McCreary County.

7

Cultural Expression in Music, Oral Tradition, and Handcrafts

The expressive culture of Appalachia generally has been treated in a way that emphasizes the persistence of ancient European elements through migration and the many environmental and cultural changes settlers experienced in the New World. Early collectors were selective, recording Child ballads and fiddle tunes from the British Isles while ignoring the indigenous development of sacred music, seeking out wonder tales and old riddles more assiduously than legends of pioneer days, Civil War stories, or contemporary occupational lore. By the 1970s there was greater interest in the oral tradition and folk music forms indigenous to Appalachia, shifting the frame of reference from survival toward change. If new forms of folk expression spring up and fewer and fewer individuals in each generation preserve ancient forms, how are these changes related to more general processes of culture change? In other words, how does the sociocultural context affect oral tradition and folk music?

That question might organize an exhaustive study of expressive culture in the Big South Fork as well as collection and analysis of representative examples from the various genres. Such a study could well fill several volumes. The present chapter attempts only to describe briefly the wealth of extant material available for documentation and study in the late 1970s, to provide some commentary on examples preserved on recording tape during the course of the folklife survey, and to offer some tentative explanations for the changing popularity of various expressive culture forms through time. By the late 1970s, because of mass media and other popular culture forms, contexts for performance of local folk traditions in the Big South Fork area had become more limited during the late twentieth century than formerly. On the other hand, incipient tourism was beginning to reverse this trend by generating new performance opportunities that encouraged musicians, storytellers, and crafters to practice these arts.

Music

The Big South Fork has a rich musical heritage, and much of its traditional music still survives, though not in isolation from popular culture. Today's Top 40 hits, Nashville-style country music, and commercial gospel recordings and broadcasts are heard more often than ballads, fiddle tunes, and old-time sacred songs. In its music as in many other respects, the Big South Fork area illustrates the impact of mass media on folk culture and points to the value of documenting these traditions.

In common usage, *folk* and *traditional* suggest that an item of culture has spread through oral transmission, circulating for such a long time that it has become part of a common heritage, losing its association with a particular author or composer and developing significant geographical variation. In fact, some of the "traditional" fiddle tunes popular in the Big South Fork area and elsewhere in the Upland South can be traced to specific nineteenth- and twentieth-century composers and to printed music sources (Wiggins 1979), although almost all contemporary performers are unaware of these origins. More recently, the folk domain has claimed compositions by popular balladeers such as Woody Guthrie, Pete Seeger, and Bob Dylan; yet many of their songs have been recorded and performed so widely that they are no longer identified with the composer or original performer. They have entered folk tradition.

FOLK ROOTS AND LITERATE TRANSMISSION OF SACRED MUSIC

The symbiotic relationship between folk tradition and elite or popular culture was especially important in shaping the distinctive sacred music heritage of the rural South. During the nineteenth century and the early twentieth century, singing masters traveled through the mountains, selling shape-note songbooks and holding singing schools. The first teachers were outsiders, but students who had completed singing school soon set themselves up as singing masters and carried this form of music education throughout the rural South. The singing schools were secular affairs generally held in the evenings at community schoolhouses, but the books contained mostly sacred songs, reflecting the origins of shape-note choral music in the Separatist churches of New England.

Daylong singing conventions held in churches became focal points in the musical lives of the shape-note singers, and ultimately official church hymnals incorporated some of the old tunes. Protestant denominations further bowed to local tradition by producing special shape-note editions of their hymnals for distribution in the rural South long after the round notes of the elite modern European musical tradition had supplanted shape-notes elsewhere in America.

Although singing masters made use of printed songbooks and gave formal music lessons, this literate tradition belonged to the rural folk; the "fasola," or four-shape, system used in the songbooks of the first half of the nineteenth century derived from the European music theory of an earlier age. After the Civil War, modified seven-shape systems, which were compatible with the seven-tone elite music theory, began to gain ground at the expense of the "fasola" tradition. The seven-shape songbooks showed changes in content as well as notation.

Fortunately, musicologist Henry Pullen Jackson discovered the sacred music tradition of the rural South while it was still fairly widespread. He carefully examined and compared all of the songbooks he could locate and published his conclusions in *White Spirituals in the Southern Uplands* (1933). Jackson identified the sources of many tunes and poems, and he collected information about composers and songbook compilers. By following songs through successive editions and through borrowing from their original sources into later song compilations, Jackson was able to make inferences about public taste and its role in turning some compositions into old favorites while relegating others to obscurity (Jackson 1933, chaps. 12–14).

Although well-known composers such as William Billings and Ananias Davisson contributed lengthy anthems as well as hymns to the "fasola" songbooks, many less famous singing masters also are represented among the composers. Not all of their work was original; some "took down" and harmonized traditional tunes like "Amazing Grace." Ballad and fiddle tune material also found its way into this body of sacred song (see Jackson 1933, chaps. 15–16). Most tunes based on a pentatonic scale probably had a folk origin, and there were many of these in the early books. Their numbers were significantly reduced in the later seven-shape songbooks, which specialized in major keys and tunes expressing "sprightly optimism" (Jackson 1933, 381).

The new material in the seven-shape songbooks reflected the popularity of camp meeting songs (see Bruce 1974). One feature of these new tunes was their rhythmic interest. Syncopation, described by Jackson as "one of the trademarks of the ragtimers and still an ingredient of most of the secular popular music" (Jackson 1933, 381–82), was not accepted by the more conservative singing masters without complaint, but it sold books. In fact, upbeat rhythms and emotional lyrics already had spilled over from the camp meeting into the old four-shape songbooks to a limited extent (see Jackson 1933, 241).

Bill Malone (1979, 67) said of the transformation of the late-nineteenth-century sacred music tradition into today's gospel music:

> *The gospel music business, which is today a major facet of the nation's entertainment industry, developed out of two aspects of nineteenth-century American*

religious history—the shape-note singing schools and the evangelical revivals; but it drew much of its dynamism and much of its personnel from the Holiness-Pentecostal movement of the late nineteenth and early twentieth centuries. By 1900 a great stream of religious songs, fed by the big-city revivals of the era, flowed into American popular culture, and in the South such songs circulated invariably in shape-note form. On an average of twice a year several publishing houses printed paperback hymnals designed for church conventions and singing schools. The publishing houses were sometimes aligned with, or adjuncts of, religious denominations, but even the independent ones defined their goals in missionary terms: the evangelizing of the nation through the power of song.

Like the singing masters before them, the early traveling gospel quartets often were affiliated with publishing houses, performing and recording to advertise the contents of the company's songbooks (Malone 1979, 67–69). By the end of the 1920s the more popular quartets had achieved recognition in their own right and were well launched into careers of commercial recording, radio, and public appearances.

SACRED MUSIC IN THE BIG SOUTH FORK AREA

The general pattern just outlined was reflected in specific developments within the Big South Fork area. Interviews indicated that singing masters were active in the area around the turn of the twentieth century. The grandfather of one elderly interviewee was a singing master in the McCreary County–Wayne County area. His granddaughter and at least one other resident of the Bell Farm area learned to play the organ and accompanied family hymn sings. Local music masters were their organ teachers.

The issue of instrumental music in churches continued to separate the more conservative Baptists from other branches of their denomination and from Pentecostal and Holiness congregations. Unaccompanied congregational singing at the Beech Grove Baptist Church in McCreary County preserved some of the feeling of the old-time singing conventions. This congregation actively preserved unaccompanied congregational singing as its only form of musical expression. Given the opportunity to host a visiting gospel group, the church members voted to restrict their performing with instruments to the church grounds. The woman who described this event admitted to liking string music in secular contexts but did not entirely dismiss the possibility that this enjoyment was sinful.

In addition to the Beech Grove congregation, Joe Hicks of Fentress County, Tennessee, and Alvin Perry of McCreary County, Kentucky, performed solo renditions of old-time sacred song in a nineteenth-century style that survived into the twentieth century. However, gospel was by far the most prevalent form of sacred music by the late twentieth century. Local groups as well as professional groups from outside the area (sometimes with kinship ties to the Big South Fork) performed live and were broadcast by the local radio stations.

SECULAR VOCAL MUSIC

Like sacred music, the secular music sung around the Big South Fork area in the 1970s developed from several distinct streams of Anglo-American musical tradition. It contained remnants of the popular music of earlier periods as well as indigenous material that originated among the "folk" themselves. Various styles and forms were represented: British and early American ballads and instrumental dance tunes brought to the region by its earliest settlers; songs reflecting facets of the Kentucky–Tennessee frontier lifestyle; lighthearted numbers that entered local folk tradition during the nineteenth century by way of the widely popular minstrel stage; and maudlin favorites from the turn of the century onward brought into the local musical tradition by way of radio or country music recordings. This music recorded the experiences that shaped the people of the Big South Fork region—lingering echoes of their ethnic origins and of the times and the cultural environments they have known.

Broadside ballads dated from the seventeenth to the nineteenth century and were composed by professionals who printed them on large sheets of paper called broadsides and peddled them in the city streets of Great Britain, Ireland, and America. In a sense, the broadside ballads were the hit songs of their day; they were quickly assimilated into folk tradition. Although some of the broadside ballads were fictitious, many were based on current events and offered political satire or accounts of murders, disasters, and outlaws. More concise than the Child ballads set in a British past, broadside narratives were sometimes told in the first person; their authors often interjected wry editorial comments or morals. The recurring themes of heroism, true or unfaithful love, and violence illuminate the popular taste of the day.

The printed broadside ballad tradition itself survived until the early twentieth century in the form of postcard-sized cards containing the printed lyrics to popular narrative or "event" songs. These were peddled by full-time musicians who, like Dick Burnett of Monticello, Kentucky, were often blind men unable to support themselves any other way. Before the advent of the phonograph record, these cards enabled listeners to learn the words to songs that they heard and liked. In fact, old-timers around the Big South Fork used the word *ballad* (or *ballet*) not in reference to the song itself, but to the song lyrics in printed form.

The area's folksong repertoire included in addition to remnants of these ballad traditions many different kinds of traditional songs: love songs, courting songs, children's songs and singing games, songs describing funny or exaggerated incidents, and songs about animals who sometimes possess human characteristics. Much of this material was published in collections of American traditional songs, but some items may well be of local origin. Except for songs about hunting, songs dealing with work-related activities were curiously absent. Occupational folksongs are an important traditional genre, but they did not appear to have been common in the Big South area, even in the coal mining sections of Scott and McCreary Counties. Tom Lowery's "Little David Blues," written during the Wilder-Davidson strike of the early 1930s, was the exception rather than the rule. The most knowledgeable area musicians said that they did not recall hearing songs about coal mining before the Merle Travis radio hits "Dark as a Dungeon" and "Sixteen Tons" came out during the 1950s.

Before the development of sound recording, people made music for themselves, just as they embraced self-sufficiency in other respects. The songs described here were an important form of leisure-time entertainment, and they helped relieve the monotony of physical labor, housework, travel, and the pangs of loneliness. The ballads, in fact, accomplished the same basic function that television fills today, providing melodrama and a passive sort of entertainment for the listeners. Jean Ritchie's autobiography, *Singing Family of the Cumberlands* (1955), describes the important place traditional songs held in family life before radio and television arrived.

Ballad singers sang alone without instrumental accompaniment. Ballads often have a haunting, plaintive sound because they are based on modal scales that do not correspond to modern major and minor scales. Consequently, modern systems of harmony are not applicable, and fretted instruments such as the guitar, which are designed on the principle of an equal distance between all whole-step intervals, simply do not sound right accompanying the modal ballads. The classic ballad-singing style itself is generally stark but discretely embellished by vibrato and grace notes. Delta Hicks sang ballads with a conspicuous lack of emotion, even during dramatic passages, so that the song itself rather than the singer occupied the spotlight. Although ballad singers may use vocal style effectively to set a mood, the subtlety and restraint of the singing reinforce the sense of emotional distance created by balladry's third-person narratives.

Unfortunately, the Big South Fork's early ballad and folksong traditions were virtually extinct in the late 1970s. Aside from Fentress County's exceptional Hicks family with their large repertoire of ballads and songs handed down for at least four generations, there were only a few individuals who could still recall and sing any of this material. The area's younger musicians did not appear to be interested in learning and singing these songs. Ballads probably were passing out of vogue even before the turn of the century, losing ground to the wave of shorter, sentimental material so popular at that time. These new songs called for musical instruments and harmony. "The Pale Wildwood Flower," "The Letter Edged in Black,"

"The Little Rosewood Casket," and other popular songs of their kind were recorded by the Carter Family and other "old-time" or "hillbilly" performers in the late 1920s and early 1930s. They have become folksongs today, but in their heyday they represented popular culture displacing an older body of folk material just as they themselves later bowed to changing taste in popular music.

INSTRUMENTAL MUSIC

Before the turn of the century, the fiddle and the five-string banjo were the principal instruments played in the Big South Fork area. The guitar was not played locally until after 1910 and remained only a secondary instrument for old-time musicians. Another bluegrass instrument, the mandolin, appeared in the area as recently as the 1940s. The dulcimer, which is popularly associated with Appalachian music, was unfamiliar to most of the local old-time musicians. The dulcimer was known in Wayne County, and one Fentress County family brought an instrument from Claiborne County, Tennessee. Those familiar with the dulcimer agreed that it was used chiefly in playing sacred music. The harmonica, or "French Harp," was popular in the past, and people also played Jew's harps and other novelty instruments purchased from mail-order houses or from peddlers. Homemade flutes and whistles were fashioned from cane or bark cylinders. But traditional instrumental music in the Big South Fork is largely the music of the fiddle and the banjo.

The Fiddle. The fiddle was used in the British Isles and the American colonies before the Big South Fork region was settled, so the earliest Euro-American settlers probably brought it into the region. It remained the fundamental instrument, next to which the banjo was of secondary importance and served mainly for accompaniment. In the 1970s, the fiddle repertoire (i.e., items still identified as "old-time fiddle tunes" even when played on another instrument) formed the Big South Fork's second major category of folk music. Like folksong, this instrumental music was a composite: it included ancient Celtic airs (e.g., "Soldier's Joy," "Billy in the Lowground," "Rocky Road to Dublin," and "Devil's Dream"), melodies that originated on the Appalachian frontier (e.g., "Cumberland Gap" and "Sally Goodin"), minstrel show numbers (e.g., "Arkansas Traveler," "Turkey in the Straw," and "Listen to the Mockingbird"), and popular tunes of the early twentieth century (e.g., "Down Yonder" and "Chicken Reel").

Breakdowns or reels made up the standard part of the local fiddle repertoire. Breakdowns are fast dance tunes played in two-four or four-four time, the sort of tunes associated with popular images of mountain fiddle music. Many of these pieces are quite old, with popular counterparts in the British Isles. Their titles are often obscure and may vary from place to place, or even from performer to performer. Titles had changed through time, according to information supplied by older musicians. Lyrics to quite a few numbers survived and sometimes shed light on the meanings of the titles. However, it is impossible to know whether the words were original or composed later to fit an instrumental tune. There are undoubtedly instances of both.

Other fiddle pieces included waltzes (slow-to-moderate tempo dance tunes in three-four time) and hornpipes, the sprightly tunes that originally accompanied a kind of solo dance brought to America in the eighteenth century. The hornpipe tunes survived even though the dance was forgotten; they were usually played fast like breakdowns.

Some fiddle pieces were not dance tunes at all but were performed as solos. These tunes contain rhythmic intricacies and modal elements that made them unsuited to accompaniment. These numbers were played between dance sets to give the dancers a break and to allow the fiddler to demonstrate his skill. "Bonaparte's Retreat" was probably the most popular survivor of this idiom.

Most fiddle tunes consist of two strains of equal length: a high-pitched part sometimes called the "fine" and a low part known as the "coarse." In performance, each part is repeated, but the structure of repeats varies from one performer to another. Most tunes begin with the fine and end on the coarse and are played over and over for as long as the dance demands or until the musicians give out. Some tunes, such as "Bonaparte's Retreat," have three parts repeated in this manner.

Big South Fork fiddlers played in various keys, with the most common keys being D, G, and A, followed by C and F. Fiddlers would occasionally use E and B-flat. Tunes tended to be fixed in certain keys: "Soldier's Joy," for example, was always played in D; "Old Joe Clark" in A; "Tennessee Wagoner" in D. Certain breakdowns like "Fire on the Mountain" and "Orange Blossom Special" rock back and forth between two keys. Alternate tunings ("round keys") in which the four open strings sound a chord are essential to some breakdowns.

Fiddles were precious heirlooms around the Big South Fork, and every old, well-played fiddle in the area had at least several stories attached to it. In the late 1970s, local musicians were still playing on some very old handmade fiddles. In the days before mail-order or store-bought instruments became easy to obtain, fiddles must have been even more cherished than in the twentieth century. The fiddle was the most difficult stringed instrument to make, but the Big South Fork had at least one well-known fiddle maker, Hiram Sharp (1885–1976), who lived in Norma in Scott County.

Fiddle-playing style is a highly idiosyncratic matter, and every good fiddler tries to cultivate a distinct sound and technique. Style tends to be transmitted through personal contact and imitation, usually between parent and child, but occasionally between an outstanding local fiddler and an eager young protégé. Fiddling, like other forms of musical expertise, has been a family tradition for the most part, and certain Big South Fork families like the Hickses, Sharps, and Davenports had longstanding reputations for producing good musicians.

In spite of individual variation among fiddlers, some generalizations about regional style are still possible. Local musicians themselves recognized two distinct patterns. In the common old-time hoedown or jig style, the fiddler might hold the instrument under his chin in the typical violin fashion or play with its bottom resting down against the ribs. The bow might be grasped at the frog or held by the shaft. The nonstandard placement of the fiddle and bowing style retain the practice used by European elite musicians of the seventeenth century. The hoedown fiddler relies on short bow strokes embellished by frequent "digs" in which the upward accentuation of a certain note is produced by applying pressure on the bow as it travels across the string. "Double-noting," in which two adjacent strings are played simultaneously to produce a drone effect, also embellishes the hoedown style. Some fiddlers, after modifying the bridge of the instrument, even employ "triple-noting."

Another manner of playing, the "smooth" style, was popularized locally by Leonard Rutherford (circa 1900–1954), a well-known Monticello musician identified by many as the region's virtuoso fiddler. Exactly where Rutherford learned the style remains unclear. In smooth fiddling, the instrument and bow are almost invariably held in the conventional violin manner. The whole bow, manipulated in slow, smooth strokes, produces a legato effect. Other technical hallmarks of this style include glides, vibrato, slurred notes, and little "double-noting." Clyde Davenport of Wayne County, Kentucky, was still performing this style at the end of the twentieth century.

Because fiddle music was an integral part of folk dancing, and because it seemed to encourage revelry, the fiddle was condemned as "the devil's instrument" during the wave of religious fervor that swept the country in the early nineteenth century. Its notoriety lingered on around the Big South Fork in conspicuous ways: in the old simile "as thick as fiddlers in Hell," in the disapproval of square dancing that persisted in some quarters, and in conservative churches' ban on musical instruments in their services. These sentiments drew on a well-established body of European folk belief connecting the fiddle with the devil. In some slyly self-conscious ways, local fiddlers maintained the tradition themselves, through the high-spirited revelry suggested by the titles of such tunes as "Devil's Dream," "Hell's Broke Loose in Georgia," or "Dance All Night with a Bottle in My Hand." The custom of putting a few sets of rattlesnake rattles inside the fiddle to keep the sound box free of cobwebs may have a related symbolic meaning.

The Banjo. Exactly when the five-string banjo entered the Big South Fork region is unclear. It assuredly must have been present by the 1870s and it may predate the Civil War. The instrument has African origins and was used by slaves in the Southeast as early as the 1750s (Epstein 1975). As African Americans became acculturated, they adapted their instrument to play Anglo American folk dance music. The Americanized banjo began to be used to accompany the fiddle. By the 1830s, a fretless model that otherwise resembled the modern instrument had evolved, and the number of strings—four melody strings plus a drone string running halfway up the neck—was standardized. Popularized by the minstrel shows as part of their burlesque of plantation life, the banjo spread among white musicians at the same time African Americans were rejecting this artifact of their heritage.

In the Appalachian region, musicians discovered that the fretless five-string banjo was well suited to playing the old modal melodies that survived in many of their songs and fiddle tunes. A number of open banjo tunings devised to facilitate the playing of certain tunes were used by Dee Hicks and other old-time banjo pickers around the Big South Fork. Homemade instruments generally were made without frets, partly because of tradition and their suitability for modal music and partly because it was difficult to install the frets properly. However, fretted banjos became universal when mail-order and store-bought instruments replaced homemade ones. Frets permitted greater accuracy in noting the instrument and made possible both the playing of chords and the playing of melody lines farther up the neck of the instrument. This innovation enhanced the development of the familiar Earl Scruggs or bluegrass three-finger banjo picking.

By the 1970s, distinctive nineteenth-century methods of banjo playing were the subject of renewed interest among fans of old-time music. The old minstrel show frailing or clawhammer style (sometimes called "knocking it" by Big South Fork musicians) was probably derived from the African American banjo tradition. In this style of playing, the right hand functions as one rigid unit, with the thumb and index finger held in a claw position. Melody strings are sounded with the index finger as the hand moves downward across the strings, and the thumb plucks the drone string as the hand moves back up on the following offbeat. Bailey (1972) saw an African influence in the inherent syncopation common to this manner of playing. This banjo style no longer survives in the Big South Fork area, although the parents of Dee Hicks's generation did play in this fashion. The prevalent old-time banjo style in the area became two-finger picking involving the right thumb and index finger, used in a manner similar to two-finger banjo styles that have been recorded in western North Carolina. The index finger picks out the melody, punctuating it with rhythmic downward brushes across the lower strings, while the thumb continues to sound the drone string on the accompanying offbeat and occasionally drops down to play a "drop thumb" lick on the second or third string. No one knew when and how this two-finger style came to replace the clawhammer style in the Big South Fork.

Banjo picking, like fiddling, is very idiosyncratic, and individual players have their own unique technical variations even if they all follow the same basic pattern. Drawing on the simpler aesthetic of an earlier time, the understated playing of the Big South Fork's old-time banjo pickers contrasted sharply with the flashy exhibitionistic "virtuosity" of the popular bluegrass banjo style.

Played together, the fiddle and the banjo were the foundation for the latter-day string band that developed after the guitar and other instruments appeared in the Big South Fork area around 1910. But into the early twentieth century, "string band" usually meant fiddle and banjo. In one playing style, the banjo closely followed the fiddle line, playing practically in unison with the fiddle. The other style used the banjo more as a rhythmic accompaniment.

SOME BIG SOUTH FORK MUSICIANS

These sketches describe some of the most influential musicians of the preceding generation as well as individuals whose music was recorded during the folklife survey project. All of these performers acquired their instrumental skills through imitation and association with other musicians. Music has always been very much a family tradition, and most of these musicians attributed their technique to a parent or another close relative. They learned their material orally with minimal reliance on written sources. Secular music has always been played by ear, regardless of whether the performer learned a tune firsthand, from the radio, or from a phonograph record. All of these had been important sources of material for the generation of musicians carrying on old-time performance traditions in 1979.

Every member of the culture experienced and related to music to some extent, but those who demonstrated greater talent and musical propensities became specialists who were depended upon to perform whenever the situation required it. Nevertheless, musicianship was only rarely a full-time specialty around the area. A talented performer would usually be compensated in some manner for musical services but would at the same time be expected to be productive at everyday tasks. Traditionally, the only individuals who became full-time musicians did so out of necessity, as did Dick Burnett of Monticello, Kentucky.

Dick Burnett and Leonard Rutherford. The traveling musician Dick Burnett and his protégé Leonard Rutherford were remembered by every old-time musician in the area and by a good many other residents as well. Burnett was born at Elk Spring Valley near Monticello, Kentucky, in 1883. At the age of seven, he began picking out religious songs on the dulcimer and soon learned to play the banjo, his principal instrument, as well as fiddle, guitar, harmonica, and accordion—a total of thirteen instruments in all (Wolfe 1974).

Burnett was blinded in 1907 at the age of twenty-four, the victim of an armed robbery in Stearns, Kentucky, and that misfortune forced him to turn to music professionally. By 1909, he was traveling and performing throughout the area, selling postcard-sized "ballets" with the words to some of his songs printed on them. One of these, "The Song of the Orphan Boy," recounted the incident in which he lost his sight. Sometime later, he published and sold copies of a little songbook containing the lyrics to six of his most popular numbers. He is said to have been quite a showman, performing card tricks and other novelties in addition to his musicianship.

Around 1914, Burnett adopted a young orphan who was to become his traveling companion and playing partner for the next thirty-five years. Leonard Rutherford was born in Somerset, Kentucky, about 1900. Dick Burnett had known his family and took the boy in after his parents died; Leonard was thirteen or fourteen at the time. Leonard helped Dick find his way around, and he later drove the car that Burnett bought for them to travel in (Wolfe 1974). In the meantime, Dick taught Leonard what he knew about music, and Leonard Rutherford grew up to become the most accomplished and respected fiddle player in the area.

Burnett and Rutherford traveled a circuit through Kentucky, Tennessee, Virginia, and West Virginia. They sometimes played as far south as Georgia and Florida and as far north as Ohio and Indiana. They performed at places and events wherever people congregated: in coal camps, at local fairs, and at county court days. Between 1926 and 1930, they recorded a number of songs for the Columbia, Gennett, and Brunswick record companies in Atlanta and in Richmond, Indiana. They apparently made a good income from the record sales and from the spare coins their listeners would contribute.

Alone, with Rutherford, or sometimes in the company of other musicians, Dick Burnett became a fixture in the towns surrounding the Big South Fork. Dee and Delta Hicks, Ralph and Clyde Troxell, and other area musicians vividly recalled him from the years between 1915 and 1950, playing on street corners or on the county courthouse lawns in Monticello, Jamestown, Oneida, or Huntsville, or at fairs in Deer Lodge, Somerset, or London, Kentucky. He wore a metal cup strapped to his leg for people to drop their coins in, and he shook his leg and rattled the cup whenever he wanted someone to throw in more money.

Burnett and Rutherford stopped performing in the early 1950s shortly before Rutherford died. Burnett dropped from sight until 1973, when Doyle Jones of WCLC radio in Jamestown rediscovered him and introduced him to Charles K. Wolfe, an authority on old-time music. Wolfe and Becky Morse, a student from Western Kentucky University, visited and interviewed Burnett a number of times before his death in 1977. Rounder Records (#1004) reissued sixteen Burnett and Rutherford recordings in 1974 with extensive notes by Wolfe (1974).

Burnett and Rutherford had a strong influence on Big South Fork musicians. During the years when they were actively performing, Burnett was the most visible musician in the area, and Rutherford was the most admired and respected. Dee Hicks once remarked: "Dick Burnett was the first singer that ever was around here," a significant observation when his meaning becomes clear. Burnett was the first musician in the area who was recognized as a full-time professional specialist, rather than as a community member who played or sang but followed a more conventional livelihood. Dick Burnett's career spanned the transition of old-time music from a folk tradition to a commercial product.

The recordings Burnett and Rutherford made in the late 1920s are classic examples of old-time country music, and their technical musicianship is impressive even today. Their close unison fiddle and banjo playing documents the traditional ensemble manner in which these instruments were played. Separately, Burnett played a fast-driving banjo in pure Appalachian frailing style and Rutherford's exceptionally smooth fiddling, with its slides and occasionally heavy syncopation, set a standard that other fiddlers still emulated fifty years later. Through their live performances and recordings, Burnett and Rutherford documented traditional fiddle tunes and popular songs of the late nineteenth and early twentieth centuries that already were part of the local folk heritage. They also recorded Burnett's own compositions and tunes learned from other musicians while traveling. They were a link between the musically active African American population around Monticello and white musicians. Among the musicians Burnett remembered were Bled Coffee, an African American fiddler who lived through the Civil War, and Shell Coffee, a banjo picker, probably Bled's grandson. The Bertrams were another African American family in Monticello who produced several musicians; Cooge and Andy Bertram played throughout the area in the 1920s and 1930s. One of the most popular Burnett and Rutherford tunes, "Lost John," was learned from a black musician.

W. L. Gregory and Clyde Davenport. Many people around Wayne County would consider either W. L. Gregory or Clyde Davenport to be Leonard Rutherford's successor as the premier fiddler of the region. Gregory, a Monticello veterinarian, sounded a lot like Rutherford, from whom he learned his technique. Gregory was born in 1905 at Rockybranch in Wayne County. Neither of his parents were musicians, but when he was about twelve years old he learned to play the fiddle and the banjo, using homemade instruments. He met and began playing with Leonard Rutherford in 1923, absorbing much of Rutherford's style and repertoire. Gregory also traveled with Dick Burnett for a while around 1929 and 1930, sometimes filling in for Rutherford.

W. L. Gregory's fiddling can be heard on the Davis Unlimited album *Monticello: Tough Mountain Music from Southern Kentucky* (DU 33014), accompanied by Clyde Davenport on banjo and his grandson Gary Gregory on guitar. Gregory and Davenport expertly re-created the old-time fiddle and banjo sound that was characteristic of Burnett and Rutherford's style. The record also spotlights Gregory's own unique banjo style on three tunes. One of these was played with a slide apparently of his own invention. Gregory also used unusual banjo tunings: he employed a key of B tuning on one cut and an F tuning on another.

Unfortunately, Clyde Davenport's fiddling is not featured on the *Monticello* album. Davenport was born at Mt. Pisgah in Wayne County about 1920 and later lived in Monticello. He began playing the fiddle at the age of nine, and the banjo when he was sixteen. Like Gregory, Davenport also learned to play on homemade instruments. Like many natives of the Big South Fork area, he later migrated to Muncie, Indiana, and performed on the radio during the years he lived there. After returning to Monticello, Davenport continued performing what collector Bobby Fulcher thought might be the most extensive repertoire of any mountain fiddler. In 1977 Fulcher recorded Clyde Davenport's fiddle tunes for the Library of Congress Archives of Folk Culture and later produced an album, *Clyde Davenport. Clydeoscope. Rare and Beautiful Tunes from the Cumberland Plateau* (County Records 788).

Eldridge "Slim" Smith. Fiddler Eldridge "Slim" Smith was born in Oneida in 1906, and although his father played the banjo, Slim did not start seriously learning music until he was about twenty-four years old. His younger brothers "Tennessee" and "Smitty" were already experienced musicians. They had a fairly successful country-and-western recording career as the Smith Brothers during the 1930s and 1940s.

Slim's first tune was "Wink That Other Eye," which he learned off the radio from Uncle Jimmy Thompson, an early fiddler on the Grand Ole Opry. He eventually acquired a large repertoire of fiddle tunes from the radio, from records, and from other local fiddlers, and he began playing at square dances around the Big South Fork area in the 1930s. He also knew and played with Burnett and Rutherford when they came through the area. In 1951 he moved to Monticello, where he continued his acquaintance with Burnett, Rutherford, and other Monticello musicians until he returned to Oneida in 1975.

The Sharp Family. The Sharp Family, who migrated from Wayne County, Kentucky, to Fentress County, Tennessee, was an important musical family in the Big South Fork area. As his nickname suggests, John Gibson "Fiddlin' John" Sharp (1894–1965) was one of the better-known local fiddlers during his lifetime. His offspring contributed notably to the perpetuation of the area's traditional music, particularly the old-time fiddle tunes. Fiddlin' John Sharp grew up on Langham Branch near Mt. Pisgah. His father, Ewell Sharp, played the fiddle and appears to have been the source for most of John Sharp's music. Two of John's brothers, Albert and Hugh, played the banjo. John Sharp worked for the Stearns Company. He married Bonnie Wood (b. 1895) and they had eight children. The Sharps moved to Fentress County about 1932 and settled in the vicinity of what is now Pickett State Park. From 1935 until World War II, Sharp, daughter Evelyn Sharp Conatser, and a banjo picker named Sherman "Red" Morris performed together as the Rock Creek Ramblers at square dances and musical events all over the area. John Sharp played with a fast, fiery combination of smoothness and drive and had a distinctive repertoire of tunes that he seldom referred to by name. Besides the fiddle, John Sharp also played the banjo, guitar, piano, harmonica, and Jew's harp. Most of his children also became musicians: Bonnie played harmonica, Evelyn the guitar and fiddle, and Opal Sharp Wright, the banjo. Son Paul Sharp became an accomplished fiddler with a sound much like his father's. Eugene Sharp played guitar and sang traditional and religious songs, while Junior Sharp played guitar with a country band. The Sharp Family Reunion, traditionally held Labor Day weekend at Pickett State Park, became locally renowned for the music that it featured and grew into the Labor Day Old-Time Music Festival at Pickett State Park.

Clyde and Ralph Troxell. Brothers Clyde Troxell (b. 1911) and Ralph Troxell (b. 1920), who lived near Rockybranch, Kentucky, belonged to another Wayne County musical family with roots in the Big South Fork area. Clyde played old-time banjo and also sang and played the guitar. Fiddler Ralph performed as part of the Rocky Toppers, the area's last old-time square-dance band, with his neighbors Ray and Louella Sharp Souders. (Louella's father was Fiddlin' John Sharp's brother Hugh.)

The Troxell brothers inherited a musical heritage from both sides of the family. Ralph and Clyde's father, Jasper Troxell (1887–1972), was a banjo picker and fiddler who came from what is now McCreary County. He married Anna Davenport (b. 1889), who grew up near Bell Farm. "Aunt Annie" Troxell's grandfather Lewis Menifee was a singing-school teacher. As a girl, Anna Davenport Troxell learned to read shape-note music and play the organ. Her father, Lewis Albert "Al" Davenport, played the fiddle, banjo, and guitar. According to Clyde, "He was the first guitar player . . . that ever was in this country." Clyde Troxell took up the banjo when he was about twelve years old, learning from his father. He developed a variation of the two-finger picking technique common to the Big South Fork area, playing a number of his father's tunes in this old-time mountain banjo playing style. Guitars were not common in the area while Clyde was growing up. He got his first guitar at sixteen or seventeen as a premium on a Lee Manufacturing Company order that his mother got together from the neighborhood.

There were a lot of musicians in the community when Clyde was learning to play; he played with the Gregorys, Bells, and with Fiddlin' John Sharp. Ralph, being younger, associated with a different set of local musicians. Ralph learned the fiddle from his father, and when he was about thirteen a teacher at Parmleysville, Col. M. W. Peters, gave him a guitar. He remembers that it was "Hawaiian" with painted decorations. Ralph Troxell's repertoire included the standard square-dance numbers popular around the Big South Fork area, but also hornpipes and some of the intricate old solo fiddle airs. Clyde Troxell and the Rocky Toppers can be heard on the album *Getting' Up the Stairs. Traditional Music from the Cumberland Plateau, Volume I* (County Records 786).

Virgil Anderson. Virgil Anderson, Ralph and Clyde Troxell's brother-in-law, was an adept banjo picker and singer of old-time songs from both traditional and recorded sources. He learned some tunes from his wife, Mabel, who also played banjo, and from her grandfather Al Davenport. He also was known as a storyteller, buck dancer, and generally colorful character around the Rockybranch area. He was recorded in the first of a series of record albums featuring music from the upper Cumberland Plateau, *Virgil Anderson . . . On the Tennessee Line* (County Records 777).

The Hicks Family. The Hicks Family of Fentress County, Tennessee, enjoyed a long-standing local reputation as musicians and storytellers, and their treasury of ballads and songs is one of the Big South Fork's most noteworthy cultural resources. Dee and Delta Hicks received national recognition in the United States and Canada for their ballad singing; Dee's brother Joe was also a musician. Joe Hicks (b. 1899) and Dee Hicks (b. 1906), sons of Daniel Hicks, were born at the old Hicks homestead on Mary's Point, at the confluence of Crooked Creek and Clear Fork near Peters Bridge. According to family tradition, the Hicks family originally came from North Carolina, and Daniel's was the third generation that lived in the Big South Fork area.

Daniel "Dan'l" Hicks was a well-known singer and musician in his day. Old-timers around Fentress County remembered him vividly as a colorful figure. Originally a hunter and trapper, Dan'l turned to farming around 1900, after the area's large game had been almost entirely depleted. A clever, energetic man who played both fiddle and banjo, Dan'l, like most of his contemporaries, had little formal education, but he supposedly was remarkably well read for the time and for the area. He seems even then to have appreciated his family's musical heritage and tried to pass on to his children many of the old ballads and songs that had been handed down since at least their great-grandparents' time. He was always ready to entertain anybody who showed up at the Hicks home. With Dee accompanying him on the banjo, Dan'l fiddled all around this part of Fentress County and nearby sections of Morgan County. They played at the fair in Deer Lodge, and Dee recalled how they won a contest at Burrville once with a rendition of "Turkey in the Straw."

Joe and Dee both learned the two-finger banjo style from their father, and from cousins Ben Hicks and Joe Wheeler Gentry. Ben Hicks was the source of Dee's "Lost Gander" piece; according to Dee, Ben learned it somewhere from an African American banjo player. Dee Hicks memorized most, but not all, of Dan'l's songs by ear, because they never had been written down. Joe also learned some of his father's repertoire, as well as picking up songs from the "ballet" cards peddled by local performers like Burnett and Rutherford; he even composed a few of his own. After moving to Armathwaite, Joe played his banjo for square dances in Allardt. Another Hicks brother, Besford, also became an accomplished singer, and their sister Lou Cromwell, a teacher, studied the old family ballads to learn the meanings of some of the archaic expressions they contained.

A close association developed between the Hickses and the Len Winningham family, who moved from Morgan County into Fentress and settled in the neighborhood around the Old Barger (now Mt. Pleasant) Baptist Church near Allardt. The Winninghams were a musical family like the Hickses. They were united by several marriages: Dee Hicks married Len's daughter Delta (b. 1910), Joe's first wife was her half sister, and Dee and Joe's sister Nancy married another Winningham relative. Delta brought a number of old ballads and songs that she had learned from her mother and sisters into the Hicks repertoire, which was vast, encompassing hundreds of different pieces representing a variety of traditional genres. From the 1920s and 1930s onward, it included country songs learned from records, radio, and television.

Bobby Fulcher of the Tennessee Department of Conservation worked with the Hicks family for a number of years and recorded between two and three hundred of their songs for the Library of Congress and the Tennessee State Library and Archives. A sample can be heard on *Dee and Delta Hicks. Ballads and Banjo Music from the Tennessee Cumberland Plateau* (County 789). *The Hicks Family, A Cumberland Singing Tradition* (Tennessee Folklore Society TFS 104) includes selections by Dee Hicks, Delta Hicks, their daughter Lily Mae Hicks, Joe Hicks, Nancy Hicks Winningham, and Besford Hicks and his family.

Joe Wheeler Gentry. Joe Wheeler Gentry was a local legend in his own time. The son of fiddler Jesse "Whitehead" Gentry and Lissie Hicks, Dan'l's sister, he was born around 1895 under a rock shelter on Clear Fork and grew up near Allardt. Old-time musicians judge him to have been the best old-time banjo picker the Big South Fork area ever produced. He reputedly could play both right- and left-handed, and he could play in both the frailing and two-finger picking styles. "Whitehead" and Joe Wheeler Gentry were well known for their musical talent around Fentress and Morgan Counties during the early 1900s. They played at dances for the English at Rugby, for the Germans at Allardt, and at Deer Lodge.

Joe Beaty. Recollections of Joe Wheeler Gentry came from Joe Beaty of Grimsley, another well-known old-time banjo player in Fentress County. Joe Beaty was born in 1905 in the Banner Springs vicinity of Fentress County. Joe's mother played the fiddle, and her uncles John Hogue and Jim Hogue were accomplished fiddlers also. Joe's father played the Jew's harp. When he was nine years old, as Joe tells it, his sister got him a banjo. "She give four dollars and seventy-five cents for it. That was a good banjo then, though. It had eight brackets. I played it 'til I plumb wore it out, 'til it plumb wore me out!" Joe learned most of his tunes from Joe Wheeler Gentry, who was his childhood friend even though he was about ten years older than Joe Beaty. He learned other tunes from another neighborhood friend, banjo player Henry Hicks, who was the son of fiddler Frank Hicks and his wife, Sena Adkins. Joe was also well acquainted with the Dan'l Hicks family, who were somehow related to Frank and Henry. Joe Beaty developed a heavily rhythmic two-finger style. His son David also learned to play the banjo and became a very good bluegrass-style player.

Harold Stanley. Harold Stanley (b. 1922) came from a distinguished musical background. His grandfather was a fiddler, and his father, Elmer Stanley, and uncle Fred Stanley were well-known musicians around the Big South Fork area. Elmer Stanley, who was born near Elgin in Scott County and later moved to Fentress County, played the fiddle and is credited as the source of Dick Burnett's popular tune "Sleeping Lulu." Fred Stanley of Stearns, Kentucky, played the banjo and guitar and performed and recorded with Bert Layne, Clayton McMichen, and the Skillet Lickers in the early 1930s.

Harold Stanley started playing the fiddle when he was thirteen. He learned some material from his father and his uncle, but like other aspiring young musicians of the period, he also learned songs from radio performances by Jimmie Rodgers, the Carter Family, and other popular artists. Clayton McMichen's records were an important influence on his developing style. Harold and Jamestown musician Doyle Jones began appearing on WHUB radio in Cookeville during the summer of 1940. As "Red" Stanley, Harold went on to perform and record with major country and bluegrass performers, including Bill Monroe and Ralph and Carter Stanley (no relation to Harold). He retired from playing professionally in 1964 and returned to Fentress County to farm.

Stanley's exceptional fiddle style borrowed elements from old-time hoedown fiddling, western swing, and even classical violin, all acquired from years of playing, practice, and contact with a variety of fiddlers and styles during his professional career.

Ralph Weaver and Rowe Parker. In 1979 Ralph Weaver and Rowe Parker were keeping the traditional Saturday night musical "get-together" alive in the Stockton section of Fentress County, with Rowe playing the bass fiddle and sons Jim Weaver and David and Boyd Parker joining in on guitar and sometimes on fiddle. The Saturday night sessions might attract a dozen friends and relatives and last until 1:00 or 2:00 A.M.

Fiddler Ralph Weaver was born in Union County, Tennessee, in 1919; his family moved to Fentress County in 1932. His mother played the fiddle and his father played fiddle and banjo, so Ralph and his two brothers grew up in a musical household. They later formed a string band and played around East Tennessee. He developed a hard-driving hoedown style and a repertoire so extensive that he rarely would repeat a tune during an evening of music making.

Rowe Parker's parents originally came from Claiborne County. They were not musicians, but Rowe and his brother got a guitar as a Lee Manufacturing Company premium and learned to play it. Rowe Parker also was one of the few dulcimer players in the Big South Fork area. His family owned a dulcimer made by Rowe's grandfather, Daniel Thomas, a preacher and music teacher in Claiborne County. As children, Rowe and his sister learned to play hymns on it.

Folk Dance

In many neighborhoods, dances were a major social function. Of course, the more conservative church members in rural settlements frowned upon dancing, but most of the larger communities like Jamestown and Allardt had dance halls. The school building or individual homes might be used for dances in smaller communities. Dances were held to celebrate holidays and other special occasions, and they often provided entertainment at the end of a "working." In some communities dances were held for their own sake, usually each Saturday night.

Dances became less frequent in the 1930s. Radio was a main contributor to their demise, but tales of drinking and violence at dances, not without basis in fact, also discouraged participation. World War II dealt the final blow: the absence of so many young men effectively brought an end to a tradition already in decline. Jamestown continued to host street dances in conjunction with Fentress County's annual Chicken Festivals and Bean Festivals, but these dances had ended by the 1960s. Many folklife survey interviewees attributed the dying interest in square dancing and old-time music to television, but a small group of enthusiasts had kept Appalachian square dancing alive around Jamestown and Monticello. Jamestown also had a Western square-dance group, but it represented another style not derived from local tradition.

SQUARE DANCING

Like folk music, folk dance in the Big South Fork area can be viewed as the product of interplay between folk culture and elite or popular culture. Appalachian square dance developed out of traditional English country dance in which the couples faced each other in two long parallel lines, a form that still survives in figures like the Virginia Reel. After being transformed into the quadrille (four couple "square") in late-seventeenth-century France, the "new" dances were reintroduced to England and crossed the Atlantic with the southern planters. From the plantation setting, quadrille dancing eventually was reabsorbed by folk culture. Damon (1952) believes that square-dance calling appeared sometime after the War of 1812, and that the familiar practice of "singing" the calls emerged during the 1870s. The French association survives in such terms for square-dance figures as allemande, promenade, sashay, and do-si-do.

Square-dance calling is an art in itself, and it is as essential to the dance as the music. The caller, who almost universally has been male, serves as master of ceremonies and maintains a great responsibility for the enjoyment of all involved, whether they be dancers, musicians, or onlookers. He must know the calls and popular dance figures thoroughly and must also be able to fit calls and dance movements to the musical phrases. The caller must be familiar with participants' tastes: the figures dancers like to do, the tunes musicians like to play, the favorites everyone likes to hear. Pacing is all-important. The caller must keep the dance running long enough for it to be exhilarating, but not so long that either dancers or musicians tire out. He should be imaginative, be able to add the right amount of variety, and be able to introduce new movements he has observed. Nothing is worse than a caller who does the same thing over and over.

Square-dance calls can take two forms. The simplest are the short, prompting calls like "Circle left," "Swing your partner," or "Do-si-do," which are interjected at the end of a musical phrase. These set up the figure to begin on the first beat of the next phrase. The long, singing call transcends mere instruction. Midway between a song and a chant, it is a rhyme timed to fit the music and is entertaining in its own right.

The following example of a singing call comes from Elmer Hurst, a Jamestown square dancer and caller who learned it from his father. Each stanza contains the directions for a different dance figure. The ones included here are all standards, and a detailed explanation of their execution can be found in Smith (1955) or other sources on Appalachian square dancing.

> *Get your partner and get them on the floor!*
>
> *Lady on the right and gent on the left, All join hands and Circle to the Left,*
> *Break and swing your corner lady, Then swing your own partner and circle four,*
> *Then do-si the ladies, Swing your partner and promenade!*
>
> *First couple out with Right Hands 'Cross, Then left and back—I told you wrong!*
> *You swing my partner and I swing yours, Swing your own partner and circle four,*
> *Do-si the ladies, Then swing your partner and promenade!*
>
> *Second couple out with Four Hands Across, The ladies bow and the gents know how,*
> *You swing my partner and I swing yours, Then swing your own and circle four,*
> *Do-si the ladies, Then swing your partner and promenade!*
>
> *The next couple out and Cage the Bird with three hands around,*
> *The bird flew out and the crow flew in, The crow flew out and we are gone again,*
> *You swing my partner and I swing yours, Swing your own and promenade!*
>
> *Next couple out and do the Ocean Wave,*
> *The first couple through, Second couple through the same old trail,*
> *Swing your corner lady, Swing your own partner and circle four,*
> *Do-si the ladies, Then swing your partner and promenade!*
>
> *The next couple out with the Lady Around the Lady and the gent also,*
> *Now lady around the gent and the gent don't go.*
> *Swing your partner when you meet her and circle four,*
> *Do-si the ladies out on the floor, Then swing your partner and promenade home.*
>
> *Take her out and give her air. You know where and I don't care.*
> *That's all there is, there ain't no more!*

BUCK DANCING

Another type of folk dancing, buck dancing, has survived better than square dancing, perhaps because it depends less on cooperative activity and learning formal dance patterns. Buck dancing is the foot-stomping, jiglike style observable at any traditional music or bluegrass festival and it is relatively easy to learn. Music is its only essential. It requires neither a caller nor a minimum of four couples, nor cooperative involvement. It may be performed by couples or by two dancers of the same sex but is frequently performed solo. The style is highly individual and original even when two dancers perform together.

Buck dancing has antecedents in the buck-and-wing dancing of the nineteenth-century minstrel shows that evolved as a parody of African American dance. The name comes from two of their popular figures, the Buck Dance and the Pigeon Wing. Emery (1972) quotes sources that describe African Americans in the early nineteenth century dancing their distinct version of the Scots-Irish jig, along with figures that may have represented elements of African animal imitation dances that had survived in plantation slave culture.

Rural whites adopted the buck-and-wing from minstrel sources and also borrowed elements from juba dancing, another old slave tradition. Juba dancers would form a circle that might rotate or remain stationary while each individual in turn entered the circle to "strut his (or her) stuff" (Emery 1972).

Oral Tradition

Verbal lore in the Big South Fork area, like folk music and folk dance, has been affected by changes in social relations and by expanding opportunities for mainstream recreation. While county festivals and fairs and more recently the Pickett State Park Old Time Music Festival have nurtured traditional music and dance, storytelling had not found its way into those late-twentieth-century entertainment contexts. Until the recent popular revival of storytelling and emergence of professional tellers, some highly entertaining genres like riddles and Jack Tales were seldom heard around the Big South Fork. On the other hand, folk belief, haint tales, family anecdotes, and legends (developed from family anecdotes in many cases) continued to flourish because their content had social or psychological relevance and local meaning that transcended mere entertainment.

RIDDLES AND FOLKTALES

The verbal genres most in danger of becoming museum pieces or dying out altogether were some classic riddles from European tradition, old folktales with parallels in the wonder tales that the Grimm Brothers collected in Germany, traditional Appalachian Jack tales, and Irishman stories. Riddles and folktales collected in Appalachia (e.g., Roberts 1959, 1974) often preserve archaic forms of speech and cultural settings much as the Child ballads do. Their point of reference is timeless or in the distant past; they are not firmly rooted in local history and experience.

A few older residents offered isolated examples of these genres in passing, but they were not easily persuaded to search the recesses of their minds for additional items or to record them. A typical response to requests for more was: "My Dad used to tell those, and I learned them from him. But it's been a long time since I told any—I don't remember."

Before convenient transportation and access to mass media brought a wealth of new ways to spend leisure time, exchange of riddles and stories at social gatherings or within the family circle was a major form of entertainment. The old general stores were fine gathering places for premier storytellers and their audiences. With the disappearance of these natural contexts for sharing riddles and folktales, these genres were laid aside. Without being told, they cannot be kept alive.

IRISHMAN STORIES

Irishman stories were the Polish jokes of an earlier day. Roberts (1959) collected a large sample of Irishman stories in Leslie County, Kentucky. No large Irish migrant population ever settled in the Big South Fork area, so persistence of the Irishman as the butt of these jokes must be viewed purely as a matter of tradition in the Big South Fork context. The content of Irishman stories does, however, draw upon familiar aspects of work and technology that the naive Irishman misinterprets.

One man, who according to a neighbor used to be famous for entertaining with Irishman stories at social gatherings, offered two examples. The first was volunteered while he was describing his own work on construction crews. It points up relations between the master workman and helpers. The Irishman apprentice when asked how he liked his new job replied that he liked it fine: "All I have to do is mix the mortar and carry up the bricks, and he (the bricklayer) does all the work." When this man was asked for more Irishman stories, he told one about an Irishman who came along a road and saw two men using a crosscut saw. He stopped the men, took their saw, broke it in two, and gave each man half with the comment: "Now you won't have to fight over it." Although the storyteller claimed that he didn't tell Irishman stories any longer and could not remember any others, it is likely that appropriate contexts would have sparked his memory as in the case of the bricklayer story. But changing technology has made the content of many old Irishman stories as unfamiliar to an audience of young people as to the hypothetical Irishman; of course, the joke depends on the audience's knowledge.

GHOST LORE, ANECDOTES, AND LEGENDS

Ghost lore, labeled "haint tales" in Big South Fork parlance, is one genre of traditional lore that has maintained its vitality. There is a high degree of consistency between recorded samples of ghost lore from the Big South Fork area (e.g., Howard 1981) and the material contained in Lynwood Montell's *Ghosts along the Cumberland* (1975). Road ghosts, mysterious sights and sounds encountered while traveling at night, haunted houses, and revenants laid to rest after their wishes are carried out figure heavily in these stories. They are often associated with familiar locations and are authenticated as actual experiences of the narrator or some relative or close friend of the narrator (cf. Montell 1975, 89–90). While describing mine disasters, murders, or deaths of relatives from natural causes, several people told of dreams, the appearance of apparitions, strange sounds, or other death omens associated with these events. Great psychological weight attaches to this death lore, and the related body of ghost lore assumes added importance as a result.

Because traditional motifs are made concrete through a context of local and personal experience, tellers and their audiences find it relatively easy to believe in ghosts if they are inclined to do so. Skeptics do not tell haint tales unless they are stories similar to items 447–57 recorded by Montell (1975, 194–99). In these stories, the source of a mysterious sound or sight is first thought to be supernatural, but the story ends on a humorous note with an explanation of the natural cause. An excellent example related by a former resident of the No Business Creek settlement is the story of the haint in a rock house who turned out to be two billy goats locking horns in combat.

Legends and anecdotes also are firmly rooted in local places and local events. Legends have their origin in historical events; therefore, they begin as anecdotes. But through oral transmission certain facts are selected, recombined, and embellished or shaped by common folkloric motifs until the anecdote becomes a better-than-real story. Legends may be placed along a continuum from almost pure fantasy (stories of abduction and rescue similar to wonder tales) to almost factual legends (stories of outlaw heroes who lived in the area so recently that eyewitness accounts of their deeds are still available).

At the "fantasy" end of this continuum, for example, are two stories with parallel structure: "The Woman Kidnapped by an Ape" and "The Woman Kidnapped by Indians." In both stories the abducted woman leaves a trail to aid the party of rescuers headed by her husband. Despite the formulaic nature of these stories, however, they are told as accounts of true happenings; in the case of the ape story, the events were recalled from a turn-of-the-century newspaper account.

At the "factual" end of the continuum are stories of violence, murder, and outlawry. Examples based on actual events that occurred during the 1930s include accounts of the Zenith strike, the murder of Cleve Spradlin in McCreary County, and the saga of Jerome Boyatt. Each narrator who told about Jerome Boyatt, with the exception of one close relative, had been an eyewitness to some but not all of the events described. Collation of these several versions of the story following the methods employed by Montell in *The Saga of Coe Ridge* (1970) served to separate fact from the fiction that has embellished it during fifty years and elucidated the process of transforming anecdote into aesthetically satisfying legend (Howell 1983a).

FOLK BELIEF

Enumerated in previous sections of this report are beliefs and lore pertaining to the weather, to the Zodiac and moon signs, to folk medicine, and to the life events of birth, marriage, and death. These items and similar ones were collected in the 1970s from middle-aged interviewees who grew up hearing them, but these people typically placed some distance between themselves and such beliefs with comments like: "I've heard that one," or "My (older relative) used to say that. . . ." These people rarely interjected folk belief into their ordinary conversation about the weather, illness, or the like.

On the other hand, several older residents, without prompting, indicated they still employed folk beliefs as a guide to scheduling work, prognosticating the weather, warding off bad luck, and the like. They cited personal experiences or observations to support the validity of the beliefs they used. No one accepted the whole body of folk belief on any topic uncritically; items that had not been validated to one's personal satisfaction were accorded considerable skepticism. Thus, for many of the older Big South Fork residents, folk belief was still a living and useful body of tradition in the late 1970s.

SPEECH

The literature on Appalachian speech is extensive and ranges from popular lists of expressions published in tourist booklets or on restaurant place mats to highly technical studies of phonology prepared by linguists. Work by Wolfram and Christian (1976) brings together and augments data collected by professional linguists, much of it published in the dialectology journal *American Speech* (Berrey 1940; Carpenter 1933; Hall 1942; and Owens 1931). The Kentuckians Josiah Combs (1916, 1919, 1931) and James Still (1929, 1930) contributed important word lists to this literature. Ethnographies too numerous to mention also contain word lists or chapters on mountain speech.

While research on phonology, lexicon, and figures of speech has been extensive, less has been done in the way of discourse analysis of narrative, oratory, and informal conversation. Any one of these topics might occupy a linguist for years. Interviews taped during the folklife survey provide excellent samples of conversation and narrative; recorded sermons are a useful sample of that oratorical style. Although it was not possible to undertake linguistic analysis of this material during the folklife survey, an extensive body of data for future research has been assembled in sound recordings of more than seventy men and women ranging in age from late twenties through mid-nineties.

Although word lists are interesting, especially to newcomers or outsiders, they call attention to the quaint and the peculiar in mountain speech. Listening to recorded samples of conversation, storytelling, and preaching, one is struck by the forcefulness, clarity, and color of verbal expression. Some interviewees were taciturn and others loquacious, but virtually everyone seemed to forget that there was a tape recorder in the room once the interview preliminaries were over. These recordings capture the natural speech patterns extremely well and display the unique features of regional speech in their appropriate communication contexts.

Handcrafters

In the late 1970s handcrafting was widely practiced. The majority of crafters produced items for home use, made gifts for relatives, and occasionally sold items to neighbors, but many also attempted to develop a local market by advertising in classified circulars or placing signs on their property. The most common women's crafts were crocheting and quilting. Among the men, woodworking was a common skill, although most men engaged in kitchen cabinet building and general carpentry rather than making woodenware and traditional furniture.

Before Big South Fork tourism developed to any extent, craftspeople had very limited markets because the population of the immediate area was small and as a whole not able to afford many nonessential purchases. Compared to the number of individuals trying to market their products, there were few independently owned craft shops in the immediate vicinity of the Big South Fork. Craft shops located in more populous parts of East Tennessee and craft fairs provided additional retail outlets for a few highly skilled and enterprising persons who sought out such opportunities. But cooperative action had been most effective in improving the economic outlook for area craftspeople. Of the two craft cooperatives operating in the 1970s, Kentucky Hills Industries was the older and stronger.

KENTUCKY HILLS INDUSTRIES

Smith and Alma Ross of Pine Knot established Kentucky Hills Industries in 1946 to provide cash income for area residents. Through a career of teaching, organizing National Youth Administration work projects, and working for the Department of Agriculture in McCreary County, Ross became disturbed by the pattern of out-migration to northern and midwestern industrial centers. Although most residents owned their homes and grew their own food, they had a very difficult time acquiring needed cash. Mr. Ross determined that lack of ability to earn needed cash within the local economy was a major factor responsible for migration.

In their travels throughout the area, the Rosses had met a number of highly skilled traditional craftspeople. These older individuals became the core of the cooperative and taught their skills to younger craftspeople on a one-to-one basis. Among the early cooperative members was Lillie Elkins, basket maker. Mrs. Elkins already had begun to market her baskets by peddling them through the hills from Ohio to Tennessee. The Rosses also discovered the woodworker Ernest Cos, whose carved and whittled wooden articles were among the cooperative's most marketable items. Other traditional objects that were still being made in the Big South Fork area included chairs, churns, and utilitarian quilts.

In 1946 with aid from the Farmers Home Administration, the Rosses opened a small retail shop near Highway 27 to market the items made by craftspeople they had identified and (in some cases) trained. Kentucky Hills Industries grew slowly until 1963, when the woodshop burned. In 1965, thirty-two member families incorporated the cooperative and since that time federal and state grants have helped finance a new woodshop, retail building, and training programs for new members. These included workshops conducted by nationally recognized artist-crafters in weaving, woodworking, pottery making, and basketry. Kentucky Hills Industries affiliated with MATCH, the Southern Highland Handicraft Guild, and the Kentucky Guild of Artists and Craftsmen in order to participate in fairs sponsored by these groups.

Most members worked in their homes or in small shops located nearby. They produced as much as they liked and worked at their own pace. The manager set quality standards and bought all marketable items outright rather than taking items on consignment. Cabinetmakers worked in the woodworking facility behind the Pine Knot shop where they could have access to expensive, heavy-duty equipment that they could not afford to purchase individually for home shops. Other crafters or members of their families staffed the Pine Knot retail store, selling to walk-in customers and preparing wholesale and mail orders for shipment.

Rerouting of traffic from U.S. 27 to Interstate 75 and subsequent deterioration of State Highway 92 forced a change in the marketing emphasis from retail to primarily wholesale. Mail-order retailing was moderately successful, but wholesale orders increased until Kentucky Hills Industries was selling to approximately two hundred crafts outlets in 1979.

Member families produced a variety of traditional Appalachian woodenware items and furniture, pottery, needlework, and hand-woven pieces. Some of the products, for example a wooden biscuit cutter and a milking stool, reproduced objects that the Rosses encountered in their early study of Big South Fork area crafts. Other designs were developed by the craftspeople themselves and adopted for the product line after successful test marketing.

Because of its wholesale marketing niche, Kentucky Hills Industries emphasized bulk production of standardized items that were proven good sellers. The cooperative helped members develop designs that could be produced efficiently and priced reasonably while still generating a fair return on the workers' investment in time and materials. This objective eliminated certain labor-intensive items like hand-made quilts from the product line. It also restricted a cooperative member's artistic freedom to a considerable extent in order to maximize earnings.

The cooperative's economic importance to members varied. In 1979, at least two of the thirty-four member families produced and marketed their crafts full time; others only supplemented their income with handcrafts. However, earnings from Kentucky Hills Industries (an average per family of $4,409 in 1978) did help these families avoid out-migration. Prior to joining the cooperative, all but two of these families had been forced to leave home to find work.

Irene Burchfield of Strunk, Kentucky, was one of twelve potters trained in the late 1960s at Kentucky Hills Industries through a Manpower Training Development Act (MTDA) grant. Of the twelve who participated in the training sessions conducted by the well-known potter Charles Counts of Rising Fawn, Georgia, Mrs. Burchfield was the only one who was still producing pottery in 1979. Although none of the other adults who had expressed an interest in learning this craft had persevered, Mrs. Burchfield's young grandson was learning how to throw miniature pots. Irene Burchfield experimented with local clays and glaze materials but ordered commercially prepared stoneware clay in order to keep up with the orders Kentucky Hills obtained from various retail shops. She typically worked long hours in her shop during the winter to stockpile for the high-demand summer period when she needed free time for working in the family's large garden.

One of the Kentucky Hills weavers, Bessie West, also had a home shop in Strunk, Kentucky. After learning to weave in the MTDA class in 1965, Mrs. West taught her two daughters to weave. Beulah West was working regularly with her mother in 1979. The two supplied the cooperative with place mats, napkins, and coasters woven in Mrs. West's original pattern named Bessie's Folly. Another daughter made tablecloths for Kentucky Hills. Mrs. West also designed and wove curtains and made traditional Appalachian woven rugs for her own use and for family members. She occasionally sold rugs through Kentucky Hills.

Alfred Byrd and his sons turned woodenware manufacture into a full-time occupation, working together in a large workshop on the family property in Strunk, Kentucky. A daughter-in-law sometimes helped with sanding and oiling small items, and a school-age son assumed these duties during vacations and in his free time. Another daughter worked in the Kentucky Hills shop at Pine Knot. Mr. Byrd had earlier left McCreary County for industrial employment, and his experience as a mechanic made it possible for him to acquire much of his woodworking equipment secondhand and do the necessary reconditioning himself. The Byrd family supplied Kentucky Hills Industries with small wooden items such as biscuit cutters, honey swirls, butter molds, candlesticks, and pipe racks. Alfred Byrd selected and cut the native hardwoods himself and took his material to Somerset, Kentucky, for milling and kiln drying. The cooperative hoped ultimately to have its own kiln-drying facility.

RUGBY CRAFT COOPERATIVE

Thirty craftspeople from Scott, Morgan, and Fentress Counties organized the Rugby Craft Cooperative in 1974. In addition to wooden and soft goods items (including quilts, afghans, small crocheted items, and dolls), the group's products included silk screening, photography, and paintings. Members marketed through a retail outlet located in the restored Board of Aid office in Rugby, through MATCH, and through participation in craft fairs. When the Board of Aid building was destroyed by fire in 1977, the craft inventory and marketing center were lost. Active participation in the cooperative organization had decreased, although individual members still marketed through MATCH, through fairs, and through privately owned and operated craft shops.

The cooperative was managed by annually elected officers and by a board of directors composed of two members from each of the three counties represented in the membership—Morgan, Scott, and Fentress. A standards committee elected from the membership maintained quality control. Ovid Tompkins, the past president of the Rugby cooperative and a MATCH officer, had facilitated arrangements to market through MATCH, a nonprofit organization that marketed Appalachian crafts in a Lexington, Kentucky, shop. Craft production was the principal occupation for O. N. Peercy of Fentress County. Mr. Peercy, who learned woodworking with hand tools when he was a child, made both small and large items, from honey swirls to rocking chairs. For most Rugby Craft Cooperative members, however, craft sales only supplemented other sources of income. Subsequent to 1979 the reconstructed Rugby Commissary became a popular sales outlet for handcrafted items purchased outright from crafters in the area or sold on consignment.

Four Families in a Changing Economy

This chapter offers detailed economic histories of four families to complement the generalized overview presented in previous chapters. Because households make and implement strategic economic decisions, the household is the context in which environmental adaptation can best be appreciated not as an abstract concept, but as the real-life consequences of many practical decisions. The family history approach also counters the tendency of classic ethnographic description to present a normative view of culture without showing the range of variation in actual behavior.

Preliminary interviews with Big South Fork residents conducted at the beginning of the folklife survey identified farming, logging, mining, and railroad work as historically important alternative occupations available in the area. Families representing these occupations were chosen as subjects for more detailed economic histories. In each case, however, the family's total economic adaptation has involved a combination of strategies through time with variation occurring in the relative importance of the several strategies used.

Each of the four case studies that follow includes a description of the family's initial settlement in the Big South Fork area, household composition, landholdings, and division of labor. Each economic history concludes with a discussion of crucial economic decisions. Names of persons and places have been changed and some details have been modified or omitted in order to protect the privacy of the families who cooperated so generously in sharing many details of their personal lives.

Members of the households whose economic histories are described here were born between 1900 and 1930. The thirty years (approximately 1915–45) during which they matured, married, and established their own households included the most intense commercial exploitation of the area's forest and mineral resources and the beginnings of decline of these extractive industries. Available economic alternatives fluctuated considerably during this period.

For at least thirty years before 1915, when the oldest individual included in these economic histories began to work away from home, the Big South Fork region had felt the impact of economic forces emanating from outside the region, a pattern that has persisted to the present. Agents of the coal and lumber companies already had purchased much of the land from local landowners and many owner-farmers had become tenants. To the extent that members of the local community no longer owned economic resources, individuals lost the ability to create new economic alternatives for themselves through control of these resources. Patterns of exchange, cooperation, and competition that had been established prior to extensive commercial exploitation were greatly altered. For example, informal customary agreement among private landowners that had permitted the free ranging of livestock shifted to more formal agreements between individual farmers and the corporate landowners.

Even at low population densities, the balance of resources necessary to achieve acceptable levels of agricultural production was always fairly delicate in this region of marginal agricultural potential. Cooperation was necessary to manage land-extensive methods of farming that would reduce the inherent risks of single-family, small-scale production. But by 1915, the individuals living in these communities no longer owned much of the land. Farm size had decreased as the land was bought up by the lumber and coal companies and by land speculators. Small farmers who lacked the knowledge and the technology necessary to employ more intensive agricultural methods were forced to seek alternative livelihood by finding some way of earning wages, by becoming tenant farmers, or by combining these strategies.

A Farm Family: Chester and Bertha Ledford

There has been a Ledford living somewhere in the Big South Fork region since about 1800 when James Ledford came through the Cumberland Gap settling first in Oil Valley, Kentucky, and then migrating south along the tributaries of the Big South Fork to Parch Corn Creek. The family says that he was a hunter and trapper who carried his frying pan and rifle as he moved from place to place. He did not do much farming; it was his children who settled down to become farmers. Chester Ledford continues to farm on part of the land grant given to his great-grandfather (James's son) after the War of 1812.

LANDHOLDINGS

In 1908, Chester Ledford's father married and obtained a lease from Stearns on part of the land that the family now owns. In 1917, he purchased the surface rights to another tract from a local family. That tract had been part of the land grant that Chester's great-grandfather obtained after the War of 1812. Chester's great-grandmother had sold it after most of her children had moved away and she could no longer maintain the property herself.

For a time, the Ledfords lived away from their own property because Stearns offered Chester's father an attractive lease on a large tract of land. When the company sold that tract, the family returned to their former home. Chester, who had just married, was able to take advantage of an opportunity to buy the original leasehold from Stearns, and he farmed this and the land-grant tract jointly with his father.

In the 1970s, the Ledfords owned surface rights to approximately 175 acres, of which about 50 acres were cleared. The cleared land was used for a vegetable garden, tobacco allotment, corn, hay (about 20 acres), and pasture (about 25 acres). The undeveloped acres were forested. Chester's father deeded his portion of this land to his son in exchange for Chester's commitment to care for his father in his old age. This occurred about twenty-five years before Chester's father died.

DIVISION OF LABOR

Chester Ledford and his wife, Bertha, both in their mid-sixties, were living alone in 1979. One son and his wife lived about forty miles away but visited once or twice a week. Labor necessary to maintain the household had generally been confined to household members, including Chester's parents when they were alive and still physically active.

The division of labor within the household was somewhat flexible. The women generally did inside work, the men tended crops and livestock, and the whole family maintained the vegetable garden. But when extra help was needed, the women helped with the plowing and with the stock, and the men helped with preparing food for canning. Occasionally when Chester worked away from home in the logwoods, he hired a local man to help with the farmwork.

HOME PRODUCTION AND SOURCES OF CASH INCOME

Chester and Bertha Ledford mixed some commercial farming with the kind of self-provisioning traditionally found in the region. They chose to incorporate only those aspects of cash economy that were compatible with traditional farming and its associated values. Their general economic strategy was always directed toward staying on their land. They produced from that land and through their own labor most of what they needed, supplemented with enough cash to pay their taxes and to purchase the limited amount of manufactured goods that they needed. The family's production system did not remain static through the decades, because the specific strategies necessary to maintain this general adaptation changed through time in response to available opportunities.

Figure 1 depicts this household's various economic pursuits arranged into an annual cycle of activities. The figure depicts the period before enforcement of stock fence laws around 1950, a time when "working in the logwoods" was also

Four Families in a Changing Economy 173

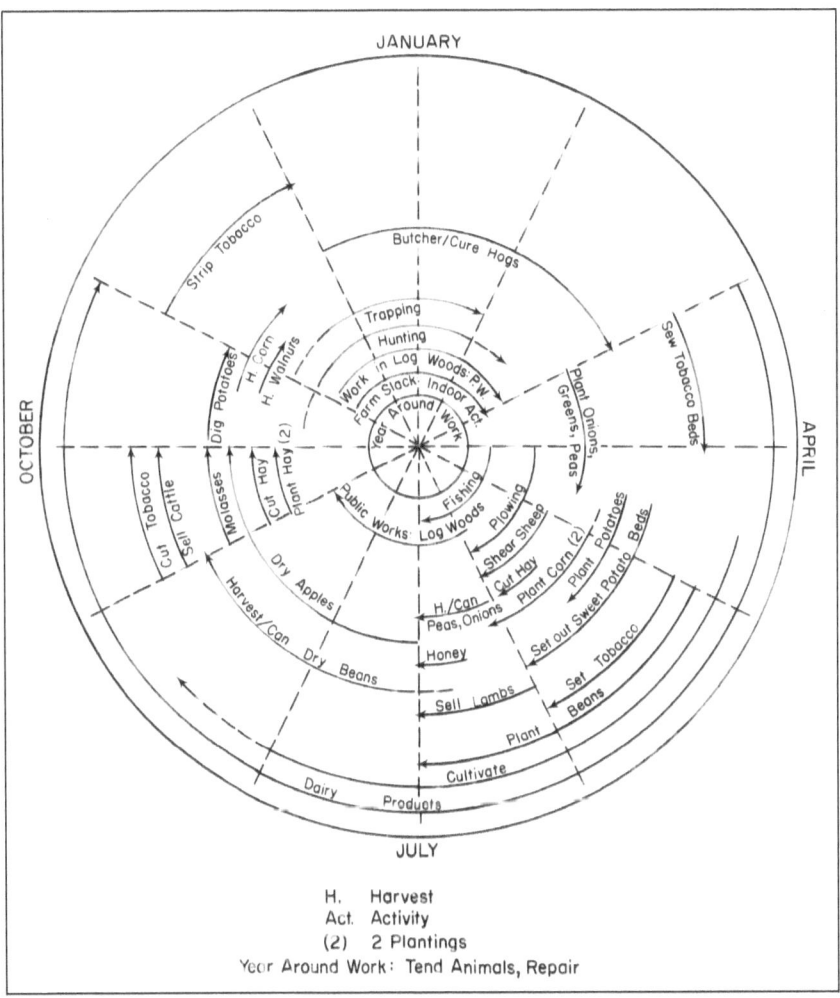

Annual cycle of farming activities.

available as a source of income. The subsistence activities shown in this diagram are fairly representative of activities undertaken by mostly self-provisioning farmers of the region between 1900 and 1950, although certainly there was variation among families in the relative importance of particular activities.

For the Ledfords, certain activities were a constant part of their economic strategies over the years. Primary activities included growing a vegetable garden, raising hogs and chickens, and preserving foodstuffs by canning and drying. The family always raised beef cattle for sale, although the number of cattle the household could maintain decreased in the 1950s after livestock fence laws were enforced. The stock fence law also caused the Ledfords to give up raising sheep.

A two-acre vegetable garden supplied the bulk of food needs for the family. Vegetables raised in 1979 included sweet corn, peas, beans, potatoes, sweet potatoes, tomatoes, cabbage, cucumbers, onions, beets, popcorn, peanuts, squash, pumpkins, rhubarb, and strawberries. Wild poke and mustard greens were gathered to supplement these garden vegetables. The Ledfords saved seed from year to year and asked neighbors for seeds of new vegetable varieties they wanted to try. Bertha canned most vegetables, although she dried fodder beans and also apples. She canned more than 230 quarts of vegetables in 1978 and 1979, a quantity more than adequate for their needs.

The Ledfords generally raised a hog each year for home consumption. Chester used to butcher and cure the hog himself sometime between December and February, the exact time depending on when the hog was fat enough and when the weather was cold enough to allow curing without spoilage. The Ledfords had given up curing pork, even though they had a smokehouse on their property, shifting instead to pressure canning in order to preserve the meat longer. A few chickens supplied the family with all the eggs they required, but they no longer kept a milk cow. Fifteen stands of bees that Chester originally captured from the wild supplied honey for the household. The extensive amount of food produced at home meant that only limited food purchases were necessary. The Ledfords even had their own corn ground into meal until the local gristmill closed.

Their beef cattle were sold at the local weekly cattle auction rather than slaughtered for home consumption. Chester tried to maintain a self-perpetuating herd fed primarily on grass, selling the animals when they reached 300 to 400 pounds. Ideally sales were made in the fall to avoid feeding over winter. He determined optimal selling times by listening to daily farm market reports on the radio. Trapping as a minor source of cash income was a constant element in the Ledfords' economic strategies.

Household members always built their own dwellings and outbuildings using timber cut from their property. Chester never harvested timber primarily to sell, although he did cut timber in the process of clearing more land for crops. The lumber produced in this way usually went into farm improvements, although small quantities were sold.

The Ledfords' barn building illustrates the integration involved in using land and labor in response to changes in economic alternatives. Once Stearns concluded its massive timber cutting operation in the area, working in the logwoods was no longer a viable alternative for Chester. In addition, enforcement of the fence law had decreased the amount of land actually available for family food production. The Ledfords wanted to stay on the farm, replacing the income Chester had brought in from part-time logging by raising more cattle for sale. In order to support more cattle, they had to clear more land for pasture and build a new barn for wintering cattle and storing fodder.

In the late spring after the crops had been planted, the family cleared the land, had their timber sawed at a sawmill, and built a large post-and-beam dairy barn, doing the construction work themselves. As a substitute for commercial paint or stain, they poured used motor oil into five-gallon vats and applied it to the structure with old mops. All buildings on the property, whether log, frame, or native stone, were constructed using patterns from the mind, materials from the land, and labor from the household.

Besides land, buildings, livestock, and their own labor, the Ledfords required few capital assets to carry out their economic activities. Farm machinery consisted of an old tractor purchased in the late 1960s. Before that, mules did the plowing and all other heavy traction tasks. The family bought the tractor when they could no longer obtain equipment and supplies needed to take care of the mules, when the mules themselves became too expensive, and when a used tractor became available at a very good price.

CHANGE THROUGH TIME

When Chester Ledford and his father began farming their properties jointly, the Stearns policy of allowing local residents to run livestock on company land greatly increased the land resources available to the family. They were able to raise beef cattle, feeder pigs, hogs, and sheep for sale. Stearns logging activities near the farm also enabled Chester to earn extra cash from part-time logging. From the late 1930s until the mid-1950s Chester worked in the logwoods during slack periods on the farm, first for Stearns and later for their contractors.

Slack times on the farm came during the summer after the crops had been planted and during the fall and winter after harvesting was complete. Chester's jobs included cutting timber, running loaders, and working in the sawmill; he was paid in cash on a daily basis. If the work was close to the farm, he came home at night; if he was logging farther away, he boarded close to the job. Boarding lasted from a few days to a maximum of two months.

The family left home only once during this period and kept their property with the intention of returning. Unlike many of their neighbors, Chester and Bertha did not leave for wage work in an urban area, but to help a relative with agricultural work in a neighboring county. They returned home when Chester's father was no longer able to maintain the farm alone. It was then that the elder Mr. Ledford deeded his property to Chester. With logging work less available than before, Chester made a full-time commitment to the farm.

Developments in the mid-1950s demanded the family's most fundamental change in economic strategy. For a variety of reasons, more intensive land utilization was required. At about the same time that fence law enforcement became effective, Stearns discontinued its policy of leasing land to local residents for their use. The Ledfords could no longer raise sheep, hogs, and feeder pigs, and they had to reduce the size of their cattle herd.

Clearing additional land for pasture compensated partially for the loss of free-range use rights, but the herd size could not be increased to former levels. A 1,048-pound tobacco allotment introduced a new source of cash income. During the 1970s the family divided the tobacco profits with a neighbor. Chester provided the land, plowed, and prepared the field, while the neighbor took care of planting, cultivating, and harvesting the crop with the help of hired hands.

When Chester began receiving a monthly Social Security check, it was the first regular check he had ever received. This plus his realization that "the only thing that stops folks like us from living this way is getting old" made it somewhat easier to accept with resignation the imminent loss of his property to the recreation area. In response to the anticipated move, he decreased crop production and the size of his herd, reduced maintenance procedures, and halted some construction projects. Chester and Bertha Ledford had reached the point in the traditional domestic cycle when they would expect to deed their property to their son, just as Chester's father had done, while continuing to contribute their labor to the farm for as long as possible, but the impending taking of the farm for the recreation area confirmed their son's decision to pursue a different occupation than farming.

DISCUSSION

When Chester Ledford's father married in 1908, the problem he faced was how to remain a farmer when he did not own any land. His initial strategy was to lease the land. Leasing certainly had its disadvantages; after many years of clearing, farming, and building activities, Mr. Ledford lost the lease and had to move when the land was sold. The money Chester earned as a logger helped his father buy a tract of recently logged land considered worthless by anyone but a plateau farmer. Chester combined farming with wage work as a logger until the area near his farm had been almost completely cut over. At that point, logging was no longer an acceptable alternative for Chester because it would have meant migration from the farm. Instead, he chose to employ more land-intensive agricultural methods.

This family never considered migration away from the region an acceptable alternative. They continued to emphasize agriculture because they had sufficient land to maintain an adequate level of farm production through the years when wage work was possible. Chester's farm remained about the size thought adequate for family farming at the time of initial settlement of the area. Of the 572 Tellico Land Grants issued between 1803 and 1853, most were between 100 and 200 acres (Jillson 1925, 443). Ancestors of the Ledfords had received land grants of 100 and 200 acres.

Although pioneer settlers soon exhausted their land and had to acquire more in order to continue farming, Chester Ledford maintained his farm through the use of fertilizers and crop rotation, increasing overall productivity while owning no more land than his ancestors. There were limits to the productivity of this land even with the use of fertilizers and crop rotation, but the family chose to accept a standard of living consistent with these limitations. They tried as much as possible to reduce their need for cash and thus the need to seek wage labor off the farm. At the same time, the natural resources of the farm were used to full advantage. For example, their building projects used lumber from their own timber and natural limestone rather than purchased materials.

In summary, the Ledfords' total economic adaptation involved the integration of strategies that allowed them to retain control of their land. They accomplished this by minimizing their need for cash and maximizing their use of available natural resources. Cash was earned primarily through the sale of livestock and tobacco and, in earlier years, through logging. The Ledfords never considered certain other economic alternatives such as permanent out-migration or making moonshine, because these were inconsistent with the family's values.

A Logging Family: Morgan and Nellie Skidmore

Among the early settlers along the Big South Fork was Jeremiah Skidmore, who settled first in Kentucky before moving south to Station Camp Creek in Tennessee. Morgan Skidmore and his wife, Nellie, in their late sixties at the time of the folklife survey, were born there and lived there until their marriage in 1933. In 1923, when Morgan Skidmore began working off his father's farm, wage work was available in the mines, in the timber industry, and on the railroad. Morgan chose to work as a logger for Stearns at the time Stearns was beginning to extend its logging railroad from Bell Farm, Kentucky, along Rock Creek into Tennessee.

LANDHOLDINGS

Morgan and Nellie Skidmore did not settle in one place for more than a few years during the first fifteen years of their marriage. They moved several times in order to be closer to the area being logged. Each time the family moved, they rented or leased a small farmstead at least large enough to support a vegetable garden, a milk cow, chickens, and a hog. Finally in the late 1940s as Stearns was about to discontinue logging operations, the family bought a 100-acre farm in Fentress County and moved there permanently. They cleared 45 acres, of which 1 acre was used for a vegetable garden and 4 to 20 acres for crops of corn, hay, and sorghum, while the remainder was pasture. Some timber was cut from the remaining acres.

In addition to the 100-acre property, the family also had an informal lease with Stearns on a large tract (greater than 1,000 acres) of Stearns property. In return for "looking out for" this tract, this acreage could be used to run livestock: hogs, sheep, and cattle. Only the cattle were brought in for the winter. In addition, the family could gather downed or dead timber and cut small quantities of timber for their own use. Looking out for the land entailed reporting any possibility of illegal logging. This arrangement provided an additional source of forest products and allowed the family to maintain livestock in far greater numbers than their own property could support. The fence law affected the Skidmores just as it did the Ledfords, but poor health also forced the Skidmores to curtail farming activity in the late 1960s.

DIVISION OF LABOR

Morgan and Nellie Skidmore were living alone in 1979. None of their five children chose to be loggers or farmers, although they had shared major responsibility for farming with their mother while Morgan worked as a logger. By the time the family bought the farm, the children were old enough to supply much of the labor necessary for running it. Morgan helped out with the farmwork when he was able, and he also hunted and trapped.

The combination of wage work and subsistence farming chosen by the Skidmores entailed fundamental changes in division of labor from the patterns of the previous generation that were largely maintained by the Ledfords. Nellie rather than Morgan assumed primary responsibility for agricultural production.

HOME PRODUCTION AND SOURCES OF CASH INCOME

As was the case with the Ledfords, the Skidmores' economic strategies were tied to the activities and policies of the Stearns Coal and Lumber Company. Primary reliance on logging as a source of income was dependent on continued availability of work; when the family finally did settle permanently on a farm, their lease arrangement with Stearns made possible a higher level of productivity.

At one time, the family raised as many as 400 laying hens and sold eggs twice a week in Jamestown. They kept between ten and thirty head of beef cattle and sold five or six a year, as well as a large herd of sheep that produced wool and meat for sale. Honey and sorghum molasses were additional sources of cash. The family gradually decreased farm production as the children began to leave home and in response to the stock fence law.

Until the late 1960s, Morgan was able to supplement his farm income by working for logging contractors. Disability had forced him to retire from this work and to curtail farming operations by 1970. Knowing that their farm would soon be taken for the recreation area, the Skidmores sold their remaining livestock, the tractor, and the horse they used for cultivating. In 1979 they still grew a vegetable garden (smaller than one acre) and kept a few chickens for domestic use. They bought a hog each fall but continued to do the butchering themselves.

Both of the Skidmores had serious health problems that made it dangerous for them to remain on the farm alone, especially in winter. They realized that it would be practical to move to town, but in spite of the advantages of electricity, running water, telephone, and refrigeration, they would have preferred to stay on their farm if they could.

DISCUSSION

The Skidmores like the Ledfords chose farming and logging as their primary economic strategies, but they placed the opposite emphasis on these pursuits. While Chester Ledford gave up logging when it would have interfered with running his farm, the entire Skidmore family moved with Morgan in response to changes in the location of logging areas. For many years they rented rather than establishing a permanent farm. The Skidmores bought a farm only in the late 1940s after almost all of the area's timber resources had been exhausted. They replaced their previous economic adaptation with a combination of self-provisioning, commercial farming, and moonshine making, supplemented by hunting and trapping.

Although the Skidmores depended primarily on wages from logging from the 1920s through the 1940s, they were able to shift their economic strategies when opportunities for steady work in logging diminished. By returning to the farming adaptation of the previous generation, the Skidmores avoided participating in the post–World War II out-migration from the area. Farm ownership gave the Skidmores the means of production necessary to survive during this time of severe shortages in economic resources. In addition, moonshine making was an acceptable alternative for the Skidmores, whereas it was not for the Ledfords.

Residents of the area justified moonshine making as a necessary source of cash income to meet taxes and other obligations, particularly during the Great Depression. This was the same argument used by earlier generations of Appalachian farmers. Morgan Skidmore said that there were times when his family would have "starved" if it had not been for the profit made from making moonshine.

A Coal Mining Family: Seldon and Jennie Lacey

Jennie Lacey knew little about the early history of her ancestors in the Big South Fork area, nor did she know much about her husband's family. Jennie had been married twice, both times to Laceys who came to Kentucky in the early 1920s from Scott County, Tennessee, to work in Stearns mines. Her second husband, Seldon, died in 1978.

Jennie's personal history was unusual. She was born in 1904, the eldest of three illegitimate children of Wilma Morrison and John Bowen. The children lived with their mother until she contracted tuberculosis and was sent away for five months when Jennie was seven. At that time, John Bowen took the children to live with his family, and he retained custody of them after Wilma recovered and returned home.

By the time Bowen died, he had become one of the wealthiest men in the county, with assets of cash, property, mortgages, and notes. He began with a small farm and expanded his interests to include large-scale farming, livestock, and timber. He built a gas-powered sawmill and gristmill and employed a number of local men to work there and on his farm. Jennie was not one of his heirs.

LANDHOLDINGS

Seldon, his father, and his brothers came to Kentucky in the early 1920s along with other Laceys from Scott County, Tennessee. They worked in the mines, farmed, and made a little moonshine. Seldon had already spent some time in Kentucky working in a sawmill. Soon after Seldon's family settled in Kentucky, he married his first wife and they bought a fifteen-acre tract, the place where Jennie was still living in 1979. One of her stepsons inherited it from his mother but deeded it to Seldon and Jennie. The family had never owned any additional land.

DIVISION OF LABOR

Growing up in John Bowen's house, Jennie did not learn the things then commonly taught to girls. Instead, she did work usually assigned to men and boys: heavy farmwork, timber cutting, and loading boxcars. She did this work at her father's insistence and in return received room and board. Jennie said, "Before I got married I had it real rough and afterwards it didn't get any better." It was only after her first marriage that an aunt taught Jennie to sew, cook, and preserve food.

Jennie and her first husband combined coal mining and subsistence farming, much as she and Seldon were to do later. They had eight children, seven of them live births. Seldon's ex-wife died shortly after Jennie and Seldon married in 1939. Jennie added Seldon's three sons by his first marriage to her family; she and Seldon had no children together.

While Seldon worked in the Stearns mines he walked to work from the family farm. The mines did not run every day, and on days off, Seldon helped with the farming. He also spent his free time hunting, his "greatest joy," according to Jennie. The farmwork was primarily Jennie's and the children's responsibility. As adults none of the children continued farming, though several remained close by in the county. After Seldon's death, Jennie lived alone.

HOME PRODUCTION AND SOURCES OF CASH INCOME

From 1939 until 1951, the Laceys depended principally on wages from coal mining and subsistence farming for a livelihood. Hunting, trapping, moonshine, the sale of beef cattle, and the sale of extra garden crops were supplementary sources of food and cash income.

While working as a miner, Seldon never chose to move his family to the camps. In addition to maintaining a vegetable garden, the Laceys were able to raise corn, chickens, a milk cow, and, when they could afford it, a hog and some beef cattle. The hog was raised for home consumption, the beef cattle for sale. After the enforcement of fence laws, the family could no longer keep beef cattle.

Trips to any town were infrequent. Any necessary purchases were made at the company store at Fidelity. Usual purchases included lard, meal, flour, salt, and coffee. Extra garden produce, usually beans, was sold or traded at the company store.

During his years as a coal miner, Seldon contracted black lung and he also had a crippling accident. These conditions forced his early retirement in 1951. When he retired, he received no pension, no disability pay, and no Social Security. The family had no savings until 1966 when they began collecting a small welfare check. The Laceys were supported by one of Seldon's sons. Their Social Security payments ranged from approximately $80 per month in 1966 to approximately $210 per month at the time of Seldon's death. Seldon had been a member of the United Mine Workers since 1945. For the last few years of his life he collected a small disability check from the union and received medical benefits that helped defray the cost of frequent hospitalizations for black lung treatment.

Seldon died at home in November 1978 while Jennie was trying to find a way to get him to the hospital. Jennie herself prepared the body in the traditional way. While living alone after being widowed, Jennie Lacey maintained close contacts with her family, especially with Seldon's youngest son and his family. Family and neighbors visited frequently, providing transportation and helping with heavy housekeeping chores.

DISCUSSION

Seldon Lacey began working away from home at approximately the same time as Morgan Skidmore, and the economic alternatives available to them were the same. Seldon ultimately chose mining, after first working for three years in sawmills in Tennessee and Kentucky. Once he chose to settle in Kentucky and work in the Stearns mines, he was subject to fluctuations in employment caused by the company's response to changing market conditions. After seven years of fairly steady work in the mines, he could never again rely on working for more than a few days a week.

The Laceys combined a number of strategies in their economic adaptation: wage work in the mines when available, subsistence farming, moonshine making, and hunting. The family made extensive use of wild plant foods and raised livestock occasionally, but their limited landholding (fifteen acres) did not permit much farming, nor did it contain enough varied resources to fill all of the family's subsistence needs.

When Seldon Lacey moved to Kentucky in the 1920s, most property already was in corporate hands. Mining was well under way, the forest had been logged extensively, population had increased considerably, and farms were small. Employment opportunities were limited to mining and related work in the area where Seldon Lacey settled. During coal industry slumps, there were few economic alternatives available to miners, especially if they lacked land.

After the 1950s, physical disabilities acquired as a consequence of mining prevented Seldon Lacey from taking any other job requiring heavy physical labor. Lack of education eliminated the potential for many other kinds of jobs, although the opportunities were few at any rate. As a result, the Laceys became economically dependent on some type of financial assistance, first from their family, then from government agencies and the union.

A Railroad Family: Jim and Dottie Farmer

By the mid-1800s, Jim Farmer's grandfather was an established farmer living near Sharp Place, southeast of Pickett State Park, in an area peripheral to what would become Stearns Coal and Lumber Company property. Around 1880 he sold that farm and bought a 200-acre tract in Fentress County near the future site of the Oneida and Western Railroad. He bought the property because it contained in addition to good farmland, a sawmill and a gristmill. Local residents brought their timber, corn, wheat, buckwheat, and rye to the mill; processing was done in return for a cash payment or a share of the product. The Farmers also had a sorghum mill, and their homestead became a social and economic center where people with business at the mills gathered to talk and where molasses stir-offs were held each fall.

Jim's father grew up here but moved to his wife's home in Scott County when he married. There he began farming and bringing up a family of eleven children. In 1907 the family moved back to the "old Farmer home place" in Fentress County. Jim's grandfather was getting too old to manage the farm and mill without help. He agreed to deed his farm to Jim's father in exchange for a promise to be cared for in his old age.

Jim's grandfather had added ownership and management of a sawmill, gristmill, and sorghum mill to his previous farming livelihood. Jim's father added wage work to these sources of income. He started working for the Oneida and Western railroad in 1915, first as a surveyor, then as a crew chief in charge of men who were laying the roadbed. His wife and children maintained the farm.

Jim Farmer was one of the middle children. His older brothers had already joined their father in railroad work when Jim decided he wanted to work for the railroad too. It paid better than logging and was not as hazardous as mining. Once he started working for the railroad, Jim never wanted to do anything else; he stayed with the Oneida and Western from 1916 until 1951. During that time, he married and brought up eleven children, just as his father had done.

LANDHOLDINGS

The Farmers owned three different tracts of land, all in Fentress County. The first, a nine-acre tract, was Jim's share of the "old Farmer home place," which Jim's father deeded to him in 1923 in exchange for monetary compensation. Jim and Dottie Farmer acquired this place while the family was moving frequently from one railroad camp to another. They built a house on the property shortly after acquiring it, but they lived there only irregularly until Jim left the railroad. Before that, the house served as a kind of home base. It gave them a place to store belongings while they moved from one section camp to another. When it was time to move to a new camp, the dining table was turned upside down and necessary items were piled on the table to be carried out of the house.

The Farmers sold their part of the old home place and left Fentress County for about two years during the early 1970s. When they returned they bought a modern house on an acre and a half in town. They also bought another tract from one of their sons, seven acres in young timber situated near but outside of the recreation area.

DIVISION OF LABOR

The Farmers' economic decisions were constrained by the frequent changes in residence that railroad work entailed and by Jim's commitment to full-time wage work. While Jim was working on the section crews, the first eight Farmer children were born. The family lived in the railroad camps where the company rented small houses to crew members. Jim worked ten-hour days and was paid on a daily basis. On days when railroad work was not available (the size of crews was scaled down to a minimum during severe winter weather), he hauled lumber or cut timber.

After 1923, Jim owned part of the Farmer home place. Whether living on the farm or in the railroad camps, Dottie and the children raised a vegetable garden and a few hogs and kept a milk cow and some chickens. Before their sons were old enough to plow for the garden, Jim did it in the evenings after he came home from work.

When living on the farm, Jim and Dottie routinely got up at 3:00 A.M. Dottie fixed Jim's breakfast and packed his dinner in an old syrup bucket. He walked up to seven miles to work, using a lantern to light his way. By the time he got home, the children were already asleep. Sometimes he did not see them during the week for weeks at a time. Dottie's most difficult time came during the early years of the marriage before she had children old enough to be companions and helpers. Later on, during the day while Jim was working, Dottie and the children worked in the garden, took care of the animals, and sometimes fished together.

Jim became a section foreman in the 1940s. He was responsible for the maintenance and repair of all track in a ten-mile section, including cleanup after accidents. Jim's crew had seven regular members, but he could call on as many as twenty-seven in an emergency following a train derailment. He began his day by taking a lever car (later a motorcar) through his section, picking up his crew along the way. He returned them home in the same manner at the end of the day. In an emergency he had to collect the crew, one by one, from their homes. His was the only home in the camp with a telephone. Whereas the family had moved sometimes two or three times a year at first, the foreman's responsibilities tied him to the section camp where Jim was always "on call." His longer work hours meant that he had even less time than before to help Dottie and the children with farming activities.

After Jim retired, the Farmers lived for a short time in Maryville, Tennessee, near a son and daughter, but they returned to Fentress County and bought a house in town where they had a vegetable garden and kept a few chickens. Jim also dug and sold roots and herbs to a local agent for a pharmaceutical company, and Dottie made and sold quilts. Although the Farmers lived alone, many of their children lived in Fentress County and visited them regularly.

HOME PRODUCTION AND SOURCES OF CASH INCOME

Railroad work was always the principal source of income for Jim Farmer's family, first through daily wages, then through a salary, and finally through a pension. The Farmers' railroad income was always supplemented by traditional subsistence activities and by some cash income from traditional sources, however. With the help of the children, Dottie grew a vegetable garden, raised hogs to supply the family, and kept a few chickens and a milk cow. With thirteen mouths to feed, they did not produce surpluses for sale. Jim Farmer was fond of hunting. Until his health would no longer permit it, he supplemented the family diet and income by hunting. Deer, raccoon, and squirrel meat were consumed at home; fox and raccoon pelts were sold to proprietors of local country stores, who in turn sold them to the traveling agents of furriers located in Louisville and other regional cities. Logging was an occasional occupation for Jim Farmer during his railroading years.

Jim left the Oneida and Western Railroad when it became obvious that the company could not survive and he could no longer obtain the equipment and supplies needed to do a proper job of track maintenance. He was in his early fifties and still wanted to work for a railroad. Leaving his family temporarily in Fentress County, Jim went north to Muncie, Indiana, where he applied for a job on the Nickel Plate Railroad. He stayed there six weeks. After he failed the company physical examination, he was retired and given a railroad pension.

The pension was small and the family needed more money, so Jim began working for logging contractors, cutting and hauling timber. Dottie took on work outside the home as well, because it was important to the Farmers that all of their children have a chance to finish high school. Dottie worked first in a local shirt factory and later in a restaurant. In retirement, the Farmers turned to traditional methods of supplementing their pension and Social Security income. They continued to grow a vegetable garden and preserved surplus by freezing. Jim collected roots and herbs for sale, and Dottie sold quilts. The Farmers purchased more foods and more manufactured items than the other families described here.

DISCUSSION

Lack of economic alternatives was never a problem for the Farmers. Although they were the oldest couple profiled in this chapter, they had most aggressively sought and chosen the widest array of economic alternatives during their years together. Their economic strategies included railroad work, logging, work in manufacturing and service industries, and both subsistence use and commercialization of elements from the traditional culture—that is, hunting, collection of medicinal plants, and quilting.

Jim Farmer's family seemed quite willing to take advantage of new work opportunities. His father and older brothers were among the Oneida and Western's earliest workers, and Jim soon followed them. He had an eighth grade education, which in the 1910s qualified him for a variety of jobs. Mining and logging were the primary sources of wage work when Jim chose railroading in 1916. He chose railroad work because it paid better than logging or sawmill work, and the mines scared him. Because of the financial benefits, the Farmers were willing to accept the frequent moves required by Jim's job and the disruption to family life and family division of labor that his long work hours caused. Whenever he could, Jim worked for logging contractors, and he continued that work well past his retirement from the railroad. When manufacturing and service jobs became available to them, the Farmers seized upon those opportunities also. Dottie started working outside the home so that her children could finish their education. During the short time that the Farmers lived outside Fentress County, Jim took a job in a car wash; he was seventy-two years old at the time.

Conclusion

A common thread of similarity underlies the apparent differences in economic adaptations of the four families described here. All were descendants of the area's early Euro-American settlers and thus shared a common cultural heritage of subsistence strategies developed by those settlers. At least one member of each household shared an ancestor with someone in the other three households.

All four families retained some elements of the traditional subsistence base; the degree of retention depended upon their access to land and natural resources and their involvement in wage work. The Ledfords, with ownership of a large farm assured, depended least on wage labor and fit it into the annual cycle of farm activities. The Skidmores chose subsistence and commercial farming only after their first strategy based on wage labor in the logwoods was no longer available. But even while logging was their primary source of income, the Skidmores produced much of their food. The Laceys, dependent on mining employment and without access to enough land to develop commercial farming, nevertheless kept a vegetable garden and raised as much livestock and poultry as they could afford. The Farmers, better educated than the others, were able to choose from the widest array of economic alternatives, but they too always produced much of their food and used traditional skills to supplement their retirement income.

Far from being a thing of the past, self-sufficiency remained a guiding principle in the Big South Fork area. Pervasive unemployment, poor pay for many of the available jobs, and widespread reliance on modest pension, Social Security, or other public assistance payments explain why minimizing cash expenditures and tapping a variety of sources of cash income continued to be adaptive for Big South Fork residents. Through the years, the people of the Big South Fork have shown admirable resourcefulness and resilience in adapting to economic change and weathering hard times.

Conclusion and Recommendations

This historical ethnography has described traditional folklife of the Big South Fork area, its origins in the largely self-provisioning farming that prevailed in the early nineteenth century, and its development through time in response to changing conditions. Knowledge of the past was the basis for predictions about how these cultural traditions might fare in the future.

The Past

Early settlers who confronted the Big South Fork environment achieved a successful adaptation through knowledge and skills shared with pioneers who migrated westward to populate other parts of the United States in the early nineteenth century. Despite the beginnings of commercial development, the Big South Fork economy remained relatively self-contained through the Civil War period. Limited transportation and commerce made self-sufficiency a necessity, and the local community composed of a few closely related families was the focus of all social interaction.

The postwar decades ended the region's isolation, however. The key to change was completion of the Cincinnati Southern Railroad across the Cumberland Plateau. This transportation link brought commerce, industry, new settlers, and new ideas into the Big South Fork area. Settlement actually continued throughout the nineteenth century and well into the twentieth, and the newcomers brought technological and social change; however, modernization did not undermine local folk traditions. On the contrary, the outsiders who made successful permanent settlers did so in part by incorporating elements of the local culture into their own lifestyles.

The Great Depression and World War II brought another upheaval. Reduced employment opportunities in local extractive industry coupled with the wartime demand for servicemen and workers in the industrial North and Midwest stimulated a mass exodus from the Big South Fork as well as other parts of Appalachia. The migrants did not leave permanently but returned home between jobs, during layoffs, or at least for vacations. Since the 1940s, succeeding generations of young people have followed their older relatives to Muncie, Indiana, and they have perpetuated this pattern of interchange and interaction between rural and urban settings. By 1980, the first generation of post–World War II migrant workers had returned home permanently to retire.

In the face of continuous interaction with the outside world for more than a century, it is not possible to explain the persistence of folk culture elements in the Big South Fork area simply as the result of isolation from mainstream American life. In addition to the old farming adaptation, available alternatives have included wage work in local and urban industry. Why then has tradition withstood the onslaught of modernization to the extent that it has?

Several economic and social factors seem to provide insight, though by no means a conclusive answer to this question. First, one should note that the stimulating effects of transportation facilities benefited farmers and local entrepreneurs as well as industrial concerns. Ready markets were opened up for commodities derived from the subsistence lifestyle and the skills it required: farm produce, roots and herbs, pelts, tanbark, home-fashioned cross ties, even moonshine.

Second, the area's largest industrial employer, Stearns Coal and Lumber Company, adopted policies that encouraged continuation of farming alongside the new wage-work alternatives. Farmers who did not own land could lease it from Stearns; and because the demand for workers varied seasonally, the company had no objections to employing farmers part time. Company employees were not required to live in company housing.

Such policies permitted workers to regard wage work as a supplement to the traditional lifestyle rather than a replacement for it. They were not forced to choose between the old and the new. When the economic boom turned to bust in the 1930s, it was relatively easy for families to resume the lives they had known before wage-work opportunities had become available.

Increasing population pressure on arable land and passage of stock fence laws forced families without sufficient landholdings to seek their fortunes away from home, but even these persons tended to regard factory work and urban living as temporary economic expedients rather than thoroughgoing changes in lifestyle.

Industrial development introduced a new settlement pattern to the Big South Fork area, the company town or camp. These settlements differed from the older aggregates of farm homesteads because they brought together in a smaller space larger numbers of people who often came from diverse backgrounds and were not bound together by kinship and long-standing attachment to place. Because the company furnished public services, the people who lived in its camps could easily occupy a quasi-urban place without developing community citizenship through civic cooperation and participation in government activities. Rather, they maintained the traditional family-based system of social relations, continued to participate in the social life of their home communities, and at the end were laid to rest in their home communities. Once the industrial raison d'être of the camps was gone, they disappeared as fast as they had sprung up. Only the older towns that had developed as county seats and commercial centers on the periphery of the Big South Fork gorge area became truly urbanized. In contrast to the camps, the farming settlements of the gorge area clung to life as long as they could in the face of external pressures eating away at them—post office and school closings, followed by closings of local stores; neglect of the old wagon roads once the state and county paved road systems were developed; and, finally, depopulation brought about by centralization of needed services in towns and along paved roads.

Economic self-sufficiency and family-based social life persisted through industrial growth, industrial decline, and out-migration. These choices certainly were encouraged by the traditional value system, but economic factors made them sensible choices as well. Historically, wage work has not provided a stable, reliable source of income. Employment in mining and the timber industry fluctuated seasonally and dwindled to almost nothing during the Great Depression. Appalachian migrants were in demand as factory workers in good times but suffered layoffs and unemployment during the recessions of past decades. In 1979, decline in the American auto industry brought many young migrants home for an extended stay; families planted larger gardens and settled down for the duration, much as they had done in the 1930s.

In addition to these economic incentives to retain survival skills, contemporary urban problems reinforce the migrants' preference for rural life at home—if not immediately, then certainly after retirement. Urban dwellers face a high cost of living with only limited opportunities for self-sufficiency activities, overcrowding, crime, pollution—the same problems that are prompting long-term urbanites as well as rural migrants to cities to appreciate the advantages of rural living.

The Future

The survey of Big South Fork folk culture revealed variable retention of traditional elements in everyday life. Practices such as hunting, gardening, and food preservation continued to be well integrated into economic and social patterns; many features of traditional construction methods were preserved even though construction materials had changed through time. On the other hand, music suffered to some extent as changing social patterns caused discontinuation of group workings and social events such as box suppers and other activities that once provided natural contexts for string band music and dancing. Verbal expression was affected more extensively than music; anecdotes and legends having their roots in personal, family, or local history survived, but the purely fanciful tales and riddles were not being transmitted to younger generations.

Self-sufficiency skills have survived better than other aspects of Big South Fork folklife because they have economic utility to young and old alike. Current economic conditions suggest that these skills will continue to have real economic importance. Even if local opportunities for steady employment improve markedly, retirees on a relatively fixed income will be able to make that income go further if they grow what food they can, make some of their own clothing and household furnishings, and use traditional skills and knowledge to earn supplemental income. Substantial tourism will expand potential markets for handcrafted items.

On the other hand, verbal expression and old-time music have become increasingly the province of the elderly because they lack an economic function and for the most part have been stripped of their original social contexts and functions. Relegation of these aspects of folk culture to the elderly is a consequence of greater mobility and more diverse recreational opportunities for today's youth as well as the impact of mass media entertainment. Mainstream popular culture has increasingly become the reference point for young people.

Working against this trend, however, was the nationwide rediscovery of ethnic and regional roots, the popular groundswell that produced the Foxfire phenomenon among young people. The historic and folklife interests incorporated into development of the recreation area can only help to strengthen this trend by publicly affirming the national value and significance of Big South Fork traditional folklife. Furthermore, a comprehensive interpretive program and similar activities within the private sector tourist industry could provide economic as well as psychological incentives for talented young people to keep alive as entertainment and education aspects of folklife that otherwise would be neglected and eventually forgotten. If development of the recreation area could become a stimulus for deliberate preservation of cultural resources, then the area's folklife might fare better than if there had been no federal intervention.

Specific recommendations pertained to (1) interpretive themes and resources; (2) additional folklife documentation; (3) land acquisition, relocation, and social impact assessment; (4) the construction phase of the recreation area; and (5) operation and management, especially of proposed lodges and special events.

Interpretive Themes and Resources

Big South Fork traditional culture evolved through the nineteenth and twentieth centuries, so many folklife themes are best treated in historical context. These include settlement history, subsistence farming, transportation, logging and sawmills, and coal mining.

SETTLEMENT HISTORY

Topics to be treated include the cultural and geographic background of settlers who inhabited the area, their routes of migration into the area and reasons for coming, and the communities they established. Opportunities exist through published local history, oral histories collected during this project, and additional research to interpret the settlement history of Station Camp and No Business communities in Tennessee and Bear Creek and Bald Knob communities in Kentucky. The history of late-nineteenth-century immigrant communities outside the recreation area boundaries also should be addressed. These include Rugby in Morgan County and Allardt in Fentress County.

SUBSISTENCE FARMING

The ecological and small-scale technology aspects of traditional subsistence farming are topics of current interest to the general public. Treatment of subsistence farming should show how early settlers attained maximum utilization of natural resources in creating a largely self-sufficient lifestyle in farming communities prior to the railroad. A picture of daily life activities and the annual round of farm and household activities should be presented.

The Oscar Blevins farm and log structures standing on the nearby Lora Blevins place are possible locations for reconstruction of subsistence farming and associated household activities and for craft and domestic skills demonstrations. The smokehouse on the Tapley property in McCreary County also could be used for interpretation. All of these sites are accessible and located in or near campgrounds.

TRANSPORTATION

Changing modes of transportation played a key role in the Big South Fork area's industrial development and subsequent decline. The area railroads, particularly the O & W, are the most obvious elements, but the transportation story also includes wagon transport and the rigors of the old wagon roads and fords. The final chapter in the transportation story concerns impacts of paved roads and automobile and truck transportation on continued viability of the area's short-line railroads and on the remote communities that were bypassed by paved roads.

LOGGING AND SAWMILLS

Treatment of this topic should include preindustrial exploitation of forest resources for domestic and commercial purposes as well as industrial logging and sawmill operations. The tanbark gathering process and the old water-powered sawmills should be described as well as activities of the Stearns Coal and Lumber Company, Tennessee Stave and Lumber Company, Cumberland Valley Lumber

Company, and Whitson Pole Road. While Tennessee Stave and Lumber Company records have not been located, the Stearns Company archives are a valuable source of information for this interpretive theme.

COAL MINING

Coverage of mining should emphasize changing mine technology, the coal camps, daily life of the coal miner's family, and effects of economic conditions on the coal industry. Development of facilities at Blue Heron and at Zenith would provide the appropriate context for interpreting mining to the public. Stearns Company archives contain abundant information for use in developing this theme.

PERFORMANCE AND DEMONSTRATION

While settlement history, subsistence farming, transportation, the timber industry, and coal mining are appropriately treated in historic context through brochures, pamphlets, exhibits, reconstructions or models, videotape and film programs, etc., three other major interpretive themes must be developed through live performance and demonstration. These are music, verbal performance, and crafts, including a variety of old-time skills that can be demonstrated.

As noted elsewhere in this section, increased tourism will likely bring a larger audience to the Pickett State Park Old-Time Music Festival held each Labor Day weekend and to the Rugby Festival held in May. In order to prevent overcrowding at these events, it might be desirable for the National Park Service to work with festival planners to hold some of the musical events at nearby recreation area facilities. In addition, the recreation area might develop a festival of its own for midsummer. Music tapes recorded during this project demonstrate that the area has many fine musicians who deserve recognition and a chance to derive some economic benefits from their talents. Providing such opportunities is the best encouragement the National Park Service can offer talented young people who are in a position but now lack any real incentives to keep their parents' and grandparents' musical traditions alive.

Regular Appalachian square dances held during the peak tourist season would be an enjoyable activity for recreation area visitors. They would have an opportunity to participate in this aspect of traditional folklife firsthand, and the bands and square-dance callers employed for these events would also benefit.

Campfire programs held in recreation area campgrounds can incorporate educational and entertaining facets of regional folklife by including storytelling sessions and presentations on regional lore and customs such as weather lore and death lore.

Crafts and other old-time skills should be presented actively through demonstrations and living exhibits as well as in showcase displays and craft shops. As suggested elsewhere, the Oscar Blevins farm would be an excellent site for such activities. A crafts fair could be held in conjunction with the midsummer music festival suggested above.

Additional Folklife Documentation

This report, the accompanying oral history tapes housed at the University of Kentucky, and detailed recommendations concerning which resource persons to consult on specific topics (not reproduced in this edition of the report) are the starting point for future focused research and documentation activities to build on the overview contained in this folklife survey. Priorities for working with resource persons must be set with several factors in mind:

1. *The immediate need to develop interpretive materials and activities around the major themes outlined above and in conjunction with the planned development areas*
2. *The need to work with older persons and those in bad health as soon as possible, whether or not their areas of expertise have top priority in the interpretive program*
3. *The need, for public relations reasons, to complete land acquisition and make large strides in constructing facilities before expecting maximum public cooperation in developing the interpretive program. A long-term research and documentation program, carried out at least in part by uniformed Park Service personnel, would be a positive contribution to understanding and good relations between the Park Service and the community*

Means of developing interpretive themes for public consumption should include brochures and pamphlets; exhibits of photographs, maps, artifacts, etc.; self-guided tours; reconstructions and models; demonstrations of crafts and old-time skills both live and through videotape, slide, or film presentations; and programs of music, verbal performance, and dance that allow for public participation. The following are some specific research and documentation activities to consider.

MUSIC

In order to take advantage of the excellent groundwork already laid and to avoid needless duplication of effort, further documentation of music should be undertaken in coordination with Bob Fulcher of the Tennessee State Parks system. Largely because of Fulcher's work at Pickett State Park and the Old-Time Music

Festivals held at the park each Labor Day, more is known of musicians from Pickett and Fentress Counties in Tennessee and Wayne County, Kentucky, than those from Scott, Morgan, or McCreary Counties. This imbalance needs to be rectified in future work.

STORY

Legends, personal and family anecdotes, and haint tales are easily collected because these stories are still told in family and other gatherings. Traditional Appalachian items such as Jack tales, Irishman stories, and old riddles are known to older storytellers but are not part of their current repertoire. Professionals based near the Big South Fork area are best situated to carry out long-term collecting of oral genres among elderly Big South Fork residents. They could work cooperatively with Park Service interpretive personnel who are based year-round in the recreation area.

CRAFTS

Photography, especially videotaping, is the most effective means of documenting craft activities and special skills like notching up logs and riving boards. However, these techniques involve the crafters as well as researchers in substantial expenditures of time and other resources. Thus, the matter of compensation needs to be addressed as well as the logistics of providing appropriate settings, supplies, materials, etc. for persons demonstrating activities that they do not normally engage in on a regular basis.

In addition to documenting crafts and skills, the Park Service should explore various means of supporting craftspeople actively. Use of local craft items in lodges and other facilities, craft shops featuring local work, craft demonstration programs, and an annual crafts fair are some suggested means to achieve this end.

ORAL HISTORY

Oral history tapes are an invaluable source of information about daily life activities not captured in other kinds of documents; they abound in human-interest material. The present oral history sample is biased toward older persons, toward people who live or once lived within the proposed recreation area boundaries, and toward the topics of settlement history, technology, and economic history. In future research this sample should be broadened in age range, geographical scope, and topical coverage.

PHOTOGRAPH ARCHIVE

Experiences during the survey indicate that over a period of years, an excellent archive of old photographs could be assembled. Most family photographs show people in neutral settings that do not convey much cultural information, but each family collection contains some exceptions, and some collections prove to be gold mines of information. Because all of the area newspapers fairly regularly publish old photographs submitted by readers, back files of newspapers (available on microfilm in the respective state libraries) would be a valuable tool in locating owners of promising photograph collections.

UNPUBLISHED WRITINGS

In comparison with published material on the Cumberland River proper, published writings on the Big South Fork are scanty. An effort should be made to locate additional primary material in the form of diaries, letters, unpublished manuscripts, church and business records, and the like. Cooperation of local historical societies should be sought in locating such materials and obtaining access to them.

HISTORICAL ARCHAEOLOGY

To date, resources and opportunities for historical archaeology within the recreation area have not been exploited. Excellent opportunities for industrial archaeology exist at Blue Heron and at Zenith, but both of these sites are rather recent. Of greater concern in the context of folklife research are the early subsistence farming settlements whose history extends back into the early nineteenth century. No living witness can give firsthand information about these settlements in their heyday, but there is still an opportunity to work with older former residents to coordinate ethnohistorical and archeological approaches to understanding these settlements.

The No Business settlement is an especially promising candidate for research of this kind. It is a typical example of the dispersed farmstead type of community established along the Big South Fork and its major tributaries by early Euro-American settlers. A number of collapsed structures are still in situ and several former residents are still living.

COOPERATIVE RESEARCH PROGRAMS

Interpretive personnel should be aware of existing community groups that share their interests and goals and should work with these groups whenever possible. These groups include local historical societies like the Litton Historical Society of Oneida and the Fentress County Historical Society; the Rugby Restoration Association; the craft cooperatives; and local civic clubs such as Kiwanis and Rotary.

Cooperation with local schools also is possible. Folklore classes taught at Oneida High School during the past few years have included Foxfire-inspired research projects. Students have obtained a variety of information from parents and grandparents (see Oneida High School n.d.). Programs of this kind should be supported and encouraged as a means of promoting an interest in traditional culture among the area's young people and as a means of augmenting the store of knowledge about the area.

Land Acquisition, Relocation, and Social Impact Assessment

Although evaluation of the land acquisition and relocation programs was not included in the scope of this research, certain problems became apparent during our initial survey of households subject to relocation and through continued contact with many of the affected individuals. These problems are discussed here because relocation does have an obvious impact on local folklife, but more importantly because this information may help to improve the land acquisition and relocation programs developed for future federal construction projects. The Big South Fork land acquisition and relocation program could have been improved by better background research on the affected population and more timely and effective communication with landowners and tenants.

BACKGROUND RESEARCH

The brief statistical compilation of social and economic data contained in the Final Environmental Impact Statement (U.S. Army Corps of Engineers 1976a) was not an adequate social impact assessment when judged by provisions set forth in the Community Development Act of 1974. There is no evidence that tenants and resident landowners were interviewed to gather basic data on land ownership patterns, settlement patterns, land use, economic pursuits, and other topics relevant to the land acquisition and relocation issue. Had such research been done, two special problems might have been foreseen: one concerns the homestead provision of the relocation program; the other concerns the magnitude of social impact on affected families.

A common land ownership practice among residents of the area meshes badly with the homestead provision as outlined in the existing relocation regulations (U.S. Army Corps of Engineers 1973). The problem is this: many older landowners are accustomed to deed over property to a child in return for care in their old age. This practice obviates the need for a will and shifts the property tax burden to the more affluent child. The child typically lives elsewhere, however, often out of state. Even though these elderly residents are just the kind of people the homestead provision was designed to help, it does not apply to them because they are no longer landowners, but tenants. The children are ineligible to homestead because they are landowners, but absentee. Had this local practice of land transfer been understood before the land acquisition program began, the policy might have been adjusted to extend the homesteading privilege to landowner-tenants in this situation. This adjustment would have brought the letter of the law in line with its intent.

Second, the statistic "number of households" tells little about the magnitude of social impact on residents. While there were thirty-four or more separate year-round households within the proposed recreation area boundaries in 1974 at the time of authorization, these households cluster into a much smaller number of extended families. In one case, as many as seven branch households of a single extended family will be subject to relocation. This fact is a natural consequence of the typical settlement pattern in which close kin live near one another. Also typical is primary reliance upon kin for emotional and material support when needed.

Loss of family land and relocation produce considerable emotional and economic stress under the best of circumstances, and these stresses are exacerbated in the Big South Fork case by the fact that many households will have no immediate kin to turn to who are not facing the same problems as themselves. This situation calls for more aid from outsiders, particularly the responsible agencies, than might otherwise be needed both to complete the process of moving and to locate suitable new residences. Extended families that now occupy households adjacent to one another will want to duplicate this arrangement when they relocate. To be effective, relocation assistance must be offered in a personal rather than bureaucratic manner.

COMMUNICATION

Better communication—that is, more direct, face-to-face communication—would have been the best means land acquisition and relocation officers could have used to improve their relations with landowners and tenants. Mass media news releases and public meetings are not sufficient means to communicate with these persons. Workers with social science skills should have begun door-to-door visits as soon as boundary lines were clearly defined so that land acquisition procedures, relocation benefits, and probable timetables could have been explained in person to everyone directly affected. In a situation where many older citizens with limited transportation facilities are involved, and where many have little formal education or experience in dealing with bureaucracies, the agencies involved must take the initiative in communication. Distributing a printed brochure describing relocation benefits is not a sufficient guarantee that the information is understood and all its implications fully grasped, nor is maintaining an office in Oneida sufficient guarantee that landowners and tenants have access to the information they need.

The long delay between authorization of the recreation area and completion of land acquisition has magnified the problem of poor communication, because it has provided ample time for misunderstandings and rumors to flourish and has prolonged the uncertainty of the families faced with land loss and relocation. The strategy of first acquiring the large Stearns landholdings has pragmatic value from a management standpoint but can be questioned from a social perspective. Ideally, the land acquisition process should have proceeded expeditiously and smoothly from an initial social impact assessment phase, to policy planning, to communication with affected landowners and tenants, to property assessment, acquisition, and relocation. Giving priority to land acquisition in overall project funding would have achieved important conservation as well as social ends: a few potentially significant structures and many acres of timber have been destroyed during the lengthy delays in land acquisition.

In sum, based on a more intensive and prolonged contact with Big South Fork area residents than McCracken's (1980), the folklife survey research team concurs substantially with many of McCracken's recommendations.

Construction Phase

This discussion deals with appropriate interpretive uses for existing structures and other cultural features, space requirements for interpretive programs and activities, and contributions local craftspeople can make during the construction phase of the project.

USE OF EXISTING STRUCTURES AND OTHER CULTURAL FEATURES

The following structures and cultural features should be maintained or restored as a part of the folklife interpretive program.

The Oneida and Western Railroad. The O & W roadbed should be restored for excursion train travel between Oneida and East Jamestown. Interpretive facilities located along the rail bed could appropriately deal with local mining and lumber operations as well as railroad history. Zenith is a prime location for such facilities.

Local opinion favors an excursion train schedule arranged so that trains depart from both East Jamestown and Oneida at intervals that will permit a visit of a few hours in the destination town. (The problem of transportation between East Jamestown and Jamestown apparently has not been addressed.) Local opinion also strongly favors night use of the railroad for commercial freight. This idea has the virtue of removing coal trucks and other freight haulers from local roads (an aesthetic benefit to tourists), saving fuel now used in hauling freight by an indirect highway route between Jamestown and Oneida and allowing the restored railroad to pay for itself, at least to some extent.

Blue Heron. Because the Blue Heron tipple represents a serious safety threat in its present state, it should be demolished or reconstructed for interpretive purposes. Its progress to date through the National Register nomination process is a strong argument in favor of restoration, and this certainly is the course favored by the folklife research team and by most local citizens, who also support location of a coal mining museum complex at the Blue Heron site. Because an interpretive center is needed to explain the tipple to the public, this is the logical place to tell the entire story of coal mining and coal camp life. A reconstructed company store could house the interpretive center and public facilities. Reconstructed mine buildings and miners' housing could be added to the complex later.

There is no development area especially well located in relation to Steams logging operations, so it might be desirable and economical to present Steams logging operations as well as mining activities at the Blue Heron interpretive center.

Log Structures. Standing log structures within the recreation area include examples of designs used from earliest settlement through the 1920s. As many of these as possible should be preserved. Their value lies not in unique architectural features and unique historical significance, but rather in their illustrating typical folk architectural designs and construction and providing the best possible background for interpreting subsistence farming and associated domestic activities to the public.

Recommendations to maintain the complex of buildings at the Parch Corn Hunting Camp for use as a primitive camp area are well taken. Although some of these buildings have been moved from other sites and modified, most are presently in good condition. The four-crib log barn is rare enough at this time to warrant its preservation on architectural grounds. The original saddlebag component of the lodge is also an interesting type not found elsewhere within the recreation area. A self-guided folk architecture exhibit could be designed around the complex of buildings at Parch Corn Hunting Camp.

Proximity of the Oscar Blevins farm to the Bandy Creek campground, current use and condition of the property, and the presence of two log buildings (circa 1900) make this the best choice for a farm life interpretive center. In addition to exhibits of household and farm implements, videotape presentations, and other museumlike means of presenting information, this center could provide demonstrations of crafts and skills such as cider making, sorghum making, soap making, shingle making, and board riving.

Because the Lora Blevins farm is nearby and easily accessible from the Oscar Blevins property, log structures there could provide an alternative or supplementary site for demonstration activities, especially during special events such as a folklife festival or crafts fair.

The Tapley property in McCreary County is the site of the Bear Creek campground. The smokehouse on that property should be preserved for its architectural and interpretive value. With some restoration, the Tapley cabin and its porches could have provided a pleasant gathering place for campground group activities, but this building already has been destroyed by fire. This loss points up the need for adequate and timely protection of remaining structures of architectural and interpretive value.

SPACE REQUIREMENTS

Space appropriate for exhibits, slide/tape or videotape presentations, campfire talks, and other conventional interpretive activities has been incorporated into preliminary designs of recreation area facilities, but additional planning to provide space for live demonstrations of crafts, music performances, square dancing, and similar activities may be needed. A large meeting room and patio areas at each of the lodges could accommodate these crafts and music activities. Fairly large pavilions in the primary campgrounds may also be desirable.

The research and documentation activities recommended above will generate files, sound recording collections, photograph collections, and similar materials that will need to be housed adequately for their preservation and convenient use. Ideally, the storage area should have both humidity and temperature control. Adequate space and facilities for constructing exhibits also will be required.

CONTRIBUTIONS OF LOCAL CRAFTSPEOPLE

Local residents, particularly craftspeople, can contribute to the construction phase of the project in various ways. First, old-timers should be consulted on the design of reconstructions that might be built at Blue Heron, Zenith, or elsewhere, and their advice on rehabilitating log structures might also be helpful.

Second, local residents can be employed in construction. There are many experienced construction workers in the area; some are versed in stone masonry, log, and post-and-beam techniques used in the area's traditional folk architecture. Full-size or scale models that might be desired for interpretive purposes could be built by local crafters. These models might include a moonshine still, a sorghum mill, a water-powered gristmill/sawmill, and the like. Objects needed for exhibits could be reproduced by local craftspeople if originals were unobtainable.

Finally, interior decoration of recreation area facilities, especially the lodges, offers many opportunities to employ local craftspeople and to create an authentic local atmosphere for these facilities. Several of the furniture designs already developed by local woodworkers would be suitable for lounge and dining room areas. Ceramic and wooden tableware for the dining rooms could be obtained from local crafters, as well as some woven items.

Operations and Management

CRAFT SHOPS

Craft shops operated by the Park Service should provide an example to private shops in the area. They should limit their stock to Appalachian craft items, emphasizing those made in Kentucky and Tennessee. The work of local craftspeople should make up as large a proportion of the stock as possible. These shops should be managed independently of the area's craft cooperatives but should advertise the existence of the cooperatives to the public through purchasing their goods at wholesale and through displaying the brochures of the cooperatives and labeling or identifying items produced by cooperative members. It is important that shop managers and salespeople be knowledgeable about the crafts they sell and that they be able to establish and implement quality standards. Well-qualified craft shop managers could improve the business and the economic opportunities of their local suppliers by periodically sponsoring workshops to help craftspeople accustomed to producing only for home consumption direct their work toward the tourist market.

FOOD SERVICE

Inclusion of some regional foods on lodge menus with brief background notes for information would be a simple but effective addition to the program of folklife interpretation.

INFORMATION CLEARINGHOUSE

Live performances and demonstrations should be an important part of the Park Service interpretive program. In addition, outside events such as singings, square dances, craft shows, county fairs, and farm auctions could provide tourists with exposure to local folklife. A calendar of such events should be maintained at each of the lodges and at the visitor centers.

PREEXISTING SPECIAL EVENTS

The Labor Day Old-Time Music Festival held each year at Pickett State Park and the Spring Festival at Rugby are two special events held close to the recreation area boundaries that are certain to attract additional visitors after recreation area construction is complete. In both cases, the present attendance levels strain parking and restroom facilities. Looking ahead, it would seem to be desirable for the National Park Service to work with planners of these events to schedule some of the activities within the recreation area. If participants were dispersed over two or three areas, the strain on facilities would be eased and the intimate atmosphere that now characterizes these events could be better preserved. The recreation area should develop its own midsummer folklife festival to showcase music and crafts.

Summary

Some aspects of traditional culture are fast disappearing from the Big South Fork area, so that timely documentation is the only means of preserving knowledge of these aspects. Others, notably crafts and music, have reached a critical stage when it is all-important to encourage talented young people to continue practicing traditional skills. If the recreation area's interpretive program provides opportunities for local people to display their knowledge and skills and receive recognition and financial reward for their efforts, this will encourage these young people to pursue activities and interests that they may now view as "old-fashioned" in a pejorative sense.

For this reason, the recommendations presented here emphasize activities such as performance and demonstration, employment opportunities, and craft sales opportunities. Some aspects at least of Big South Fork folklife can and should be perpetuated in living form rather than simply preserved through documentation. A program actively encouraging continuance of traditional skills addresses not only the need to mitigate cultural impacts in the most effective way, but also the goal of economic development that was the original stimulus for a federal project in the Big South Fork area.

Postscript 2002

To thoroughly assess how creation of the Big South Fork National River and Recreation Area has affected local people and culture would require systematic research more extensive than the 1979–80 folklife documentation project. The brief comments that follow are personal observations and impressions, not research findings.

Cultural Heritage Interpretation

The National Park Service has developed a rich and diverse program of natural and cultural heritage interpretation and environmental education. Year-round visitors who stop by one of the visitor centers or stay at Bandy Creek or Blue Heron can enjoy displays and collect print information pertaining to subsistence farming, logging and sawmills, and coal mining. Seasonal festivals and special programs celebrate cultural heritage and attract additional visitors to the recreation area. These include a demonstration and celebration of spring planting and farm life at the Lora Blevins place near Bandy Creek Campground; Cumberland Heritage Day, a fall celebration of traditional lore and skills held at Blue Heron; and "Haunting in the Hills," a storytelling festival with side attractions of crafts and music held each fall at Bandy Creek. This event has grown to become the largest free storytelling event in the Southeast.

In addition to regular programs in campgrounds, rangers also provide hands-on experiences in natural and cultural history and environmental education to school groups who visit the recreation area. They also take programs out into the schools, senior citizen centers, and festival events of surrounding communities. Many people have been involved over the years, but most notable is ranger Howard Duncan, whose first-person long-hunter interpretation brings stories of the region's preindustrial past to life. Appalachian people often have been critical of outsiders' patronizing interpretations of the culture. Howard Duncan is a native of this region who was a popular teacher and school principal before joining the National Park Service. He is both a respectful and authentic interpreter of local culture and history and a wonderful entertainer. On Pioneer Days in the recreation area or in pioneer encampments set up at regional festivals, Howard Duncan and his wife, Ranger Sue Duncan, demonstrate the knowledge and skills men and women needed for daily life. Festival events provide opportunities for artists and craftspeople, musicians, and storytellers to demonstrate their talents and teach them in workshops.

Facilities

The most ambitious project in cultural heritage interpretation at Big South Fork has been stabilization of the old coal tipple at Blue Heron, Kentucky, and development of a museum complex around it. Exhibits in a pavilion near the tipple provide history of the Stearns Coal and Lumber Company's timber operations as well as coal mining. Ghost structures mark the approximate locations of the company store, church, school, and superintendent's house. During planning of the recreation area, there was a groundswell of public support for a museum attraction at Blue Heron. Retired miners, their families, and other residents of McCreary County became key participants in developing the museum through donating artifacts for displays, recording recollections to provide the verbal interpretation in each ghost structure, and sometimes being on hand to share experiences with tourists.

Cessation of all industrial activity following transfer of Stearns Company land to the federal government meant abandonment of the last few miles of the Kentucky and Tennessee Railroad that were still in use in the 1970s. That made it possible to restore the railroad as a tourist attraction operated cooperatively by a private concession and the National Park Service. Although there is automobile access to Blue Heron, the Big South Fork Scenic Railway is the most colorful and authentic way to visit the site. The depot in Stearns, the company store, and the headquarters building are the core of private heritage tourism development in the former capital of Stearns operations. Recently, local investors acquired and restored the Worley mine camp to provide a novel bed and breakfast experience for visitors to the area. The presence of the recreation area as a magnet for visitors has stimulated similar nongovernmental cultural heritage initiatives in Tennessee, particularly in and around Rugby and Allardt. No facilities for interpretation have yet been developed for the Oneida and Western Railroad or Zenith.

Many of my recommendations concerning facilities and opportunities for interpretation are moot because plans to construct a lodge in Kentucky and one in Tennessee never were realized. Back in 1979, many local residents were skeptical that the Big South Fork's outdoor recreation attractions would draw enough visitors or keep them in the area long enough to boost the economy. They wanted a tourist attraction at Blue Heron, restoration of the Oneida and Western as an excursion railroad (and perhaps a nighttime freight hauler), federally funded highway improvements, and the lodges. They wanted the recreation area to provide tourist attractions that would help their counties overcome chronic underemployment.

In fact, economic growth based on private entrepreneurship and collaboration among state and local government and nonprofit heritage and arts organizations probably has been more effective in stimulating economic revitalization than if the National Park Service were competing to provide lodging, food, and other services through concessions.

Change and Cultural Persistence

Longtime residents were right to doubt that outdoor recreation and tourism would become a panacea for the region's chronic economic woes. Unemployment rates in these counties continue to be high in comparison to state averages. The Big South Fork National River and Recreation Area's annual visitation grew slowly and did not break the one million barrier until 2001. But a windshield tour of the region reveals dramatic changes since 1979—better roads, a great deal of new home construction, and national franchise businesses. As their history would suggest, residents of these counties have been resilient and resourceful in meeting the challenges and taking advantage of opportunities the recreation area has brought.

Modernization and economic development have improved quality of life in the region without undermining values and identity. Thanks to the comprehensive program of cultural heritage interpretation provided by the National Park Service, it would be virtually impossible for someone to visit the area and leave without knowledge of local history and appreciation for the people who lived along the Big South Fork and the lives they led prior to creation of the recreation area. As I hoped, attention focused on local history and culture by the National Park Service and visitors' positive response has fostered local pride in regional culture and spawned additional heritage conservation projects. In this sense, Big South Fork folk culture is alive and well in the twenty-first century.

Appendix 1:

Household Survey

This appendix includes the questionnaire used in conducting a household survey of families residing within the recreation area boundaries in July of 1979. One adult member of each household was asked to respond for the household, but often two respondents worked separately with two researchers, one answering the questions in parts A and C of the interview while the other completed the architectural survey (part B).

The researchers asked all questions verbally and recorded answers on the worksheets reproduced on the following pages. No part of the survey was a paper-and-pencil questionnaire for the residents. Questions were posed in the general order in which they appear on the work forms, but the wording was not always uniform. The work forms should be considered a guide to a structured interview rather than a questionnaire in the strict sense of the term.

Following the work forms is a tabulation of survey responses that are easily quantified. The primary purpose of the survey was not to gather statistical data but to identify elements of the folk culture to be documented and resource persons who might contribute to the folklife project in various ways.

A

(Introduction)
1. Do you or anyone you know: (who, what, where)
    1. Play a musical instrument
    2. Sing traditional songs—ballads
    3. Know old-time stories
    4. Know old-time dances
    5. Make furniture
    6. Whittle or carve in wood
    7. Spin
    8. Weave
    9. Quilt

        10. Make baskets
        11. Make dolls, toys, or miniature furniture
        12. Make musical instruments
        13. Make pottery
        14. Do needlework, crochet, or knit
        15. Make tools
        16. Do blacksmithing
        17. (other)
    2. Do you have any examples of their work?
    3. Do you remember if anyone in your family ever made or did these kinds of things?
        a. If they did, was it only for family use, or did they trade or sell the products?
    4. Do you have any old furniture, tools, or other things that belonged to your parents, grandparents, or other relatives?
        a. What can you tell us about the history of these things, who made them, when did they make them, etc.?

B

Further Study
General Architecture
(Introduction)
[Complete 1–7 below for residence and each additional standing structure on property]
1. What is this structure used for?
2. What is it made of?
3. When was it built?
4. Do you know who built it?
5. How many rooms does this structure have? (sketch)
    What is each room used for?
6. Have there been any additions or changes made since built?
    a. What are they?
    b. When were they done?
    c. Why were they done?
7. Have you changed the structure in any way?
    What—When—Why?
8. If you could change anything you wanted to about this house what would you change?
9. What's the best thing about living in this house?
10. What's the worst thing?
11. If you could live anywhere you wanted to, where would you live?

Cemetery
(Introduction)
12. Do you have a cemetery on the property?
13. Do you know of any early cemeteries?
    Description:
    Location:

C

1. How many people live in this house?
2. What are their ages?
3. How are they related?
4. How long have you lived here?
5. Do you own or rent this place?
6. Where have you lived before?
7. Do you know who lived here before you?
8. Do you own any other property?
   Where?
   What is it used for?
9. Do you have relatives living nearby?
   Where?
10. Do you have relatives in other parts of Tennessee (Kentucky)?

C2

11. How long has your family lived in Tennessee (Kentucky)?
    a. Where did they come from?
    b. Do you know why they came?
12. Have any of your family moved away from the area?
    a. Do they come back to visit?
13. What things does your family do together?

C3

14. How often do you get together with your relatives who live nearby?
    For what activities?
15. How often do you get together with neighbors who aren't relatives?
    For what activities?
16. Do you belong to a church? Which church? Where is it?
    a. Have you always belonged to this church?
    b. Do most of your relatives living around here belong to your church?
17. In what kinds of church activities does your family participate?

C4

18. What are the present occupations of the adults in the house?
    Is it a year-round job?
    Have they always done this? If not, what were their previous occupations?
19. What kinds of chores does each member of the household do?
20. Do you buy most of your food, clothes, tools. etc?
21. Do you trade at a local country store?
    Which one?
    What kinds of things do you buy there?
22. Do you ever go to larger towns to shop?
    Where?
    What kinds of things do you buy there?

C5

23. Do you use mail order?
    From where?
    What kinds of things do you order this way?
24. Have you ever, do you now, or do you know anyone who (for positive responses—who, what, how often, time of year):
    a. Collects fuel for use, sale, or trade?
    b. Cuts timber for use, sale, or trade?
    c. Gathers plants for use, sale, or trade?
    d. Hunts, fishes, or traps for use, sale, or trade?
    e. Keeps bees or hunts for wild honey for use, sale, or trade?
25. Do you know anyone who gathers plants to help someone who is sick?
26. Do you grow any crops for sale or trade? What do you grow? How much?

C6

27. Have you ever raised animals for food—meat, eggs, dairy products? What did you raise? When did you do it?
28. Do you have a garden to grow food for use at home?
    a. What do you grow there?
    b. How much of the family's food comes from the garden?
    c. How do you choose what to grow?
    d. Do you preserve any of the food from your garden? How? How much? Who taught you?

C7

29. Did your parents do any of the things we've mentioned—hunt, etc?
30. Are your children learning any of these things?
31. Do you ever help out neighbors or relatives with work around their place? Who? What do you do? When? How are you repaid?

TABULATION OF HOUSEHOLD SURVEY RESPONSES

Survey Responses

County	Completed Surveys	To Be Returned	Refusals	Failure to Contact	Vacation Home
McCreary	5	1	1		
Fentress	4				
Scott	14	1	2	7	2
Total	23	2	3	7	2

Number of Occupants per Household

County	Number of Responses	Range	Mean	Median
McCreary	5	1–10	5.6	5
Fentress	4	1–6	3.5	
Scott	14	1–7	3.4	4

Household Composition

County	Type 1	Type 2	Type 3	Type 4
McCreary	4	1	3	
Fentress	3			1
Scott	18	2		

Definitions: Type 1: composed of husband, wife, and children. Type 2: composed of widow(er) and children. Type 3: composed of brother and sister. Type 4: composed of single (including divorced) person and children.

Time on Tract
(in Years)

County	Number of Responses	Range	Mean	Median
McCreary	7	1–30	12.4	10
Fentress	4	3–39		
Scott	23	1–30	9.3	7

Tract Ownership or Rental

County	Own	Rent	Other
McCreary	5	1	1
Fentress	4		
Scott	21	2	
Total	30	3	1

Residence History

County	Type 1	Type 2	Type 3	Type 4	Type 5
McCreary	1	2	1	1	
Fentress	1		3		
Scott		4	3	2	4

Definitions: Type 1: Born on tract and continuous residence there. Type 2: Born in county and continuous residence but not on present tract. Type 3: Returned to county of birth after a period of residence elsewhere. Type 4: Born outside of and moved to county of residence; kin ties in county. Type 5: Born outside of and moved to county of residence; no kin ties in county.

Current Occupations
(Counties Combined)

Occupation	Number of Households
Farming	3
Contract Lumbering	5
Wage Work	8
Retired	5
Welfare/Pension	8

Participation in Traditional Subsistence Activities

Activity	Now—Yes	Now—No	Used to Do It
Collect fuel	11	12	
Cut timber	9	11	3
Collect wild plants	13	9	1
Hunt and/or fish	19	2	2
Keep bees	5	16	6
Collect medicinal herbs	1	19	3

Amount of Food Grown on Tract
(Counties Combined)

Amount	Number of Households
None	2
Some	6
About half	
Most or all	14

Sale of Crops and Livestock
(Counties Combined)

Activity	Now—Yes	Now—No	Used to Do It
Sell Crops	9	11	3
Sell Livestock	2		

Food Preservation Techniques
(Counties Combined)

Technique	Now—Yes	Now—No	Used to Do It
Canning	13	2	1
Freezing	8		
Drying	2		

Rank Order of Garden Crops Reported
(Counties Combined)

Crop	Number of Times Reported
Beans	13
Tomatoes	11
Cabbage	11
Potatoes	9
Corn	9
Onions	8
Cucumbers	7
Beets	4
Okra	4
Carrots	3
Lettuce	3

Other reported crops: popcorn, turnips, peppers, melons, mustard, strawberries
Orchard crops reported: apples, pears, peaches.

Most Frequent Reasons for Families "Getting Together"
(Counties Combined)

Activity	Number of Times Reported
Fishing	11
Visiting (talking)	8
Hunting	6
Family dinners	5
Reunions	4

Other reported activities: swimming, hiking, funerals, working, picnics, camping, portraits, music making, storytelling, volleyball, badminton, horseshoes, barbecues.

Church Membership Responses for Households
(Counties Combined)

Question	Yes	No
Church membership?	18	4
Always belonged to that church?	12	5
Do other relatives belong to the same church?	10	4

Appendix 2:
Cemetery Inventory

This inventory includes sixteen cemeteries located inside the recreation area boundaries, plus an additional twenty-two cemeteries located outside but close to the recreation area. These additional cemeteries were included in a survey conducted during the fall and winter of 1979–80 in order to expand the picture of settlement chronology, locate and document additional examples of noteworthy grave markers and decorations, and alert resource managers to possible impacts of the recreation area on these cemeteries and citizens' access to them. Comments from field observations in 1979–80 supplement information gathered by Coastal Zone Resources and published in their Natural Resource Atlas, Big South Fork National River and Recreation Area, produced for the U.S. Army Corps of Engineers, Nashville District, March 1979. Coastal Zone Resources site numbers for cemeteries within recreation area boundaries are given in these entries so that data from the two sources can easily be integrated. Cemeteries are listed in numerical order. The numbers are keyed to the accompanying map.

County historical societies have undertaken extensive cemetery inventory projects during the past twenty years and have posted much of the information on the Internet.

1. NANCY GRAVES CEMETERY, WILSON RIDGE RD., MCCREARY COUNTY, KENTUCKY.
USGS Quad: Barthell, KY 1954
Coordinates: 4062000N 718000E

An extremely large cemetery of 200–300 graves, many without markers but some with rather elaborate commercial monuments dating from 1900 to the present. Every blade of grass is cleared from the graves and the spaces between them.

Predominant families include Winchester, King, Dougherty, Ross, Waters, Watters, Wilson, Phillips, Lewis, Maxwell, Whitehead, Troxell, Hill, Slaven.

2. WINCHESTER CEMETERY, NEAR GREGORY, MCCREARY COUNTY, KENTUCKY.

USGS Quad: Barthell, KY 1954
Coordinates: 4060500N 713500E

This cemetery is on the south side of the road from Bell Farm through Gregory to White Oak Junction. It is unusual because it lies in a very low area between Rock Creek and the road. At the east end of the cemetery is the grave of William P. Troxel (1879–1896). Between this commercial monument and others belonging to the Winchester family is an area of thirty to fifty graves marked by fieldstones. Scratched on one of these is THE DO / of SARAH / FOSTER.

Joseph Winchester (1859–1885), oldest monument
William Winchester (1827–1890)
Marinda, wife of Wm. Winchester (1825–1903)
Alie Winchester (1889–1919)
Nancy Isabell Spradlin, da of Wm. Winchester (1883–1913)
Lora, da of Peck and Dora Winchester (1909-1911)
Dora Troxell Winchester (1886–1919)
Lucie Troxel (homemade cast concrete marker without dates)
Barbara Troxel (1870–1957)
John Foster (1857–1907)
Sarah J. Foster (1852–1920)
Nancy Foster (1829–1903)
OF (?) (Dec. Feb. 8, 1887) (homemade carved inscription and hand motif)
Other names represented with death dates 1899–1977: Bell, Cellears, Hamilton, Abbott, Hall, Watson

3. HILL CEMETERY, NEAR BELL FARM, MCCREARY COUNTY, KENTUCKY.

USGS Quad: Bell Farm, KY 1954
Coordinates: 4060000N 709000E

Small family cemetery grown up in weeds but recently decorated. Consists of four graves marked by uninscribed fieldstones and the following commercial stones with short epitaphs:

Sarah A. Hill (1864–1930)
W. M. Hill (1847–1933)
Gladys Hill (1929–1930)

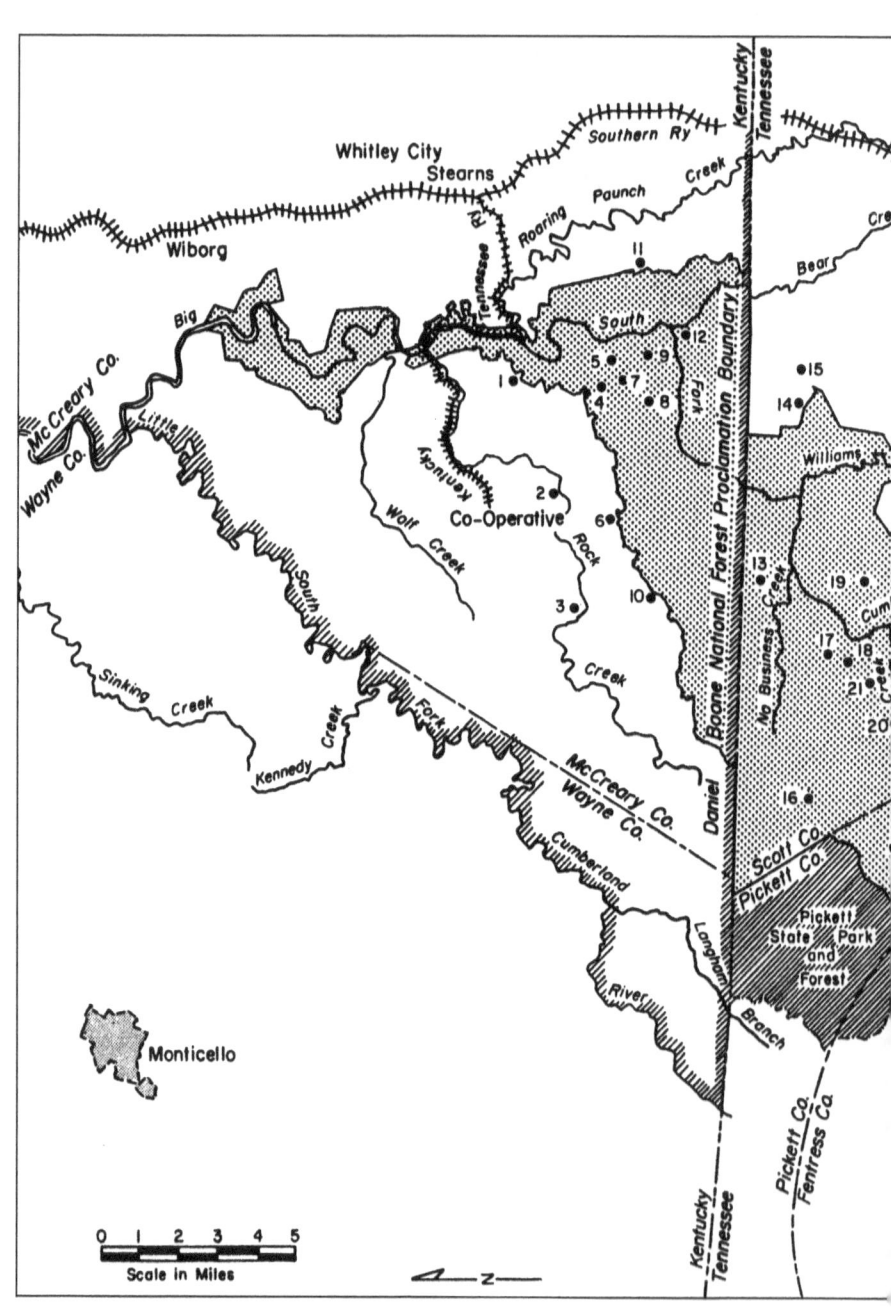

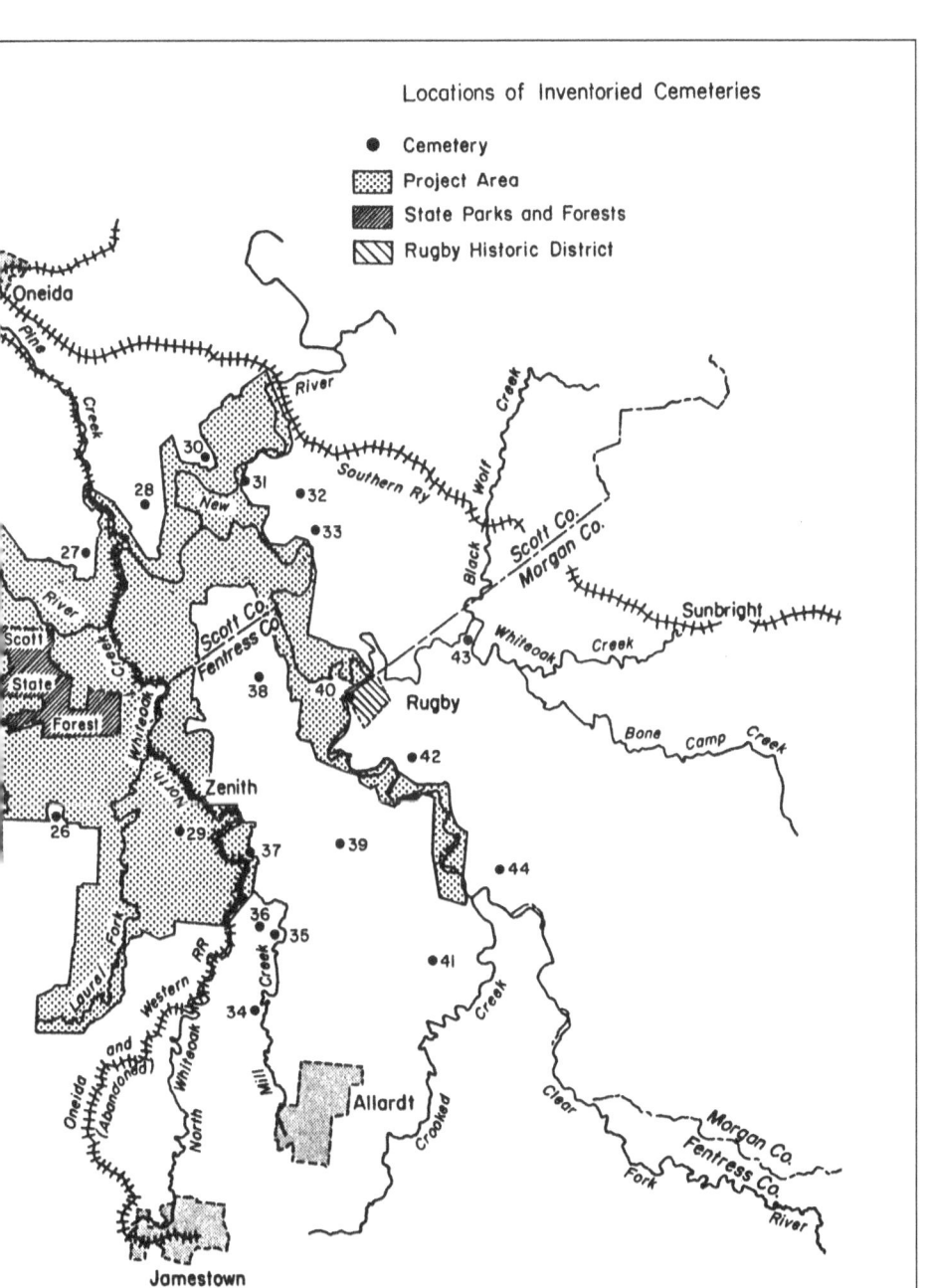

Bud Roy Hill (1931–1932)
Arlie Hill (1904–1950)
James R. Hill (b. and d. 1970)

4. BARRS CEMETERY, SOUTH OF BEECH GROVE CHURCH, MCCREARY COUNTY, KENTUCKY.

USGS Quad: Barthell, KY 1954
Coordinates: 4059250N 717946E
CZR site: 546

Cemetery is unnamed on USGS map; identified as Barrs Cemetery by Crit King Sr. It is divided into two sections. The section near the road contains the following:

Hattie M. Watts (1893–1901)
Gila Hill (1857–1907)
Doyle Coil (b. and d. 1921)
Thelma Coil (b. and d. 1923)
Ike Hill (no dates)
May Hill (no dates)
Ollie Hill (1890–1955)
Dug Coil (d. 1937)
TH/ B 6 25 1891/ D 8 26 1892
The back section contains the following:
Ren Waters (1891–1907)
George P. Waters (1888–1907)
Martha, wife of Charlie Trammell (1894–1926)
Virtie Waters (b. and d. 1932)
Tapley Waters (1882–1972)
Elaney, his wife (1876–1949)
Lenville Roysden (1941–1944)
Dissie Roysden (1918–1973)
Lillie Jane Watters (1896–1972)
Henry Waters (1892–1953)
Beverly Sue Vaughn (b. and d. 1961)

5. WATERS CEMETERY, SOUTH OF BARRS CEMETERY, MCCREARY COUNTY, KENTUCKY.

USGS Quad: Barthell, KY 1954
Coordinates: 4058130N 719067E
CZR site: 545

Small family cemetery not visited.

6. POWELL KIDD CEMETERY, BALD KNOB–BEECH GROVE RD., MCCREARY COUNTY, KENTUCKY.

USGS Quad: Barthell, KY 1954
Coordinates: 4058000N 714000E

Cemetery contains about one hundred graves. Some areas are grown up in weeds but others are well maintained. A number of graves marked only by uninscribed fieldstones. Little use before 1900 is indicated by monument dates, but no monuments bear Kidd family name. Some spouses remain to be buried in joint graves.

Jhon [sic] Watson (1878–1897)
Watson (d. 1888)
Spens Watson (1885–1896)
James F. Watson (1822–195 [sic])
Col [Colonel] Watson (b. and d. 1912)
Nancy Watson (1888–1921)
J. W. Watson (1871–1935)
Jasper Watson (1890–1943)
Wm. Watson (1892–1901)
Pollie Watson (d. 1920)
Ambers Spradlin (1831–1901)
Sallie Spradlin (1831–1885)
Elizabeth (Spradlin), wife of F. M. Miller (1854–1920)
George W., son of F. M. and Eliz. Miller (1879–1901)
Mary E. Spradlin (1868–1938)
G. W. Spradlin (1876–1933)
Roenie Spradlin (1903–[illegible])
Lizzie Spradlin (1900–1921)
Virgie Spradlin (1914–1918)
Hattie, wife of Cleve Spradlin (1904–1923)
Dorta Chasteen Spradlin (1925–1926)
Burials for members of these families date from 1920–1950: Cooper, Winchester, Ross, Shoopman, Dobbs, Boyatt, Ledbetter, York, Jones, Adkins, and Foster.

7. KING CEMETERY, NEAR CECIL LEDBETTER PROPERTY, MCCREARY COUNTY, KENTUCKY.

USGS Quad: Barthell, KY 1954
Coordinates: 4057593N 718080E
CZR site: 543

Although this cemetery contains Newt King's grave, Crit King Sr. refers to the other King Cemetery (no. 9) as the Newt King Cemetery because Newt King established it near his homeplace. This cemetery is fenced, well maintained, and has permanent benches for graveside rites installed inside the fencing.

Newton King (1876–1923)
Estel King (1927–1935)
Delilah King (1869–1940)
Joe Lewis Dolen (1886–1958)
Elbert Dolen (1920–1973)
Cora F. Dolen (1896–1978)
Georgia D. [Dolen?] Taylor (1928–1962)
Lillie Mae Boyatt (1941–1942)
Jimmie Boyatt (1888–1956)
June E. dau of Mr. and Mrs. W. A. Boyatt (b. and d. 1950)
Infant son of W. A. and Evelyn Boyatt (b. and d. 1941)
Edna Ledbetter (1924–1976)
Cecil Ledbetter (1919–1976)
Karen Ann Watson (b. and d. 1955)
Carla Faye Watson (1934)
Wm. Alfred Watson (1929–1976)
Sharon Ann Watson (b. and d. 1959)
Bobby Glen, son of Mr. and Mrs. Elmer Watson (b. and d. 1952)
Cephus Watson (1905–1978)
Mother—Malinda Ross (1881–1947)
Erma Watson (1909–1936)
Arizona Wilson (1886–1928)

8. HILL CEMETERY, NEAR CECIL LEDBETTER PROPERTY, MCCREARY COUNTY, KENTUCKY.

USGS Quad: Barthell, KY 1954 Coordinates: 4057042N 717892E
CZR site no. 542

A small cemetery, grown up in weeds, containing fourteen graves. The following have inscribed markers:
Bertie Roscoe Watson (1892–1960)
Dadalea Roysden (b. and d. 1942)
Arthur E. Watson (1919–1943)
Berry Hill (1811–1902)
Berry Hill (1867–1884)
Rebecca Spradlin (1843–1923)
W. M. Ross (1889–1929)
Gertie Watson (1888–1975)

9. NEWT KING CEMETERY, ACCESSIBLE BY PRIVATE ROAD THROUGH ALFRED KING PROPERTY, MCCREARY COUNTY, KENTUCKY.

USGS Quad: Barthell, KY 1954
Coordinates: 4056930N 719587E
CZR site: 544

Newt King established this cemetery on his property. It contains fewer than thirty graves and is now grown up in weeds and undecorated, but remnants of benches for graveside rites are still visible on the slope below the cemetery.

Winfield Troxel, d. 1912*
Roe King (1912–1919)
Pete King (1879–1925)
Pete King's mother, Lillie King (1839–1925)
Naida Lee King (1926–1927)
*The birth date of 1804 is in error, according to Crit King Sr. Troxel was in young middle age when Newt King shot him in an argument.

10. GEORGE KIDD CEMETERY, LAUREL HILL COMMUNITY, MCCREARY COUNTY, KENTUCKY.

USGS Quad: Bell Farm, KY 1954
Coordinates: 4056400N 709900E

Not visited; just a few family graves, according to General Slaven and Will J. Miller. These include three George Kidds—George Raucher, Long George, and George Goady. The last person to be buried here was Jerry Lee Kidd, about 1930.

11. TROXEL CEMETERY, BESIDE FIRST OTTER CREEK UNITED BAPTIST CHURCH, ESTABLISHED IN 1865, MCCREARY COUNTY, KENTUCKY.

USGS Quad: Barthell, KY 1954
Coordinates: 4057000N 723000E

This cemetery has a new section used extensively during the 1970s and an older section containing many Troxel and Mays burials from the 1920s and 1930s. Older monuments include the following:

Flemmon C. Troxel (1871–1882)
Tapley (d. 1897)
King (d. 1896)
Riseden (1903)
Jane Worley (1854–1907)
Joshua Ross (d. 1919)

Fred Ross (d. 1918)
Hettie, dau. of Lizzie Mays (1895–1899)
George, son of Dewey and Lottie Blevins (b. and d. 1922)

12. DOLEN CEMETERY, ON TAPLEY RIDGE NEAR THE MOUTH OF BEAR CREEK, MCCREARY COUNTY, KENTUCKY.

USGS Quad: Barthell, KY 1954
Coordinates: vicinity of 4056000N 720700E

Two residents described this cemetery, but it is not mapped on the USGS Quad sheet, county highway map, or CZR map. Not located when the area was inspected on foot.

13. NO BUSINESS CEMETERY, IN FLOODPLAIN OF NO BUSINESS CREEK, SCOTT COUNTY, TENNESSEE.

USGS Quad: Barthell SW, TN–KY 1955
Coordinates: 4051830N 709355E
CZR site: 757

This cemetery is located on a bank that was partly destroyed by a landslide. Some remains were reburied in the Terry Cemetery (no. 17). Remains of a few grave markers are visible but badly eroded. A resident mentioned a second cemetery at No Business containing mostly the Nim Slaven family. This cemetery was about 1.5 miles upstream. It was not located.

———— Smith (d. 1841[?])
Nancy Smith (d. 1862)

14. BOYATT-SLAVEN CEMETERY, WEST OF FOSTER CROSSROADS, SCOTT COUNTY, TENNESSEE.

USGS Quad: Oneida North, TN–KY 1955
Coordinates: 40507000N 717400E

Not mapped on quad sheet; appears on county highway map without name. About fifty graves, mostly Boyatt and Slaven families, predominantly early twentieth century. Some Spanish American War veterans. Burials probably now occur in Foster Crossroads Cemetery.

15. FOSTER CROSSROADS CEMETERY, BESIDE FOSTER CROSSROADS BAPTIST CHURCH, SCOTT COUNTY, TENNESSEE.

USGS Quad: Oneida North, TN–KY 1955
Coordinates: 4051000N 718000E

At the top of the cemetery hill are many graves marked only by fieldstones. Those with dated monuments are post-1900. Families most represented include Boyatt, Watters, Bell, Slaven, and Foster. Burials include Jerome Boyatt (1911–1933), and Hollis Bell, Scott County's World War II purple heart recipient who was killed in action.

16. BLEVINS CEMETERY (HATTIE CEMETERY), NORTHEAST OF DIVIDE ROAD, SCOTT COUNTY, TENNESSEE.
USGS Quad: Sharp Place, TN–KY 1955
Coordinates: 4050590N 700815E
CZR site: 931

This cemetery contains fifty to sixty graves, most marked only by uninscribed fieldstones. Burials date from 1878 to 1959, but the cemetery has been recently cleaned. Ten rows of benches for graveside rites are still in place across the logging road from the cemetery.

Isaac Blevins (?–1878)
Serepta Blevins (1844–1887)
Melirina Blevins (18?–1905)
Marin Frances Blevins (1880–1903)
Amp Blevins (1887–1926)
Minnie Blevins (1913–1941)
Orpha Miller (1915–1917)
Lewis Buck (1841–1903)
Sarah Buck (?–1914)
June Blevins Slaven (1871–1902)
Granville Slaven (1857–1930)
Polly Ann Slaven (1858–1932)
George Crabtree (1899–1925)
Isaac Crabtree's infants (1941, 1942)
Joel Crabtree (1904–1954)
Hiram Crabtree (1857–1959)

17. TERRY CEMETERY, ON NO BUSINESS ROAD, SCOTT COUNTY, TENNESSEE.
USGS Quad: Barthell SW, TN–KY 1955
Coordinates: 4050045N 707210E
CZR site: 1266

This cemetery is no longer in use but is visited regularly, mowed, and decorated. There are a number of graves marked only by uninscribed fieldstones, and these include the Terry family graves, according to Mrs. General Slaven. Families represented on monuments include Slaven, Kidd, Watson, Miller, and Roysden; dates 1890–1954. Many of the Slaven markers include photographs in plastic insets. These burials are the following:

Millie E. Slaven (1868–1944)
Charley Slaven (1881–1960)
Dewey Slaven (1885–1960)
Martha Slaven (1900–1947)
Nimrod Slaven (1863–1927)
Marion Slaven (1906–1930)
Viola Slaven (1941–1954)
Reason Slaven (1906–1951)

The graves of Rev. Isham R. Roysdon (1867–1935) and his wife, Minnie Maudie (1888–1946), are covered by a simple grave house made of pole uprights and a tin roof. This shed structure was built to replace a more elaborate log grave house after it rotted and fell in, according to Mrs. General Slaven.

18. HELEN BLEVINS CEMETERY, ON THE NORTH SIDE OF PARCH CORN CREEK, SCOTT COUNTY, TENNESSEE.

USGS Quad: Barthell SW, TN–KY 1955
Coordinates: 4048164N 707700E
CZR site: 1244

A small cemetery grown up in weeds.

Jonathan Blevins (1779–1883) and two wives, Katy Troxell and Sarah Minton (marker erected by descendants in 1976)
Julie Ann, dau. of K. and N. E. King (1875–1900)
May G., dau. of K. and N. E. King (b. and d. 1891)
Infant son of K. and N. E. King (b. and d. 1879)

19. SLAVEN CEMETERY, WILLIAMS CREEK ROAD, NEAR CHIMNEY ROCKS, SCOTT COUNTY, TENNESSEE.

USGS Quad: Barthell SW, TN–KY 1955
Coordinates: 4048000N 709605E
CZR site: 1316

This cemetery is fenced but grown up in weeds and saplings and not decorated. There are many unmarked rocks but also some interesting home carved monuments. There are approximately thirty graves.

Ab—— Slaven (?–1877)
John W. Slaven (1839–1878)
John William Slaven (1884–1920)
Polly Slaven (1838–1918)
Onva Slaven (1906–1927)
Ruth Slaven
A. B. Smith (1834–1899)
Wm. Smith (1831–1892)
Anderson Smith (1800–1890)
Sarah Smith (1796–1888)
Floyd Smith (?–1933)
Preston Smith (?–1931)
Victoria Blevins (1905)
Sarah Blevins (1906–1920)
Harvey Blevins (1879–1919)
Emily Buck (1880–1926)
Lieuvada, dau F. M. and Eliz Miller (1893–1894)
Lottie Crabtree (1912–1936)
Shirley Faye, infant daughter of Lottie Crabtree (1936)

20. HATFIELD CEMETERY, BOTTOMLAND OF STATION CAMP CREEK, SCOTT COUNTY, TENNESSEE.
USGS Quad: Barthell SW, TN-KY 1955
Coordinates: 4046270N 705718E
CZR site: 1715

A small cemetery grown up in brush; about twelve graves. Named for William Riley Hatfield (1824–1892), supposedly related to the West Virginia Hatfields. W. R. Hatfield's epitaph:

> *He died in the full triumph of a living faith.*
> *He sead for nun of his friends not to grieve*
> *After Him. For if they had ar pretty a*
> *Home to go to, they would not grieve after him.*

Jonathan Burke (1797–1875)
Elizabeth Troxel Burke, wife of Jonathan Burke
Cutshort John Troxel
Patsy Winchester, mother of several of Cutshort John's children
Nearby on ridge above Charitt Creek are graves of two Tackett boys. One stone is marked MA 3 1863; the other is unmarked.

21. OWENS CEMETERY, ON STATION CAMP CREEK FLOODPLAIN, SCOTT COUNTY, TENNESSEE.

USGS Quad: Barthell SW, TN–KY 1955
Coordinates: 4046760N 706802E
CZR site: 1248

Eight members of the Owens family; two unmarked stones; two homemade markers for parents, and four commercial stones for children. Parents' markers said to have been made by Armistead Blevins.

[Father] William W. Owens (1825–1903)
Samantha Owens (b. [illegible]–1888)
James Owens [illegible dates]
George W. Owens (1892–1900)
Sarah L. Owens (1884–1889)
Electa Owens (1890–1896)
Larry Owens (1882–1892)

22. GRAVE HILL CEMETERY, ON GRAVE HILL ROAD NORTH OF ONEIDA, SCOTT COUNTY, TENNESSEE.

USGS Quad: Oneida North, TN 1955
Coordinates: 4047000N 718000E

A large, well-kept cemetery of at least one hundred graves; in use from 1881 to the present. About half of the graves have inscribed monuments. Early use by the Marcum, Foster, Phillips, and Thomas families, with continuing use by the Thomases and Phillipses; other families represented include Blevins, Slaven, Terry, and Watson.

23. THOMPSON CEMETERY, NEAR MIDDLE CREEK CAMP AREA, FENTRESS COUNTY, TENNESSEE.

USGS Quad: Sharp Place, TN–KY 1955
Coordinates: 4044138N 699150E
CZR site: 1562

A fenced, well-kept cemetery of about thirty to forty graves. A quarter of these belong to members of the Thompson family, who have continued to use the cemetery through the 1970s. Some use by the Roysden, Slaven, and Watson families. Oldest monument for Elvira (1860–1895) and J. A. Roysdan [sic] (1859–1937). Cemetery is not named on Quad sheet.

24. WEST CEMETERY, WILLIAMS CREEK ROAD, SCOTT COUNTY, TENNESSEE.
USGS Quad: Oneida North, TN 1955
Coordinates: 4044000N 714000E

A large well-kept, cemetery in use from 1923 to the present. Mostly large commercial markers with West, Slaven, Buck, and Burke families predominating. Not noted on Quad sheet.

25. JACOB BLEVINS CEMETERY, NORTH OF LEATHERWOOD FORD ROAD, SCOTT COUNTY, TENNESSEE.
USGS Quad: Honey Creek, TN 1952
Coordinates: 4041287N 705174E
CZR site: 56

A well-maintained, active cemetery of fifty to seventy-five burials with room available for expansion. First burial Jacob Blevins (d. 1869). Families represented include Blevins, Litton, Phillips, Slaven, King, Watson, Roysden.

26. JESS ROYSDEN (ALTICREST) CEMETERY, ON LEATHERWOOD ROAD, FENTRESS COUNTY, TENNESSEE.
USGS Quad: Stockton, TN 1954
Coordinates: 4039000N 700000E

Misnamed Royalston Cemetery on Quad sheet. A large, well-kept, fenced cemetery in use from 1918 to the present. About one hundred graves, most with commercial markers; one unmarked grave is a rock cairn. Well-represented families include Roysden, Hale, Hicks, Terry, Dishman, Burke, Koger, Blevins, Slaven. Other families represented include Hughes, Crabtree, Davis, Geer, Duvall, Buck, Miller.

27. SMITH CEMETERY, SOUTH OF LEATHERWOOD ROAD NEAR POWER LINE, SCOTT COUNTY, TENNESSEE.
USGS Quad: Honey Creek, TN 1952

Coordinates: 4038000N 712000E
Nine graves in a cleared area, only two of which have inscribed monuments. Another cemetery located south-southeast of this one is on private property. Neither named on Quad sheet.

Wm. Smith (1860–1931)
Sarah Smith (1865–1933)

28. PHILLIPS CEMETERY, SOUTHWEST OF ONEIDA AIRPORT, SCOTT COUNTY, TENNESSEE.

USGS Quad: Oneida South, TN 1952
Coordinates: 4035500N 714500E

Used as Phillips family plot since 1931. Used by Long and Davidson families as well as Phillips family in the 1970s.

29. CHRISTIAN CEMETERY, NORTH OF O & W ROADBED, ACCESSIBLE BY TRAIL ALONG WEST BANK OF PANTHER BRANCH, FENTRESS COUNTY, TENNESSEE.

USGS Quad: Stockton, TN 1954
Coordinates: 4033290N 700975E
CZR site: 2333

A few graves marked by fieldstones and one marked by Robbins paving brick; some sunken graves. Only one grave has been decorated recently.

Silvana Litton Sammons (1882–1922)
Mary, wife of A. G. Smith (1866–1932)

30. SULPHUR SPRINGS CEMETERY, WEST OF HELENWOOD, SCOTT COUNTY, TENNESSEE.

USGS Quad: Oneida South, TN 1952
Coordinates: 4032700N 716000E

A small, overgrown cemetery with little decoration and no evidence of recent upkeep. In use 1902–1947.

31. WRIGHT CEMETERY, 1.2 MILES NORTH OF TERRY CEMETERY (NO. 32), SCOTT COUNTY, TENNESSEE.

USGS Quad: Oneida South, TN 1952
Coordinates: 4031200N 715200E

Four, possibly five, graves of children who died in 1918; located in front yard within fifty feet of a house.

32. TERRY CEMETERY, 0.7 MILE NORTH OF BLACK CREEK CHURCH, SCOTT COUNTY, TENNESSEE.

USGS Quad: Oneida South, TN 1952
Coordinates: 4029500N 714900E

This cemetery is marked but not named on the Quad sheet. There are only three graves, all members of the Terry family, d. 1918, 1937, and 1967.

33. BLACK CREEK CROSSROADS CEMETERY, BEHIND BLACK CREEK CROSSROADS CHURCH, SCOTT COUNTY, TENNESSEE.

USGS Quad: Oneida South, TN 1952
Coordinates: 4029600N 713300E

A large, active, well-maintained cemetery in use from the 1890s to the present.

34. STOCKTON CEMETERY, SOUTH OF C & M STORE AT STOCKTON, FENTRESS COUNTY, TENNESSEE.

USGS Quad: Stockton, TN 1954
Coordinates: 4030500N 694300E

Located but not named on Quad sheet. Notable features are graves of Stockton family members with slabs forming a pitched roof between head and foot stones, and a brush arbor with benches and lectern in place for graveside rites.

James Stockton (1842–1853)
Dosha Stockton (1844–1852)
Ben Randals Stockton (1846–1920)
Ann Schilling Stockton (1855–1918)
Isaac Stockton (1808–1888)
Lemuel Stockton (1817–1847)
Dosha Randals (1783–1852)
Richard Stockton (1848–1862)

35. TERRY AND POTTER CEMETERIES, OPPOSITE ONE ANOTHER ON STOCKTON ROAD, FENTRESS COUNTY, TENNESSEE.

USGS Quad: Stockton, TN 1954
Coordinates: 4030300N 697250E

Both cemeteries are fenced, well-kept, and decorated. Fewer than forty graves each, currently in use.

36. TOMPKINS CEMETERY, SOUTH OF COUNTY ROAD 4241, FENTRESS COUNTY, TENNESSEE.

USGS Quad: Stockton, TN 1954
Coordinates: 4030200N 700900E

A well-kept cemetery in continuous use since 1887. Oldest monument marks the grave of Berta L., son of S. A. and E. A. Tompkins (b. and d. 1887). Older graves of Noah Buck and his wife are supposed to be located near this cemetery but were not found during inspection. Note error in name on Quad sheet (Thompkin).

37. MT. HELEN CEMETERY, SOUTH OF MT. HELEN CHURCH, FENTRESS COUNTY, TENNESSEE.

USGS Quad: Honey Creek, TN 1952
Coordinates: 4029800N 705600E

Large, well-kept cemetery of 100–200 graves, in use since 1910s.

38. FELLOWSHIP CHURCH CEMETERY, ARMATHWAITE, FENTRESS COUNTY, TENNESSEE.

USGS Quad: Burrville, TN 1954
Coordinates: 4027800N 700800E

Large, well-kept cemetery in continuous use since 1890s. Families represented include Goad, Voiles, Hull, Choate, Smith, Tompkins, Brooks, Garrett, Pierce.

39. NASH CEMETERY—ON A MARKED ROAD SOUTH OF HIGHWAY 52, ABOUT ONE MILE EAST OF FELLOWSHIP CHURCH—is not shown on the Quad sheet or the county highway map. It contains about seventy-five graves of the Voiles, Brooks, Hull, Sewell, Garrett, Pierce, and Tompkins families, including graves of Cordell Hull's grandparents: Allen Brock Hull (1811–1902) and Syrena Hull (1811–1897).

40. LAUREL DALE CEMETERY, RUGBY, MORGAN COUNTY, TENNESSEE.

USGS Quad: Rugby, TN 1952
Coordinates: 4027000N 706000E

A large cemetery with many graves marked only by metal markers supplied by funeral homes; most paper inserts are illegible. Recent monuments have been erected for members of the Bertram, Berry, and Frogge families. Monuments from the old Rugby period are often elaborate. Families connected with old Rugby include Oberheu, Lourie, Brooks, Walton, Fletcher, Alexander, Wilson, Gilliat, and Dimling. Graves of English settlers include the following:

Margaret E. Hughes (1797–1887)
Walter Gardner (1853–1885)
Osmond Frederic Dakeyne (1851–1881)
J. S. Winkley (d. 1882, aged 43 years)

41. WRIGHT CEMETERY, WEST OF SHIRLEY, FENTRESS COUNTY, TENNESSEE.

USGS Quad: Burrville, TN 1954
Coordinates: 4024500N 697000E

Located in the middle of a pasture; fenced, but grown up in grass and briars and not currently in use. Used by the Wright family 1880–1967; Jones family 1901–1947; Patten family 1910–1930; Westmoreland family 1890s.

Nancy M, wife of Enoch Wright (d. 1889, aged 65)
Enoch Wesley Wright (1835–1897)
Cratan Wright (1852–1914)
Mary Wright (1861–1943)
Children of Cratan and Mary Wright (d. 1885, 1880, 1890, 1894)
Clifton Wright (d. 1967)

42. BREWSTER CEMETERY, BREWSTERTOWN, MORGAN COUNTY, TENNESSEE.

USGS Quad: Rugby, TN 1952
Coordinates: 4024500N 703500E

A well-kept, modestly decorated cemetery in use from 1910 to the present by members of the Brewster, Monday, and Berry families. Somewhat less representation of the Crabtree, Gunter, Ramsey, and York families. A number of unmarked fieldstones.

43. CARPENTER CEMETERY, ON NYDECK ROAD, MORGAN COUNTY, TENNESSEE.

USGS Quad: Rugby, TN 1952
Coordinates: 4022000N 708000E

Sign indicates that this is the Carpenter Cemetery; named Nydeck on Quad sheet. A weedy cemetery with little decoration; mostly nineteenth century burials, but one 1977 burial. Several monuments have extensive epitaphs uncommon in Big South Fork area cemeteries. There are a number of rock cairns, mostly unmarked. Two have markers at the head:

Margaret, wife of William Smith (d. 1860, aged 61 years)
EM/ A7 1899

The oldest grave appears to be a raised cairn overlaid with a solid slab of stone. A partly obliterated inscription on the edge of this slab appears to read: GR^X dec June 29 / 1855 Age 39 yea.

Hiram B. Webb (1846–1855)
James Webb (1847–1862)
Martan [sic] Webb (1855–1862)
Martha Webb (1845–1876)
Nancy Webb (1849–1862)
Samuel Webb (1842–1889)
Consider Carpenter (1797–1869)
Susannah, wife of Consider Carpenter (1800–1892)
Mary N., wife of J. F. Paul (1825–1871)
Catharine B. Paul (1836–1896)
Andrew Lewellen (1793–1875)

Malinda, wife of Andrew Lewellen (1792–1876)
Franklin Rose (1868–1895)
Cynthia W. Rose (d. 1892, about 23 years old)
Mary S. Goff (1833–1877)
John Young (1812–1876)
John M. Young (1872–1874)
Infant Twin Young (1876)
Nancy Young (1815–1881)
Flora M. Young (1877–1881)
Mary Jane Young (1886–1894)
Eva Ray Young (1893)
Daniel C. Young (1847–1935)
Shirley Young (1936–1939)
James Young (1912–1977)
Ben L. York (1872–1875)
Mary S. York (1862–1896)
Henry M York (1837–1920)
Nancy C. York (1838–1925)
Lizzie Davis (1871–1893)
F. B. Davis (1838–1913)
Pollie, wife of F. B. Davis (1835–1909)
John M. Davis (1873–1918)
Madaline Beatrice Blevins (b. and d. 1899)
Mrs. Orlena F. Blevins (1879–1899)
Louisa Jones (1835–1893)
Jeremiah Jones (1825–1900)
Margaret M. Watts (b. and d. 1891)
Annie Brewster (b. and d. 1901)
Martin S. Brewster (1881–1913)
Mary C. Brewster (1852–1917)
J. W. Brewster (1861–1934)
J. Thomas Brewster (1855–1941)
Wesley C. Peters (1861–1906)
Javan L. Albertson (1887–1909)
Bglr. Charles Pearson (1846–1930)

44. MT. VERNON CEMETERY, NEXT TO MT. VERNON METHODIST CHURCH, BURRVILLE, MORGAN COUNTY, TENNESSEE.

USGS Quad: Burrville, TN 1954
Coordinates: 4019000N 702000E

A very large cemetery divided into a new section west of the church in use 1940s to present, and an older section behind and east of the church heavily used 1910–1940. Prominent names occurring before 1900 are Peters, Alexander, Wright, Pittman, Davidson, and Jones. There are many commercial markers with lengthy epitaphs.

The oldest grave appears to be that of James Davidson (1824–1866). Rev. A. B. Wright, the well-known Methodist circuit rider, is buried here. Pre-1900 markers:

James Davidson (1824–1886)
A. B. Wright (1826–1893)
J. O. Peters (1875–1896)
Wilburn Alexander (b. and d. 1899)
Inez Alexander (1864–1894)
Margaret Pittman (1840–1882)
Daniel Pittman (1832–1890)
Jeremiah Wright (1811–1888)
Two infants of Z. T. and Nancy Johnson (1890, 1899)
Peters infant (b. and d. 1879)
Rina W. Peters, wife of A. G. Peters (d. 1897, aged 46 years)
Wife of J. S. Greer (1871–1899)
Francis Davidson Hull (1853–1874)
Rebecca Davidson (1825–1886)
Hannah Jane, wife of Jas. M. Jones (1819–1898)
Patience Davidson, wife of Rufus Jones (1851–1889)
Ida M. Peters (1882–1886)
James H. Peters (d. 1888, aged 69 years)
Rachel N., wife of George B. Lyon (1867–1897)

Appendix 3:
Tables

Table 1

POPULATION OF THE BIG SOUTH FORK AREA, 1850–1978

Year	Fentress	Scott	Wayne	Whitley	McCreary
1850	4,454	1,905	8,692	7,447	
1880	5,941	6,021	12,512	12,000	
1890	5,226	9,794	12,852	17,540	
1900	7,446	12,947	17,518	31,982	
1920	10,436	13,411	16,208	27,749	11,676
1930	11,036	14,080			14,627
1940	14,262	17,362			16,451
1950	14,917	15,966			16,660
1960	13,288	15,413			12,463
1970	12,593	14,762			12,548
1975	13,950	16,553			14,342
1978	14,600	17,800			

SOURCES: U.S. Dept. of Commerce, Bureau of the Census. Census of Population: 1850–1970; U.S. Dept. of Commerce, Bureau of the Census. County and City Data Book: 1977; East Tennessee Development District. Estimates for 1978.

Table 2

TOTAL AND FOREIGN-BORN POPULATION OF THE BIG SOUTH FORK AREA, 1850–1870

	1850		1860		1870	
	Total Pop.	Foreign Born	Total Pop.	Foreign Born	Total Pop.	Foreign Born
Fentress	4,454	1	4,867	15	—	—
Jamestown	336	1	417	—	344	5
Station Camp	126	—	124	—	103	—
Scott	1,905	—	3,460	12	4,717	—
Big South Fork	205	—	238	—	238	—
Huntsville	—	—	615	—	705	—
Black Creek	—	—	260	—	317	—
Chitwoods	—	—	654	—	712	—
Pulaski	14,195	39	15,671	66	—	—
Somerset	—	—	—	—	4,276	11
Wayne	8,692	13	9,272	21	10,602	—
Monticello	—	—	—	—	2,759	16
Slickford	—	—	—	—	1,718	1
Southford	—	—	—	—	1,117	2
Mill Springs	—	—	—	—	1,940	5
Rock Creek	—	—	—	—	339	—
Whitley	7,447	3	7,579	6	8,278	—
Williamsburg	—	—	—	—	1,210	1
Marsh Creek	—	—	—	—	1,639	2

SOURCE: U.S. Dept. of Commerce, Bureau of the Census. Census of Population: 1850–70. Washington, D.C.: U.S. Government Printing Office.

Table 3

MIGRATION TRENDS IN THE BSF, 1950–1975

	Fentress	Scott	McCreary
1950–60 net migration		-29.0	-43.0
1960–70 net migration	-18.7	-18.1	-13.0
1970–75 net migration	+5.9	+7.7	+9.7

SOURCES: U.S. Dept. of Commerce, Bureau of the Census. County and City Data Book, 1972, 1977.

Table 4

AGRICULTURAL AND WAGE LABOR, 1900

	Fentress	Scott	Wayne	Whitley
No. of households	1,137	1,034	2,792	4,829
% farm households	87	68	82	70
No. of wage earners	15	224	25	267
Total wages	$4,658	$6,4577	$7,230	$91,752
Value of products	$42,675	$27,5390	$91,248	$610,526

SOURCE: U.S. Dept. of Commerce, Bureau of the Census. Census of Manufacturers: 1900. Washington, D.C.: U.S. Government Printing Office, 1902.

Table 5

MANUFACTURING ESTABLISHMENTS IN THE BSF AREA, 1860

County	Kinds of Establishments[a]	No. of Establishments	No. of Employees
Fentress	None	0	0
Scott	None	0	0
Wayne	Flour and meal	9	11
	Lumber	6	7
	Liquor distilled	5	17
	Wool carding	3	14
	Leather	3	4
Whitley	Lumber	3	8
	Flour and meal	3	3
	Bituminous coal	1	8
	Blacksmith	1	3
	Leather	1	2
	Saddlery	1	2
	Boots	1	2
	Blacksmith	1	3
	Bituminous coal	1	8
Pulaski	Bituminous coal	9	63
	Flour and meal	4	6
	Lumber	3	12
	Boots	3	8
	Leather	2	7
	Carriage	1	5
	Millinery/dressmaking	1	5
	Printing	1	4
	Furniture	1	2
	Hats	1	2

NOTE: [a]In Rank Order.

SOURCE: U.S. Dept. of Commerce, Bureau of the Census. Manufacturers of the U.S.: 1860. Washington, D.C.: U.S. Government Printing Office, 1865.

Table 6

NUMBER OF FARMS IN THE BSF AREA, 1900–1970

	Fentress	Scott	Wayne	Whitley	McCreary
1900	972	1,389	2,304	3,111	
1910	1,019	1,490	2,670	3,430	
1920	1,214	1,344	2,448	2,614	1,161
1930	987	1,124			1,058
1940	1,740	1,507			1,675
1959	1,018	709			1,162
1964	926	428			na
1974	815	294			149

No. of farms with
sales @ $2,500,

| 1974 | 251 | 108 | | | 32 |

SOURCE: U.S. Dept. of Commerce, Bureau of the Census. Census of Agriculture: 1900–1974. Washington, D.C.: U.S. Government Printing Office.

Table 7

AVERAGE FARM SIZE (ACRES) IN THE BSF AREA, 1900–1974

	Fentress	Scott	Wayne	Whitley	McCreary
1900	182.4	118.6	124.3	89.0	
1920	118.4	81.2	110.5	87.5	74.8
1930	81.0	67.0		57.0	
1959	103.9	84.4			39.4
1964	133.5	163.9			na
1974	157.0	148.0			99.0

SOURCE: U.S. Dept. of Commerce, Bureau of the Census. Census of Agriculture: 1900–1974. Washington, D.C.: U.S. Government Printing Office.

Table 8
FARM/NONFARM POPULATION DISTRIBUTION: 1930–1970

	1930	1940	1950	1960	1970
FENTRESS					
% farm	52.2	70.6	61.1	25	20.38
% nonfarm	47.8	29.4	38.9	75	79.62
SCOTT					
% farm	44.6	49.5	45.4	9.8	6.8
% nonfarm	55.4	50.5	54.6	90.2	93.2
MCCREARY					
% farm	42.9	55	40.9	8.9	2.8
% nonfarm	57.1	45	59.1	91.1	97.2

SOURCE: U.S. Dept. of Commerce, Bureau of the Census. Census of Population: 1930–70. Washington, D.C.: U.S. Government Printing Office.

Table 9
TYPES OF FARMS IN THE BSF AREA, 1930

Types of Farms	Number of Farms (% of total)		
	Fentress	Scott	McCreary
All	987	1,124	1,058
General	68 (6.9)	82 (7.3)	45 (4.0)
Crop specialty			4 (0.4)
Dairy			8 (0.8)
Animal specialty	9 (0.9)	4 (0.4)	11 (1.0)
Self-sufficiency	665 (67.4)	654 (58.2)	647 (61.1)
Part-time	184 (18.6)	333 (29.6)	237 (22.4)
Forest product	18 (1.8)	19 (1.7)	7 (0.7)
Feedlot, livestock dealer		5 (0.4)	2 (0.2)
Unclassified	29 (2.9)	26 (2.3)	97 (9.2)

SOURCE: U.S. Dept. of Commerce, Bureau of the Census. Census of Agriculture: 1930. Washington, D.C.: U.S. Government Printing Office, 1932.

Table 10

PERCENTAGE DISTRIBUTION OF TOTAL VALUE OF FARM PRODUCTS SOLD, TRADED, OR USED BY FARM HOUSEHOLDS, 1930–1940

Farm Product	Scott 1930	Scott 1940	Fentress 1930	Fentress 1940	McCreary 1930	McCreary 1940
Livestock and livestock products sold or traded	18.3	14.6	21.6	16.6	18.0	11.2
Livestock	10.4	8.0	15.3	11.2	10.6	4.9
Livestock products	7.9	6.5	6.3	5.4	7.4	6.3
Dairy products		2.2		1.3		3.1
Poultry products		3.4		3.7		2.7
Other		0.9		0.4		0.6
Crops sold or traded	9.0	5.6	5.7	19.4	8.1	5.5
Field crops		4.9		18.5		4.1
Vegetables		0.1		0.5		0.1
Fruits and nuts		0.7		0.5		1.3
Forest products sold	6.6	1.5		1.8	4.5	2.0
Farm products used by farm households	66.1	78.2	61.6	62.2	69.3	81.2

Source: U.S. Dept. of Commerce, Bureau of the Census. Census of Agriculture: 1940. Washington, D.C.: U.S. Government Printing Office, 1943.

Table 11

TRENDS IN INDUSTRIAL EMPLOYMENT: 1940–1977

FENTRESS COUNTY, TENNESSEE

No. Employed (% of total)	1940	%	1950	%	1960	%	1970	%	1977	%
Agriculture, forestry, and fisheries	2,007	63.8	1,524	42.7	563	16.9	528	13.7	—	—
Mining	448	14.2	392	11.0	123	3.7	18	0.5	24	1.1
Construction	102	3.2	187	5.2	151	4.5	305	7.9	30	1.3
Manufacturing	11	0.3	624	17.5	1,325	39.9	1,400	36.0	1,492	68.6
Transportation	54	1.7	70	2.0	84	2.5	60	1.5	30	1.3
Wholesale and retail trade	172	5.5	258	7.2	439	13.2	442	11.4	255	11.7
Finance	9	0.3	13	0.4	23	0.7	83	2.1	—	—
Service	289	9.2	392	11.0	591	17.8	969	25.0	342	15.7
All others	54	1.7	109	3.0	25	0.8	80	2.0	—	—
Total	3,416	100.0	3,569	100.0	3,324	100.0	3,885	100.0	2,175	100.0

SOURCES: U.S. Dept. of Commerce, Bureau of the Census. Census of Population: 1940–70. Washington, D.C.: U.S. Government Printing Office. For 1977: Estimates, East Tennessee Development District.

Table 12
TRENDS IN INDUSTRIAL EMPLOYMENT, 1940–1977, SCOTT COUNTY, TENNESSEE

No. Employed (% of total)	1940	%	1950	%	1960	%	1970	%	1977	%
Agriculture, forestry, and fisheries	1,754	50.7	864	21.6	208	6.0	259	6.5	—	—
Mining	391	11.3	656	16.4	519	14.9	138	3.4	660	25.5
Construction	97	2.8	148	3.7	171	4.9	170	4.2	85	3.2
Manufacturing	88	2.5	992	24.8	974	27.9	1,317	32.9	916	35.4
Transportation	288	8.3	322	8.0	205	5.9	182	4.5	—	0.9
Wholesale and retail trade	265	7.7	425	10.6	504	14.4	632	15.8	442	17.1
Finance	13	0.4	16	0.4	54	1.5	93	2.3	—	—
Service	518	16.0	482	12.0	715	20.5	1,089	27.2	657	25.4
All others	48	1.4	89	2.2	142	4.1	131	3.3	—	—
Total	3,462	100.0	3,994	100.0	3,492	100.0	4,011	100.0	2,586	100.0

SOURCES: U.S. Dept. of Commerce, Bureau of the Census. Census of Population: 1940–70. Washington, D.C.: U.S. Government Printing Office. For 1977: Estimates, East Tennessee Development District.

Table 13

TRENDS IN INDUSTRIAL EMPLOYMENT: 1940–1970, MCCREARY COUNTY, KENTUCKY

No. Employed (% of total)	1940	%	1950	%	1960	%	1970	%
Agriculture, forestry, and fisheries	1,220	35.9	489	15.3	164	9.3	122	5.2
Mining	1,223	35.9	885	27.7	322	16.4	216	9.3
Construction	99	2.9	162	5.0	137	7.0	168	7.2
Manufacturing	25	0.7	491	15.4	279	14.2	586	25.2
Transportation	148	4.4	188	5.9	197	10.0	74	3.2
Wholesale and retail trade	272	8.0	472	14.8	296	15.0	325	14.0
Finance	8	0.2	14	0.4	12	0.6	36	1.5
Service	341	10.0	418	13.1	416	21.1	764	32.9
All others	62	1.8	75	2.3	144	7.3	33	1.4
Total	3,398	100.0	3,194	100.0	1,967	100.0	2,324	100.0

SOURCES: U.S. Dept. of Commerce, Bureau of the Census. Census of Population: 1940–70. Washington, D.C.: U.S. Government Printing Office.

Table 14

TRENDS IN MINING EMPLOYMENT IN THE BSF, 1940–1970

No. Employed	1940	1950	1960	1970
Fentress	383	392	123	18
Scott	387	656	519	138
McCreary	1222	885	322	216

SOURCE: U.S. Dept. of Commerce, Bureau of the Census. Census of Population: 1940–1970. Washington, D.C.: U.S. Government Printing Office.

Table 15

TRENDS IN FORESTRY EMPLOYMENT IN THE BSF, 1940–1960

Number Employed (% change)	1940	1950	1960
Fentress	507	27 (-94.7)	20 (-25.9)
Scott	844	25 (-97)	7 (-25.9)
McCreary	344	13 (-96)	28 (+53.6)

SOURCE: U.S. Dept. of Commerce, Bureau of the Census. Census of Population: 1940–1960. Washington, D.C.: U.S. Government Printing Office.

Table 16

TRENDS IN MANUFACTURING EMPLOYMENT IN THE BSF: 1940–1970

No. Employed	1940	1950	1960	1970
Fentress: Mfg. total	11	624	1325	1400
Furniture	—	589	208	315
Food and kindred	3	3	127	131
Textiles	2	1	924	807
Scott: Mfg. total	88	992	974	1317
Furniture	—	884	588	857
Food and kindred	5	6	21	9
Textiles	60	74	309	276
McCreary: Mfg. total	25	491	279	586
Furniture	1	437	179	214
Food and kindred	1	10	16	—
Textiles	1	1	40	171

SOURCE: U.S. Dept. of Commerce, Bureau of the Census. Census of Population: 1940–1970. Washington, D.C.: U.S. Government Printing Office.

Table 17

FARM STATISTICS, 1974

	Fentress	Scott	McCreary
No. (%) farms with sales @ $2500	251 (48.7)	108 (36.7)	32 (21.5)
% value of farm products sold by farms with sales @ $2,500:			
Crops	22.4	15.2	50.0
Dairy	9.0	26.3	—
Livestock	25.8	46.0	44.3
Poultry	50.9	36.9	1.3

SOURCE: U.S. Department of Commerce, Bureau of the Census. Census of Agriculture: 1974. Washington, D.C.: U.S. Government Printing Office, 1977.

Table 18

CURRENT FARM OPERATOR STATISTICS, 1974

	Fentress	Scott	McCreary
Farm population: 1970	2,567	822	352
% of farm operators residing on farm operated	64.9	66.7	74.5
% of farm operators working 100 days off farm	46.2	51.0	44.3

SOURCE: U.S. Dept. of Commerce, Bureau of the Census. Census of Agriculture: 1974. Washington, D.C.: U.S. Government Printing Office, 1976.

Table 19

UNEMPLOYMENT RATES IN THE BSF AREA, 1970–1978

	Unemployment Rate (%)		
	1970	1974	1978
Fentress	6.2	14.3	10.3
Scott	8.7	25.0	8.1
McCreary	10.0	5.8	6.8
Tennessee	4.4	5.8	6.8
Kentucky	4.6	na	6.2
U.S.	4.9	5.6	5.8

SOURCES: U.S. Dept. of Commerce, Bureau of the Census. County and City Data Book: 1977. Washington, D.C.: U.S. Government Printing Office, 1978. For 1978: East Tennessee Development District, personal communication, 1979.

Table 20

FAMILY INCOMES BELOW POVERTY LEVEL (1970) AND PUBLIC ASSISTANCE (1975)

	Fentress	Scott	McCreary
No. of family incomes below poverty level (1970)	3,200	3,800	3,000
% below poverty level	42%	42%	54%
Total recipients of public assistance (1975)	535	1,639	1,690
Average family income per month	$115	$110	$188
Total Recipients SSI	935	1,094	634
Total Recipients Social Security monthly benefits, including disability and health insurance	2,861	3,444	2,950
Average retiree income per month	$157	$169	$179
Total recipients food stamps	2,798	5,356	4,495

SOURCES: U.S. Dept. of Commerce, Bureau of the Census. County and City Data Book: 1977. Washington, D.C.: U.S. Government Printing Office, 1978. Tennessee Dept. of Public Welfare. Statistics: 1975. Nashville, Tennessee, 1975. Kentucky Department of Human Resources. 1975: Public Assistance in Kentucky. PA–264. Report Series. Frankfort, Ky., 1975.

Table 21

PER CAPITA INCOME, 1970-1977

	Per Capita Income (% change)			
	1970	**1974**	**1977**	**% change 1970–77**
Fentress	$1,264	$1,966 (66)	$2994 (52)	137
Scott	$1,481	$2,517 (70)	$3604 (43)	143
McCreary	$1,236	$1,915 (55)		
Tennessee	$2,464	$3,821 (55)	$5801 (52)	135
Kentucky	$2,425			
U.S.	$3,348	$4,646	$6,009	

SOURCES: U.S. Dept. of Commerce, Bureau of the Census. *County and City Data Book: 1977*. Washington, D.C.: U.S. Government Printing Office, 1978. For 1977 in Tennessee only: Estimates, East Tennessee Development District.

Table 22

AVAILABLE WILD PLANT FOODS

Identification	Use
Acer negundo Box elder	Sap used as substitute for sugar maple in making maple syrup; less sweet
Acer rubrum Red maple; swamp maple	Sap used as substitute for sugar maple in making maple syrup; less sweet
Acer saccharum Sugar maple; rock maple	Primary source of maple sugar and syrup; trees tapped for sap in late winter/early spring and boiled down to produce syrup and granular sugar; white settlers may have learned the technique from Indians
Allium canadense Meadow garlic; wild garlic	Uses similar to cultivated garlic
Amaranthus hybridus Slender pigweed	Young leaves cook as "sallet greens" in early spring
Arctium minus Burdock	Leaf stalks and young flower stalks may be peeled and eaten raw or prepared like asparagus; root peeled and boiled
Arisæma tryphyllum Jack-in-the-pulpit; Indian turnip	Fleshy root is starchy but extremely burning; burning sensation may be eliminated by first boiling and drying the root, then grinding it into a meal; collected in spring and summer
Arundaria gigantea (*A. macrosperma*) Large cane	Seeds used by both Indians and early settlers as a wheat substitute; young shoots may be prepared as a potherb

Table 22 *(continued)*

AVAILABLE WILD PLANT FOODS

Identification	Use
Asclepias syriaca Milkweed	Potherb; gather when a few inches high and boil two or three times
Asclepias tuberosa Butterfly weed	Indians ate pods, stems, and fleshy roots
Asimina triloba Papaw; custard apple	Fruit ripens in late autumn
Asparagus officinalis Asparagus	Escaped from cultivation; flower-bud stalk eaten; seeds can be used as coffee substitute
Barbarea verna Crow's foot; winter cress	Greens used raw in early spring
Berberis canadense American barberry	Similar to the European-Asian *Berberis vulgaris*, but has smaller and fewer berries; berries ripen in early autumn and are used to make jelly
Benzoin aestivale Spicewood; spicebush	Aromatic leaves, twigs, bark used for tea; a popular beverage during the Civil War
Betula lenta Sweet birch; black birch	Cambium of tree or roots is eaten fresh or dried, gathered most easily in spring; tea made from young twigs has a wintergreen flavor like the bark; sap collected in April may be made into sugar but is only half as sweet as sugar maple

Table 22 (continued)
AVAILABLE WILD PLANT FOODS

Identification	Use
Brassica nigra Black mustard	Young tops cooked as potherb; seeds a condiment
Caccinium vacillans Blue huckleberry, (low bush)	Tasty berries ripen in July and August
Cardamine pennsylvanica Pennsylvania bitter cress	Eaten raw; a substitute for watercress
Carya glabra Pignut hickory	Nuts are large but sometimes bitter
Carya ovata Shagbark hickory	Nuts vary in quality from tree to tree; Indians pounded nuts and shells to powder and added water to make a liquor called *pawhiccora*, hence the name
Castanea dentata American chestnut	Nuts were roasted and eaten; blight now attacks saplings before they reach maturity
Castanea pumila Chinquapin	Sweet nuts about half the size of chestnuts
Celtis occidentalis Hackberry	Berries ripen in September and remain on the tree and edible all winter

Table 22 (continued)

AVAILABLE WILD PLANT FOODS

Identification	Use
Chenopodium album Lamb's quarters; wild spinach	Potherb
Cichorum intibua Chicory	Chicory; gather in early spring as a potherb; roasted, ground roots added to coffee
Cirsium maculosa (C. maticum) Bullweed; swamp thistle	Young shoots boiled as potherb
Claytonia virginica Spring beauty	Small starchy bulbs prized by Indians
Commelina communis Dayflower	Escaped from cultivation; used as potherb in Europe
Corylus americana American hazelnut	Nuts ripen in August, stay on bush if not eaten by chipmunks, etc.
Dentaria diphylla (D. laciniata) Pepper-root	Root used as mustardy relish
Diospyros virginiana Persimmon; possum apple	Fruit edible usually only after frost; Indians may have taught settlers to make persimmon bread

Table 22 (continued)

AVAILABLE WILD PLANT FOODS

Identification	Use
Erythronium americanum Yellow adder's tongue	Leaves sometimes used for greens; bulb edible when cooked
Fagus grandifolia American beech	Small nuts ripe in autumn; trees must be large before they bear, especially in the South
Gaultheria procumbens Wintergreen; teaberry	Young leaves and red berries (winter) both edible; tea made from leaves
Glycyrrhiza lepidota Wild licorice	Fleshy roots resemble those of European licorice, *G. glabra*; chewed by Indians
Ipomoea pandurata Wild potato vine	Has a 10–20 pound fleshy root which may be cooked like sweet potato
Juglans cinerea Butternut; white walnut	Nuts become rancid if not used quickly after harvest; sap may be tapped as maple; nut husks and inner bark used for brown dye
Juglans nigra Black walnut	Nuts gathered in fall; husks used for brown dye
Laportea canadensis Wood nettle	Potherb; tender during most of growing season

Table 22 (continued)

AVAILABLE WILD PLANT FOODS

Identification	Use
Latuca canadensis Wild lettuce; horseweed	Potherb; boiled in two waters
Lepidium virginicum Peppergrass	Mustard family; used as garnish or salad green
Liquidambar styraciflua Sweet gum	Wounded tree exudes a resinous gum called copal-balsam, used as a chewing gum
Medeola virginiana Indian cucumber root	Tuberous root has cucumber-like taste uncooked; used by Indians
Mitchella repens Partridge berry; twinberry	Edible red berries stay on plants through the winter
Monarda didyma Bee-balm; Oswego tea	Leaves brewed into tea with strong mint flavor
Monarda fistulosa Wild bergamot	Leaves brewed into tea with strong mint flavor
Morus rubra Red mulberry	Berries ripen in late spring; insipid flavor, but available earlier than other berries

Table 22 (continued)

AVAILABLE WILD PLANT FOODS

Identification	Use
Nyssa multiflora Sour gum; black gum	Acid fruits may be used for preserves; flowers are excellent bee forage
Oenethera biennis Evening primrose	Boiled roots are edible; young shoots may be eaten raw
Onoclea sensibilis Sensitive fern	Young fronds taken just before they unfold are used as a potherb
Oxalis violacea Violet wood sorrel	Acid-flavored leaves eaten raw
Passiflora lutea Yellow passion flower	Pulpy fruit with purple juice ripens in September; unique flavor described by Medsger as "not first-class"
Peltandra virginicaa Green arrow arum	Bulbous 3-4 pound root has biting Indian turnip flavor; Indians prepared by roasting 1-2 days in ground pits, then grinding into meal
Phytolacca decandra Poke	Young shoots taken in early spring and prepared like spinach; care must be taken not to gather portions of root, which is poisonous at all times; red berry juice used for ink
Pinus strobus White pine	Sticky pitch is a poor substitute for spruce gum

Table 22 *(continued)*

AVAILABLE WILD PLANT FOODS

Identification	Use
Polyphyllum peltatum May apple; wild lemon	Fruit that ripens in July or August can be eaten in small quantities
Polygonatum biflorum True Solomon's seal	Shoot may be gathered in spring and used as potherb; starchy root eaten by Indians
Pteris aquilina Bracken, brake, eagle fern	Young stalks gathered prior to unfolding used as potherb
Quercus alba White oak	Annual crop of acorns in September; ground into coarse flour
Quercus primusa Rock chestnut oak	Acorns ground into meal, sometimes after roasting meal was soaked in water to remove tannin, then molded into cakes
Rhus canadensis (Fragrant sumac) *Rhus copallina* (Mountain sumac) *Rhus glabra* (Scarlet sumac)	Bright red fruits of all these species ripen in autumn and can be soaked in water to make a refreshing drink, "Indian lemonade"
Robinia pseudo-acacia Locust tree; black locust	Seed pods mature in fall and stay on tree through winter; seeds gathered by Indians and cooked with meat
Rubus allegheniensis Mountain or high bush blackberry	Fruits ripen in July and August; can be dried as well as used fresh and canned

Table 23

AVAILABLE MEDICINAL PLANTS

Identification[a]	Official Use[b]	Local Use[c]
Alnus sp. Alder	None	Bark boiled; drunk to regulate blood pressure or as ingredient in tea for flu
Acorus calamus Calamus, sweet flag	Calamus N.F.—dried rhizome, gathered in spring; carminative, aromatic bitter, stimulant; used in dyspepsia and colic	Rhizome chewed or made into tea for stomach ailments, incipient ulcers; headache remedy, especially sinus headache
Aletris farinosa Stargrass	Aletris—dried rhizome and root harvested in autumn of second or third year; uterine sedative	Not used locally; gathered and sold
Allium sativum Garlic	Allium—syrup diaphoretic, diuretic, expectorant; poultice in bronchitis	Not used medicinally, but onion (*Allium cepa*) used in poultice for sore throat, fever, pneumonia; as teething palliative; bruised onions worn around neck or kept in sickroom as disease preventive
Apocynum cannabium Black Indian hemp; hemp dogbane	Apocynum N.F.—strong cardiac stimulant and diuretic used in dropsy	No local use reported
Aralia spinosa Spikenard	Aralia N.F.—stimulant and diaphoretic; constituent of white pine syrup (q.v.)	No local use reported

Table 23 (continued)

AVAILABLE MEDICINAL PLANTS

Identification[a]	Official Use[b]	Local Use[c]
Aristolochia serpentaria Virginia snakeroot	Serpentaria N.F.—constituent of Compound Cinchona Tincture N.F.; aromatic bitter	No local use reported
Asarum arifolium Heart leaf	None	Chewed or made into tea as remedy for heart trouble; plaster for burns
Asarum canadense Wild ginger	*Asarum*—dried rhizome and roots dug in spring; aromatic bitter and carminative	Not used locally; gathered and sold
Asclepias tuberosa Butterfly weed; pleurisy root	*Asclepias*—dried root used as diuretic, expectorant, and alterative	Tea made from root used for lung congestion
Atropa belladonna Nightshade	Belladonna Root N.F.; Belladonna Leaf N.F.—anodyne, relieves pain by suppressing sensory nerve endings; antiasthmatic; muscle relaxant; decreases secretion	Plant tops macerated in sweet milk as lotion for poison ivy
Baptista tinctoria Wild indigo	*Baptista*—root gathered in fall; ingredient in dentifrices; infusion used topically on skin ulcers	Not used locally; gathered and sold in large quantities

Table 23 (continued)
AVAILABLE MEDICINAL PLANTS

Identification[a]	Official Use[b]	Local Use[c]
Benzoin aestivale Spicewood	None	Tea made from young twigs and bark as cure for hives
Betula lenta Sweet birch	Sweet Birch Oil Compound Resorcinol Ointment N.F.—oil of bark and young twigs antirheumatic and flavoring; distilled tar antiseptic and parasiticide used for eczema and other skin disease	Bark and twigs boiled in water used to make soap; imparted fragrance (and possibly mild medicinal qualities)
Brassica nigra Mustard	Black Mustard U.S.P.—naturalized exotic; seed a rubefacient and counterirritant applied externally; emetic	Mustard seed used in tea to cure child's wheezing; no reported use of mustard plasters
Capsicum sp. Red pepper	Unguentum Capsici N.F.—counterirritant; also stimulant and stomachic	Red pepper soaked in kerosene for rheumatism; used as snuff or in tea to induce labor
Carya ovata Shagbark hickory	None	Bark boiled with brown sugar to make a syrup for cough associated with measles
Castanea dentata Chestnut	Castanea—dried leaves gathered in autumn; astringent and tonic	Boil leaves to ooze and bathe burns with this salve; chestnut leaf poultice

Table 23 (continued)

AVAILABLE MEDICINAL PLANTS

Identification[a]	Official Use[b]	Local Use[c]
Caulophyllum thalictroides Blue cohosh; papoose root	Caulophyllum N.F.—dried rhizome and root anti-spasmodic, emmenagogue, oxytocic	No local use reported
Chamaelirium luteum False unicorn root; blazing star	Helonias—dried root; diuretic and anthelmintic; of questionable value as uterine tonic	No local use reported
Chenopodium ambrosioides Jerusalem oak; goosefoot	Chenopodium Oil N.F.—dried fruits; anthelmintic for round worms and hookworms	Tea given to children as anthelmintic
Chimaphila umbellata Spotted wintergreen; ratsbane	Chimaphila—dried leaf; diuretic, astringent; mild disinfectant to urinary tract	Tea made from leaves given as cold remedy and for nerves
Chionanthus virginicus Fringe tree	Chionanthus H.P.—fresh bark of roots collected in autumn; bitter tonic, diuretic, aperient	No local use reported
Cimicifuga racemosa Black snakeroot; bugbane	Cimicifuga N.F.—dried rhizome and root; antirheumatic, remedy for neuralgia, dysmenorrhea	Tea used for stomach ache

Table 23 (continued)

AVAILABLE MEDICINAL PLANTS

Identification[a]	Official Use[b]	Local Use[c]
Conium maculatum Poison hemlock	Conium, Extractum Conii—fruits collected during second year's growth; poison employed in small dose as motor depressant and anodyne in tetanus, convulsions, delirium tremens	No local use reported
Cornus florida Dogwood	Dogwood—listed in Youngken as nonofficial medicinal bark; use not given	Tea made from bark and root for arthritis and for chills; tea made from buds and twigs as blood purifier
Corylus americana Sweet hazel	None	Tea made from bark a cold remedy
Cypripedium calcoelus Lady slipper	Lady slipper—listed in Youngken as a nonofficial medicinal root; formerly used as nervine and antispasmodic	Not used locally but gathered and sold
Dicentra canadensis Dutchmen's britches	Corydalis—dried tubers contain alkaloids used as a bitter principle and as a preanesthetic in veterinary practice	No local use reported
Dioscorea paniculata Wild yam	Dioscorea—dried rhizome gathered in autumn; diuretic and expectorant; used for bilious colic	No local use reported

Table 23 (continued)

AVAILABLE MEDICINAL PLANTS

Identification[a]	Official Use[b]	Local Use[c]
Dryopteris marginalis Male fern, marginal shield fern	Aspidum U.S.P.—rhizomes and stipes gathered in autumn; taenifuge	No local use reported
Epigaea repens Trailing arbutus	None	Tea for kidney trouble
Euonymous atropurpureus Wahoo; burning bush	Euonymus H.P.; Euonymus N.P.—root bark cholagogue; cathartic in torpid liver and constipation	No local use reported
Eupatorium incarnatum Swamp root; lavender-flowered trumpetweed	None	Tea for kidney trouble; kidney stones
Eupatorium perfoliatum Boneset	Eupatorium N.F.—dried leaves and flowering tops gathered in late summer; diaphoretic in systemic colds	Tea for cold, flu, headache, chills, and fever
Ferula foetida Asafetida	Asafetida N.F.—imported resin used as stimulant, carminative, nervine, laxative	Worn around neck as disease preventive and toothache remedy; applied to chest with onion and kerosene as cold remedy; given in warm milk for colic

Table 23 (continued)

AVAILABLE MEDICINAL PLANTS

Identification[a]	Official Use[b]	Local Use[c]
Gaultheria procumbens Wintergreen; teaberry	Oil of Wintergreen, Methyl Salicylate—oil distilled from leaves best harvested in September; stimulant, rubefacient, antirheumatic, flavoring agent	Leaves chewed as cold remedy; taken with honey to build blood
Geranium maculatum Wild geranium	Geranium H.P.—dried or fresh rhizome collected in autumn; astringent	No local use recorded
Gillenia stipulata Indian hysic; ipecac	None (the official Ipecac is imported from South America)	Emetic and purgative
Gnaphalium obtusifolium Life everlasting	Gnaphalium—infusion used domestically for flu and diarrhea; applied to bruises as poultice	Tea for flu, pneumonia; made into tea or smoked to relieve nasal congestion
Goodyera pubescens Rattlesnake plantain; ratsbane	None	Tea for kidney trouble, cold, aches, and pains
Hamamalis virginiana Witch hazel	Hamamelis Leaf N.F.—dried leaf collected in autumn; astringent and haemostatic	No local use reported

Table 23 (continued)

AVAILABLE MEDICINAL PLANTS

Identification[a]	Official Use[b]	Local Use[c]
Hedeoma pulegioides Pennyroyal	Hedeoma—dried leaves and tops gathered in summer; oil a mosquito repellent; home use of infusion as stimulant, carminative, emmenagogue	Tea for fever, diarrhea; infusion sprinkled on beans to repel beetles; crushed leaves rubbed on body to repel seed ticks and chiggers
Hydrastis canadensis Goldenseal, yellow root	Hydrastis N.F.—dried rhizome and root collected during third or fourth year; alterative to mucous membranes; treatment for gastrointestinal upset, inflammation of vaginal and urinary tract; Hydrastine hydrochloride N.F.— for colds, nosebleed	Tea or chewed root for indigestion, ulcers, sore throat, lung trouble; mixed with tallow for sore lips, hand salve
Ilex opaca Holly	None; Medsger notes use of toasted leaf for tea by Indians; I. vomitoria (Yaupon) was the Black Drink	Tea for fever, ash mixed with tallow for baby's thrash
Impatiens capensis and *I. pallida* Jewelweed	None	Juice of stems soothes poison ivy, prevents eruption
Juglans cinera White walnut	Juglans—dried inner bark collected in autumn; mild cathartic in habitual constipation	Laxative tea; fresh bark peeled upward for emetic tea; bark applied to forehead for headache
Juglans nigra Black walnut	None	Fresh leaves used as flea-repellent animal bedding

Table 23 (continued)
AVAILABLE MEDICINAL PLANTS

Identification[a]	Official Use[b]	Local Use[c]
Juniperus virginiana Red cedar	No official substance; wood and wood chips insect repellent	Cedar chests for clothes and bedding
Liquidambar styraciflua Sweet gum	Storax U.S.P.—balsam that forms on wounded trunk; constituent of Coumpound Benzoin Tincture U.S.P.—a stimulating expectorant	No local use reported
Lobelia inflata Lobelia	Lobelia N.F.—dried leaves and tops collected after fruit capsules partly inflated; contains poison lobeline, in small dose an expectorant in asthma and chronic bronchitis	Tea used to induce vomiting; smoked for narcotic effect similar to *Cannabis*; gathered for sale
Marrubium vulgare Horehound	Marrubium—dried leaves and flower tops; plant naturalized in U.S. but local supply probably purchased; bitter tonic and expectorant in domestic medicine	Tea for cough; mixed with molasses for hoarseness
Mitchella repens Partridge berry; buck vine; baby berry	Youngken lists entire plant as drug without giving use	Possibly used as uterine stimulant, abortifacient
Monarda fistulosa Wild bergamot	Contains some of the volatile oil pulegone obtained from *Hedeoma pulegioides*	No local use reported

Table 23 (continued)

AVAILABLE MEDICINAL PLANTS

Identification[a]	Official Use[b]	Local Use[c]
Monarda punctata Horsemint	Contains Thymol U.S.P. (found primarily in thyme)— anthelmintic for hookworm, internal antiseptic, antiseptic and deodorant in mouth wash	Tea for flu, cold
Nepata cataria Catnip	Cataria N.F.—dried leaves and flowering tops gathered late summer; carminative and stimulant	Tea to calm infants, cure hives
Nepata hederacea Ground ivy	None	Tea to reduce fever, cure hives, quiet a baby's nerves and make it sleep
Nicotiana tabacum Tobacco	Rutin—decreases capillary fragility	Wet tobacco applied to bee stings; chewed to counteract effects of snakebite
Panax quinquefolium Ginseng	Ginseng—dried roots dug in autumn when plants are 3–7 years old; lay use as stimulant and aromatic bitter	Root chewed for stomach upset, nerves; gathered for sale
Phytolacca americana Poke	Phytolacca—dried root dug in autumn; alterative in chronic rheumatism and emetic	Root steeped in whiskey or applied as poultice for rheumatism; poke root tea as bath to cure itch; pokeberry to cure chills

Table 23 *(continued)*

AVAILABLE MEDICINAL PLANTS

Identification[a]	Official Use[b]	Local Use[c]
Pinus echinata Short-leaf pine	Turpentine N.F.—purified for internal use as diuretic and counterirritant; Compound Rosin Cerate N.F.—salve and liniment	Chest plasters for colds, pneumonia; lick the cork of the turpentine bottle to prevent flu; taken with sugar or castor oil for worms; liniment; salve for cuts
Pinus rigida Pitch pine	Pine Tar Ointment U.S.P.—stimulating antiseptic in skin disease; Rectified Tar Oil N.F.; Compound Tar Ointment N.F.; Pine Tar Syrup N.F.	Pine resin plaster for kidney trouble; drink water off tar barrel for a cough; pine resin plaster or burning pine torches for disease prevention
Pinus strobus White pine	Compound White Pine Syrup N.F.—stripped, dried inner bark; stimulating expectorant	Cough syrup made from needles or from bark and buds; pine needle tea as tonic; white pine resin as salve
Plantago major Broad-leafed plantain	None	Poultice to draw out blood poison
Platanus occidentalis Sycamore	None	Sycamore chip tea for measles; tea cures bad blood that causes boils
Podophyllum peltatum May apple	Podophyllum N.F.—dried rhizomes and roots collected in spring or autumn, preferably spring; cholagogue cathartic	Rhizomes and roots eaten for indigestion, rheumatism; gathered for sale

Table 23 (continued)

AVAILABLE MEDICINAL PLANTS

Identification[a]	Official Use[b]	Local Use[c]
Polygala senega Seneca snakeroot	Senega N.F.—dried root dug in autumn; expectorant for bronchitis	No local use reported; gathered for sale
Populus candicans Balm of Gilead	Poplar Bud N.F.—air dried, closed winter leaf bud; stimulant and expectorant in Compound Syrup of White Pine	Buds fried in mutton tallow as salve for sores
Prunella vulgaris Heal-all; self-heal	None	Tea for sore throat
Prunus virginiana Wild cherry	Wild cherry U.S.P., Wild Cherry Syrup U.S.P.—stem bark a stimulating expectorant	Tea for cough, flu, general tonic
Prunus americana Wild plum	None	Bark used in tea for childhood asthma
Pyrus angustifolia; P. coronaria Crab apple	None	Tea made from bark for asthma

Table 23 *(continued)*

AVAILABLE MEDICINAL PLANTS

Identification[a]	Official Use[b]	Local Use[c]
Quercus alba White oak	Quercus—dried inner bark; astringent	No local use reported
Rheum officinale Rhubarb	Rhubarb U.S.P.—dried rhizome; purgative with secondary astringent action in indigestion	Grown in gardens; stalks eaten for laxative property
Rhus glabra Smooth upland sumac	Rhus glabra—dried ripe fruit collected in autumn; astringent gargle and refrigerant	No local use reported
Rubus allegheniensis Blackberry	Rubi Fructus—berries flavoring agent and astringent	Blackberry vinegar and sugar for coughs
Rumex obtusifolius Yellow dock	Youngken lists as nonofficial medicinal root without giving use	Blood purifier and cure for spongy gums; leaf fried in grease a salve for cuts
Rumex acetostella Sour dock; sheep sorrel	None	Leaves fried in grease a salve for cuts

Table 23 *(continued)*

AVAILABLE MEDICINAL PLANTS

Identification[a]	Official Use[b]	Local Use[c]
Ruta graviolens Rue	Rue—dried leaves; calmative remedy for colic and atonic amennorhea; large doses irritant	Tea for stomach trouble and worms
Salix fragilis Willow	Salix, Salicin N.F.—bark stripped in spring and dried; simple bitter and antirheumatic	No local use reported
Sambucus canadensis Elder	Sambucus—air dried flower gathered in summer, mostly imported from Europe; diaphoretic and stimulant	Elderberry syrup for worms in children
Sanguinaria canadensis Bloodroot	Sanguinaria N.F.—dried rhizome collected in early summer; emetic and stimulating expectorant	Not used locally but gathered for sale
Sassafras albidum Sassafras	Sassafras N.F., Oil of Sassafras U.S.P.— bark of root gathered in early spring or autumn; aromatic, stimulant, diaphoretic; oil of sassafras also antiseptic in nasal and throat sprays, an ant repellent	Blood thinner; ingredient in a tea for flu
Solanum carolinense Horse nettle	Solanum—air dried ripe berries sedative in treatment of epilepsy	No local use reported

Table 23 (continued)
AVAILABLE MEDICINAL PLANTS

Identification[a]	Official Use[b]	Local Use[c]
Spigelia marilandica Pink root	Spigelia H.P.—dried rhizomes and root; anthelmintic	Worm medicine for children; gathered for sale
Taraxacum officinale Dandelion	Taraxacum N.F.—dried rhizomes and root dug early spring or fall; simple bitter and mild laxative	No local medicinal use reported
Tephrosia virginiana Devil's shoe string; goat's rue	Tephrosia—dried root; contains rotenone, an insecticide	No local use reported
Tilia americana American linden	None	Inner bark used as poultice to draw infection out of wounds
Tussilago farfara Colt's foot	Farfara—dried leaf, gathered June and July; used for home treatment of coughs	No local use reported
Ulmus fulva Slippery elm	Elm N.F.—dried inner bark, collected in spring; demulcent and emollient; powdered drug a poultice	Freshly stripped bark used locally as a poultice; chewed for indigestion

Table 23 (continued)
AVAILABLE MEDICINAL PLANTS

Identification[a]	Official Use[b]	Local Use[c]
Verbascum thapsus Mullein	Mullein Leaves—dry leaves; demulcent and emollient	Cough syrup ingredient
Verbena hastata Verbena; blue vervain; wild hyssop	Verbena—dried tops cut when in bloom; hot infusion in diaphoretic, tonic, and expectorant	No local use reported
Viburnum prunifolium Black haw	Viburnum prunifolium N.F.—dried bark of root or stem; uterine sedative used in threatened miscarriage	No local use reported
Viburnum nudum Shonny haw	Contains some of the glycoside found in *V. prunifolium* and has similar effects on small animals	No local use reported; collected for sale
Zingiber officinale Ginger	Ginger U.S.P.—powdered condiment from Jamaica, Africa, or S. Asia; carminative, stimulant	Commercial ginger added to whiskey is taken for hoarseness or as a daily arthritis medicine; ginger tea given to induce labor

SOURCE: "Plants and Animals of the Big South Fork National River and Recreation Area," appendix C of the BSFNRRA Final Environmental Impact Statement, 1976. Some plants mentioned by interviewees were added.

NOTES: [a]Correlation of scientific and common names verified in Youngen (1950); Medsger (1939); Wharton and Barbour (1971); Duncan and Foote (1975); and *Webster's Third International Dictionary, Unabridged*. [b]Notes on official medicinal use were drawn from Youngken (1950). These include name of drug, notation of official acceptance in the United States Pharmacopeia (U.S.P.), National Formulary (N.F.), or Homeopathic Formulary (H.F.), part of plant used and when collected, and medicinal effects. [c]Notes on fold uses come from interviewees or from E. G. Rogers's *Early Folk Medicinal Practices in Tennessee* (1941).

Table 24
YEARS OF OPERATION OF STEARNS COAL MINES

Barthell 1	1903–1933	Cooperative	1922–1950
Comargo	1905–1919	Blue Heron 18	1938–1961
Worley 3	1905–1911	Mine 19	1963
Worley 4	1905–1953	Mine 20	1965
Yamacraw 10	1907–1930	Mine 21	1964–1967
Yamacraw 11	1910–1949	Mine 22	1965–1966
Worley 12	1917–1918	Mine 23	1965–1966
Exodus 14	1918	Mine 24	1967–1968
Mine 15	1923–1944	Mine 25	1967–1968
Oz Mine 16	1924–1927	Mine 26	1968
Mine 16-2	1958–1965	Mine 11-A	1967
Fidelity-A	1916–1937	Justus	1968–1975

Source: Stearns Archives.

Appendix 4:
Bibliographic Resources

This section reprints the bibliography that was compiled in 1980 as a resource for interpretive program planners. The bibliography has not been updated to include the numerous works published since 1980. It is divided into topical sections, and their arrangement roughly follows the organization of the report text. References cited in this revised edition of the report are listed separately at the end of this volume.

This list of bibliographic resources includes a section of general works on Appalachia and the Cumberland Plateau. Only the best overview volumes, ethnographies, and fictional works were included, with fiction further restricted to works with a Cumberland Plateau setting. Lists of regional journals and bibliographies point the way to additional references.

History resources include a list of local and county history published in monographic form, with the many works on Rugby listed separately. The nature and quality of these works varies greatly. Selected magazine and newspaper sources for additional local history information also are included in this section. Not listed are unpublished sources such as county documents, for example, birth and marriage records, deeds and plats, court records, and wills and estate inventories.

This list is organized topically, as follows:

THEORY AND METHOD

Background Data
    Big South Fork Documents
    Water, Soil, and Mineral Resources
    Population and Economic Statistics

Appalachia and the Cumberland Plateau
    Overviews
    Regional Journals
    Ethnographies
    Fiction
    Bibliography

History
  Exploration and Settlement
  Local and County History
  Rugby History
  Magazine and Newspaper Sources
  Historic Maps

Economic Development
  Timber Industry
  Coal Industry
  Railroads

Folklife Topics
  Folk Medicine and Botanic Resources
  Material Culture and Domestic Technology
  Social Custom
  Religion
  Music
  Dance
  Verbal Lore
  Folk Belief
  Language

Theory and Method

Baum, Willa K.
1972   *Oral History for the Local Historical Society.* 2d. ed. Nashville: American Association for State and Local History.
Bowditch, George
1971   Cataloging Photographs. *Technical Leaflet 57.* Nashville: American Association for State and Local History.
Brunvand, Jan
1968   *The Study of American Folklore: An Introduction.* New York: Norton.
Comeaux, Malcolm L.
1972   *Atchafalaya Swamp Life: Settlement and Folk Occupations.* Baton Rouge: Louisiana State Univ. School of Geoscience. Geoscience and Man, v. 2.
Dorson, Richard M.
1972   Concepts of Folklore and Folklife Studies. In *Folklore and Folklife,* ed. R. Dorson. Chicago: Univ. of Chicago Press.

Driver, H. E., and W. C. Massey
1957   Comparative Studies of North American Indians. American Philosophical Society Transactions, n.s. 47(2).

Evans, E. Estyn
1972   The Cultural Geographer and Folklife Research. In *Folklore and Folklife*, ed. R. Dorson. Chicago: Univ. of Chicago Press.

Goldstein, Kenneth S.
1964   *A Guide for Field Workers in Folklore*. Hatboro, Pa.: Folklore Associates.

Higgs, J. W. Y.
1963   *Folk Life Collection and Classification*. London: Museum Association.

Ives, Edward D.
1976   Argyle Boom. *Northeast Folklore* XVII.
1980   *The Tape-Recorded Interview. A Manual for Field Workers in Folklore and Oral History*. Knoxville: Univ. of Tennessee Press.

Kniffen, Fred B.
1976   American Cultural Geography and Folk Life. In *American Folklife*, ed. D. Yoder. Austin: Univ. of Texas Press.

Kroeber, A. L.
1939   *Cultural and Natural Areas of Native North America*. Berkeley: Univ. of California Press.

List, George
1972   Fieldwork: Recording Traditional Music. In *Folklore and Folklife*, ed. R. Dorson. Chicago: Univ. of Chicago Press.

MacDonald, Donald A.
1972   Fieldwork: Collecting Oral Literature. In *Folklore and Folklife*, ed. R. Dorson. Chicago: Univ. of Chicago Press.

Montell, William Lynwood
1970   *The Saga of Coe Ridge: A Study in Oral History*. Knoxville: Univ. of Tennessee Press.

Pearsall, Marion
1966   Cultures of the American South. *Anthropological Quarterly* 39 (2): 128–41.

Redfield, Robert
1947   The Folk Society. *American Journal of Sociology* 52:293–308.

Roberts, Warren E.
1972   Fieldwork: Recording Material Culture. In *Folklore and Folklife*, ed. R. Dorson. Chicago: Univ. of Chicago Press.

Steward, Julian H.
1955   *Theory of Culture Change*. Urbana: Univ. of Illinois Press.

Thornton, Ralph
1973   Me and Fannie: The Oral Autobiography of Ralph Thornton of Topsfield, Maine. *Northeast Folklore* XIV.
Tyrrell, William G.
1966   Tape-Recording Local History. *Technical Leaflet* 35. Nashville: American Association for State and Local History.
Yoder, Don
1963   The Folklife Studies Movement. *Pennsylvania Folklife* 13 (3): 43–56.
1976   Folklife Studies in American Scholarship. In *American Folklife*, ed. D. Yoder. Austin: Univ. of Texas Press.

Background Data

BIG SOUTH FORK DOCUMENTS

McCracken, Robert D.
1980   Social and Psychological Responses to Government Land Acquisition on the South Fork of the Cumberland River. Unpublished ms.
U.S. Army Corps of Engineers, Nashville District
1976a   *Big South Fork National River and Recreation Area: Final Environmental Impact Statement.* Nashville: U.S. Army Corps of Engineers.
1976b   *Big South Fork National River and Recreation Area: General Design Memorandum. DM 1.* Nashville: U.S. Army Corps of Engineers.
1976c   *Big South Fork National River and Recreation Area: Report on Blue Heron Mining Community.* Nashville: U.S. Army Corps of Engineers.
U.S. Army Corps of Engineers, Office of the Chief
1973   Relocation Benefits to Persons Displaced by Army Land Acquisition. Pamphlet. Washington: Office of the Chief of Engineers, Dept. of the Army.

WATER, SOIL, AND MINERAL RESOURCES

Byrne, J. G., et al.
1970   *Soil Survey of the McCreary–Whitley Area, Kentucky.* Washington: U.S. Dept. of Agriculture, Soil Conservation Service.
Kernodle, M., J. Wilson, and M. Mallory
1974   *Water Resources of the South Fork Cumberland River, Tennessee.* Nashville: Tennessee Dept. of Conservation, Division of Water Resources.
Killebrew, Joseph Buckner
1876   *Mineral and Agricultural Resources of the Portion of Tennessee along the Cincinnati Southern and Knoxville and Ohio Railroads.* Nashville: Tavel, Eastman, and Howell.

Pomerence, J. B.
1964   *Geology of the Barthell Quadrangle and Part of the Oneida North Quadrangle, Kentucky.* Washington: U.S. Dept. of the Interior. Geological Survey.
1968   *Mineral Resources of the Appalachian Region.* U.S. Geological Survey Professional Papers 580. Washington, D. C.

POPULATION AND ECONOMIC STATISTICS

East Tennessee Development District
1979   Draft, The Big South Fork Population and Economy. Knoxville: East Tennessee Development District.
1980   Public Facility and Service Needs Around the Big South Fork National River and Recreation Area. Knoxville: East Tennessee Development District.

Kentucky Dept. of Human Resources
1975   Public Assistance in Kentucky. PA-264 Report Series. Frankfort.

Lake Cumberland Development District
1973   McCreary County Comprehensive Plan. Jamestown, Kentucky.

Tennessee Dept. of Public Welfare
1975   Statistics. Nashville.

U.S. Dept. of Commerce. Bureau of the Census
1850–1970 Decennial Census of Population.
1850–1940 Decennial Census of Agriculture.
1954, 1959,
1964, 1974 Census of Agriculture.
1860   Census of Manufacturers.
1973   Census of Business.
1972, 1977 City and County Data Book.

Univ. of Tennessee Technical Assistance Center
1975   *Economic Profile of Fentress County.* Knoxville: Univ. of Tennessee.

Appalachia and the Cumberland Plateau

OVERVIEWS

Campbell, John C.
1921   *The Southern Highlander and His Homeland.* New ed. Lexington: Univ. of Kentucky Press, 1969.

Ford, Thomas R., ed.
1962   *The Southern Appalachian Region: A Survey.* Lexington: Univ. of Kentucky Press.

Kephart, Horace
[1922]1976 *Our Southern Highlanders.* New ed. Knoxville: Univ. of Tennessee Press.
Lewis, Helen, ed.
1978 *Colonialism in Modern America: The Appalachian Case.* Boone, N.C.: Appalachian Consortium Press.
McKinney, Gordon B.
1978 *Southern Mountain Republicans, 1865–1900: Politics and the Appalachian Community.* Chapel Hill: Univ. of North Carolina Press.
Plunkett, H. Dudley, and Mary Jean Bowman
1973 *Elites and Change in the Kentucky Mountains.* Lexington: Univ. Press of Kentucky.
Shackleford, Laurel, and Bill Weinberg, eds.
1977 *Our Appalachia: An Oral History.* New York: Hill and Wang.
Weller, Jack E.
1965 *Yesterday's People: Life in Contemporary Appalachia.* Lexington: Univ. Press of Kentucky.
Wigginton, Elliot, ed.
1972–81 *The Foxfire Books.* Garden City, N.Y.: Anchor Books.
William, Cratis D.
1961 The Southern Mountaineer in Fact and Fiction. Ph.D. diss., New York Univ. Ann Arbor, Mich.: Univ. Microfilms.

REGIONAL JOURNALS

Appalachian Heritage. Alice Lloyd College, Pippa Passes, Ky.
Appalachian Journal. Appalachian State Univ., Boone, N.C.
Mountain Life and Work. Berea College, Berea, Ky.
Mountain Living. Franklin, N.C.

ETHNOGRAPHIES

Hicks, George L.
1976 *Appalachian Valley.* New York: Holt, Rinehart, Winston.
Pearsall, Marion
1959 *Little Smoky Ridge: The Natural History of a Southern Appalachian Neighborhood.* Tuscaloosa: Univ. of Alabama Press.
Stephenson, John B.
1968 *Shiloh: A Mountain Community.* Lexington: Univ. of Kentucky Press.
Surface, Bill
1971 *The Hollow.* New York: Coward-McCann.

FICTION

Arnow, Harriette Simpson
1949   *Hunter's Horn*. New York: Macmillan.
[1954] 1972   *The Dollmaker*. Reissue. New York: Avon.
Still, James
[1940] 1978   *River of Earth*. Lexington: Univ. Press of Kentucky.
1977   *Sporty Creek: A Novel About an Appalachian Boyhood*. New York: Putnam.

BIBLIOGRAPHY

Bennett, George E.
1975   *Appalachian Books and Media for Public and College Libraries*. Morgantown: West Virginia Univ. Library.
Hutchins Library, Weatherford Hammond Mountain Collection
1975   *Mountain Fiction from Abernethy to Zugsmith . . . 1832 to 1975*. Berea, Ky.: Hutchins Library.
Ross, Charlotte T.
1976   *Bibliography of Southern Appalachia*. Boone, N.C.: Appalachian Consortium Press.
Smith, Sam B.
1974   *Tennessee History, A Bibliography*. Knoxville: Univ. of Tennessee Press.
West Virginia Univ. Library
1975   *Appalachian Bibliography*. 3 vols. Morgantown: West Virginia Univ. Library.

History

EXPLORATION AND SETTLEMENT

Arnow, Harriette Simpson
1960   *Seedtime on the Cumberland*. New York: Macmillan.
1963   *The Flowering of the Cumberland*. New York: Macmillan.
Caruso, John
1959   *The Appalachian Frontier: America's First Surge Westward*. Indianapolis: Bobbs-Merrill.
Dunaway, Wayland F.
1944   *Scotch Irish of Colonial Pennsylvania*. Chapel Hill: Univ. of North Carolina Press.
Jillson, Willard
1925   *The Kentucky Land Grants*. Filson Club Publication 33. Louisville: John P. Morton Co.

Leyburn, James G.
1962   *The Scotch-Irish: A Social History.* Chapel Hill: Univ. of North Carolina Press.
McCague, James
1973   *The Cumberland.* New York: Holt, Rinehart, Winston.
Speed, Thomas
1886   *The Wilderness Road: A Description of the Routes of Travel by Which the Pioneers and Early Settlers First Came to Kentucky.* Filson Club Publication 2. Louisville: John P. Morton.

LOCAL AND COUNTY HISTORY

Allardt Neighbor
1925   The History of Allardt. *Allardt Neighbor,* September 1925.
Arnow, Harriette Simpson
1976   *Old Burnside.* Lexington: Univ. Press of Kentucky.
Clarke, James N., and Annetta Gernt
1925   History of Allardt. *Tennessee Historical Magazine* 9:185–89.
Cowan, Sam K.
1941   *Sergeant York and His People.* New York: Grosset & Dunlap. Reprinted for Fentress County Historical Society. Jamestown, Tenn.: Fentress County Publishing Co.
Freytag, Ethel, and Glena Kreis Ott
1970   *A History of Morgan County, Tennessee.* N.p. Specialty Printing Co.
Hogue, Albert R.
1916   *History of Fentress County, Tennessee: The Old Home of Mark Twain's Ancestors.* Nashville: Williams Printing Co.
1933   *One Hundred Years in the Cumberland Mountains along the Continental Line.* McMinnville, Tenn.: Standard Printing Co.
1950   *Mark Twain's Obedstown and Knobs of Tennessee. A History of Jamestown and Fentress County, Tennessee.* Jamestown, Tenn.: Cumberland Printing Co.
Huddleston, Tim
1968   *Pioneer Families of Pickett County, Tennessee.* Collegedale, Tenn.: College Press.
1973   *History of Pickett County, Tennessee.* Collegedale, Tenn.: College Press.
Johnson, Augusta Phillips
1939   *A History of Wayne County, Kentucky: 1800–1900.* Louisville: Standard Printing Co.

Perry, L. E.
1979   *McCreary County Conquest: A Narrative History.* Whitley City, Ky.: author.

Sanderson, Esther Sharp
1958   *County Scott and Its Mountain Folk.* Huntsville, Tenn.: author.
1974   *Scott County, Gem of the Cumberlands.* Huntsville, Tenn.: author.

Stagg, Brian L.
1964   *Deer Lodge, Tennessee. Its Little-Known History.* Published by author.

RUGBY HISTORY

Brooks, Nelly Lender
1941   Rugby in Tennessee. Typewritten ms.

Hughes, Emily
1975   *Dissipations at Uffington House.* (Letters 1881–1887. Introduction and notes by John R. Debruyn.) Memphis: Memphis State Univ..

Hughes, Thomas
1880   Rugby, Morgan County, Tennessee, Settlement Founded October 5, 1880, by the Board of Aid to Land Ownership, (limited) of London, England. Presidential address. Cincinnati: R. Clarke.
1881   *Rugby, Tennessee: Being Some Account of the Settlement Founded on the Cumberland Plateau.* New York: G. Munroe. London: Macmillan.

Miller, Ernest Ivan
1941   *The English Settlement at Rugby.* Knoxville: Univ. of Tennessee College of Agriculture. Rural Research Series Monograph 120.

Rugby Papers
1872–1942 Microfilm of Account Books and Business Papers. 9 reels. Nashville: Tennessee State Library and Archives.

Rugby Restoration Association
1972   *Rugby's History.* Rugby, Tenn.: Rugby Restoration Association.

Stagg, Brian L.
1968   Tennessee's Rugby Colony. *Tennessee Historical Quarterly* 27:209–24.
1973   *The Distant Eden: Tennessee's Rugby Colony.* Rugby, Tenn.: Paylor Publications.

Stott, Kathleen
1939   *Rugby, Tennessee: An Attempted Utopia.* Nashville: WPA Historical Records Survey.

Walton, Sarah L.
195–   *Memories of Rugby Colony.* N.p.

Wichmann, Patricia Guion
192–   *Rugby, A Great Man's Dream.* N.p.
1959   *Christ Church, Episcopal, Rugby, Tennessee; A Short History.* N.p.

MAGAZINE AND NEWSPAPER SOURCES

American Historical Magazine and Tennessee Historical Society Quarterly, 1896–1904.
Fentress County Leader-Times.
Filson Club History Quarterly, 1926–present.
Kentucky State Historical Society Register, 1902–present.
McCreary County Record.
Miscellaneous issues of the *Plateau Gazette*, *Rugby Gazette*, and *Sunbright Dispatch*, 1881–1890.
(Oneida, Tenn.) *Independent Herald.*
Publications of the Filson Club, Louisville, Kentucky, 1884–1922.
Scott County News.
Tennessee Historical Magazine, 1915–1937.

HISTORIC MAPS

Colton, G. W., and C. B. Colton
1886   Colton's Map of the State of Tennessee. New York: Colton.
Colton, Joseph Hutchins
1855–74 Colton's Kentucky and Tennessee. New York: J. H. Colton. (Seven maps 1855, 1859, 1863, 1866, 1869, 1870, 1874.)
1865   Township Map of the State of Kentucky and Tennessee. New York: J. H. Colton.
Melish, John
1814   *Description of Roads in the U.S.: 1814. The Traveller's Directory through the United States; Containing a Descriptive of All the Principal Roads . . .* Philadelphia: author.
Mendenhall, E.
1864   Railway and County Map of Tennessee Exhibiting the Locations of the Counties, Cities, Villages, Post Offices, Railway Stations, etc. Cincinnati: E. Mendenhall.
Mitchell, S. A.
1860   County Map of Kentucky and Tennessee. In *Mitchell's New General Atlas.* Philadelphia: S. A. Mitchell.
Myer, William E.
1971   *Indian Trails of the Southeast.* Nashville: Blue and Gray Press.

Rhea, Matthew
1832 Map of the State of Tennessee, Taken from a Survey by Matthew Rhea. N.p.

Tanner, Henry Schenck
1829 *Memoir on the Recent Surveys, Observations, and Internal Improvements in the United States, with Brief Notices of the New Counties, Towns, Villages, Canals, and Railroads, Never Before Delineated.* Philadelphia: author.
1839 A New Map of Kentucky, with Its Roads and Distances from Place to Place along the Stage and Steam Boat Routes. In Tanner's *New American Atlas.* Philadelphia.

U.S. Dept. of Agriculture
1966 General Soil Map of Tennessee. Rev. ed. Washington.

U.S. Post Office Dept.
1883 Post Route Map: Kentucky and Tennessee. Washington.

Young, James Hamilton
1826 Kentucky and Tennessee. In G. Armroyd's *Connected View of the Whole Internal Navigation of the U.S.* Philadelphia: H. C. Carey and I. Lea.
1838 The Tourist's Pocket Map of the State of Tennessee, Exhibiting Its Internal Improvements. N.p.

Economic Development

DeLozier, Mary Jean
1978 Heritage of the Upper Cumberland: Good Ole Days Work and Play. *Tennessee Technological University Alumnus* 25 (12): 4–5.

Carson, Gerald
1954 *The Old Country Store.* New York: Oxford Univ. Press.

Clark, Thomas D.
1944 *Pills, Petticoats and Plows: The Southern Country Store.* Indianapolis: Bobbs-Merrill.

Freeman, Graydon L.
1955 *The Country Store.* Watkins Glen, N.Y.: Century House.

Hawkins, A. W.
1882 *Handbook of Tennessee.* Knoxville: Whig and Chronicle Steam Book and Job Printing Office.

Kentucky Petroleum Councilor
1970 1818 McCreary County Well Cited by General Assembly. *Kentucky Petroleum Councilor,* March, p. 5.

Kinne, W. A.
1929 *The Gum Tree Story.* Stearns, Ky.: Stearns Coal and Lumber Co.

McCreary County Record
1975   Stearns Coal and Lumber Co. and the Justus Mine. Special issue, October 16, 1975.
McWhirter, A. J.
1885   *Revised Handbook of Tennessee.* Nashville: Albert B. Tavel, Printer to the State.
Stearns Coal and Lumber Company
1903–1975   Company records on employment and production. Stearns Coal and Lumber Company Archives, Stearns, Ky.
1938   200 *Square Miles.* Stearns, Ky.: Stearns Coal and Lumber Co.
Stearns Co-operator, The
1915   The Stearns Coal and Lumber Company. *The Stearns Co-operator,* Nov. 15, p. 18.
Stoffle, Richard W.
1972   Whither the Country Store? *Ethnohistory* 19 (1): 63–72.
Verhoeff, Mary
1911   *The Kentucky Mountains, Transportation and Commerce, 1750–1911. A Study in the Economic History of a Coal Field.* Filson Club Publication 26. Louisville: John P. Morton Co.

TIMBER INDUSTRY

Andrews, Ralph Warren
1956   *Glory Days of Logging.* New York: Bonanza Books.
Brown, Arthur A.
1887   *Lumbering on the Cumberland: A Romance Taken from Life.* Cincinnati: Lumber Worker Co.
Brown, Nelson
1947   *Lumber: Manufacture, Conditioning, Grading, Distribution and Use.* New York: John Wiley.
Bryant, Ralph Clement
1922   *Lumber, Its Manufacture and Distribution.* New York: J. Wiley and Sons.
1923   *Logging: The Principles and General Methods of Operation in the U.S.* 2d edition. New York: J. Wiley and Sons.
Clarkson, Roy B.
1964   *Tumult on the Mountains: Lumbering in West Virginia, 1770–1920.* Parsons, W. Va.: McClain.
Holbrook, Stewart H.
1961   *Holy Old Mackinaw: A Natural History of the American Lumberjack.* New York: Macmillan.

Labbe, John T. and Vernon Goe
1961   *Railroads in the Woods.* Berkeley, Calif.: Howell-North.

COAL INDUSTRY

Caudill, Harry
1963   *Night Comes to the Cumberlands.* Boston: Little, Brown.
Coleman, McAlister
1969   *Men and Coal.* New York: Arno and New York Times.
Colton, Henry
1883   Report on the Coal Mines of Tennessee and Other Minerals, to A. W. Hawkins, Commissioner of Agriculture, Statistics, and Mines. Nashville: Albert B. Tavel, Printer to the State.
Culbertson, Ben
1972   *The Ghost of Blue Heron.* Louisville, Ky.: Courier-Journal and Times Magazine.
Green, Archie
1972   *Only a Miner: Studies in Recorded Coal-Mining Songs.* Urbana: Univ. of Illinois Press.
Hinrichs, A. F.
1923   *The United Mine Workers of America and the Non-Union Coal Fields.* New York: Columbia Univ. Press.
Husband, Joseph
1910   *A Year in a Coal-Mine.* Boston: Houghton-Mifflin.
Kneeland, Frank H.
1926   *Preliminaries of Coal Mining.* New York: McGraw Hill.
Korson, George
1927   *Songs and Ballads of the Anthracite Miner.* New York: Frederick H. Hitchcock.
1964   *Minstrels of the Mine Patch.* Hatsboro, Pa.: Folklore Associates.
1965   *Coal Dust on the Fiddle.* Hatsboro, Pa.: Folklore Associates.
Lantz, Herman
1958   *People of Coal Town.* New York: Columbia Univ. Press.
Leamon, Anthony
1975   Coal Mining in Tennessee. Information Circular 17. Nashville: Tennessee Dept. of Conservation, Division of Geology.
Peterson, Bill
1972   *Coaltown Revisited: An Appalachian Notebook.* Chicago: Henry Regnery Co.
Ross, Malcolm
1933   *Machine Age in the Hills.* New York: Macmillan.

RAILROADS

Harshaw, Lou
1977   *Trains, Trestles, and Tunnels: Railroads of the Southern Appalachians.* Asheville, N.C.: Hexagon.

Kalisher, Simpson
1961   *Railroad Men: A Book of Photographs and Collected Stories.* New York: Clarke and Way.

Lanier, Alton B.
1974   The Railroad That Changed More Than Its Motive Power. *Trains* 34 (l): 20–26.

Sulzer, Elmer
1968   *Ghost Railroads of Kentucky.* Indianapolis: V. A. Jones.
1975   *Ghost Railroads of Tennessee.* Indianapolis: V. A. Jones.

Folklife Topics

FOLK MEDICINE AND BOTANIC RESOURCES

Duncan, Wilbur H., and Leonard Foote
1975   *Wildflowers of the Southeastern United States.* Athens: Univ. of Georgia Press.

Garrett, Ruby Burriss
1978   Traditional Southern Appalachian Dental Practices. In *Glimpses of Southern Appalachian Folk Culture,* ed. C. Faulkner and C. Buckles. Tennessee Anthropological Association Miscellaneous Paper 3. Chattanooga, Tenn.: Tribute Press.

Keeler, Harriet
1969   *Our Northern Shrubs.* New York: Dover.

Krochmal, Arnold, and Connie Krochmal
1973   *A Guide to the Medicinal Plants of the United States.* New York: Quadrangle.

Martin, Roxie
1947   Old Remedies Collected in the Blue Ridge Mountains. *Journal of American Folklore* 60:184–85.

Medsger, Oliver Perry
[1939]1978 *Edible Wild Plants.* New York: Collier Macmillan.

Mullins, Gladys
1973   Herbs of the Southern Highlands and Their Medicinal Use. *Kentucky Folklore Record* 19:36–41.

Norris, Ruby
1958   Folk Medicine of Cumberland County. *Kentucky Folklore Record* 4:101–10.

Parr, Jerry S.
1962   Folk Cures in Middle Tennessee. *Tennessee Folklore Society Bulletin* 28:8–12.
Rogers, E. G.
1941   *Early Folk Medical Practices in Tennessee.* Murfreesboro, Tenn.: Mid-South Publishing Co. for the Tennessee Folklore Society.
Vogel, Virgil J.
1970   *American Indian Medicine.* Norman: Univ. of Oklahoma Press.
Wharton, Mary E., and Roger Barbour
1971   *A Guide to the Wildflowers and Ferns of Kentucky.* Lexington: Univ. of Kentucky Press.
Youngken, Heber W.
1950   *Textbook of Pharmacognosy.* 6th ed. Philadelphia: Blakiston.

MATERIAL CULTURE AND DOMESTIC TECHNOLOGY

Allardt, Tennessee, Presbyterian Missionary Society
n.d.   *The Allardt Cook Book.* N.p.
Ball, Donald B.
1977a   Observations of the Form and Function of Middle Tennessee Gravehouses. *Tennessee Anthropologist* 2 (1): 29–62.
1977b   Wooden Gravemarkers: Neglected Items of Material Culture. *Tennessee Folklore Society Bulletin* 43 (4): 167–85.
Eaton, Allen H.
1937   *Handicrafts of the Southern Highlands.* New York: Dover.
Glassie, Henry
1965   Southern Mountain Houses: A Study in American Folk Culture. Master's thesis, State Univ. of New York College.
1968   *Pattern in the Material Folk Culture of the Eastern United States.* Philadelphia: Univ. of Pennsylvania Press.
1975   *Folk Housing in Middle Virginia.* Knoxville: Univ. of Tennessee Press.
Goodrich, Frances Louisa
1931   *Mountain Homespun.* New Haven: Yale Univ. Press.
Horwitz, Elinor Lander
1974   *Mountain People, Mountain Crafts.* Philadelphia: Lippincott.
Montell, William Lynwood, and Michael Morse
1976   *Kentucky Folk Architecture.* Lexington: Univ. Press of Kentucky.
Parris, John
1978   *Mountain Cooking.* Asheville, N.C.: Citizen Times Publishing Co.

Reed, Clyde
1979   A Night on New River at the Reed Fish Trap. *Tennessee Anthropological Association Newsletter* 4 (1): 1–7.
Riedl, Norbert F., Donald Ball, and Anthony Cavender
1976   *A Survey of Traditional Architecture and Related Material Folk Culture Patterns in the Normandy Reservoir, Coffee County, Tennessee.* Univ. of Tennessee Dept. of Anthropology Report of Investigations 17. Knoxville: Univ. of Tennessee Press.
Sloane, Eric
1964   *A Museum of Early American Tools.* New York: Ballantine Books.

SOCIAL CUSTOM

Ball, Donald B.
1975   Social Activities Associated with Two Rural Cemeteries in Coffee County, Tennessee. *Tennessee Folklore Society Bulletin* 41 (3): 93–98.
Bettis, Myra, Michael Blackwell, Robert Hoffmann, Patty Sonka, and Loretta Swingle
1978   The Care of the East Tennessee Dead. In *Glimpses of Southern Appalachian Folk Culture,* ed. C. Faulkner and C. Buckles. Tennessee Anthropological Association Miscellaneous Paper 3. Chattanooga, Tenn.: Tribute Press.
Conn, Philip
1978   Traditional Courtship and Marriage Customs in the Appalachian South. In *Glimpses of Southern Appalachian Folk Culture,* ed. C. Faulkner and C. Buckles. Tennessee Anthropological Association Miscellaneous Paper 3. Chattanooga, Tenn.: Tribute Press.
Lambert, Dean
1961   Mountain Funerals. *Mountain Life and Work* 37 (1): 43–50.
Long, Grady
1961   Folk Customs in Southeast Tennessee. *Tennessee Folklore Society Bulletin* 27:76–84.
Matthews, Elmora Messer
1965   *Neighbor and Kin: Life in a Tennessee Ridge Community.* Nashville: Vanderbilt Univ. Press.
Murray, Lena David
1935   *Schoolhouse in the Foothills.* New York: Simon & Schuster.
Smathers, Michael
1970   Suspicion and Community in Appalachia. In *Appalachia in Transition,* ed. M. Glenn. St. Louis: Bethany Press.

RELIGION

Boles, John B.
1972 *The Great Revival, 1787–1805: The Origins of the Southern Evangelical Mind.* Lexington: Univ. Press of Kentucky.

Bruce, Dickson D., Jr.
1974 *And They All Sang Hallelujah.* Knoxville: Univ. of Tennessee Press.

Clark, Elmer T.
1955 The Small Sects in the Mountains. In *Religion in the Appalachian Mountains*, ed. W. Weatherford. Berea, Ky.: Berea College Centennial Publications.

Gerrard, Nathan L.
1970 Churches of the Stationary Poor in Southern Appalachia. In *Change in Rural Appalachia: Implications for Action Programs*, ed. J. Photiadis and H. Schwarzweller. Philadelphia: Univ. of Pennsylvania Press.

Hooker, Elizabeth R.
1933 *Religion in the Highlands.* New York: Polygraphic Co. of America.

Humphrey, Richard A.
1974 Development of Religion in Southern Appalachia: The Personal Quality. *Appalachian Journal* 3 (1): 244–54.
1978 Mountain Revival Methods. *Appalachian Heritage* 5:23–28.

Johnson, Charles A.
1955 *The Frontier Camp Meeting: Religion's Harvest Time.* Dallas: Southern Methodist Univ. Press.

Jones, Loyal
1976 Mountain Religion: The Outsider's View. *Mountain Review* 2 (3).
1977 Old-Time Baptists and Mainline Christianity. In *An Appalachian Symposium*, ed. J. W. Williamson. Boone: Appalachian State Univ. Press.
1977 Studying Mountain Religion. *Appalachian Journal* 5 (1): 125–30.

Kane, Stephen M.
1974 Holy Ghost People: The Snake-Handlers of Southern Appalachia. *Appalachian Journal* 1:255–62.

Kerr, James M.
1978 A Pastor's View of Religion in Appalachia. In *Religion in Appalachia*, ed. J. Photiadis. Morgantown: West Virginia Univ. Press.

La Barre, Weston
1962 *They Shall Take Up Serpents: The Psychology of the Southern Snake-Handling Cult.* Minneapolis: Univ. of Minnesota Press.

Mullins, Frieda, and Diana Hall
1973   Old Regular Baptist Footwashin'. *Appalachian Heritage* 1 (4): 20–21.
Parker, Gerald K.
1970   Folk Religion in Southern Appalachia. Ph.D. diss., Southern Baptist Theological Seminary.
Photiadis, John D.
1978   *Religion in Appalachia: Theological, Social and Psychological Dimensions and Correlates.* Morgantown: West Virginia Univ. Center for Extension and Continuing Education.
Sweet, William W.
1931   *Religion on the American Frontier: The Baptists.* New York: Holt.
Weatherford, W. D., ed.
1955   *Religion in the Appalachian Mountains.* Berea, Ky.: Berea College Centennial Publications.

MUSIC

Bailey, Jay
1972   Historical Origin and Stylistic Developments of the Five-String Banjo. *Journal of American Folklore* 85:58–65.
Child, Francis J.
1882–98   *The English and Scottish Popular Ballads.* 5 vols. Boston: Houghton-Mifflin.
Coffin, Tristram P.
1977   *The British Traditional Ballad in North America.* Rev. ed. Austin: Univ. of Texas Press.
Cox, John Harrington
1925   *Folk Songs of the South.* Cambridge: Harvard Univ. Press.
Davis, Arthur Kyle, Jr.
1929   *Traditional Ballads of Virginia.* Cambridge: Harvard Univ. Press.
Epstein, Dena J.
1975   The Folk Banjo: A Documentary History. *Ethnomusicology* 19 (3): 347–71.
Green, Archie
1979   String Bands. Graphics 51. *John Edwards Memorial Foundation Quarterly* 15 (56): 215–24.
Henry, Mellinger E.
1938   *Folksongs from the Southern Highlands.* New York: J. J. Augustin.
Irwin, John Rice
1979   *Musical Instruments of the Southern Appalachian Mountains.* Norris, Tenn.: Museum of Appalachia Press.

Jackson, George Pullen
1933   *White Spirituals in the Southern Uplands.* New ed. New York: Dover, 1965.

Malone, Bill C.
1979   *Southern Music, American Music.* Lexington: Univ. Press of Kentucky.

Morse, Becky
1976a   Interview with Richard Burnett and James Corder, December 8. Available at Wayne County Library, Monticello, Ky.
1976b   Interview with Richard Burnett and Georgia Burnett, August 24. Available at Wayne County Library, Monticello, Ky.
1976c   Mean Music of Monticello: A Study of Performance and Style. Unpublished manuscript available at Wayne County Library, Monticello, Ky.
1976d   Richard Burnett, Musician, Singer: A Life History. Unpublished Manuscript available at Wayne County Library, Monticello, Ky.

Randolph, Vance
1946–49   *Ozark Folksongs.* 3 vols. Columbia: Missouri Historical Society.

Ritchie, Jean
1955   *Singing Family of the Cumberlands.* New York: Oak Publications.

Sharp, Cecil J.
1932   *English Folk Songs from the Southern Appalachians.* London: Oxford Univ. Press.

Wiggins, Gene
1979   Popular Music and the Fiddler. *John Edwards Memorial Foundation Quarterly* 15 (55): 144–52.

Wolfe, Charles K.
1974   Burnett and Rutherford: A Ramblin' Reckless Hobo. (Booklet accompanying Rounder album 1004.)
1977   *Tennessee Strings: The Story of Country Music in Tennessee.* Knoxville: Univ. of Tennessee Press.

DANCE

Chase, Richard
1938   *Old Songs and Singing Games.* New York: Dover, 1972.
1949   *Singing Games and Playparty Games.* New York: Dover, 1967.

Damon, S. Foster
1952   The History of Square Dancing. *Proceedings of the American Antiquarian Society* 62:63–98.

Emery, Lynne Fauley
1972   *Black Dance in the United States from 1619 to 1970.* Palo Alto, Calif.: National Press Books.

McDowell, Lucien, and Flora McDowell
1938   *Folk Dances of Tennessee.* Ann Arbor, Mich.: Edwards Bros.
Smith, Frank H.
1955   *The Appalachian Square Dance.* Berea, Ky.: Berea College Press.

VERBAL LORE

Blair, Marion E.
1938   The Prevalence of Older English Proverbs in Blount County, Tennessee. *Tennessee Folklore Society Bulletin* 4:1–24.
Campbell, Marie
1960   *Cloud Walking.* Bloomington: Indiana Univ. Press.
Carter, Isabel Gordon
1934   Mountain White Riddles. *Journal of American Folklore* 47:76–81.
Chase, Richard
1948   *The Grandfather Tales.* Boston: Houghton-Mifflin.
1950   *The Jack Tales.* Boston: Houghton-Mifflin.
Farr, T. J.
1935   Riddles of Middle Tennessee. *Tennessee Folklore Society Bulletin* 1 (3).
Montell, William Lynwood
1975   *Ghosts along the Cumberland.* Knoxville: Univ. of Tennessee Press.
Redfield, W. A.
1937   A Collection of Middle Tennessee Riddles. *Southern Folklore Quarterly* 1 (3): 35–51.
Roberts, Leonard W.
1959   *Up Cutshin and Down Greasy: Folkways of a Kentucky Family.* Lexington: Univ. of Kentucky Press.
1974   *Sang Branch Settlers: Folksongs and Tales of a Kentucky Mountain Family.* Austin: Univ. of Texas Press.
White, Newman I., ed.
1952   *The Frank C. Brown Collection of North Carolina Folklore.* Durham: Duke Univ. Press.

FOLK BELIEF

Anderson, U.
1937   A Comparative Study of Some of the Older Beliefs and Usages of East Tennessee. *Tennessee Folklore Society Bulletin* 3:1–7.
Carter, Roland D.
1944   Mountain Superstitions. *Tennessee Folklore Society Bulletin* 10:1–6.
Combs, Josiah H.
1914   Sympathetic Magic in the Kentucky Mountains. *Journal of American Folklore* 27:328–30.

Farr, T. J.
1935   Riddles and Superstitions of Middle Tennessee. *Journal of American Folklore* 48:318–37.
1938   Middle Tennessee Folk Beliefs Concerning Love and Marriage. *Southern Folklore Quarterly* 2 (3): 165–74.
1939   Tennessee Folk Belief Concerning Children. *Journal of American Folklore* 52:112–16.

Fowler, David C., and Mary Gene Fowler
1950   More Kentucky Superstitions. *Southern Folklore Quarterly* 24:170–76.

Frazier, Neal
1936   A Collection of Middle Tennessee Superstitions. *Tennessee Folklore Society Bulletin* 2.

Hatcher, Mildred
1955   Superstitions in Middle Tennessee. *Southern Folklore Quarterly* 19:150–55.

Haun, Mildred
1967   The Traditions of Cocke County. *Tennessee Folklore Society Bulletin* 33:72–79.

McGlasson, Cleo
1941   Superstitions and Folk Beliefs of Overton County. *Tennessee Folklore Society Bulletin* 7 (2): 13–27.

Montell, William Lynwood
1966   Death Beliefs from the Kentucky Foothills. *Kentucky Folklore Record* 12:81–86.

Morton, Joan
1978   Superstitions and Beliefs Concerning Babies in Southern Appalachia. In *Glimpses of Southern Appalachian Folk Culture*, ed. C. Faulkner and C. Buckles. Tennessee Anthropological Association Miscellaneous Paper 3. Chattanooga, Tenn.: Tribute Press.

O'Dell, Ruth
1944   Signs and Superstitions. *Tennessee Folklore Society Bulletin* 10:1–6.

Oneida High School
n.d.   Mountain Magic, Volumes I and II. Booklets prepared by students in folklore classes of Mrs. Linda Stewart. Mimeographed.

Redfield, W. Adelbert
1937   Superstitions and Folk Beliefs. *Tennessee Folklore Society Bulletin* 3:11–40.

Rogers, E. G.
1950   Guideposts to Fortune. *Tennessee Folklore Society Bulletin* 16:31–37.

Shearin, H. G.
1911	Superstitions in the Cumberland Mountains. *Journal of American Folklore* 24:319–22.
Thomas, Daniel L., and Lucy Thomas
1920	*Kentucky Superstitions.* Princeton, N.J.: Princeton Univ. Press.
Wells, J. C.
1893	Weather and Moon Superstitions in Tennessee. *Journal of American Folklore* 6:298–300.
Whitt, A. L., and Mary McGlasson
1973	*Snakelore.* Frankfort, Ky.: Whippoorwill Press.
Wilson, Gordon
1966	Folk Beliefs about People. *Tennessee Folklore Society Bulletin* 32:31, 40.

LANGUAGE

Berrey, Lester
1940	Southern Mountain Dialect. *American Speech* 15:45–55.
Bray, Rose
1950	Disappearing Dialect. *Antioch Review* 10:279–88.
Brown, Calvin S.
1916	Word List from Tennessee. *Dialect Notes* 4 (5): 345–46.
Carpenter, Charles
1933	Variation in the Southern Mountain Dialect. *American Speech* 8 (1): 22–25.
Combs, Josiah H.
1916	Old, Early and Elizabethan English in the Southern Mountains. *Dialect Notes* 4 (4): 283–97.
1919	A Word-List from the South. *Dialect Notes* 5 (2): 31–40.
1931	The Language of the Southern Highlanders. *Modern Language Association Publications* 46 (4): 1302–23.
Edson, H. A., and E. M. Fairchild
1900	Tennessee Mountain Word-List. *Dialect Notes* 1 (8): 370–77.
Farr, T. J.
1936	Folk Speech of Middle Tennessee. *American Speech* 11 (3): 275–76.
1939	The Language of the Tennessee Mountain Regions. *American Speech* 14:89–92.
Fink, Paul M.
1941	Some East Tennessee Place Names. *Tennessee Folklore Society Bulletin* 7 (3–4): 40–50.
Fruit, J. P.
1890	Kentucky Words and Phrases. *Dialect Notes* 1 (2): 63–69.
1896	Kentucky Words. *Dialect Notes* 1 (5): 230–34.

Hackenberg, Robert Gregory
1976   *Appalachian English: A Sociolinguistic Study.* Ann Arbor, Mich.: Univ. Microfilms.
Hall, Joseph Sargent
1942   *Phonetics of Great Smoky Mountain Speech.* New York: King's Crown Press. American Speech Reprints and Monographs 4.
Owens, Bess Alice
1931   Folk Speech of the Cumberlands. *American Speech* 7 (2): 89–95.
Pollard, Mary O.
1915   Terms from the Tennessee Mountains. *Dialect Notes* 4 (2): 242–43.
Shearin, Hubert G.
1911   An Eastern Kentucky Dialect Word-List. *Dialect Notes* 3 (7): 537–40.
Still, James A.
1929   Place Names in the Cumberland Mountains. *American Speech* 5 (2): 113.
1930   Christian Names in the Cumberlands. *American Speech* 5 (4): 306–7.
Wolfram, Walt
1977   On the Linguistic Study of Appalachian Speech. *Appalachian Journal* 5 (1): 92–99.
Wolfram, Walt, and Donna Christian
1976   *Appalachian Speech.* Arlington, Va.: Center for Applied Linguistics.

References Cited

Allardt Neighbor
1925 The History of Allardt. *Allardt Neighbor*, September 1925.
Allen, Barbara, and Lynwood Montell
1981 *From Memory to History*. Nashville: American Association for State and Local History.
Arnow, Harriette Simpson
1949 *Hunter's Horn*. New York: Macmillan.
1954 *The Dollmaker*. New York: Avon.
1960 *Seedtime on the Cumberland*. New York: Macmillan.
1963 *The Flowering of the Cumberland*. New York: Macmillan.
1977 *Old Burnside*. Lexington: Univ. Press of Kentucky.
Bailey, Jay
1972 Historical Origin and Stylistic Developments of the Five-String Banjo. *Journal of American Folklore* 85:58–65.
Ball, Donald B.
1977a Observations of the Form and Function of Middle Tennessee Gravehouses. *Tennessee Anthropologist* 2 (1): 29–62.
1977b Wooden Gravemarkers: Neglected Items of Material Culture. *Tennessee Folklore Society Bulletin* 43 (4): 167–85.
Berrey, Lester
1940 Southern Mountain Dialect. *American Speech* 15:45–55.
Boles, John B.
1972 *The Great Revival, 1787–1805: The Origins of the Southern Evangelical Mind*. Lexington: Univ. Press of Kentucky.
Brown, Nelson
1947 *Lumber: Manufacture, Conditioning, Grading, Distribution and Use*. New York: John Wiley.

Bruce, Dickson D., Jr.
1974	*And They All Sang Hallelujah.* Knoxville: Univ. of Tennessee Press.
Building Conservation Technology
1984	Master Plan for the Development, Management, and Protection of the Rugby Colony Historic Area. Nashville, Tenn.: U.S. Army Corps of Engineers.
Bush, Florence Cope
1992	*Dorie: Woman of the Mountains.* Knoxville: Univ. of Tennessee Press.
Byrne, J. G., et al.
1970	*Soil Survey of the McCreary–Whitley Area, Kentucky.* Washington: U.S. Dept. of Agriculture, Soil Conservation Service.
Campbell, John C.
[1921]1969	*The Southern Highlander and His Homeland.* New ed. Lexington: Univ. of Kentucky Press.
Carpenter, Charles
1933	Variation in the Southern Mountain Dialect. *American Speech* 8 (1): 22–25.
Carson, Gerald
1954	*The Old Country Store.* New York: Oxford Univ. Press.
Caudill, Harry
1963	*Night Comes to the Cumberlands.* Boston: Little, Brown.
Coleman, McAlister
1969	*Men and Coal.* New York: Arno and New York Times.
Colton, Henry
1883	Report on the Coal Mines of Tennessee and Other Minerals, to A. W. Hawkins, Commissioner of Agriculture, Statistics, and Mines. Nashville: Albert B. Tavel, Printer to the State.
Colton, Joseph Hutchins
1855–74	*Colton's Kentucky and Tennessee* (seven maps dated 1855, 1859, 1863, 1866, 1869, 1870, 1874). New York: J. H. Colton.
Combs, Josiah H.
1916	Old, Early and Elizabethan English in the Southern Mountains. *Dialect Notes* 4 (4): 283–97.
1919	A Word-List from the South. *Dialect Notes* 5 (2): 31–40.
1931	The Language of the Southern Highlanders. *Modern Language Association Publications* 46 (4): 1302–23.
Conn, Philip
1978	Traditional Courtship and Marriage Customs in the Appalachian South. In *Glimpses of Southern Appalachian Folk Culture,* ed. C. Faulkner

and C. Buckles, 34–42. Tennessee Anthropological Association Miscellaneous Paper 3. Chattanooga, Tenn.: Tribute Press.

Damon, S. Foster
1952 The History of Square Dancing. *Proceedings of the American Antiquarian Society* 62:63–98.

DeLozier, Mary Jean
1978 Heritage of the Upper Cumberland: Good Ole Days Work and Play. *Tennessee Technological University Alumnus* 25 (12): 4–5.

East Tennessee Development District
1979 The Big South Fork Population and Economy (Draft Report). Knoxville: East Tennessee Development District.
1980 Public Facility and Service Needs Around the Big South Fork National River and Recreation Area. Knoxville: East Tennessee Development District.

Emery, Lynne Fauley
1972 *Black Dance in the United States from 1619 to 1970.* Palo Alto, Calif.: National Press Books.

Epstein, Dena J.
1975 The Folk Banjo: A Documentary History. *Ethnomusicology* 19 (3): 347–71.

Ferguson, Terry A.
1988 Lithic Analysis and the Discovery of Prehistoric Man–Land Relationships in the Uplands of the Big South Fork of the Tennessee Cumberland Plateau. Ph.D. diss., Univ. of Tennessee.

Ferguson, Terry A., Michael W. Morris, Robert A Pace, Jeffrey W. Gardner, and Robert W. Hoffman
1986 *An Archaeological Reconnaissance and Testing of Indirect Impact Areas within Selected Development Sites of the Big South Fork National River and Recreation Area.* Knoxville: Dept. of Anthropology, Univ. of Tennessee.

Ford, Thomas R., ed.
1962 *The Southern Appalachian Region: A Survey.* Lexington: Univ. of Kentucky Press.

Freytag, Ethel, and Glena Kreis Ott
1970 *A History of Morgan County, Tennessee.* N.p. Specialty Printing Co.

Glassie, Henry
1968 *Pattern in the Material Folk Culture of the Eastern United States.* Philadelphia: Univ. of Pennsylvania Press.

Green, Archie
1972 *Only a Miner: Studies in Recorded Coal-Mining Songs.* Urbana: Univ. of Illinois Press.

Hall, Joseph Sargent
1942   *Phonetics of Great Smoky Mt. Speech.* New York: King's Crown Press. American Speech Reprints and Monographs 4.
Hawkins, A. W.
1882   *Handbook of Tennessee.* Knoxville: Whig and Chronicle Steam Book and Job Printing Office.
Hogue, Albert R.
1950   *Mark Twain's Obedstown and Knobs of Tennessee. A History of Jamestown and Fentress County, Tennessee.* Jamestown, Tenn.: Cumberland Printing Co.
Holbrook, Stewart H.
1961   *Holy Old Mackinaw: A Natural History of the American Lumberjack.* New York: Macmillan.
Howard, Brenda Lee
1981   A Collection of Ghost Stories from Fentress County, Tennessee. Unpublished student paper, Univ. of Tennessee, Knoxville.
Howell, Benita J.
1983a   Folk History as a Mirror of Class Values: The Saga of Jerome Boyatt. *Tennessee Anthropologist* 8 (1): 1–19.
1983b   Implications of the Cultural Conservation Report for Social Impact Assessment. *Human Organization* 42 (4): 346–50.
1984   Folklife Research in Environmental Planning. In *Applied Social Science for Environmental Planning,* ed. W. Millsap, 127–39. Boulder, Colo.: Westview Press.
1987   Folklife in Planning. *Cultural Resources Management Bulletin* 10 (1): 14–15, 29.
1989   The Anthropologist as Advocate for Local Interests in National Park Planning. In *International Perspectives on Cultural Parks. Proceedings of the First World Conference, 1984,* 275–79. N.p.: Colorado Historical Society and U.S. National Park Service.
1990   Mediating Environmental Policy Conflicts in Appalachian Communities. In *Environment in Appalachia, Proceedings from the 1989 Conference on Appalachia,* 99–105. Lexington: Appalachian Center, Univ. of Kentucky.
1993   Social Impact Assessment and Cultural Conservation: Implications for Local Public Involvement in Planning. In *Environmental Analysis. The NEPA Experience,* ed. S. G. Hildebrand and J. B. Cannon, 274–88. Boca Raton, Fla.: Lewis Publishers.
1994   Folklife, Cultural Conservation, and Environmental Planning. In *Putting Folklore to Use,* ed. M. O. Jones, 94–114. Lexington: Univ. Press of Kentucky.

1998 National Recreation Areas in Appalachia: Citizen Participation in Planning and Management. In *Culture: The Missing Element in Conservation and Development*, ed. R. J. Hoage and K. Moran, 51–65. Dubuque, Iowa: Kendall/Hunt.

Hughes, Thomas
1881 *Rugby, Tennessee: Being Some Account of the Settlement Founded on the Cumberland Plateau*. New York: G. Munroe; London: Macmillan.

Husband, Joseph
1910 *A Year in a Coal-Mine*. Boston: Houghton-Mifflin.

Hutchinson, Steven K., Ellen A. Dugan, and Richard S. Levy
1982 *An Inventory and Evaluation of Architectural and Engineering Resources of the Big South Fork National River and Recreation Area, Tennessee and Kentucky*. Lexington, Ky.: Environmental Consultants.

Ives, Edward D.
1976 Argyle Boom. *Northeast Folklore* XVII.

Jackson, George Pullen
1933 *White Spirituals in the Southern Uplands*. New ed. New York: Dover, 1965.

Jillson, Willard
1925 *The Kentucky Land Grants*. Filson Club Publication 33. Louisville: John P. Morton Co.

Johnson, Charles A.
1955 *The Frontier Camp Meeting: Religion's Harvest Time*. Dallas: Southern Methodist Univ. Press.

Kane, Stephen M.
1974 Holy Ghost People: The Snake-Handlers of Southern Appalachia. *Appalachian Journal* 1:255–62.

Kentucky Petroleum Councilor
1970 1818 McCreary County Well Cited by General Assembly. *Kentucky Petroleum Councilor*, March, p. 5.

Kephart, Horace
[1913] 1976 *Our Southern Highlanders*. New ed. Knoxville: Univ. of Tennessee Press.

Kernodle, M., J. Wilson, and M. Mallory
1974 *Water Resources of the South Fork Cumberland River, Tennessee*. Nashville: Tennessee Dept. of Conservation, Division of Water Resources.

Killebrew, Joseph Buckner
1876 *Mineral and Agricultural Resources of the Portion of Tennessee along the Cincinnati Southern and Knoxville and Ohio Railroads*. Nashville: Tavel, Eastman, and Howell.

Kinne, W. A.
1929 *The Gum Tree Story*. Stearns, Ky.: Stearns Coal and Lumber Company.

Korson, George
1927 *Songs and Ballads of the Anthracite Miner.* New York: Frederick H. Hitchcock.
1964 *Minstrels of the Mine Patch.* 3d printing. Hatsboro, Pa.: Folklore Associates.
1965 *Coal Dust on the Fiddle.* Hatsboro, Pa.: Folklore Associates.
La Barre, Weston
1962 *They Shall Take Up Serpents: The Psychology of the Southern Snake-Handling Cult.* Minneapolis: Univ. of Minnesota Press.
Leyburn, James G.
1962 *The Scotch-Irish: A Social History.* Chapel Hill: Univ. of North Carolina Press.
Long, Grady
1961 Folk Customs in Southeast Tennessee. *Tennessee Folklore Society Bulletin* 27:76–84.
Loomis, Ormond H.
1983 *Cultural Conservation: The Protection of Cultural Heritage in the United States.* Washington, D.C.: Library of Congress, American Folklife Center.
Malone, Bill C.
1979 *Southern Music, American Music.* Lexington: Univ. Press of Kentucky.
Matthews, Elmora Messer
1965 *Neighbor and Kin. Life in a Tennessee Ridge Community.* Nashville: Vanderbilt Univ. Press.
McBride, Kim A.
1993 *A Background Archival and Oral Historical Study of the Barthell Coal Camp, McCreary County, Kentucky.* Lexington: Program for Cultural Resource Assessment, Univ. of Kentucky.
McCague, James
1973 *The Cumberland.* New York: Holt, Rinehart, Winston.
McCreary County Record
1975 Stearns Coal and Lumber Co. and the Justus Mine. Special issue. October 16, 1975.
McWhirter, A. J.
1885 *Revised Handbook of Tennessee.* Nashville: Albert B. Tavel, Printer to the State.
Melish, John
1814 *Description of Roads in the U.S.* Philadelphia: author.
Miller, Wihry, and Lee, Inc., for U.S. Army Corps of Engineers, Nashville District
1980 *Big South Fork National River and Recreation Area. Master Plan.* 3 vols. Nashville: U.S. Army Corps of Engineers.

Mitchell, S. A.
1860   County Map of Kentucky and Tennessee. *Mitchell's New General Atlas.* Philadelphia: S. A. Mitchell.
Montell, William Lynwood
1966   Death Beliefs from the Kentucky Foothills. *Kentucky Folklore Record* 12:81–86.
1970   *The Saga of Coe Ridge: A Study in Oral History.* Knoxville: Univ. of Tennessee Press.
1975   *Ghosts along the Cumberland.* Knoxville: Univ. of Tennessee Press.
Montell, William Lynwood, and Michael Morse
1976   *Kentucky Folk Architecture.* Lexington: Univ. Press of Kentucky.
Morton, Joan
1978   Superstitions and Beliefs concerning Babies in Southern Appalachia. In *Glimpses of Southern Appalachian Folk Culture,* ed. C. Faulkner and C. Buckles, 1–19. Tennessee Anthropological Association Miscellaneous Paper 3. Chattanooga, Tenn.: Tribute Press.
Myer, William E.
1971   *Indian Trails of the Southeast.* Nashville: Blue and Gray Press.
Oneida High School
n.d.   Mountain Magic, Volumes I and II. Booklets prepared by students in folklore classes of Mrs. Linda Stewart. Mimeographed.
Owens, Bess Alice
1931   Folk Speech of the Cumberlands. *American Speech* 7 (2): 89–95.
Parker, Gerald K.
1970   Folk Religion in Southern Appalachia. Ph.D. diss., Southern Baptist Theological Seminary.
Parris, John
1978   *Mountain Cooking.* Asheville, N.C.: Citizen Times Publishing Co.
Pearsall, Marion
1966   Cultures of the American South. *Anthropological Quarterly* 39 (2): 128–41.
Perry, L. E.
1979   *McCreary County Conquest: A Narrative History.* Whitley City, Ky.: author.
Pomerence, J. B.
1964   *Geology of the Barthell Quadrangle and Part of the Oneida North Quadrangle, Kentucky.* Washington: U.S. Geological Survey. (Map GQ-314)
Redfield, Robert
1947   The Folk Society. *American Journal of Sociology* 52:293–308.
Reed, Clyde
1979   A Night on New River at the Reed Fish Trap. *Tennessee Anthropological Association Newsletter* 4 (1): 1–7.

Riedl, Norbert F., Donald Ball, and Anthony Cavender
1976   *A Survey of Traditional Architecture and Related Material Folk Culture Patterns in the Normandy Reservoir, Coffee County, Tennessee.* Univ. of Tennessee Dept. of Anthropology Report of Investigations 17.

Ritchie, Jean
1955   *Singing Family of the Cumberlands.* New York: Oak Publications.

Roberts, Leonard W.
1959   *Up Cutshin and Down Greasy: Folkways of a Kentucky Family.* Lexington: Univ. of Kentucky Press.

Rogers, E. G.
1941   *Early Folk Medical Practices in Tennessee.* Murfreesboro: Mid-South Publishing Co. for the Tennessee Folklore Society.

Rugby Restoration Association
1972   *Rugby's History.* Rugby, Tenn.: Rugby Restoration Association.

Sanderson, Esther Sharp
1958   *County Scott and Its Mountain Folk.* Huntsville, Tenn.: author.

Smith, Frank H.
1955   *The Appalachian Square Dance.* Berea, Ky.: Berea College Press.

Speed, Thomas
1886   *The Wilderness Road: A Description of the Routes of Travel by Which the Pioneers and Early Settlers First Came to Kentucky.* Filson Club Publication 2. Louisville: John P. Morton.

Stearns Coal and Lumber Co.
1938   *200 Square Miles.* Stearns, Ky.: Stearns Coal and Lumber Co.

Still, James A.
1929   Place Names in the Cumberland Mountains. *American Speech* 5 (2): 113.
1930   Christian Names in the Cumberlands. *American Speech* 5 (4): 306–7.

Sulzer, Elmer
[1968]1998   *Ghost Railroads of Kentucky.* Indianapolis: V. A. Jones. Reprint, Bloomington: Indiana Univ. Press.
[1975]1998   *Ghost Railroads of Tennessee.* Indianapolis: V. A. Jones. Reprint, Bloomington: Indiana Univ. Press.

Sweet, William W.
1931   *Religion on the American Frontier: The Baptists.* New York: Holt.

Tanner, Henry Schenck
1829   *Memoir on the Recent Surveys, Observations, and Internal Improvements, in the United States, with Brief Notices of the New Counties, Towns, Villages, Canals, and Railroads, Never before Delineated.* Philadelphia: author.
1839   *New American Atlas.* Philadelphia: author.

Thornton, Ralph
1973   Me and Fannie: The Oral Autobiography of Ralph Thornton of Topsfield, Maine. *Northeast Folklore* XIV.
U.S. Amy Corps of Engineers, Nashville District
1976a   *Big South Fork National River and Recreation Area: Final Environmental Impact Statement.* Nashville: U.S. Amy Corps of Engineers.
1976b   *Big South Fork National River and Recreation Area: General Design Memorandum. DM 1.* Nashville: U.S. Army Corps of Engineers.
Verhoeff, Mary
1911   *The Kentucky Mountains, Transportation and Commerce, 1750–1911. A Study in the Economic History of a Coal Field.* Filson Club Publication 26. Louisville: John P. Morton Co.
Weller, Jack E.
1965   *Yesterday's People: Life in Contemporary Appalachia.* Lexington: Univ. Press of Kentucky.
Wiggins, Gene
1979   Popular Music and the Fiddler. *John Edwards Memorial Foundation Quarterly* 15 (55): 144–52.
Wigginton, Elliot, ed.
1972–81   *The Foxfire Books.* Garden City, N.Y.: Anchor Books.
Wolfram, Walt, and Donna Christian
1976   *Appalachian Speech.* Arlington, Va.: Center for Applied Linguistics.
Young, James Hamilton
1826   Kentucky and Tennessee. In *Connected View of the Whole Internal Navigation of the U.S.,* comp. G. Armroyd. Philadelphia: H. C. Carey and I. Lea.
Youngken, Heber W.
1950   *Textbook of Pharmacognosy.* 6th ed. Philadelphia: Blakiston.

Index

A. C. French Company, 70
Adkins, Sena, 158
African Americans: banjo tradition, 150; dance traditions, 161–62; musicians, 153; railroad crews, 102
Allardt, Tenn., 3, 21
American ballads, 145
Anderson, Billy Dean, 35
Anderson, J. T., 100
Anderson, Mabel Troxell, 156
Anderson, O. H., 100
Anderson, Virgil, 156
Anderson, W. C., 100
annual cycle, farming, 172–73
Appalachian stereotypes, 4–5, 134
applejack, 63–64
applied ethnography, 13
Archer Mancourt Company, 70
archives, recommendations, 194–95, 200
Armathwaite, Tenn., 131

backwoods lifeways, 46
ballads, 145–46
banjo, 145–51
Baptists, history, 123–24
barn types, 49–50

Barren Fork Mining and Coal Company, 26, 89
Barrs Cemetery, McCreary Co., Ky., 200
barter, 67–68
Barthell, Ky., 83, 85
Beaty, Joe, 158
Beatty, Martin, 92
Beech Grove Baptist Church, 144
bees and bee keeping, 37, 61
Bell Farm, Ky., 73, 92, 96, 98, 112, 115
Bertram, Andy, 153
Bertram, Cooge, 153
Big South Fork Bridge, 102–3, 105
Big South Fork National River and Recreation Area: enabling legislation, 1; festivals, 203; folklife themes and resources, 190–93, 198–202; interpretive programs, 203–5
Big South Fork Scenic Railway, 97, 204
birth customs and beliefs, 116
Black Creek Crossroads Cemetery, Scott Co., Tenn., 231
black lung, 80
blacksmithing, 47–48

Blevins, John, 50
Blevins, Jonathan, 20, 23
Blevins, Lora, 51
Blevins (Hattie) Cemetery, Scott Co., Tenn., 225
Block Brothers Company, 69
Blue Diamond Coal Company, 87–89
Blue Heron, Ky., 27, 83, 86, 88, 112
Blue Heron interpretation, 198–99, 204
Blue Heron tipple, 82
boardinghouses, 69, 76, 86
Boyatt, Jerome, 99, 135
Boyatt-Slaven Cemetery, Scott Co., Tenn., 224
brattice construction, 80
Brewster Cemetery, Morgan Co., Tenn., 233
Briar Point, Tenn., 108
British ballads, 145
broadside ballads, 145
brooms and broom making, 55
Bruce, Leslie C., 95
Bryant, Louis, 84
Bryant coal mines, 96
Buck, John (Woolyhead), 68
Buck, Nancy, 68
buck dancing, 161–62
Burchfield, Irene, 168
burial customs and beliefs, 119, 120–22
Burnett, Dick, 145, 151–53
Burnett and Rutherford, 152–53
Burnside, Ky., 70
Butler, J. E., 95
Byrd, Alfred, 168

camp meeting songs, 143
cannel coal, 90–91

Carpenter Cemetery, Morgan Co., Tenn., 233–34
cash income, household strategies, 175–76, 178–79, 180–81, 184–85
cemetery inventory, 9, 216–35
Charit Creek Lodge, 51
chestnut mast, 37
Chicago Veneer Company, 70
Christian, Tenn., 101, 102, 108
Christian, Wales, 100, 108
Christian Cemetery, Fentress Co., Tenn., 230
church association meetings, 127
church denominations, 122, 123–24
church homecoming, 127
church services, 126
churching, 137–38
Cincinnati Southern Railroad: and commercial development, 25; and extractive industry, 26
Civil War, 2, 21
Civilian Conservation Corps, 78
clawhammer banjo style, 150
climate, 17
clothing, home production, 53–54
coal camps, living conditions, 85–86
coal mine accidents, 83–84
coal miners: economic strategies, 179–82; mobility, 112; paycheck deductions, 86
coal mining: draft animals, 81; interpretive themes, 192; mechanization, 81–82; occupational lore, 84; technology, 79–83; working conditions, 80–82
coal production and employment, 88–89
Coffee, Bled, 153
Coffee, Shell, 153

coffin making, 119
Comargo, Ky., 85
Comargo Coal Company, 85
company stores, 87
Conatser, Evelyn Sharp, 155
congregational singing, 144
construction skills, 47
contract logging, 79
Cooperative, Ky., 27, 85, 97, 112
cooperative research programs, 195–96
Copeland, Albert, 74, 76
Cos, Ernest, 166
county formation, 132–33
Court Day, 136–37
courts, 135–36
courtship, 114, 116
coverlet weaving, 54
crafts: documentation recommendations, 194; as income source, 167–68; marketing cooperatives, 166–69; shops, 200–201; training, 166, 168
Cromwell, Lou Hicks, 157
Crooke Coal and Coke Company, 26
Crown-Healy Company, 101
crude oil, cultural uses, 34
cultural continuity and change, 187–89
cultural heritage conservation, 11–12
cultural resource management, 3–4, 6, 13
Cumberland house type, 51
Cumberland Valley Lumber Company, 75, 77–78, 107

dairy production, 63
dance, 159–62

data sources, folklife survey: census, 6; historical documents, 6, 9–10; oral history, 9; regional literature, 10
Davenport, Clyde, 149, 153–54
Davenport, Lewis Albert (Al), 155–56
Davidson, M. H., 100
Davidson-Wilder mines, 81
death customs and beliefs, 119–20, 122
death lore, 122, 163–64
Decoration Day, 120–21
division of labor, household, 172, 178, 180, 183–84
dogtrot house type, 50–51
Dolen Cemetery, McCreary Co., Ky., 224
domestic manufactures, 24
Doss Spur, 74–75, 101, 109
Douglas, Willie, 104
dowsing, 93
Dr. Medico, 118
drift mouth mines, 80
Duncan, Howard, 203–4
Duncan, Sue, 204
Durrell, J. B., 89

Eagle Coal Company, 26
Eagle Construction Company, 102
East Jamestown, Tenn., 100, 103, 109
East Laurel, Tenn., 90, 107–8
ecological anthropology, 4
economic adaptation, household, 174–77, 179, 181–82, 185–87
economic development and decline, 2–3
economic forces, 171
economic revitalization, 205
elections, 133–34

Elkins, Lillie, 166
employment data, 26, 29–30, 238, 243–47
English foodways, 58
environmental impact assessment, 11
Euro-American exploration and settlement, 18–21
expressive culture: popular culture influences, 141–43, 146–47, 159–60; traditional survivals, 141, 146, 149, 162
extractive industry, 25–26

Fairview, Tenn., 68–69
family loyalty, 135, 138
family reunions, 113
farm location, 33
farmers, economic strategies, 171–77
farming: and coal mining, 85, 87; communities, 111–12; crops, 24; economic strategies, 171–77; as interpretive theme, 191; livestock, 56; settlement pattern, 33; statistical data, 28–30, 240–42, 247–48; subsistence production, 23–24
fasola shape note system, 143
Fellowship Church Cemetery, Fentress Co., Tenn., 232
Fentress County, Tenn., settlement, 112
Fentress County Bean Festival, 159
Fentress County Chicken Festival, 159
fiber processing, 53
fiddle: in folklore, 149; instrument making, 148; playing styles, 148–49; repertoire, 147–48
fidelity, Ky., 27, 85

fieldwork, 6–8
fishing, 36
Fletcher, Laodicia (Aunt Dicey), 54
folk architecture principles, 52
folk belief, attitudes toward, 164–65
folk construction, 52–53
folk culture, retention of, 189–90, 201, 202
folk religion, 125
folk transmission, 142
folklife interpretation: festivals, 199, 201; performance and demonstration, 192–93, 200
folklife survey: research methods, 5–9; scope of work, 4
food preservation, 57–60
foods, 56–63
forest products, 70–71
Foster Crossroads Cemetery, Scott Co., Tenn., 224–25
four-shape music notation, 143
funerals, 119–20

garden crops, 57
Gentry, Jesse (Whitehead), 157–58
Gentry, Joe Wheeler, 157–58
geology, 16
George Kidd Cemetery, McCreary Co., Ky., 223
George P. Taylor Company, 68
German foodways, 58, 63
Gernt, 77, 90, 101, 103, 107
Gernt, Arthur, 110
Gernt, Hugo, 110
Gernt Lumber Company, 107
ghost lore, 163–64
Gibbs, Mark A., 95
Gilreath, William O., 130
Glenmary, Tenn., 69, 79, 92, 102

gospel music, 143–44
government, attitudes toward, 134
grave cleaning, 121
Grave Hill Cemetery, Scott Co., Tenn., 228
grave houses, 121
grave markers, 121
graveside rites, 120
Gregory, W. L., 153–54
gristmills, 60
ground water, 18
gunpowder manufacture, 34

H. C. Whitson Company, 109
Hagemeyer, Bartlett, 100
Hagemeyer, Tenn., 89, 108
Hagemeyer, Hall, 100
Hagemeyer Flooring Mill, 75
Hagemeyer Mine, 90, 108
haint tales, 163–64
Hall, Samuel, 23
Hatfield Cemetery, Scott Co., Tenn., 227
Head-of-Wolf, Tenn., 74, 109
healers, 118
Helen Blevins Cemetery, Scott Co., Tenn., 226
Helenwood, Tenn., 79, 80
Helenwood Coal Company, 26
Hicks, Ben, 157
Hicks, Besford, 157
Hicks, Daniel, 156
Hicks, Dee, 150, 156–57
Hicks, Delta Winningham, 146, 157
Hicks, Frank, 158
Hicks, Henry, 158
Hicks, Joe, 144, 156–57
Hicks, Lily Mae, 157
Hicks, Lissie, 157

Hill Cemetery, McCreary Co., Ky., 217, 222
historic preservation goals, 10–11
historic structures evaluation, 8
historical anthropology, 10
historical archaeology, 195
historical legends, 164
Hiwassee Land Company, 78
hoedown fiddle style, 149
Hogue, Jim, 158
Hogue, John, 158
hospitals, attitudes toward, 116, 119
house types, 48, 50–52
household economic strategies, 172–86
household manufactures, 172–75, 178–79, 180–81, 184–85
household survey, 6–7, 207–15
Hugarth, Tenn., 110
Hughes, Thomas, 2, 24–25
Huling, Marcus, 20, 91–92
Hull, Cordell, 74
Hull, Uncle Billy, 74
hunting, 23, 36–37
Hurst, Elmer, 160–61

I-house type, 52
immigration, 2–3, 5, 21–22
income, statistical data, 31, 249–50
Indian trails, 2, 19
industrialization, cultural impacts, 187–89
infare dinner, 117
instrumental music, 147–59
interviews, xv–xvii, 7–8
Irishman stories, 163

Jacob Blevins Cemetery, Scott Co., Tenn., 229

Jamestown, Tenn., 69, 91, 100, 110
Jess Roysden (Alticrest) Cemetery, Scott Co., 229
Jewel Ridge Coal Company, 90, 101
john boats, 35
Jones, Doyle, 158
Justus Mine, 87

Kentucky and Tennessee Railroad, 27, 73–74, 84–85, 94–96; logging extension, 96–97; officers, 95; route, 94–97; shop, 98–99
Kentucky Guild of Artists and Craftsmen, 167
Kentucky Hills Industries, 53, 166–68
Kentucky Lumber Company, 70
King Cemetery, McCreary Co., Ky., 221–22
kinship, 113–14, 135, 138
Koppers Company, 78

Labor Day Old-Time Music Festival, 155
labor exchange, 67, 114
labor violence, 91
land acquisition and relocation, 12, 196–98
land grants, 1, 19–20
landholding patterns, 171–72, 177–78, 180, 182–83
Larmee, Christian, 95, 98–99
Laurel Dale Cemetery, Morgan Co., Tenn., 232
law enforcement, 133–34
Layne, Bert, 158
legal disputes, 135–36
legends, local, 164
Ligon Mine, 107

limestone, cultural uses, 34
log construction, 48–51
log structures: Charit Creek, 49–51; Lora Blevins farm, 49–50; Maxine Loudin property, 52; Oscar Blevins farm, 50; Tapley property, 50
log transport, 70, 73–74, 75–76, 95
loggers, economic strategies, 177–79
logging and sawmills, interpretation, 191–92
logging railroad, Stearns Coal and Lumber Company, 96–97
Logsdon, Cal, 135
Long Hunters, 18–19
Lost Silver Mine legend, 34
Lowery, Tom, 146
lunar signs, 41–45
lye soap making, 55

M. I. Thompson Lumber Company, 74–75, 107
mail order trade, 69
manufacturing establishments, 25, 239
marking of infants, 116
Marlow Mine, 82, 90, 108
marriage customs, 113, 116–18
MATCH, 167, 169
May Meetings, 127
McCreary County, Ky., settlement, 20, 111–12
McCreary County Miner's Union, 89
McMichin, Clayton, 158
medical doctors, attitudes toward, 116, 119
medicinal plants, 38–39, 259–74
Menifee, Lewis, 155
Michigan Lumber Company, 75, 109

midwifery, 116
Mill Creek (old East Jamestown), Tenn., 108–9
Miller, France, 68
mineral resources, 16, 33–34
missions controversy, 124
mobile homes, folk modification, 52
Monticello, Ky., musical traditions, 151, 153–54
Monticello-Huntsville Pike, 111–12
moonshine making, 64–66; attitudes toward, 134
Morgan, John, 71
Morgan County, Tenn., settlement, 21
Morris, E. W., 106
Morris, Sherman, 155
Mounce, John, 20
Mt. Helen Cemetery, Fentress Co., Tenn., 232
Mt. Vernon Cemetery, Morgan Co., Tenn., 234–35
music: commercial recordings, 153–54, 156–57; documentation recommendations, 193–94; family tradition, 151; folklife survey archives, 8
mutual aid, 114, 118

Nancy Graves Cemetery, McCreary Co., Ky., 121, 216–17
narrative genres, 162–64
Nash Cemetery, Fentress Co., Tenn., 232
National Environmental Policy Act, 11
Native American occupation, 2
needlework, 53
Newt King Cemetery, McCreary Co., Ky., 223
No Business, Tenn., 68, 86

No Business Cemetery, Scott Co., Tenn., 224

occupational lore: coal industry, 83–84; railroad industry, 98–99, 105; timber industry, 76–77
oil wells, 20; 91–93
Oneida, Tenn., 68, 79, 100, 104, 105
Oneida and Western Railroad, 27–28, 100–10; abandonment, 101; coal mines, 89–91; freight hauling, 100–101, 106–10; headquarters, 100; interpretation, 198; machine shop, 106; officers and shareholders, 100; rolling stock, 103, 104–5; route, 100–101, 106–10; section crews,102–4
Oneida Wood Industries, 79
open-range grazing, 24
oral history: documentation recommendations, 194; folklife survey collection, 8
oral tradition, social context, 162–63
outlaw heroes, 135
out-migration, 22–23, 238
Owens Cemetery, Scott Co., Tenn., 228

Paint Cliff, Ky., 85, 88
Paint Cliff Coal Company, 85
Parker, Boyd, 159
Parker, David, 159
Parker, Rowe, 159
Peercy, O. N., 169
Pemberton, Grover, 75, 106
Perry, Alvin, 144
persimmon beer, 38, 63
Phillips Cemetery, Scott Co., Tenn., 230

Pickett State Park and Forest, 27, 78
pie suppers, 114–15, 129
Pine Knot, Ky., 71, 79
pole roads, 75–76
political campaigns, 133–34
population: and industrial development, 22; and resources, 171; trends, 22–23, 236–38
Potter, Tenn., 89, 107
Potter Mine, 90
pottery making, 168
Powell-Kidd Cemetery, McCreary Co., Ky., 120, 221
preaching, 125
Premier Coal Company, 85
Presbyterian Academy, Huntsville, Tenn., 130
Primitive Baptists, 124
public assistance, 31, 249

quilting, 54

railroad accidents, 99–100, 105
railroad construction: Kentucky and Tennessee, 94–96; Oneida and Western, 101–2; Stearns logging railroad, 98
railroad crossties, home production, 70
railroad work, 98–100, 102–4, 106
railroad workers, economic strategies, 182–85
Ray, William Bradley, 100
recipes, 57–61
Redmon Mountain, 98–99
Reed Station, 106
reforestation, 78
Regular Baptists, 123–24
religious beliefs, 123–25
religious broadcasts, 127

residence and livelihood, 175–76, 179, 181, 182–85
return migration, 23
revivals, 126
riddles, 162
Rock Creek Ramblers, 155
rock houses, cultural uses, 34
Rocky Toppers, 155–56
rolling stores, 69
root cellars, 62
Ross, Alma, 166
Ross, Smith, 166
Rugby, Tenn., 2, 21, 54
Rugby Commissary, 169
Rugby Craft Cooperative, 168–69
Rugby Land Company, 78
Russell, A. J., 95
Rutherford, Leonard, 149, 151–53

sacred music, 142–45
saddlebag house type, 51
salt exploration and manufacture, 20, 34
saltpeter, 34
sandstone, cultural uses, 34
sawmills, 71–73, 79, 96, 106, 109
school march, 129
schools: consolidation, 127, 130–31; construction, 130–31; county and state support, 129–31; one-room, 127–29
Scott County, Tenn. settlement, 20, 112
Scott State Forest, 78
scrip, 86
Separate Baptists, 123–24
settlement history, interpretive theme, 191
settlement pattern, 111–12
seven-shape music notation, 143

Sharp, Albert, 155
Sharp, Eugene, 155
Sharp, Ewell, 154
Sharp, Hiram, 148
Sharp, Hugh, 155
Sharp, John Gibson (Fiddlin' John), 154
Sharp, Junior, 155
Sharp, Paul, 155
Sharp Family Reunion, 155
Sharp Place, Tenn., 77
shivaree, 117–18
shoe making, 54–55
shouting in church, 126
singing schools, 142
slaughtering hogs, 58–59
Slaven, Ed, 91
Slaven, Elisha, 20
Slaven, Richard Harve, 20
Slaven Cemetery, Scott Co., Tenn., 226
Slick Ford, Ky., 75–76
Smith, Eldridge (Slim), 155
Smith, Wolford, 91
Smith Cemetery, Scott Co., Tenn., 229
Smith Switch, Tenn., 104, 106
smokehouses, 50
smoking meat, 59
smooth fiddle style, 149
social activities, 114–15
social control, 132, 137–38
social impact assessment, 196–97
social interaction patterns, 113–14
social support, 115–19
sociocultural change, 4–5, 187–89
soil types, 16–17
song genres, 145–46
songbooks, 143

Southeast Archeological Center, 3–4
Southern Highland Handicraft Guild, 167
Southern Wood Piedmont Company, 79
Speck, D. M., 100, 107
Speck, Tenn., 107
speech, 165
spelling bees, 129
Spradlin, Hen, 92
springhouses, 50
springs, 35
square dancing, 160–61
squatters' rights, 26–27
Stanley, Elmer, 158
Stanley, Fred, 158
Stanley, Harold (Red), 158–59
state line, disputed, 132
Stearns, Justus S., 26, 72
Stearns, Ky., 97, 151
Stearns, Robert L., 84
Stearns Coal and Lumber Company: bandmill, 72–73, 96; boardinghouses, 76; coal operations, 81–89, 275; employee recreation, 115; employees, 26–27; land tenants, 27, 188; logging camps, 74; logging railroad, 73–74, 98–100; Store 14, 97–98; timber operations, 72–74
Stearns Hotel, 88
stock fence laws, 57, 188
Stockton, Tenn., 75, 109
Stockton Cemetery, Fentress Co., Tenn., 231
storekeeping, 67–70, 107
storytelling: documentation recommendations, 194; festival, 203; revival, 162

street dances, 159–60
Sulphur Springs Cemetery, Scott Co., Tenn., 230

tanbark production, 71
Tatesville, Ky., log boom, 96
Tays, John, 107, 109
teachers and teacher training, 129
Tellico Land Grants, 19–20
tenant house type, 51
Tennessee Stave and Lumber Company, 27–28, 74–75, 100, 109
Terry and Potter Cemeteries, Fentress Co, Tenn., 231
Terry Cemetery, Scott Co., Tenn., 121, 225–26, 230
Thompson, Jim L., 75, 107
Thompson, Herb, 107
Thompson, Ide, 107
Thompson Cemetery, Scott Co., Tenn., 228
three-finger banjo picking, 150
Tibbals flooring, 79
timber industry, 71–72, 78–79
Tompkins, Ovid, 169
Tompkins blacksmith shop, 47–48
Tompkins Cemetery, Fentress Co., Tenn., 231
Toomey, Tenn., 107
topography, 15–16
tourism, 155, 162, 166, 192
tourist attractions, 203–5
tram roads, 75–76
transportation, 21, 68–69 191
trapping, 37
tree species, cultural uses, 35–36
Troxel Cemetery, McCreary Co., Ky., 223–24

Troxell, Anna Davenport, 155
Troxell, Clyde, 155–56
Troxell, Jasper, 155
Troxell, Ralph, 155–56
two-finger banjo picking, 150
Two-Seed-in-the-Spirit Baptists, 124

unemployment statistics, 31, 248
union organizers, 88–89, 91
United Baptists, 124

verbal expression, 165
Verdun, Tenn., 106
violence, 134, 138–40

wakes, 119–20
walnut processing (cottage industry), 69
water resources, 17–18
water supply, 35
Waters Cemetery, McCreary Co., Ky., 220
Wayne Co., Ky., settlement, 1, 20
weather lore, 39–40
Weaver, Jim, 159
Weaver, Ralph, 159
weaving, 53–54, 168
Webb Hammock Company, 90, 108
West, Bessie, 168
West, Beulah, 168
West, E. Rye, 83
West Cemetery, Scott Co., Tenn., 229
whiskey making, 64–66
White Oak Junction, Ky., 85
Whitson Lumber Company, 75
Whitson Pole Road, 75–76, 109
wild plant foods, 37–38, 57, 251–58
Wilder, Robert, 90

Wilder-Davidson strike, 146
wildlife resources, 36–37
Winchester Cemetery, McCreary Co., Ky., 217
Winningham, Len, 157
Winningham, Nancy Hicks, 157
Wolf Creek Dam, 101
Wolf River incline, 109
Wood, Bonnie, 155
Woods, Cap, 91, 105
woodworking, 35–36, 167–69
workings, 114
Worley, Ky., 80, 85, 204
Worley mine disaster, 83–84
worship practice, 125–27

Wright, Opal Sharp, 155
Wright Cemetery: Scott County, Tenn., 230; Fentress Co., Tenn., 232–33

Yamacraw, Ky., 85
Yamacraw Bridge, 95–96
York, Alvin C., 117, 130
York, Gracie, 117
York Institute, 130

Zenith, Tenn., 77, 83, 105, 108
Zenith mines, 90–91
Zimmerman, Andrew, 20, 91–92
zodiac signs, 41–45

www.ingramcontent.com/pod-product-compliance
Lightning Source LLC
Chambersburg PA
CBHW030300080526
44584CB00012B/389